GENERATIONS AND CHANGE

GENERATIONS AND CHANGE

Genealogical Perspectives
in Social History

edited by
ROBERT M. TAYLOR, JR.
Indiana Historical Society

and
RALPH J. CRANDALL
New England Historic Genealogical Society

MERCER

ISBN 0-86554-168-X

Generations and Change
Copyright © 1986
Mercer University Press, Macon GA 31207
All rights reserved
Printed in the United States of America

The paper used in this publication meets
the minimum requirements of American National Standard
for Information Sciences—Permanence of Paper
for Printed Library Materials, ANSI Z39.48-1984.

Library of Congress Cataloging-in-Publication Data
Main entry under title:
Generations and change.

Includes index.
1. History—Research—United States—Addresses,
essays, lectures. 2. Social history—Research—
United States—Addresses, essays, lectures.
3. Genealogy—Methodology—Addresses, essays, lectures.
4. Social sciences—Biographical methods—Addresses,
essays, lectures. I. Taylor, Robert M., 1941–
II. Crandall, Ralph J.
D16.G44   1986   907′.2   85-15579
ISBN 0-86554-168-X

CONTENTS

FOREWORD.. ix
PREFACE... xi

PART I
BRIDGING HISTORY AND GENEALOGY

CHAPTER 1
HISTORIANS AND GENEALOGISTS:
AN EMERGING COMMUNITY OF INTEREST
Robert M. Taylor, Jr. and Ralph J. Crandall................................ 3

CHAPTER 2
HISTORY AND GENEALOGY:
PATTERNS OF CHANGE
AND PROSPECTS FOR COOPERATION
Samuel P. Hays 29

CHAPTER 3
ANTHROPOLOGY, GENEALOGY, AND HISTORY:
A RESEARCH LOG
John W. Adams and Alice Bee Kasakoff.....................................53

CHAPTER 4
THE PLACE OF GENEALOGY
IN THE CURRICULUM OF THE SOCIAL SCIENCES
Robert Charles Anderson 79

CHAPTER 5
ETHNICITY AND THE SOUTHERN GENEALOGIST:
MYTHS AND MISCONCEPTIONS,
RESOURCES AND OPPORTUNITIES
Elizabeth Shown Mills 89

PART II
GENEALOGICAL APPROACHES
TO COMMUNITY AND FAMILY RESEARCH

CHAPTER 6
RECONSTRUCTING CATHOLIC FAMILY HISTORY
    James M. O'Toole 111

CHAPTER 7
GENEALOGIES AS EVIDENCE
IN HISTORICAL KINSHIP STUDIES:
A GERMAN EXAMPLE
    Andrejs Plakans 125

CHAPTER 8
THE STABILITY RATIO:
AN INDEX OF COMMUNITY COHESIVENESS
IN NINETEENTH-CENTURY MORMON TOWNS
    Dean L. May, Lee L. Bean, Mark H. Skolnick 141

CHAPTER 9
THE MASSACHUSETTS TOWNS
AND THE LEGISLATURE, 1691–1776:
CONTRIBUTIONS OF GENEALOGY
TO COLLECTIVE BIOGRAPHY
    John A. Schutz 159

CHAPTER 10
"BELOVID WIFE" AND "INVEIGLED AFFECTIONS":
MARRIAGE PATTERNS
IN EARLY ROWLEY, MASSACHUSETTS
    Patricia Trainor O'Malley 181

CHAPTER 11
THE FERTILITY TRANSITION IN NEW ENGLAND:
THE CASE OF HAMPTON, NEW HAMPSHIRE, 1655–1840
    Lawrence J. Kilbourne 203

CHAPTER 12
FORENAMES AND THE FAMILY IN NEW ENGLAND:
AN EXERCISE IN HISTORICAL ONOMASTICS
    David Hackett Fischer 215

CHAPTER 13
"IN NOMINE AVI": CHILD-NAMING PATTERNS
IN A CHESAPEAKE COUNTY, 1650–1750
    Darrett B. Rutman and Anita H. Rutman 243

PART III
GENEALOGY IN MIGRATION RESEARCH

CHAPTER 14
MIGRATION, KINSHIP, AND THE INTEGRATION
OF COLONIAL NEW ENGLAND SOCIETY:
THREE GENERATIONS OF THE DANFORTH FAMILY
  Virginia DeJohn Anderson... 269

CHAPTER 15
THE WILSONS MOVE WEST:
FAMILY CONTINUANCE AND STRAIN
AFTER MIGRATION
  Claudia L. Bushman.. 291

CHAPTER 16
PROBLEMS AND POSSIBILITIES
OF INDIVIDUAL-LEVEL TRACING
IN GERMAN-AMERICAN MIGRATION RESEARCH
  Walter D. Kamphoefner.. 311

CONTRIBUTORS... 325
INDEX.. 327

To

Sue
Julia
Linda
Elizabeth
Meredith
Catherine

FOREWORD

The English term *historical genealogy* indicates the broader view and stresses the close relationship between these two disciplines. When the genealogist sets down a lineage of "begats" and "begottens" with documentation and gives it perspective and place in history, he has embarked on historical genealogy. When the genealogist continues to interpret the meaning of the past in connection with this array of relatives, the richer rewards of historical genealogy are earned.

In the course of his research, the historian too compiles and organizes data; however, here the total process also demands analysis of the subject. The historian, utilizing a spectrum of sources to probe the political, economic, and social relations of the time, goes far beyond data on pedigrees. The genealogist, on the other hand, might be directly concerned with personal names in a narrow area. Yet there can be conditions, as now exist, when similar interests forge a new relationship. The social historian's concerns about family and kinship and the genealogist's desire to supplement the pedigree with a credible story line furnish a context for interaction.

Historians and genealogists have important functions that can be performed effectively by understanding that cooperation entails mutual benefit. Workers in both fields must be prepared to test the authenticity of the records and assess the comparative value of documents in order to determine the facts.

How all this is being accomplished is set forth in the splendid papers that follow. The efforts of Bob Taylor and Ralph Crandall to get this work in print have resulted in a major contribution to historical genealogy.

Willard Heiss

PREFACE

A distinguishing mark of historical writing and teaching is the prominent place given to social history. Future historiographers will probably characterize the present as the era of the "new" social history wherein scholars, equipped with the latest methodologies, balanced the historical record by giving due attention to the lives and institutions of common folk. Central to much of today's social history, and "relevant to all," according to Peter Stearns, is the family.[1] The description and analysis of family historical development came into its own in the 1960s and 1970s, intersecting with other subfields of social history. This furnished the kind of historical perspective to research on the family that was long established in other social-scientific disciplines.[2] No longer the silent or assumed partner in studies of individuals, groups, and institutions, the family is being accorded its rightful place as a significant variable in the evolution of society.

Concurrent with the emergence and diffusion of social history and family research, another group, largely outside the classroom, has been engaged in the genealogical reconstruction of families. Though by no means a new activity, genealogy registered a substantial upsurge of practitioners in the 1970s. Harried librarians have been hard pressed for space

---

[1] Peter N. Stearns, "Toward a Wider Vision: Trends in Social History," in *The Past before Us, Contemporary Historical Writing in the United States*, ed. Michael Kammen (Ithaca NY: Cornell University Press, 1980) 222.

[2] For example, present efforts by social scientists to create an academic field of "Famology" take into account the accomplishments of family historians. See Wesley R. Burr and Geoggrey K. Leigh, "Famology: A New Discipline," *Journal of Marriage and the Family* 45 (1983): 467-80.

and resources to accommodate the waves of ancestor seekers. Claiming the label of "family historian" years before members of academia adopted the tag, genealogists have brought forth thousands of updated and new lineages.

The extraordinary expansion of sociohistorical research in our colleges and universities, in conjunction with the "search for generational memory" by a considerable portion of the general public, has renewed discussions about the relation of historical scholarship to genealogy.[3] As social historians are exploring the patterns of daily life in the contexts of community, workplace, and family, and as genealogists are uncovering lines of descent that mesh the individual in a web of kinship, family, and communal associations, it is not surprising that after a century of mutual indifference, historians and genealogists have begun a new dialogue. Historians are investigating genealogies as major sources of social data, and genealogists are becoming more aware of the methodological and substantive treatments of the family and its environments produced by historians and by other social scientists.

The essays in this volume address the subject of the benefits of genealogy as an information base for social history. It is not often that historians overlook a long-standing body of evidence, especially one that dovetails with current research needs. Reasons for the neglect of genealogy within the academic community will be taken up in the following essays. Suffice it to say that during the recent expansions of social history and genealogical study a small number of researchers—representing diverse vocations and academic pursuits, and working independently for the most part—identified genealogy as a worthwhile tool. For some, particularly historical demographers, anthropologists, even geneticists, it was a matter of resurrecting or reevaluating previously tried genealogical approaches within their respective specialties. For historians to give fresh attention to genealogy involved, first, a basic conceptual shift to a social-scientific perspective and, second, the acknowledgment that thorough investigations of social change required the kind of longitudinal record intrinsic to genealogies. The articles in this collection, many of which appear in print for the first time, offer fresh assessments of, and innovative uses

---

[3]Tamara K. Hareven, "The Search for Generational Memory: Tribal Rites in Industrial Society," *Daedalus* 107 (1978): 137.

for, genealogies. The volume familiarizes the reader with highlights of past and present genealogical activity, gauges genealogy's strengths and weaknesses as a reservoir of personal data, and provides examples of genealogies employed in serious historical inquiry.

The first selection surveys the origins and evolution of American genealogy and its connection with past and present historical research and writing. The classic statement on the benefit of enjoining genealogy and history is the 1975 article, replicated here, by Samuel P. Hays, who makes the case that the new social history is simply "genealogy writ large." Anthropologists John W. Adams and Alice Bee Kasakoff report on why they turned from investigating preliterate societies to studying New England towns, and on the role of genealogy in the transition. From the professional genealogist's point of view, Robert C. Anderson argues for the inclusion of genealogy among the auxiliary disciplines of history and of the social sciences generally, and advises that genealogy be increasingly taught at the collegiate level. He goes on to suggest that a superficial understanding of modern genealogy by academic professionals has precluded meaningful exchange. Genealogist Elizabeth Shown Mills next examines myths that Southern genealogists have held regarding their region's social structure—myths about historical relations that genealogists have largely accepted and carried over into research. Mills calls for a reconsideration of data sources that were previously of limited interest to white genealogists.

Students have long been interested in the structure and function of family and community, but too often their analyses have been limited to vignettes and not the changes over a period of time. James O'Toole imaginatively describes the kinds of records an average nineteenth-century Roman Catholic would generate over a lifetime. Andrejs Plakans outlines the steps necessary for the historian to transfer anthropological techniques of kinship investigation to the study of towns. Genealogies, according to Plakans, supply the content for "historical maps" of relationships over a considerable time. These networks can be examined for long-term changes in kinship interaction. The idea of religious commitment as a stabilizing force in past communities informs the study of nineteenth-century Utah Mormon towns by Dean May, Lee Bean, and Mark Skolnick. The authors measure the evolution of several communities through the longitudinal data on population housed in the extensive Mormon genealogical archives. A "stability ratio" captures the degree of permanence of the resident families between 1850 and 1910. The influence of towns on political outlooks is central to John A. Schutz's collective biography of some 2,500 Massachusetts legislators in the 1691-1775 period. Schutz explains how power was distributed among the lawmakers by focusing on the characteristics of age, class, occupation, wealth, and geography.

The next series of articles focuses more directly on the family. Historian Patricia O'Malley researches marriage patterns in seventeenth-century Rowley, Massachusetts. More specifically, she profiles the nuptial habits of three generations. The author observes that the extent of choice in the selection of partners anticipates modern marriage custom. Lawrence Kilbourne's investigation of 281 family careers in Hampton, New Hampshire, between 1750 and 1850, supports recent findings that the fertility decline in America predates the industrial revolution.

One of the most inventive and significant uses of genealogies is in the research on child-naming, or onomastics. The study of naming practices provides clues to social and cultural change. Historian David Hackett Fischer views onomastics as a means of specifying a chronology for the study of family history, which is rather vaguely arranged. Fischer examines the names of children in 1,000 Concord, Massachusetts, households over two centuries. He detects three successive naming systems, which he interprets as corresponding to three successive ideas of the family. In another important article on child-naming, Darrett and Anita Rutman take an incisive look at the application of names in Middlesex County, Virginia, from 1650 to 1750. The authors intriguingly allude to the possibility of regional differences in child-naming in colonial America.

Several of the papers included here note opportunities provided by genealogy for research on migration. Concluding this volume are three essays that engage the subject directly. Virginia DeJohn Anderson employs genealogies of three generations of the New England Danforth family to establish that interfamily migration served as an integrating mechanism for early New England society. Claudia Bushman describes the long-distance relationships of the Wilson and Corbit families of Odessa, Delaware, in the nineteenth century. Though geographically remote from one another, the ties of the first generation did not deteriorate; however, the strain of distance, changing occupations, and life-style gradually eroded kin cohesiveness. Finally, Walter D. Kamphoefner investigates intercontinental migrations of a group of Missouri Germans. By using individual-level tracing through genealogies of more than 100 families, Kamphoefner is able to entertain questions pertaining to ethnic persistence and change among Germans settling in Missouri during the nineteenth century.

The basic message embedded in this collection is that genealogies offer a means to enlarge upon or go beyond routine social-history studies because of the longitudinal nature of genealogical information. The probation period for genealogy is, we think, over. It is a matter now, as this volume intends, to not only bring genealogy into the mainstream of historical sources, but to demonstrate the serviceability of genealogy to historians who want the processes of life to be the fulcrum of their work.

We would like to express our gratitude to W. W. Norton and Company for permission to reprint portions of *A Place in Time: Explicatus* (1984) by Darrett B. Rutman and Anita H. Rutman; to David Hackett Fischer for permission to reprint "Forenames and the Family in New England: An Exercise in Historical Onomastics," *Chronos* 1 (Fall 1981): 76-111; to *Delaware History* for permission to reproduce parts of "The Wilson Family in Delaware and Indiana," by Claudia Bushman from *Delaware History* 20 (1982): 27-49; and to Samuel P. Hays and *Prologue: The Journal of the National Archives* for republication of "History and Genealogy: Patterns of Change and Prospects for Cooperation," by Samuel P. Hays from *Prologue: The Journal of the National Archives* 7 (1975): 39-43, 81-84, 187-91. We particularly want to thank the Family History Section of the Indiana Historical Society for its assistance in the publication of this volume.

Part I

BRIDGING HISTORY AND GENEALOGY

Chapter One

HISTORIANS AND GENEALOGISTS: AN EMERGING COMMUNITY OF INTEREST

Robert M. Taylor, Jr.
and Ralph J. Crandall

Genealogy, the spoken or written evidence of ancestral lines, has a history of its own, a chronology that extends from ancient accounts of kings descended from mythical gods to present-day pedigrees designed on computers. A brief consideration of human curiosity about our parentage, and of the ways societies have handled such issues as leadership succession, inheritance, and marriage, rules out genealogy as a recent invention. In America, the impetus to research family trees did not suddenly materialize during the Bicentennial celebration or follow the publication of Alex Haley's book *Roots*. Traces of today's seasoned genealogy can be found in the seventeenth century, but not before the mid-nineteenth century is it possible to detect the emergence of a vigorous genealogy having the potential for widespread appeal. Thereafter the story is one of fluctuating popularity, evolving standards of professionalism, increased heterogeneity of participants, and a century-long disassociation from mainstream history. The following essay sketches these central features of genealogy's past.

The history of genealogy in America has yet to be written. The personal nature of genealogical research, its straightforward methodology, and the long absence of professional oversight perhaps account for genealogists neglecting the development of their craft. Historians also have overlooked genealogy; even as a manifestation of popular culture, they generally have thought it to be little more than an amateurish pastime. What follows, therefore, is an initial attempt to depict and interpret the pattern of genealogy's growth.[1]

Few persons compiled genealogies prior to the Revolutionary War. Wealthy colonists possessed heraldic insignia and pedigrees, but the average East Coast settler remained uninformed or disinterested. Knowledge of biblical genealogies, the oral transmission of information on forebears, and the recording of births, marriages, and deaths in family Bibles was as near as most colonists came to exhibiting a genealogical bent. Inside the courtroom, though, things were different; there judgments often took into account the minutiae of descent. The twenty-four-page Stebbins genealogy, printed in 1771, is commonly accepted as America's first published genealogy.[2]

Political independence and the triumph of democratic ideology both restrained and fostered genealogy. The popular distaste for social distinc-

---

[1]The following writings provide details pertinent to a history of American genealogy: Milton Rubincam, ed., *Genealogical Research: Methods and Sources*, 2 vols. (Washington: American Society of Genealogy, 1980) 1:5-12; idem, "Genealogy for All People," *National Genealogical Society Quarterly* 66 (1978): 243-51; Walter Lee Sheppard, Jr., "A Bicentennial Look at Genealogy Methods, Performance, Education, and Thinking," ibid. 65 (1977): 3-15; Russell E. Bidlack, "Genealogy as It Relates to Library Service," *ALA Yearbook, 1978* (Chicago: American Library Association, 1978) xxiii-xxx; H. Minot Pitman, "The Progress of Genealogical Literature in America," *National Genealogical Society Quarterly* 50 (1962): 3-7; Meredith B. Colket, Jr., "Some Trends in Genealogy," ibid. 68 (1980): 3-7; Lester J. Cappon, "Genealogy: Handmaid of History," *Special Publications of the National Genealogical Society*, no. 17 (1957): 1-9; Alexander J. Wall, "American Genealogical Research: Its Beginning and Growth," *Papers of the Bibliographical Society of America* 36 (1942): 305-14; Peter Andrews, "Genealogy: The Search for a Personal Past," *American Heritage* 33 (August/September 1982): 10-17.

[2]Luke Stebbins, *The Genealogy of Mr. Samuel Stebbins and Hannah His Wife from the Year 1701 to 1771* (Harford, 1771). Some writers contend that James Blake, Jr.'s appendix to his *Memoirs of Roger Clap* (Boston, 1731) should be designated the earliest-printed compilation. See Rubincam, "Genealogy for All People," 244.

tions based on heredity functioned as a powerful norm to discourage ancestor research, which could be construed as a means to establish privilege by descent. Moreover, the ordinary citizen, like his colonial predecessors, had a new history to make. Present achievements and future prospects mattered, not recalling events or recovering lineages. The press of building a nation and the pursuit of individual attainment accorded little time for probing family links. And yet for all the earnest voicing of equalitarian values, the exercise of freedom corresponded nicely with the human impulse to differentiate oneself from others. The basic American penchant for proclaiming equality while practicing exclusiveness spurred genealogical inquiry. The implicit goal of realizing social distance could be carried out by attesting to an illustrious bloodline in the guise of family pride. Visitors from abroad expecting to witness a republican utopia expressed disbelief at the extent of social climbing and the number of newspaper advertisements offering to produce titled lineages and coats of arms.[3] A growing body of affluent Americans, self-conscious of ignoble origins, sought social and cultural certification from Europe. Transatlantic schooling, travel, commerce, and marriage stimulated a stateside market for genealogy.

More crucial than aristocratic pretensions for establishing and sustaining genealogical research was the expansion of public record keeping and the formation of local and state historical societies. Meanwhile, antiquarians were busy incorporating in their tomes of "useful knowledge" the filiations of the leading families. By 1830 more than one dozen genealogies had appeared in print, highlighted by John Farmer's *A Genealogical Register of New England* (1829), a pathbreaking work in the use of manuscripts and local records.

Not until the 1840s, however, did genealogy garner the kind of advocacy necessary to insure its progress. The key event occurred in 1845 with the establishment in Boston of the New England Historic Genealogical Society (NEHGS). Lemuel Shattuck, chronicler of Concord's history, genealogist, and founder of the American Statistical Association, played a major role in the society's organization. The purpose of the society was to collect, preserve, and occasionally publish genealogical and

---

[3]Thomas D. Clark, "The Great Visitation to American Democracy," *Mississippi Valley Historical Review* 44 (1957): 26.

historical matter relating to early New England families.[4] In 1847 the NEHGS inaugurated the *New England Historical and Genealogical Register*, the nation's first quarterly devoted to genealogical studies. Within the succeeding decade ninety-six primary genealogies appeared in the *Register*. In the same period, eighty-four other lineages surfaced nationwide, seventy-three of these published in New England. In addition, genealogical information turned up in local histories and registers, in listings of gravestone markings, in memoirs and funeral sermons, and in newspapers.[5] There also were issued several compilations of European immigrant names, thus facilitating the linkage of American and Old World families.[6]

Augmenting the increasing range of source materials was the publication, on the eve of the Civil War, of the first of four volumes of James Savage's *Genealogical Dictionary of the First Settlers of New England*. Savage, a Boston city official, state legislator, Harvard overseer, and antiquary, devoted years to assembling this classic work of genealogical research. Another pioneering effort was William H. Whitmore's *Handbook of American Genealogy*, an 1862 catalog of annotated genealogies containing 170 items.[7]

In the fifty-year span between the Civil War and World War I, genealogy's clientele multiplied dramatically as measured by organizational fervor, library resources, and readership. By 1870 NEHGS holdings totaled 8,000 books and 26,000 pamphlets pertaining to historical and genealogical subjects.[8] In the preceding year, 1869, the New York Genealogical and Biographical Society was founded along with its journal, the *Record*. The enthusiasm for organization spread westward, reaching Pennsylvania in 1892 and Utah in 1894. The debut of the National Genealogical Society in 1903 symbolizes the breadth of popularity ge-

---

[4]William Carroll Hill, *A Century of Genealogical Progress. Being a History of the New England Historic Genealogical Society, 1845-1945* (Boston: The New England Historic Genealogical Society, 1945) 10.

[5]*North American Review* (April 1856): 475.

[6]Wall, "American Genealogical Research," 309.

[7]James Savage, *A Genealogical Dictionary of the First Settlers of New England*, . . . 4 vols. (Albany: J. Munsell, 1862). William Henry Whitmore, *A Handbook of American Genealogy* . . . (Albany: J. Munsell, 1862).

[8]Hill, *History of the New England Historic Genealogical Society*, 20.

nealogy had acquired. Between 1890 and 1909 the Library of Congress added 2,340 American family genealogies, increasing its stock to 3,795 volumes, a far cry from the 203 genealogies on the shelves in 1860.[9] Patrons crowded library reading rooms. The New York Public Library handled request slips for 33,542 items in its genealogy section in one twelve-month period during 1900-1901. In 1915 the library dispensed five times as many sources and registered 26,129 researchers.[10] Membership in the Genealogical Society of Utah grew from 48 in 1895 to 2,500 in 1915.[11]

Why in this space of time was there such a thirst for tracing lineages? One contemporary reckoned that America had developed a leisure class with time to cultivate aristocratic tastes, resulting in "scarcely a family of any pretension which does not boast its pedigree and escutcheon, and, in many cases, a gallery of ancestral portraits."[12] Quite apart from the usefulness of genealogy to an enhanced self-image is the fact that genealogical research did require time and money.

Though leisure and wealth furnished the wherewithal for some to practice genealogy and the dictates of high society often supplied a motive, for others there was a different reason: events and circumstances of this period evoked a retrospective mood. For the first time, it appears, Americans confessed to having a national history, and genealogy was one of several manifestations of a deepening public desire to plumb that history.[13] The emergence of new sources of genealogical information—pioneer associations, family reunions, county "mug" books, patriotic and hereditary associations—also reflects the new appreciation of history. The novel concern for bygone days is evinced in the heightened dedication to preservation and conservation. The Civil War had created social fissions

---

[9]Robert M. Taylor, Jr., "Summoning the Wandering Tribes: Genealogy and Family Reunions in American History," *Journal of Social History* 16:2 (1982): 23.

[10]Figures are taken from the "Statistics of Readers and Volumes Consulted," in the annual reports of the *Bulletin of the New York Public Library*.

[11]Charles W. Penrose, "The Genealogical Society of Utah," *Utah Genealogical and Historical Magazine* 7 (1916): 9.

[12]John D. Champlin, Jr., "The Manufacture of Ancestors," *Forum* 10 (January 1891): 565-72.

[13]See *Reunion of the Dickinson Family at Amherst, Massachusetts, . . . 1883 . . .* (n.p., Binghampton Publishing Co., 1884) 192.

and psychic wounds that in the course of widening or healing were well remembered. In addition, a flurry of city and town bicentennials, along with the national birthday of 1876 and Chicago's Columbia Exposition of 1892-1893, served to remind persons of whose shoulders they stood on and whose dreams they aspired to fulfill. All such occurrences jogged the collective memory of a portion of Americans and helped pave the way for genealogical study.

The rapid social and economic changes, propelling the nation into its second century, gave rise to an apprehensiveness that further accentuated the era's concern with the past and with genealogical enterprise. Increasing numbers of largely old-stock natives were troubled by their knowledge of an urban, impersonal, and heterogeneous society. For an older generation the sense of malaise centered on the loss of esteem, a common enough condition, but one now backed by contemporary medical and scientific findings.[14] If obsolescence threatened the aged, the deviations of youth frightened the parental generation. The private and protective character of the modernizing household made parents oversensitive to their forfeiture of control over offsprings, who scattered across the country and exhibited unconventional attitudes and behavior. Concern mounted as sons elected not to follow the father's occupation, as daughters grew more restive, and as children opted for unmarried, childless, or divorced roles.

Still others feared most the undermining of the nation's Anglo-Saxon institutions and culture by the influx of immigrants from Eastern Europe. Anarchy, aliens, and alcohol stood as the evil trinity poised to destroy the Republic. Cities, unhealthy and depraved, bred the malignancy. In this context genealogy reaffirmed and justified nordic hegemony in social and cultural affairs at a time "when 'respectable' citizens showed a concern with caste, race, and ancestry to an extent which has not been seen in America before or since."[15] Fears of race suicide, attributed to a precipitous decline in births and to massive immigrations of non-Western Europeans, influenced the creation of patriotic and hereditary societies, and vindicated the

---

[14]See, for example, W. Andrew Achenbaum, *Old Age in the New Land: The American Experience since 1790* (Baltimore: Johns Hopkins University Press, 1978) 39-54, and David Hackett Fischer, *Growing Old in America* (New York: Oxford University Press, 1977).

[15]Kenneth M. Ludmerer, *Genetics and American Society: A Historical Appraisal* (Baltimore: Johns Hopkins University Press, 1972) 24.

study of eugenics. The family tree served as an admission ticket to the scores of associations composed of descendants of pioneers and war veterans. Mostly established in the 1890s, these organizations frankly credited their success to the alarming presence of the new foreign element. Genealogists and historians, moreover, supported the efforts of eugenicists to document racial differences in character, temperament, and intelligence, and to see laws passed restricting immigration and permitting sterilization. Students of heredity courted genealogists because lineages were required for research. Genealogists embraced the proponents of race meliorism because of compatible goals; eugenicists gave a seemingly scientific base to notions of race supremacy and accommodated genealogists' wish for social relevancy.[16]

With misgivings about the individual's place in a complex world, about the solidity of the family unit, and about the locus of power in a pluralistic society, individuals reached out to living kin for assistance and reclaimed appropriate experiences of ancestors for guideposts. Katherine Ellis observes that as things appeared to worsen during this time, "The pursuit of stability, domesticity, and a sure knowledge of one's parentage became an integral part of middle-class culture."[17] Through genealogies,

---

[16]"It is as positive as time itself," a writer observed in 1909, "that future civilizations will require by law examinations into heredity before granting the privileges of entering into the serious and sacred matrimonial relations, and the basis for these examinations will be a perfected system of genealogical investigations" ("The Inauguration of Genealogy as the Science of Heredity," *Journal of American History* 3 [1909]: 145). See also Charles K. Bolton, "Genealogy and History," *Annual Report of the American Historical Association for the Year 1912* (Washington, 1914) 202-16; Paul Popenoe, "Genealogy and Eugenics," *Utah Genealogical and Historical Magazine* 6 (1915): 202-18; Louis Dublin, "The Significance of the Declining Birth Rate," ibid. 9 (1918): 113-23.

Historical interpretations regarding the confluence of "race suicide," hereditary societies, eugenics, and genealogy include: Wesley Frank Craven, *The Legend of the Founding Fathers* (Ithaca: Cornell University Press, 1956) 102-77; Rowland Berthoff, *An Unsettled People: Social Order and Disorder in American History* (New York: Harper & Row, 1971) 426-38; Barbara Miller Solomon, *Ancestors and Immigrants* (Cambridge: Harvard University Press, 1956); Wallace Evan Davies, *Patriotism on Parade: The Story of Veterans' and Hereditary Organizations in America, 1783-1900* (Cambridge: Harvard University Press, 1956); Charles E. Rosenberg, *No Other Gods: on Science and American Social Thought* (Baltimore: Johns Hopkins University Press, 1976); Mark H. Haller, *Eugenics: Hereditarian Attitudes in American Thought* (New Brunswick NJ: Rutgers University Press, 1963).

[17]Katherine Ellis, "The Limits of Domesticity in the Nineteenth-Century Novel," *Feminist Studies* 2 (1975): 57.

associations, and family reunions, the perplexed sought to recover an identity, to forge a kin cohesiveness, and to produce ancestral models of courage and unblemished character.

As genealogies were increasingly looked upon as indispensable testimonies to social status, family strength, and racial purity, genealogists favored dismissing oral histories in favor of the "reliable" written record. No longer, they argued, could family traditions—that mixture of fact and fancy orally communicated across generations—tutor the moral and psychological needs of the new age. The Carter family historian found it "necessary to make a holocaust of the stumps and brush of warped and twisted traditions."[18] A spokesman at the Bartholomew family reunion advised that "we should desire to have our family history accurate and complete, and not resting upon mere tradition."[19] Wharton Dickinson noted in 1883 that written genealogies, documenting the family past, could supply an authentic account of "what has been done in the past, and what is now being done," in order for families to know "what must be done in the future."[20]

Genealogy caught on for reasons other than nostalgia or insecurity. Curiosity or the pleasure of the hunt compelled some individuals. A desire to fill out the history of their community or locale prompted others. An obligation to avoid future legal disputes over property distribution induced still others to register lineages. In Utah, an aggregation was marching to a different drummer. The Church of Jesus Christ of Latter-day Saints was instructing its flock on the urgent and grave religious duty of genealogical study. Mormon doctrine permitted the living to perform vicarious acts of salvation for deceased ancestors. It was incumbent upon the believer to identify his ancestors in order to "bind" them to the church. The tenet of the perpetuity of the soul's existence and advancement, and the responsibility of the living for the salvation of the dead propelled the Mormons'

---

[18]*The Carter Family Reunion at Woburn, Mass., June 11, 1884* (Boston: Coburn Bros. & Snow, 1884) 32.

[19]*Address of the Hon. Andrew J. Bartholomew of Southbridge, Mass., . . . on the Occasion of the First Reunion of the Descendants of Lieut. William Bartholomew* (Boston: Coburn Bros., 1882) 30.

[20]*Reunion of the Dickinson Family at Amherst, Massachusetts, . . .* 192.

aggressive acquisition of family records and advanced their international reputation as the Mecca for genealogical work.

Genealogy held little attraction, however, for a wide spectrum of Americans. Few advocates could be found among the young, the poor, the new urban immigrant with ties abroad, the politically disenfranchised, or structurally diverse family systems found, for example, among blacks or Native Americans. These groups had minimum affinity with the established Northeastern families and their geographically dispersed descendants who monopolized the content and practice of genealogy.

Nevertheless, it is clear that in the latter nineteenth and early twentieth centuries genealogy realized its first major phase of development.[21] On the strength of the gains, plans were underway by 1912 to hold an International Congress of Genealogy. The congress met in San Francisco in July 1915 in connection with the Panama-Pacific International Exposition. Sixty-six organizations, including genealogical, historical, and patriotic societies, plus family associations, sent 297 delegates. The congress, and the issues considered—eugenics, government preservation of vital records, methods and quality of research, establishment of information networks—was a fitting capstone to the establishment of American genealogy.[22]

The subsequent war effort stalled genealogy's growth (as suggested in Figure 1). Yet the accompanying flush of Americanism and nativism, the loss of family members, and a kind of "trench genealogy" shared in barracks and on battlefields fed the renewal of genealogical inquiry after the armistice. Eugenics attained its height of popularity in the zenophobic atmosphere that immediately followed the war. The *Wisconsin Magazine of History* advised its readers in 1923 that the "only hope of improving the race is through 'selective breeding,' " and that questions dealing with racial superiority and traits "may often profitably be considered with the aid of data compiled and worked out in genealogical study."[23] Other contri-

---

[21]See Penrose, "The Genealogical Society of Utah," 8-11, and Sheppard, "A Bicentennial Look at Genealogy," 9.

[22]Papers delivered at the congress and a description of the proceedings are in the 1915 volume of the *Utah Genealogical and Historical Magazine*.

[23]Arthur Adams, "The Historical Society and Genealogical Research," *Wisconsin Magazine of History* 7 (September 1923): 59.

butions to genealogy's recovery in the 1920s included the 1919 publication of the Library of Congress index to 6,965 American and British
genealogies, and the first of seven volumes of the massive *Compendium of
American Genealogy* in 1925.[24] In addition, important commemorations
stimulated ancestor research, such as the Mayflower Celebrations of 1919,
memorializing the 300th anniversary of that famous immigration, and the
nation's sesquicentennial birthday in 1926.

The economically depressed years of the 1930s reveal erratic trends
in genealogy. The financial squeeze constricted genealogical-society
memberships, which were perhaps a luxury to forgo. Like the Pennsylvania society (Figure 1), for example, the membership of the New England
Historic Genealogical Society decreased after a peak in 1930 and recovered only after World War II.[25] Still, the momentum in publications
and research, begun in the 1920s, did not wane. An ever-widening body
of study aids, research centers, and organizations brought genealogy within
reach of more and more persons. Of major significance was the opening
in 1935 of the National Archives, the appearance of the *Dictionary of
American Biography*, the first how-to manuals, the indexing and historical-
records survey projects of the Works Progress Administration, and the debut of magazines and journals.[26] While some organizations floundered,
others started up or expanded. The Federation of American Family Associations originated in 1930; a 1931 directory listed more than 500 constituents. Sixty-two patriotic and hereditary societies were active in 1936,
no doubt invigorated by the 1932 bicentennial of George Washington's
birth. Around this time Donald L. Jacobus, a dominant figure in genealogy for fifty years, unveiled a "new school" of genealogists committed to

---

[24][J. C. M. Hanson], *American and English Genealogies in the Library of Congress*
(Washington: Government Printing Office, 1919): Frederick A. Virkus, ed., *The Abridged
Compendium of American Genealogy. First Families of America. A Genealogical Encyclopedia
of the United States*, 7 vols. (Chicago: A. N. Marquis & Co., 1925-1942).

[25]Membership statistics for the NEHGS are found in the "Report of the Committee
on Membership" in the "Annual Report" in the *Register*.

[26]The multivolume *Dictionary of American Biography* (*DAB*) was published between
1928 and 1936. Gilbert Harry Doane's *Searching for Your Ancestors: The Why and How of
Genealogy* (New York: Whittlesey House, 1937) was one of the first major training manuals. Its fifth edition, with James B. Bell as coauthor, came out in 1980. Lester J. Cappon
estimated that thirty new genealogical periodicals were issued between the world wars
("Genealogy: Handmaid of History," 7).

upgrading professional standards.[27] To this end, the American Society of Genealogists was established in 1940, composed of fifty elected fellows and dedicated to professional betterment and educational programs.

For the first time, genealogy caught the attention of America's literary and cultural critics. Magazines such as the *American Mercury,* the *Literary Digest,* and *Colophon* carried articles on the genealogical phenomenon. Marquis Childs ridiculed the application of business techniques to the selling of family history. Cedric Larson thought genealogy had "achieved such popularity and respectability . . . as to rival philately, numismatics, and golf as the avocation of a countless multitude." Edna Cleve found the "genealogical novel" a popular form among fiction writers.[28]

The Second World War checked genealogy's development, moreso than the previous world conflict. Appeals on war's eve to probe ancestral lives for Christian and democratic values to counter totalitarianism failed to preserve genealogy's momentum.[29] Regaining the impetus in the war's aftermath took longer than before. The most noteworthy advances between 1945 and 1965 occurred in the areas of instruction and professionalization. Meredith B. Colket, Jr. organized in 1950 the Institute of Genealogical Research, an annual three-week training course jointly

---

[27]Donald L. Jacobus brought out his *Genealogy as Pastime and Profession* in 1930 (New Haven: Tuttle, Morehouse & Taylor Co.). It is considered the first professional instructional book. In 1932 he expanded the compass of his *New Haven Genealogical Magazine,* begun in 1922, and renamed it the *American Genealogist.*

[28]Marquis W. Childs, "The Genealogy Business," *American Mercury* 19 (1930): 348-54; Cedric Larson, "The Rising Tide of Genealogical Publication in America," *Colophon* 3 (Winter 1938): 100; Edna Cleve, "Some Genealogical Novels," *Wilson Bulletin for Librarians* 7 (1933): 298-300. See also "Ancestor Hunts: Dust of Family Closets Stirred in Wave of Genealogical Sleuthing," *Literary Digest* 123 (1 May 1937): 21-23. Genealogy was intimately linked with the contemporary rage for writing biographies, with the *Dictionary of American Biography* being the most obvious manifestation of what Francis P. Weisenburger referred to as "the personal element in history" in an article so entitled in the *Ohio State Archaeological and Historical Quarterly* 48 (1939): 153-63. Colleges, Dartmouth in particular, furnished courses on American biography. For an enlightening portrayal of the ways genealogy affected the life and work of one of America's foremost modern poets, see Milton J. Bates, "To Realize the Past: Wallace Stevens' Genealogical Study," *American Literature* 52 (January 1981): 607-27.

[29]See, for instance, Harold J. Grimm, "The Genealogist as Historian," *Ohio State Archaeological and Historical Quarterly* 49 (1940): 281.

sponsored by the National Archives and the American University. The American Society of Genealogists introduced in 1960 its influential text, *Genealogical Research, Methods and Sources;* and in 1964 this same group, along with the National Genealogical Society, created the Board for Certification of Genealogists.[30]

The most recent surge of genealogy far surpassed any past periods of marked vitality. Beginning with the Civil War Centennial in the mid-1960s, this newest wave of genealogical interest officially began at the first World Conference on Records held at Salt Lake City in 1969. By the time of the Bicentennial and the publication of *Roots,* the vogue for genealogy had assumed tidal proportions. By the 1980s at least one-half million Americans and Canadians were considered to be active genealogists. One thousand genealogical societies existed in the two countries. Around 300,000 Americans held memberships in such organizations.[31] The Genealogical Society of Pennsylvania, which had about 400 members in 1960, counted 1,715 members in 1979. Patronage in state archives shared similar increases. The 4,600 readers in the Georgia archives in 1970 expanded to 17,500 by 1980.[32] Several hundred newspapers and nongenealogical magazines featured genealogical columns. As many as 50,000 family genealogies were in print or in manuscript.[33] Readers could choose from among 1,000 genealogical periodicals.[34]

We can assume that given these recent trends, genealogical activity between 1980 and 1985 has continued to multiply. Its growth has added new job classifications, publishing houses, bookstores, and a variety of support services from travel packages to computer programming. Media coverage has been widespread. Conferences and courses have prolifer-

---

[30]Such a national board to pass on credentials had been suggested as early as 1910. See John R. Totten, "Science of Genealogy. The Growing Interest in This Study in the United States," *New York Genealogical and Biographical Record* 41 (1910): 138-39.

[31]Mary Keysor Meyer, ed., *Directory of Genealogical Societies in the U.S.A. and Canada,* 3d ed. (Arlington Heights IL: AHM Publishing Corporation, 1978).

[32]Betty Doak Elder, "The Need to Know: Amateur Genealogists Pose Problems for State Repositories," *History News: American Association for State and Local History* 36 (May 1981): 8.

[33]Williard Heiss, "Ancestoritis," Indianapolis *News,* 4 August 1979.

[34]Kip Sperry, *A Survey of American Genealogical Periodicals and Periodical Indexes* (Detroit: Gale Research Co., 1977).

ated. This growth indicates genealogy's appeal to a broad range of the populace. Whereas upper-class native white Americans generally carried on genealogical work in times past, the last fifteen years have witnessed participation that cuts across age, sex, ethnic, and socioeconomic lines.[35]

As genealogy has ripened over the last century, it has been compared periodically with the field of history. Prior to the Civil War, the relation between genealogy and history rarely occasioned comment because the genealogist, biographer, historian, and antiquarian usually were one and the same person. In the late 1800s historical writing splintered into roughly three orientations. The local historian chronicled the town and the county. Genealogy came to be a popular pastime, and its devotees, with notable exceptions, gave attention to the bare bones of lives—names, places and dates of births, marriages, and deaths. History proper became associated with teachers in colleges and universities and with their professional organizations. These classroom historians might mention local manners and customs, or popular movements, but typically the student learned about great events and the movers and shakers of past eras. The historian gave scant consideration to ordinary persons, their environment, social and familial relations, work and play.

A broadly segmented coverage of history resulted from this threefold apportionment of investigation. Detached from one another's scholarship, the academic historian, the local historian, and the genealogist pursued their chosen specialties, generally disregarding the interdependence of institutions, community, and family. The artificial partitioning of the historical experience finally began to break down in the 1960s and 1970s as a "new" social history probed and exalted common people, and as the case study in local history became the mode of operation.

In the meantime, the genealogist and the professional historian had little positive communication. Prejudice and misunderstanding hindered finding a common ground for serious give-and-take. The stereotype of the

---

[35]Rubincam surveys the advances in Mexican-American, Jewish, black, and Native American genealogy in his article "Genealogy for All People." As for the traditional age bias, Ronald Reed noted several years ago that in his community of Carterville, Illinois, the "age of the researcher makes little difference: our collection is used by the seventh grader and a great-great-grandmother." ("A Selected Bibliography for the Establishment of a Small Genealogy Collection for Medium-size Public Libraries in Illinois," *Illinois Libraries* 59 [April 1977]: 271-72).

genealogist as "the little old lady in gum shoes," and its variants, was almost impenetrable. More often than not the historian assumed that genealogy was an amateurish avocation coveted by enthusiasts too engrossed
in chasing down a famous relative to be nonsubjective, and too unversed
in rigorous proof methods to avoid sloppy work. The genealogist re-
proached the historian for holding only vague notions of what genealogists did; for not acknowledging genealogists' skills in records research; and
for rejecting genealogy as a legitimate historical undertaking.[36]

The historian correctly recognized that the goal of genealogy was the
pedigree, the orderly listing and numbering of a line of descendants through
several generations. The unembellished pedigree, or charted lineage,
commonly pictured as the "family tree," is what one historian had in mind
when he surmised that the genealogist "produces only charts crammed with
more notes and dates, bearing obscure numbers, and signifying little to the
historian."[37] Until recently, most historians could not imagine the information value of a pedigree for their research except as an occasional biographical aid.

The pedigree defined the compass of genealogical work for the historian and for many genealogists. Yet through the years leading genealogists have counseled, as in 1915, that "a pedigree is valuable, but immensely
more so when associated with the lives of its component members, or as
may be said clothed with flesh and blood."[38] To gather every scrap of information pertinent to the names on a pedigree chart, and to fashion life

---

[36]See Totten, "Science of Genealogy," 130; Frederic J. Haskin, "Modern Profession
of Genealogy," *Utah Genealogical and Historical Magazine* 5 (1914): 14; idem, "American
Societies Based on Genealogical Descent," ibid. 8 (1917): 39-40; M. R. [Milton Rubin-
cam], "The Genealogist's Contributions to History," *National Genealogical Society Quarterly* 40 (1952): 106-107. An epigram in the *Genealogical Helper* 1 (November 1947): 10,
raised the matter of reverse snobbery: "There is no more snobbery in wishing to trace the
family tree back to its roots and branches than in pretending to be superior to such research."

[37]Theodore L. Agnew, Review of *Three Hundred Years American: The Epic of a Family
from Seventeenth-Century New England to Twentieth-Century Midwest*, by Alice F. Jackson
and Bettina Jackson, in the *Mississippi Valley Historical Review* 39 (June 1952): 109.

[38]Henry Byron Phillips, "International Congress of Genealogy Day," *Utah Genealogical and Historical Magazine* 6 (1915): 166. As Charles K. Bolton wrote in 1913, "Are we
genealogists writing the lives of people or are we copying records?" ("The New Genealogy," ibid. 4 [1913]: 127).

histories or a detailed narrative of a lineage's development, is the heart of the genealogical craft. "Many genealogists, falsely so called, do lack a true historical spirit, have no understanding of historical method, and have no vision beyond the compiling of names and dates, . . . but a genealogy that doesn't rise above them and reach beyond them has small, if any, excuse for being."[39] Lester J. Cappon, in 1957, concluded that "the study of genealogy is something larger than the particular genealogy itself, it is the history of a family in both its immediate relationship and its wider impact on society."[40]

These genealogists did not casually apply the terms *family history* or *historical genealogy* to denote their work. People made history, they argued: to be acquainted with family backgrounds could illuminate the actions and motivations underlying, for example, the process of community growth or decline, or even the diplomacy of great nations. Backed by the oft-quoted statement of historian John Fiske that "without genealogy, the study of history is lifeless and incomplete," genealogists heralded their endeavor as the cornerstone of history.[41]

Regardless of how persistently genealogists labored to convince historians (and perhaps themselves) that their efforts merited serious review, cooperation between the two disciplines rested primarily on changes in the focus of historians' research. Such changes occurred in the 1960s and 1970s when a new breed of social historians turned to localized data, converted into machine-readable form, as a means of defining society's behavioral patterns.[42] In the process of digging up and experimenting with community and family materials, genealogy received fresh consideration.

---

[39]Arthur Adams, "The Development of Genealogical Study through a Century," in Hill, *A Century of Genealogical Progress,* 65.

[40]Cappon, "Genealogy: Handmaid of History," 1. See also Rubincam, "The Genealogist's Contributions to History," 107.

[41]G. W. Dial, "The Value of Genealogy," *New England Magazine,* n.s. 33 (September 1905-February 1906): 288; Phillips, "International Congress of Genealogy Day," 167-68.

[42]For discussion of the "new" social history, see Peter N. Sterns, "Toward a Wider Vision: Trends in Social History," in *The Past before Us: Contemporary Historical Writing in the United States,* ed. Michael Kammen (Ithaca: Cornell University Press, 1980): 201-30; idem, "The New Social History: An Overview," in *Ordinary People and Everyday Life: Perspectives on the New Social History,* ed. James B. Gardner and George Rollie Adams (Nashville: The American Association for State and Local History, 1983) 3-21.

In the mid-1960s historians, dealing with population and family structures of colonial New England communities, initiated a reassessment of genealogy's usefulness in historical research. These scholars shared Philip Greven's observation that "historians must seek to explore the basic structure and character of society through close, detailed examination of individuals, families, and groups in particular communities and localities."[43] Most colonial historians did not employ the family information already available in published genealogies. They preferred to develop data bases, and to do so they adopted the strategy of "family reconstitution," which Dan Scott Smith calls "essentially statistical genealogy."[44] Originating in Canada and Europe in the 1950s and 1960s, family reconstitution is the construction of genealogies by fusing separate listings of births, marriages, and deaths—a procedure demographer Richard Vann recognizes as one employed by genealogists.[45] In fact, the Cambridge Group for the History of Population and Social Structure, a pioneer in family reconstruction founded in England in 1964, regularly consulted genealogists in devising their worksheets.[46]

The technique of family reconstitution and its similarity to genealogical practice, led some historians and demographers in the late 1960s to express cautious optimism about the utility of family accounts produced by genealogists. Greven proposed that the lineages published in several prominent genealogical journals "could provide an astonishing amount of information about the lives of early Americans."[47] Among records useful

---

[43]Philip Greven, Jr., *Four Generations: Population, Land, and Family in Colonial Andover, Massachusetts* (Ithaca: Cornell University Press, 1970).

[44]Daniel Scott Smith, "Parental Power and Marriage Patterns: An Analysis of Historical Trends in Hingham, Massachusetts," *Journal of Marriage and the Family* 35 (1973): 422.

[45]Richard T. Vann, "The New Demographic History," in *International Handbook of Historical Studies: Contemporary Research and Theory,* ed. Georg G. Iggers and Harold T. Parker (Westport: Greenwood Press, 1979) 33.

[46]Of considerable influence to American historians were the works of E. A. Wrigley, ed., *An Introduction to English Historical Demography from the Sixteenth to the Nineteenth Century* (New York: Basic Books, 1966), and D. V. Glass and D. E. C. Eversley, eds., *Population in History: Essays in Historical Demography* (Chicago: Aldine Publishing Co., 1965).

[47]Philip J. Greven, Jr., "Historical Demography and Colonial America," *William and Mary Quarterly* 24 (1967): 441.

to demographers, T. H. Hollingsworth ranked genealogies eighth, but he added that "genealogy-based demographic studies have their special interest since the data are usually relatively complete."[48] At the World Conference on Records in 1969, Dan Steel suggested that genealogy had attained new respectability as a result of its testing by demographers.[49] Historian Edward Saveth thought library shelves were filled with particularly worthless padded genealogies, although he went on to say that unadorned genealogy could be "helpful in the study of family mobility and in the techniques of family reconstruction."[50] Fellow historian Michael Kamman wrote that genealogies, "when used in clusters," could have "considerable value for certain types of serious research."[51]

The publication in 1970 of book-length versions of the New England town studies by Greven, John Demos, and Kenneth Lockridge prompted demands for more local and family history.[52] Calls went out for closer cooperation between historians and genealogists. Van Beck Hall told the Western Pennsylvania Historical Society in 1971 that the new social history, in revitalizing the study of local and family history, would allow closer working relationships between professional and amateur historians and genealogists.[53] In noting the requirements that the new family history would make on America's archives, Richard Jensen urged genealogists, ar-

---

[48]T. H. Hollingsworth, *Historical Demography* (Ithaca: Cornell University Press, 1969) 60.

[49]D. J. Steel, "Demography, Genetics and Genealogy," 1 (World Conference on Records and Genealogical Seminar, Salt Lake City, Utah, USA, 5-8 August 1969, Area B).

[50]Edward N. Saveth, "The Problem of American Family History," *American Quarterly* 21 (1969): 313.

[51]Michael Kamman, "Politics, Science and Society in Colonial America. An Essay Review of Recent Approaches and Neglected Opportunities," *Journal of Social History* 3 (Fall 1969): 63-81.

[52]Greven, *Four Generations*; John Demos, *A Little Commonwealth: Family Life in Plymouth Colony* (New York: Oxford University Press, 1970): Kenneth A. Lockridge, *A New England Town, the First Hundred Years: Dedham, Massachusetts, 1636-1736* (New York: W. W. Norton, 1970).

[53]Van Beck Hall, "New Approaches to Local History," *Western Pennsylvania Historical Magazine* 55 (1972): 239-48.

chivists, and family historians to work together.[54] In 1975, on the eve of the Bicentennial, five leading historical journals carried articles that dealt with the question of genealogy and history.[55]

Since 1975 gestures toward a more cordial and effectual association of historians and genealogists have come from a number of directions. Of greatest relevance are those developments that appear to have had special significance in drawing historians' attention to genealogists' accomplishments. Some years ago historians turned to the computer in order to handle large assortments of bits of information. More recently, genealogists have availed themselves of computers to list, index, and update raw generational materials. As a result, there exists a great deal of career data in a form that is convenient for historians to use in studying collective social and family behavior. With both sides using the same tool, it's apparent that the computer is functioning as a third party joining mutual interests.[56]

Another active agent is the so-called public historian, the trained historian employed in historical societies, archives, and libraries, for instance. These professionals not only report the quality and quantity of local and genealogical documents at hand, they also probe their institutions' collections for research topics and publish genealogically based studies.[57]

---

[54]Richard Jensen, "Archives and Ancestors: The Study of the American Family" (paper delivered at the Society of American Archivists, annual meeting, San Francisco CA, December 1973).

[55]Richard S. Lackey, "Genealogical Research: An Assessment of Potential Value," *Prologue: Journal of the National Archives* 7 (1975): 221-25; Samuel P. Hays, "History and Genealogy: Patterns of Change and Prospects for Cooperation," ibid. 7 (1975): 39-43, 81-84, 187-91; Jay P. Anglin, "The Fundamentals of Genealogy: A Neglected and Fertile New Field for Professional Historians," *Southern Quarterly* 13 (1975): 145-50; Larry R. Gerlach and Michael L. Nicholls, "The Mormon Genealogical Society and Research Opportunities in Early American History," *William and Mary Quarterly* 32 (1975): 625-29; Larry T. Wimmer and Clayne L. Pope, "The Genealogical Society Library of Salt Lake City: A Source of Data for Economic and Social Historians," *Historical Methods Newsletter* 8 (1975): 51-58.

[56]See Connie Lamb, "Computers and Genealogy: A Survey of the Literature," *Genealogical Journal* 12 (Winter 1983-1984): 151-61.

[57]See Richard J. Cox, "Genealogy and Public History: New Genealogical Guides and Their Implications for Public Historians," *Public Historian* 6 (Spring 1984): 91-98.

In schools, teachers find greater student enthusiasm for history if the subject is approached through the pupil's own family genealogy. At the college level, some 300 courses in genealogy and family history, compared with 30 a decade ago, are being offered in the regular or extension curriculums. Along these lines, programs and publications emanating from research libraries and universities, such as Newberry Library's Family and Community Center, and the University of Utah's Center for Historical Population Studies, have exposed historians to genealogies. Genealogical journals, especially the *New England Historical and Genealogical Register* and the *Genealogical Journal,* have been receptive to pieces by historians who demonstrate the way genealogies can shed light on substantive historical questions.[58]

As a historical source, a genealogy embodies two incomparable characteristics. It specifies the particulars of lives both over time and within the crucial context of kinship. These intrinsic qualities of longitudinality and consanguinity are in the final analysis what give genealogy the exceptional capability of aiding modern historical studies. To actually observe life processes is a major reason social historians are attracted to genealogies. Scholars researching patterns of past family behavior have relied heavily on census-type materials because of their uniformity and breadth. It has become increasingly clear, though, that the census used alone presents only a cross-sectional view, a snapshot of family experi-

---

[58]The *Register* has published such pieces as John J. Waters, "The Traditional World of the New England Peasant: A View from Seventeenth Century Barnstable," 130 (1976): 3-21; Timothy Breen, "Transfer of Culture: Chance and Design in Shaping Massachusetts Bay, 1630-1660," 132 (1978): 3-17; Thomas R. Cole, "Family, Settlement, and Migration in Southeastern Massachusetts, 1650-1850: The Case for Regional Analysis," 132 (1978): 171-85; Robert M. Taylor, Jr., "Genealogical Sources in American Social History Research: A Reappraisal," 135 (1981): 3-15; John J. Waters, "Naming and Kinship in New England: Guilford Patterns and Usage, 1693-1759," 138 (1984): 161-81.

The *Genealogical Journal* has included Ralph J. Crandall, "A Neglected Resource: The Value of Genealogy to the Study of the Nineteenth-Century Family in America," 9 (1980): 165-81; Richard S. Lackey, "The Value of Genealogy and Family History," 9 (1980): 153-64; Robert Charles Anderson, "Genealogy and Record Linkage," 9 (1980): 3-8; idem, "The Genealogist and the Demographer," 9 (1980): 182-97; Peter R. Knights, "The Facts of Lives; or, Whatever Happened to 2,808 Nineteenth-Century Bostonians," 12 (1983-1984): 162-73.

ence.[59] To capture the diversity and richness of family life, some historians adopted a family-cycle model that defined a sequence of developmental stages from marriage to widowhood, and they compiled age-specific groups from successive censuses to approximate family change. The life-cycle approach, however, still obscures family dynamics because it overlooks other significant dimensions of family life not enumerated in censuses, and it ignores those life histories that do not conform to preconceived stages.[60]

Other historians have employed a "life course" approach, a more comprehensive view than the life-cycle analysis. The life-course study is concerned with the timing of changes over an individual's lifetime, and how these transitions are affected by and coordinated with flux in family careers, transpiring historical contexts, and the person's cumulative history. This sensible yet complex avenue to researching past behavior is not, of course, designed to clarify an individual's activity, but rather the patterned activity of aggregates. With this intent the concept falters in implementation because of the difficulties in locating data sets containing the desired detailed and running records of individuals and families. Using some combination of censuses, linked vital records, and oral histories, the few demonstrations of life-course research thus far published have had to resort at some point to simulating or inferring life processes.[61] It would seem

---

[59]Particularly influential in the methodology of household research was the English historical sociologist Peter Laslett. Laslett's suspicions about the reliability of nonquantitative sources to illumine past family behavior led him to urge studying the dominant forms of family organization using census lists. See especially his introduction to *Household and Family in Past Time* (Cambridge: Cambridge University Press, 1972). See also Maris A. Vinovskis, "Recent Trends in American Historical Demography: Some Methodological and Conceptual Considerations," *Studies in American Historical Demography*, ed. Maris A. Vinovskis (New York: Academic Press, 1978) 1-25. Louise A. Tilly and Miriam Cohen discuss the pros and cons of census-based research in "Does the Family Have a History? A Review of Theory and Practice in Family History," *Social Science History* 6 (1982): 134-37.

[60]An explanation and application of life-cycle analysis is given in Graham B. Spanier and Paul C. Glick, "The Life Cycle of American Families: An Expanded Analysis," *Journal of Family History* 5 (1980): 97-111.

[61]Dan Scott Smith has defined the life-course approach as a "diffuse and often metaphorical way of discussing lives over time." ("Life Course, Norms, and the Family System of Older Americans in 1900," *Journal of American History* 4 [Fall 1979]: 285). Tamara Hareven discusses the life-course strategy in her introduction to *Transitions: The Family and the Life Course in Historical Perspective*, ed. Tamara Hareven (New York: Academic Press, 1978). See also Hareven's *Family Time and Industrial Time: The Relationship between the Family and Work in a New England Industrial Community* (Cambridge: Cambridge University Press, 1982), and Clyde Griffen's review of this work in *Social Science History* 8 (1984): 313-20.

that here, as with other current strategies for uncovering change in family experience, efforts to surmount the usual source limitations should take into account genealogies.

A systematic appropriation of information in genealogies can also help to close a gap in migration studies by recording an individual's residence changes, an advantage not accorded the typical census-based migration study. The career data often found in genealogies empower the investigator to examine the character of lifelong geographic mobility, including migration rates, distances and destinations, chain migration and clustering, and migration selectivity (why some move and others do not). Knowing dates and locations of movement enables immediate linkage with other kinds of records, including censuses, which can add biographical particulars along with clues to unraveling the causes and effects of migration.

Trailing families over distance and time more often than not entails taking up the matter of kinship. Despite the impressive findings compiled by social scientists on the instrumental role of kin in migration, historians have yet to do more than acknowledge their failure to address the subject adequately. Kinship is a unique and crucial dimension of social structure, and almost instinctively we know that our view of family and community is incomplete if kin ties are overlooked.

Historians should be knowledgeable about kinship terminology and set about investigating kin roles, the size and makeup of kin groups, the functioning of kin ties in various contexts, and the effect changing social and demographic conditions have on the composition and operation of kinship. Making use of network-analysis techniques could be fruitful here. Finding sources to execute kin studies has been a major stumbling block. Again, genealogies command the sort of horizontal and vertical kin connections that facilitate kinship analysis. As Andrejs Plakans makes clear in his essay below and in other articles, genealogies, however fashioned, constitute a time depth of relationships that enhances meanings of kinship deduced from less applicable sources.[62]

The genealogical lens projects a series of actions and images that allows questions of how much and how many to be correlated with questions such as how deep, how remote, or how durable. In other words, besides

---

[62]Andrejs Plakans, "Ties of Kinship and Kinship Roles in an Historic Eastern European Peasant Community: A Synchronic Analysis," *Journal of Family History* 7 (1982): 55. For an incisive look at network analysis and the ways historians can benefit from it, see Darrett B. Rutman, "Community Study," *Historical Methods* 13 (Winter 1980): 29-41.

having the potential to disclose the broad external form of a kinship group, genealogies can also cue researchers to attitudes and values underlying the interaction within and between generations. Distribution patterns in occupation, residence, religious affiliation, elderly care, kinship aid, organizational fellowship, and other variables can expose structural transitions and suggest the mind-sets responsible for these changing courses of behavior. [63]

Depending on the extent of and reason for incorporating genealogies in historical scholarship, their use raises serious methodological considerations. It is one thing to dip into genealogies for selective or supplemental data on particular individuals or households. It is quite another thing to take full advantage of the longitudinal character of genealogies in a systematic fashion. The alignment of descent compels the student not only to redefine the family in order to encompass the kin connection, but to mark off kinship boundaries, an arbitrary decision at best. Furthermore, genealogies differentiate segments of time by the turnover of generations, which can be confusing. Glen Elder, Jr., the architect of the life-course perspective, observes that "genealogical status . . . is a very poor index of historical location." [64] Persons may represent different generations but be the same age and mature in a common environment, while others may be in the same generation but be widely separated in age and lack shared historical references. If quantification is integral to the research design, what measurement techniques fit the chain of evidence genealogies exhibit?

These operational matters, and others, have been addressed by historians, demographers, and anthropologists. [65] We can expect further refinements as genealogies gain a wider scholarly audience. In order to attract that larger audience, it must continually be stressed that genealogists care about accuracy and documentation. Today's genealogist knows that an

---

[63]See Patrick H. Hutton, "The History of Mentalities: The New Map of Cultural History," History and Theory 20 (1981): 237-59; Lawrence Stone, "Family History in the 1980s," Journal of Interdisciplinary History 12 (Summer 1981): 71-74.

[64]Maris Vinovskis, "From Household Size to the Life Course: Some Observations on Recent Trends in Family History," American Behavioral Scientist 21 (1977): 267-69; Glen H. Elder, Jr., "Family History and the Life Course," in Hareven, Transitions, 41.

[65]For example, see the essays in Genealogical Demography, ed. Bennett Dyke and Warren T. Morrill (New York: Academic Press, 1980), and the articles in the special issue on anthropology and family history of the Journal of Family History 9:3 (1984).

unsubstantiated lineage is not only personally unacceptable, but may produce false leads or gaps within the final product. The some seventy-five instructional manuals thus far produced and the college-level courses established to train the amateur in genealogical methods attest to the genealogical community's concern for high standards of scholarship. Further, because of the professionalization of genealogy in the last half-century, much of the published genealogical research has been compiled by certified genealogists and reflects their understanding of family-history resources and documentation.

Moreover, genealogists should be urged to record every piece of information uncovered on individuals and families. Besides accuracy and authenticity, the comprehensiveness of an information base is of prime interest to the historian. In particular, the lives of persons still living, or those deceased but still vividly remembered by the living, should be accorded a detailed examination. In twenty to fifty years, these kinds of career descriptions, along with the secondary analysis of sociological and governmental family materials, will furnish historians the basic information with which to recover the makeup and culture of the twentieth-century family.

Also important, finally, is that genealogists be encouraged to write family-history narratives, to take that pedigree chart and expand it into a full-scale group biography. After many years of laboriously researching and compiling materials on a family, an intimate knowledge of that family has been acquired that would be forever beyond the time and resources of the historian. To put into an organized narrative the details on, and impressions about, the family would in itself represent a valuable contribution to American historiography; but it would be of inestimable value to the professional historian. When composing these narratives genealogists should be encouraged to mine the relevant historical literature, to become acquainted with recent data relative to community, family, and kin, and to eschew the extremes of sterile numbers and pointless anecdotes.

In depicting the history of American genealogy and its relationship with the historical profession, we may have exaggerated the degree of either its alienation or compatibility. Certainly we know too little of genealogy's past to tell the the whole story, and the sheer profusion of present social-history research practically guarantees our having overlooked some illustrations of problems and advantages in uniting history and genealogy. The point of the essay, however, should be clear. Genealogies represent a maligned and ignored body of source material on the family that only recently has engaged the social historian. Looking for alternative means to disentangle the meaning of the family in past times, a small number of historians latched onto genealogy and invented methods of working with the data. Out of this have come some imaginative uses of genealogies and, most important, studies that are longitudinal in intent and in execution. The handling of change is central to the historical enterprise, and the move toward appropriating genealogies seems to be a major advance in this regard and one beneficial to both historians and genealogists.

FIGURE 1

TRENDS IN GENEALOGICAL ACTIVITY, 1915-1965

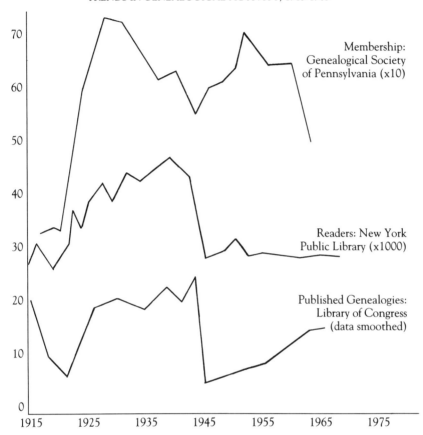

Membership:
Genealogical Society
of Pennsylvania (x10)

Readers: New York
Public Library (x1000)

Published Genealogies:
Library of Congress
(data smoothed)

Data drawn from "Annual Reports," *Pennsylvania Genealogical Magazine;* "Statistics of Readers and Volumes Consulted," *Annual Reports, Bulletin of the New York Public Library;* Marion J. Kaminkow, comp., *Genealogies in the Library of Congress. A Bibliography,* 2 vols. (Baltimore, 1972).

Chapter Two

HISTORY AND GENEALOGY: PATTERNS OF CHANGE AND PROSPECTS FOR COOPERATION

Samuel P. Hays

During the past decade or so a number of significant developments have occurred in both the history and genealogy fields. For the most part these trends have remained separate. The traditional separation of their activities, often accompanied by mutual disdain, has allowed historians to pay only slight attention to genealogy and has divorced genealogists from the professional work of historians. A quick review of their publications indicates the degree to which both work in separate worlds.[1] Yet developments in these fields are moving in similar directions, sufficient to give rise to the notion that closer cooperation between them would be mu-

---

[1]See, for contrast, *The Genealogical Helper* (Logan, Utah) and the *Journal of Social History* (Pittsburgh).

tually advantageous.[2] When the social historian begins to work with family history and to focus on a broader network of kinship relationships over time, and the genealogist begins to spend time and effort in indexing the same manuscript census returns that historians use, it is time for the two groups to examine their common ground.

This essay attempts to foster such a relationship. It comes from the author's long involvement in both fields. On the one hand, I have devoted considerable attention to working out concepts and research resources for a more grass-roots type of social history; on the other, my first interest in history, some four decades ago, was through genealogy, which became a hobby that has persisted. As social history has come to focus on family-related institutions, I have found the information from genealogical investigations to be very helpful in dealing with matters such as migration and vertical mobility, changes in family size and life cycle, and the impact of modernization on traditional values and practices in religion, family, and recreation. All this suggests the enormously valuable role that a more informed and imaginative genealogy could play in broadening historical inquiry and insight.

At the same time, I have been involved in attempts to make usable the large quantity of historical evidence about the ordinary everyday activities of people—available in archives of local, state, and national governments, as well as private sources—in order to provide the research base for more effective social history. I have been impressed with the fact that genealogists have gone after such records to a far greater extent than have historians. The federal manuscript census returns were used effectively initially by genealogists, and their work in indexing them for more rapid use has been prodigious. The focus on the county courthouse, where the great majority of the vital materials for social history still lies, has occupied the attention of genealogists far more than that of historians. In fact, the disdain frequently expressed by historians concerning the usefulness of these records, which have often been allowed to decay by neglect, borders on irresponsibility.

There is immediate need for a closer relationship between the new social history and the new genealogy. On one side, the concerns of his-

---

[2]Historians will be especially interested in Phillip R. Kunz, ed., *Selected Papers in Genealogical Research*, Institute of Genealogical Studies, Brigham Young University (ca. 1972), which are studies in social history that draw upon the archives of the Mormon Church.

torians can add a wider dimension to genealogy, and on the other side the work of genealogists can provide crucial evidence for social history. Both, in turn, rely on the same records and could benefit from a common approach to preserving and organizing historical sources and to making them accessible.

The new trend in American social history stems from dissatisfaction with a narrow political history that was preoccupied with the big event, the dramatic and highly publicized episode. The traditional focus has been on the presidents, the wars, the dramatic election, the prominent writer. Now there is more interest in society as a whole. Since the concern of history now encompasses everyone in the social order, there is a concerted attempt to seek information about as many in the entire population and as much about their activities as possible. During the last decade, for example, county, township, and precinct election returns have been used extensively to analyze voting patterns at the smallest geopolitical level.[3] One township or one ward votes differently from another, and the pattern persists over the years—why? Such an approach seeks to relate variations in voting to differences in group cultural values. But even this data is not individualized, and recently there has been an effort to ferret out what information remains in poll lists, which are individualized records of whether people voted or how they voted.[4] All this reflects a shift in emphasis toward the grass-roots and day-to-day human affairs.

Other aspects of grass-roots social life soon came under scrutiny. The most extensive recent foray into the manuscript census returns has come from historians who study geographical and vertical mobility. This research requires information about individuals, for which the manuscript census returns are the most complete source. A number of these studies

---

[3]A good introduction to such studies is Joel H. Silbey and Samuel T. McSeveney, *Voters, Parties, and Elections: Quantitative Essays in the History of American Popular Voting Behaviour* (Lexington MA, 1972). A study based on urban small-unit voting data is John L. Shover, "The Emergence of a Two-Party System in Republican Philadelphia, 1924-1936," *Journal of American History* 50 (March 1974): 985-1002.

[4]A review of current poll-book research and a case study of Greene County IL is John M. Rozette and Paul E. McAllister, "Voting Behaviour in the Late Jacksonian Period: The Conceptual and Methodological Significance of Poll Book Research," paper delivered at the sixth annual conference on social and political history at the State University of New York, College at Brockport.

examine the degree of migration in and out of a community.[5] How many people there at the beginning of the decade leave by the end, or how many there at the end of the decade are newcomers? The evidence demonstrates a high degree of moving about, far more so than we had previously believed. But the studies are limited because the manuscript census does not tell how far a person moved; it might have been only into the next county, or it could have been several states distant. Mere departures, if added up, might give a false notion of extensive movement or in other ways distort the conclusions.

This problem immediately raises the possibility of genealogical inquiry that focuses on the life span of individuals and generations. I am speaking of mini-mini biographies from birth to death, which implicitly rivet attention on the place of residence in between. Full genealogical information would provide just the kind of data that migration studies require. Moreover, some of the most promising approaches to the vexing problem of "Where did they go?" use genealogical materials. One such study, now underway, is based upon pension records of Civil War soldiers from Allegheny County, Pennsylvania.[6] The pension records indicate their place of birth, their moves thereafter, and their place of death. From this research project the patterns of migration—the number and distance of moves—for at least one group of people will be described. Since moves are a fact of life, much effort is spent by the genealogist trying to fill in the data lacking in the records. How simple it would be if each individual who moved had been required to record the place to which he went or from which he came.

The new social history has brought a variety of inquiries into the history of the family.[7] What have been the changes over the years in the size of family, the spacing of children, the activities and roles of young people, the middle-aged, and older people? Recent interest in youth and the elderly has stimulated new historical research in those fields. One hears of

---

[5]The difficulties of tracing migration within the United States are dealt with effectively in Stephan Thernstrom and Peter R. Knights, "Men in Motion: Some Data and Speculations about Urban Population Mobility in Nineteenth-Century America," *Journal of Interdisciplinary History* 1 (Autumn 1970): 7-35.

[6]Dissertation undertaken by David Pistolessi at the University of Pittsburgh.

[7]See, for example, Michael Gordon, ed., *The American Family in Social-Historical Perspective* (New York, 1973).

"life-cycle" as an important way of looking at more general social change. Light is being shed on the social relationships among members of the family, between husband and wife, and between parents and children. Also being described is the gradual change from male dominance to more co-ordinate relationships between parents and changes in patterns of child rearing from the adult-centered to the child-centered to the adult-directed. Interest in the history of the family has given rise to a variety of conferences and there is a newsletter to stimulate communication among interested researchers.[8]

Social history has focused increasingly on vertical mobility, the changing occupational and educational levels of Americans as they move up or down the ladder.[9] Who moves up or down and who doesn't? Analysis has remained for the most part on the level of broad social characteristics: what percentage of people at one occupational level have children who move up or down to another; similarly, what percentage of people at one level of education have children who reach another level? All this can be examined with more insight within the context of the family. What is the family climate for occupational or educational mobility? Is there a drive for more education for the children or not? To what extent are occupations passed on from father to son and to what extent is there an effort to move out of old patterns into new ones? Within the same family, changes in education and occupation vary with different children. And certainly the historical trend can be visualized as a sequence of general changes within several generations of the genealogical family.

The new interest in ethnic history has also stimulated research on the individual, the family, and the close network of community and kinship relationships that are reinforced by a common ethnic or racial background.[10] The concern for ethnic or racial identity can be explored in a

---

[8]*The Family in Historical Perspective: An International Newsletter,* ed. Tamara K. Hareven and published by the Newberry Library, Chicago IL. Subscriptions are available through the Department of History, Clark University, Worcester MA 01610.

[9]Two excellent examples of work on vertical mobility are Howard P. Chudacoff, *Mobile Americans: Residential and Social Mobility in Omaha, 1880-1920* (New York, 1972) and Stephan Thernstrom, *The Other Bostonians: Poverty and Progress in the American Metropolis, 1880-1970* (Cambridge MA, 1973).

[10]A review of recent trends in one aspect of ethnic history is Robert P. Swierenga, "Ethnocultural Political Analysis: A New Approach to American Ethnic Studies," *Journal of American Studies* 5 (April 1971): 59-79.

general and aggregate manner with evidence drawn from ethnic sources, such as newspapers and religious documents, the writings of ethnic leaders, or the fortunes of ethnic institutions. One can approach ethnic and cultural history through the medium of ideology, the self-conscious expression of identity. Yet the more fundamental context is the family itself, and the process by which cultural values are retained or modified as they are passed from one generation to the next. The impact of modernizing tendencies on traditional ethnocultural loyalties can frequently be observed most clearly in the genealogical biography. Awareness of this has prompted an increasing number of teachers to ask their students to write such genealogies, as a means of developing ideas about enduring historical processes affecting ethnicity, religion, and the family.[11]

More recently the history of women has received increasing attention.[12] Historians have long neglected many aspects of this subject, assuming that the history of women was covered adequately in general histories. But younger scholars have demonstrated that this is not at all the case. As they have investigated the role of women in the family, the community, religion, work, organizations, and public affairs—such as the antislavery crusade of the pre-Civil War years—their research has opened a variety of new fields of social history. The history of women is infused with many elements of the new social history: a concern with grass-roots life rather than national events and leaders and an interest in patterns of experience, life, and thought.

Current interest in social history is evident in ways too numerous to detail here: in a shift of focus in the history of religion from theology and denominational controversy to religious values as an important reflection of human outlooks and preferences; in a new interest in the history of youth and childhood on the one hand and the elderly on the other; in a marked shift in labor history from preoccupation with trade unions to a focus on work and the human setting of work; in recording the history of the com-

---

[11]See Allen F. Davis and Jim Watts, *Generations: Your Family in Modern American History* (New York, 1974), a manual for stimulating student research in family history, and Samuel P. Hays, "History and the Changing University Curriculum," *The History Teacher* (November 1974): 64-72.

[12]An example of the new interest in the history of women is Susan Kleinberg, "Technocracy's Stepdaughters: The Impact of Industrialization upon Working-Class Women, Pittsburgh, 1865-1890" (Dissertation, University of Pittsburgh, 1973).

munity, or that network of personal relationships that develops within the small geographical context of the home and its related institutions. Once the perspective shifted from national events and national history to social life within the entire society, then the appropriate subjects for historical research encompassed all its activities.

A great number of questions being posed now by social historians focus on the family, its generational sequences and its kinship networks. What is being suggested is that a wide range of historical processes can be understood if seen within the context of patterns of relationships fashioned by the individual family and of the intergenerational continuities or discontinuities brought out by genealogy. Rootedness within a community or migration can best be understood as choices not of isolated individuals but of individuals with different kinds and degrees of family relationships. Continuity or discontinuity of values, of customs and traditions, and of old and new perspectives can be seen in the degree to which one generation passes on those characteristics to another or ventures into new and different paths. Involvement in the processes of modernization, including education, new occupations, and new social attachments, is a differential process in which change can be best understood within the context of family values and activities.

Insofar as improved historical understanding can proceed in this fashion, and it certainly has enormous potential, the historian is moving towards the concerns of the genealogist. In terms of common subject matter, the approach logically calls for a variant of family reconstitution to include several generations, what one might term "genealogical reconstitution." The format could be an extension of the family genealogical charts so familiar to the genealogist and the family-reconstitution charts developed by the Cambridge Group for the History of Population and Social Structure in England.[13] The basic data as well as the method of compilation for ready use could be worked out jointly by historians and genealogists. One such effort has already been promoted by bringing together family histories written by college students under the direction of history

---

[13]The reader should examine *Local Population Studies,* a periodical based on the Cambridge Group's demographic studies. It serves as a link between historians studying local demography and the research center at Cambridge and is published twice yearly in association with the Nottingham University Department of Adult Education, Nottingham, England.

teachers; but the success of this venture, because of its large, nationwide scale, seems questionable. A more workable form of cooperative genealogical reconstitution might well focus on mobilizing resources for community genealogy.

All this emphasizes information about individuals rather than collections of statistics and calls for the historian to take a major interest in preserving records of individuals. Until recently the majority of such records were local, rather than state and national. They were collected daily by local agencies in carrying out the functions of government. The few that were generated by national governmental activities, such as military service records and the federal census, have been the most carefully preserved and widely used. But only recently have historians begun to utilize such records, especially census records for migration studies, and rarely has the concern for individual data concentrated on use of state and local records.

In this area genealogists have taken the lead. They have spent an enormous amount of energy in making the individual records available. There is hardly a manuscript census index among the several hundred counties that have been indexed for 1850 that has not been a product of genealogical activity.[14] Only one such project, to my knowledge, has been initiated by professional historians. For a host of counties there are now indexes to marriage records, early land records and deeds, mortality schedules, wills and probate proceedings, and tombstone inscriptions. In view of what needs to be done, the work so far is only a beginning, but compared with the state of affairs two decades ago, the change is remarkable. It now seems accurate to state that if one wishes to become acquainted with the world of local records and the data about individuals in them, one turns to genealogical organizations, publications, and publishers.[15]

Historians and genealogists have been working independently of each other, and most historians do not see the wisdom of a closer relationship.

---

[14]Progress in indexing can be followed regularly in the *Genealogical Helper*. For example, a genealogist, Sam McDowell of Richland IN, is indexing surnames in the 1850 federal population census for Kentucky. Others are indexing entire states for 1800, 1810, and 1820, or counties for later years. Few go beyond 1850.

[15]Two such publishers are the Genealogical Publishing Co., Inc. of Baltimore MD and Polyanthos, Inc. of New Orleans LA.

Nonetheless, the new social history could profit greatly if the energies and activities of genealogists and local historians could be coordinated with those of historians. A major requirement is that historians develop a more active interest in genealogy and community history through the medium of genealogical reconstitution. Historians should use their influence and resources to encourage the preservation and use of local and family records. Moreover, they should promote inquiry into state and national records that provide genealogical information. The efforts of genealogists could be aided by the cooperation of historians.

The expansion of higher education in the past several decades, not only through the college and university but also in the community colleges, provides an excellent opportunity for historians in those institutions to encourage community history and genealogy. To encourage their students to write family genealogies as case studies of long-term social change is one method. Another is for the institution to use its influence to see that these records are preserved. The development of effective oral-history programs that have a broad social context and are not limited to the leaders of the community is still another. In varied ways an institution of higher education can work closely with genealogists in the community to mobilize the resources that are of value to genealogists and historians.

If there is a new social history, there is also a new genealogy. The sharply increased level of organizational activity and publications indicates that genealogy is far more popular and pervasive now than in years past. Circulation of the *Genealogical Helper,* the most widely known of the new publications, has grown rapidly in the past decade, and numerous state and regional organizations have produced magazines.[16] These serve as communication links whereby those searching for information about individuals and families can advertise their needs in the form of a query with the hope that it will be read by someone possessing the information. Query columns have become popular features of local newspapers and special

---

[16]*The Genealogical Helper,* founded in 1947, had a paid circulation of 24,000 in November 1974. Some organizations are statewide, such as the Virginia Genealogical Society of Richmond; some are regional within a state, such as the West-Central Kentucky Family Research Association of Owensboro; and some are county organizations, such as the Knox County (IL) Genealogical Society organized in 1972. Organizations and individual genealogists produce a variety of publications to foster communication between those seeking information and those who might have it. One example is *The Southern Genealogist's Exchange Quarterly and Michigan Heritage.*

magazines.[17] This more intensive activity reflects important shifts in genealogical inquiry. Until very recently the most significant genealogical work was carried on by patriotic organizations, of which the Daughters of the American Revolution was the most important. But that activity has been eclipsed and, while the DAR still plays a significant role, its concerns and services have been superseded by a wider range of genealogical activities. If there is a center of genealogical inquiry today, it is in Utah, where a host of genealogical enterprises have grown up around efforts of the Church of Jesus Christ of Latter-day Saints to preserve ancestral records from all over the world. The *Genealogical Helper* is published in Logan, Utah. But despite the Mormon role in genealogy, this center of activity has not nearly the dominant influence that the DAR had in the past. Genealogical work is now spread throughout the nation.

One might sketch the apparent historical sequence of genealogical activity. Originally it was confined for the most part to exclusive societies of America's past elite—those who could trace their ancestry to the Mayflower or to the officer corps of the American Revolution in the Society of Cincinnatus. New organizations in the latter part of the nineteenth century, such as DAR, extended the range of inquiry to the descendants of all who participated in the Revolution, even in state militias, and if only for a few days, no matter what their social position or origin. It was the DAR that brought the Scotch-Irish into the genealogical fold. Yet for the DAR the genealogical world was confined to those who were descendants of eighteenth-century immigrants who came before 1783; and as time went on, they constituted a more exclusive and limited group in the face of growing numbers of postrevolutionary migrants and their descendants. What had at one point in history expanded the scope of genealogical interest served in later years to limit it.

The recent burst of energy in the area of genealogy constitutes a marked change from the DAR perspective. No longer is the search for ancestors tied so strongly to their involvement in historic episodes. The Mormons' interest in the ancestors of any present member or future convert of the church has expanded the range of genealogical inquiry to a far broader number of people. Genealogical work by church members has

---

[17]One of the most widely circulated is in the *Tri-State Trader* published in Knightstown IN.

tended to stimulate research into ancestors and families of Western migrants far more than those of post-1890 immigrants to the U.S. For example, there is a magazine devoted entirely to the search for ancestors and relatives in Scandinavian countries.[18] Yet there have been important developments for the families of later immigrants. The Mormon records include materials from Southern and Eastern Europe, and the *Genealogical Helper* contains articles to aid in the search for forebears in Poland and Italy, relations among Eastern European Jews, and the ancestors of American blacks.[19] Full development of genealogical inquiry for these newer Americans is yet to come; its beginnings have already been stimulated, though. The drive for identification with an exclusive and select ancestry has been replaced by an interest in ancestry as such. The search for cultural roots is dominated by the desire to find out about one's particular past, no matter what that past might be.

All this has been accompanied by another subtle yet significant shift: a change in perspective from tracing one's family back to some point in the past to tracing it forward through history from more remote ancestors to the present. The search for ancestors, of course, continues; filling in gaps in the family tree remains a major objective of every genealogist. While many of the earlier searches for Revolutionary War ancestors stopped when proof of ancestry had been pinned down, today there is increasing interest in working out patterns of descent through children and grandchildren down to the present generation. There is a growing desire for the researcher to be able to visualize himself not simply as having a remotely historical family connection but as having kinship with hundreds, even thousands, of people tied together by a common ancestry.

There is an important change in direction here that has brought the genealogist's perspective closer to that of the historian. The historian inevitably focuses on the flow of history: on change from some point in

---

[18]*The Scandinavian Genealogical Helper* is published by Everton Publishers. See also Charles A. Hall, ed., *The Atlantic Bridge to Germany*, vol. 1, *Baden-Wuerttemberg*, and vol. 2, *Hessen and Rheinland Pfalz*, and Hall, *A Genealogical Guide and Atlas of Silesia* (in press), all published by Everton.

[19]See, for example, Peggy J. Murrell, "Black Genealogy," *Genealogical Helper* 26:5 (September 1972): 180, 415-17; Phyllis P. Preece, "Guide to Genealogical Research in Italy," ibid. 27:1 (January 1983): 409; Larry O. Jensen, "Genealogical Research in Poland," ibid. 28:1 (January 1974): 1406.

the past moving toward the present. Much of the older genealogical thrust was contrary to this perspective. It looked backward with a limited vision that was content to stop once a remote ancestor had been found. However, the new genealogy has reversed this. More and more, genealogists are shifting to a frame of mind similar to that of the historian. The flow of thought is from a previous generation to a succeeding one, from parents to children, from the past to a point closer to the present. Until this shift occurred it was difficult for the historian and the genealogist to share a similar point of view. But the change now under way in genealogical perspective makes cooperation far more feasible.

This shift in perspective has prompted the genealogist to focus on two problems familiar to the historian. The first is migration. To the historian, movement in space appears to be one of the important processes in examining the continuity or discontinuity of human institutions. While one can observe outmigration, not knowing where the migrants went leads to painfully limited conclusions. For the genealogist, lack of knowledge about migration is a fundamental obstacle. The task at hand is to acquire information about migrants in their new homes; without knowledge of their destinations, the family history is truncated. If this problem cannot be solved, then the entire inquiry fails. No wonder one of the many genealogical magazines is called *The Ridge Runners: A Magazine of Migration.*[20] It is concerned with genealogy in the middle belt of states from Virginia and North Carolina on the East Coast through Kentucky, Tennessee, southern Indiana and Illinois, Missouri, and Arkansas to the Ozark region. The area shows a coherent pattern of migration. Again, a recent genealogical publication contains an inquiry concerning the migration routes traveled by early Scotch-Irish settlers. Migration has become a subject of great interest to social historians. Genealogy, viewing history from the bottom up, through individual and kinship movements, provides evidence of migration as a process in human lives.

The genealogist has devoted considerable energy to overcoming this obstacle, and the U.S. manuscript census has been the main instrument for doing it. Until recent years this was confined to searching through the

---

[20]*The Ridge Runners* is published by William A. Yates of Sparta MO. Another local source is the "Emigrant Registry," a file of persons who have lived in a given locality and moved away, with information about their destination. Such a file is maintained for New Jersey.

census for names of individuals in the county where they were thought to live. More recently, statewide census indexes and the federal soundex for 1880, though limited in coverage, have assisted in this. The statewide printed index to the 1850 Ohio manuscript census enables one to find an individual name quickly. Similar indexes are available for Indiana and Illinois, though in card files rather than in printed form. If each state had its censuses indexed in this way, the facts of migration would be far more readily available.[21]

The second perspective that comes from the newer genealogical inquiry is a sense of place and of the persistence of a family in a given place. Such a perspective is salutary in an intellectual climate in which we are prone to describe only motion, continual movement of individuals through space and time. Despite the important fact of movement, many individuals put down roots and played an important role in the development of community institutions. Thus, while in many cases the genealogist searches for kin who have migrated, in many other cases the search takes the form of intensive investigation of records in one locality covering a long period of time. From this comes an understanding of the relationships among families within a given community. Within fifty, let alone a hundred years, the kinship context of community life takes on great significance. It is greater for rural than for urban communities. It is impressive that the new burst of genealogical inquiry has been responsible for the most significant movement in the twentieth century to preserve and make available community records. A host of county histories and atlases have been reprinted; local census records have been indexed; cemeteries have been located and headstone inscriptions transcribed; and wills and deeds, marriage records, birth and death records have been indexed.[22] Most of this has occurred through local undertakings that seek to promote a heightened sense of community history.

---

[21]The opening of the 1900 census promises to be a boon for the genealogist and historian tracing the destinations of individuals. It contains a statewide soundex index for each state. One such project is already being conducted; see Charles Stephenson, "Tracing Those Who Left: Mobility Studies and the Soundex Indexes to the U.S. Census," *Journal of Urban History* 1:1 (November 1974): 73-84.

[22]The West-Central Kentucky Family Research Association, Owensboro, for example, is now in its fourth volume of transcriptions and indexes to records in the nineteen counties of its territory.

Out of these perspectives comes an awareness of a number of historical problems that professional historians have not yet emphasized and which can be illuminated considerably through genealogical inquiry. One is the selective process in horizontal and vertical mobility. Generally these matters are described in terms of broad social categories. Those who migrate are those with fewer community ties, the younger, unmarried, non-property-owning members of the community. Those who are better off economically tend to move upward in the occupational and social order more rapidly than those less well off. Yet focusing on family genealogy brings sharply to the fore a recognition of individual differences within these social groups. Within a single family, in which individual members are apparently in the same social circumstances, some migrate and others do not; some move to the city from the rural areas for better jobs and others do not; some reach higher levels of education and others do not. Genealogy sharpens the constant differentiating process that has gone on in American history, involving both general social characteristics and individualizing characteristics.

Closely related to the patterns of individual variation is a process of sequential community formation. As a community develops, some members of the early families remain to form persisting economic, social, political, and religious institutions, while others move on to become part of a new community elsewhere. To trace a family, as it moved westward from Connecticut in the 1770s, for example, might well mean tracing each generation as it set down roots in a different locality—the first in eastern New York, the next in western New York, the next in Wisconsin, and the next in North Dakota. While the individual process is one of continual movement, the family process is one of differentiation. To look only at migrants can be misleading; the process involves the differential and sequential establishment of communities with some family members migrating and others remaining.

Finally, genealogical inquiry fosters a greater sensitivity about the relationship of institutions to individual migration. In the nineteenth century, movement within the United States seems to have been confined to relatively short distances and within small-scale institutions. A sequence of short-distance rural migrations was far more common than movement over a thousand miles of terrain; movement to a town or city usually occurred when it was nearby and where the opportunities were readily perceived or known by word of mouth. For nineteenth-century rural migrants, the movement was inexorably westward, rarely south or north, and even more rarely to the east. By the twentieth century, however, considerable long-distance and even reverse migration had set in, mediated by large-scale institutions. After a long sequence of westward movements, families began after World War II to move in a variety of directions. Individuals became involved in institutions of national scope that enticed or transferred them in ways that could not be predicted. For some, higher education led to more higher education elsewhere; professional training led to job opportunities elsewhere; employment in a national corporation transferred one in any of a number of directions; and service in the armed forces took one far beyond the community of origin. A series of involvements in nationwide institutions resulted in a pattern of movement far different from the regular sequence in the nineteenth century of farm to westward farm or farm or small town to city.

The degree to which the new genealogy has fulfilled its promise should not be overemphasized. There is much in the records and history of family and kinship that genealogists have not yet developed. It seems to me that the major contributions they have made are twofold: first, the reorientation toward the sequence of descendants rather than a single, illustrious ancestor; and second, the perspective of migration, and the differentiating processes of migration between individuals and institutions of movement and those of community development. Yet genealogists can go much further. Just as I would urge historians to work alongside genealogists, so I would urge genealogists to broaden the context of their family histories to make them more meaningful inquiries. Thus far few family historians have gone beyond brief thumbnail biographies concerned with birth, death, marriage, children, and perhaps migration and occupation. Some facts about education are beginning to creep in, but there is little about religion, the specifics of educational or occupational institutions, recreational activities, the nature of work or community activities, or physical descriptions of housing, farm, or community. It is time that genealogists expand their bare-bone biographies into accounts in which the family members come alive as human beings.

From the archivist's point of view, the intersection of the new social history and the new genealogy requires a look from the bottom up rather than from the top down. Archivists are accustomed to thinking of records in terms of the government agencies that produced them. This is the way they are ordered in the process of being created, the way they are sent to the archives, and the way they are described and controlled. The minimal approach to records is to describe their contents as administrative records, in the style of the National Archives record groups, for example, or of the WPA descriptions of state and local records. The more useful descriptions go beyond this to the details of the agency's goals and methods of operation.

From government records one can reconstruct two processes in the interaction between the agency that produced the records and the individual whose activities were recorded. First, one can visualize an agency reaching out to draw people into some administrative process. Poll lists are made during every election to prevent double voting; the county orphans' court requires guardianship to take care of those whose parents have died; property owners are required to pay their taxes regularly; the individual liable for military service must report and enlist if physically fit or be put on a disability list. These records are not simply records of administrative action; they also reflect a process by which the "arm of the law" reaches out to require the individual to do something for the purposes of government. Who does government reach out to? Obviously, the more individuals the government involves, the larger the number of records generated and the better their possibilities for either extensive social description or genealogical discovery.

There is yet another aspect to archival records, and that is the individual who is drawn into some act of record by a government agency. In their daily lives individuals work, buy and sell, own property, are born, marry, die, and are buried, vote, go to school, transfer property, will and inherit, migrate to a new area, town, city, or county—in short, engage in innumerable activities that altogether make up the history of their lives. That history is played out within a given community. Individuals are not merely the product of manipulation by governmental activity; they also carry on a variety of daily activities that the historian and the genealogist can reconstruct imaginatively. Evidence about these activities is often lacking, but since many of them involve government action, considerable evidence is available from public sources to describe much of the course of daily human life.

This is the vantage point of the genealogist. In its earlier phases genealogy was concerned primarily with the facts of birth, marriage, death, and child-parent relationships, and all this mainly of ancestors. In other words, the dominant perspective was that people were born, married, had children, and died. Since much of the earlier genealogy was concerned with proving the involvement of an ancestor in a war, war-service records were crucial. As genealogy moves to an interest in descendants and the web of kinship relationships, however, the range of individuals about whom information is desired expands to the entire population. Hence the U.S. manuscript census returns have become the most important single source of evidence for genealogists, and much energy has been devoted to making those returns more readily available through indexing. From this a far wider range of records—including poll lists, land transfers, property taxes— came to be exploited in order to prove the presence of an individual in a given place at a given time.

It may well be that in the future school records will be the most important single source of genealogical data, for they contain information about the parent-child relationships so vital to family reconstitution. Even now the school enumerations of a number of states—for example, Indiana beginning in 1843—provide not only the names of parents but often the names of each school-age child as well. Student records of application and admission to colleges and universities will become of increasing importance.

Because genealogists are prone to follow individuals throughout their lives, they inevitably develop a sense of history from the individual outward and from the bottom up. Their perspective focuses on the individual in daily life, in work and in play, in religion, in birth, marriage and death, in place of burial, in daily movement and movement over the years. Until recent years most of the records about such activities were generated at the level of local government, in the township and the county, for it was there that the individual in the daily round of life came into greatest contact with government. In the early development of a rural community, local elections often called out more voters than did state or national elections. Most records about individuals in the nineteenth century and earlier are thus at the local level, and it is no wonder that genealogists have flocked to those records to reconstruct life histories.

As time passed new layers of governmental activity were established at the state and especially the federal level, thereby increasing the information about individuals in the archives of those governments. Earlier federal records of this kind have long been important genealogical sources—census, war service, immigration, and land records especially. A few additional types of records have been added more recently, notably income tax and social security data. Despite the increase in federal functions, however, it is significant that many personalized records remain at the local level. As I have indicated, perhaps the most important additional local record for genealogical purposes will be school records because of their crucial information about child-parent relationships. Individualized data in local archives will probably remain the most extensive source of information useful to both the new social history and the new genealogy.

All this requires a perspectival shift from the context of the administrative system within which the records were created to one of individuals as they move through life and come into contact with governmental processes. Many of the new aids to research in public records written by genealogists and for genealogists have this perspective. From one point of view, these guides merely provide genealogists a way of knowing about the existence of records. But the material selected and the way in which it is presented reveal something more than just old material in a new guise. The guides reflect a desire to facilitate the current investigator's ability to reach and follow lives in the form of mini-biographies and with a focus not on celebrated events but day-to-day affairs. To make his records more useful to genealogists, the modern-day archivist must imaginatively reconstruct the daily lives of people and the possible ways in which they came into contact with legal processes, and then ferret through the existing records to see which human processes are reflected in them.

From this perspective the traditional organizing principles of archivists are more of a hindrance than a help. Those principles reflect the formal processes of governmental organization and not the human processes inherent in daily life. If one is interested in the history of public administration or of law as an institution, such a perspective is adequate. But the new social history and the new genealogy require a vastly different approach. The context of history is the ebb and flow of human life and not of the administrative agency, and for this the starting point is the individual rather than the processes of government. The terminal points are not acts of the legislature but birth and death, and the in-between steps are not processes of public administration but processes of human maturation (from childhood to adulthood to old age), of human movement and migration, of human affairs such as work, leisure, religion, and family. Moreover, the archival records remaining are not the comprehensive story but only pieces of it, only that small portion of the larger ebb and flow of human life that was written down as the individual came into contact with the law.

The new social history is simply the new genealogy writ large, and it requires for its historical base a similar archival approach. No longer can the historical researcher justify a project on the grounds that it exploits a given body of records. This is inadequate simply because the dimensions of a historical problem are quite independent of the system that collected the historical information. It is the accumulation of activities in the lives of many individuals that adds up to social history.

A historian's records are not different from those required by the genealogist, but they are required in a different format, one that can process the happenings in the lives of many people, not just one family. And the archival perspective should be the same, a shift from the agency creating the records to the transformations in human life. The archival record is merely an artifact, a momentary product of a given act in time and space, and not a reflection of the context of life itself. It should be used as a window through which the broader events of life may be visualized and reconstructed. Such a perspective is required for the archivist to increase the usefulness of records for both the historian and the genealogist.

The interests and activities of the social historian, the genealogist, and the archivist converge in the records and resources needed for research. I have provided suggestions enough about this; let me stress several aspects of cooperative activity that are of special and immediate concern.

First is the need for much greater attention to the preservation of local records. This is an old refrain, but it requires repeating until more is done about it. Local records are in a most uneven state of preservation, with most falling on the deplorable side. In some states, during the past few years, action has been taken to do something about this, but for the most part it has not led to tangible results. Local records remain in a chaotic state of access. Resources for effective preservation of local records simply have not been made available. I am distressed especially by the limited concern about the matter on the part of professional historians. Too many have their eyes on the national event and the personal manuscripts of the prominent individual and thus give too little concern to the average citizen and day-to-day activities as reflected in the local records. Moreover, much local historical activity is more concerned with the preservation of buildings and the creation of museums than with the records of history. Genealogists are the most important influences for a different approach, and historians should be willing to work with them on this common objective.

A second major problem confronting both genealogists and historians is the compilation of biographical material. Genealogists are interested in family biography—that is, of family members or generations—while historians are more interested in collective biography, information about many individuals in a given occupational category. For this information, both genealogists and historians have relied heavily on the biographical compilations in early county histories. But such compilations after 1920 are few and far between, and as a result future researchers will have precious little biographical material on which to rely for research after that time. An ongoing cooperative venture—joining historians, genealogists, and archivists—of compiling biographical information about ordinary people in towns, counties, and cities across the nation is of critical importance for both genealogical and historical research.

There are several possible approaches to this. One is an extension of the clipping and filing of obituaries that has been undertaken by some public libraries. The task is a simple one that takes only persistent effort for a continuous program, an effort that might well capture the same volunteer energies so admirably displayed by genealogists. Another lies in oral history, which is focused on short biographies of many people rather than intensive information about prominent figures. Oral history could well be focused on family biography, and genealogists might become as involved in the preparation of material by and about the living as well as about the dead. Perhaps one could envisage trained volunteer groups of oral-history associates who could develop this source of information. Still another idea might be adult-education classes in writing individual and family biographies as a way of being involved in both genealogy and history. Certainly the leisure-time energies that have been such an important element in modern life could be focused on the task of compiling contemporary biographical information for use by later researchers.

The third task deserves more emphasis and will involve a cooperative effort to make individualized data more accessible for both genealogical and social research. Much data of this kind is available, but considerable indexing is necessary to make it accessible. The manuscript-census returns are an excellent example of the possibilities. This is the major mass-data file approached via computer by both historians and genealogists. But each has gone his own way and the work done by one is not useful to the other.

If it were done cooperatively, with the needs of both in mind, the result would be more effective.

The social historian has usually drawn a sample from the census for research, but a sample is meaningless to the genealogist. After all, any one individual might be just the one who is being sought. The genealogist, on the other hand, has been preoccupied with indexing the census in such a way as to limit its usefulness for the historian. Most such projects pertain to a single county, and are without much relevance for projects in other areas. Often the information is limited to the name and the census manuscript's location, so the researcher must then go to the manuscript record to find other data.[23] These are useful genealogical tools but hardly of the level required for historical research on a great number of individuals. Historical research requires quick access to all the data in the record, not just the surname, and a system of indexing capable of merging data in different geographical areas into one body.[24]

The solution to this problem is to computerize manuscript-census data, all of it, in the same format. It can then be alphabetized by individual name for any one geographical unit; the data for one unit can be merged with that for another into one combined system; and all the characteristics of individuals in the census can be analyzed in the aggregate as well as individually. Such a project has been under way for some time in the Pennsylvania cities of Pittsburgh and Allegheney. Sponsored by the History Department and the Social Science Information Center of the University of Pittsburgh, the project has already made the 1860 census available for both genealogical and social research; computerization of the data for 1850, 1870, and 1880 for the same cities is in process. This data is used by faculty and students at the University of Pittsburgh for social research; alphabetized printouts have also been made available to libraries in Pittsburgh and are used by genealogists.[25]

---

[23]The index for the Ohio census of 1850, the largest statewide index available, cites name, county, township, and page. The reader must use the manuscript census to recover the full schedule of information.

[24]Several private firms have computerized census data for given states and census years, most of them prior to 1850; for a fee they will search their files for surnames. See the *Genealogical Helper* for advertisements.

[25]Copies of the 1860 printout are available at the Historical Society of Western Pennsylvania, the Pennsylvania Room of the Carnegie Library of Pittsburgh, and the Archives of Industrial Society in the Hillman Library, University of Pittsburgh. Printouts of the other three census years will be deposited there when completed.

The advantages of this system are manifold. For the genealogist, the information in the printout is complete; there is no need to go back to the microfilm copy except to verify the accuracy of an entry. Moreover, as other areas are computerized in the future, they can be merged easily into one alphabetized format. For the historian, the format makes possible the collection of data that would describe the different wards and subcommunities of the city, occupations of individuals and their geographical location, and a variety of other characteristics. Addition of other areas to the file will facilitate comparative historical research. Such a system could be applied to any county in the nation for the same census years and be equally useful to both genealogists and historians.

The census is only one of many individualized records that could be computerized for ready access to the mutual advantage of both genealogists and historians.[26] Archivists, moreover, should be deeply involved in this venture, for the records so created will be a highly significant addition to their resources for both historical and genealogical research. It might well be time to come together and work out a common schedule of computerization to facilitate both individualized and social research. Veterans' service and pension records should have a high priority. Pension records are usually sought only by genealogists and usually for one or a few individuals. The servicing of these records has been organized to respond to this type of use. The request that the National Archives assemble the records of several thousand veterans for social research, as happened in Allegheny County, Pennsylvania, sorely taxed its facilities. Clearly the Archives is not now prepared for extensive social research into veterans' records for the nineteenth century. Yet those records contain invaluable information for both the genealogist and the social historian. Now that a program and coding system has been worked out for a group of Civil War veterans, it is feasible for projects to be undertaken to computerize more extensive amounts of the same material. These could well be undertaken concurrently by archivists, genealogists, and historians.

Genealogists and social historians have not been accustomed to thinking that their needs and objectives converge in a common set of interests. This lack of contact is becoming a liability. This is especially so as

---

[26]One computerized index already available is Philip W. McMullin, "Grassroots of America: A Computerized Index to the American State Papers: Land Grants and Claims (1789-1837)."

historians become more interested in building up social description through individualized information from local records while genealogists use the same records in pursuing the rapidly growing field of family history. Intergenerational reconstruction of the family is a task that both pursue but which so far has led to little cooperative effort. The possibilities are enormous and eminently worthwhile. It is hoped that the separate ways of the past will soon give way to joint activities of great benefit to both.

Chapter Three

ANTHROPOLOGY, GENEALOGY, AND HISTORY: A RESEARCH LOG

John W. Adams
Alice Bee Kasakoff

Genealogy does not resemble the evolution of a species and does not map the destiny of a people. On the contrary, to follow the complex course of descent is to maintain passing events in their proper dispersion; it is to identify the accidents, the minute deviations—or conversely, the complete reversals—the errors, the false appraisals, and the faulty calculations that gave birth to those things that continue to exist and have value for us; it is to discover that truth or being do not lie at the root of what we know and what we are, but the exteriority of accidents.

—Michel Foucault, *Nietzsche, Genealogy, History*

Today no anthropologist would study a living community without collecting at least a few oral genealogies—if only because the very act of collecting them places him in a line of descent from his professional forebears. When the Cambridge University psychologist W. H. R. Rivers introduced their use to anthropology in the 1890s, it was to solve a specific research problem in the field of kinship. He had been confronted with strange-seeming kinship systems in the South Seas and so tried to "put them on the map" of what he knew about the meaning of our words for "father" and "mother." This he did by assembling a native's genealogy, then asking what the native called each person on his family tree. It was exactly what Lemuel Shattuck of Concord, Massachusetts, had done, and reported on, fifty years earlier in the first volume of *The New England Historic Genealogical Register*, except that Shattuck had used his own pedigree to display the strange kin-term usages of his ancestors.[1]

Rivers occupies a pivotal position in the transition to modern anthropology because his work on genealogies led him to an interest in the concrete that foreshadowed the functionalist obsession with fieldwork. In fact, he carried out one of the first modern ethnographic field studies. Yet he was also as passionately interested in history as the older anthropologists.

Rivers thought that in societies where the same kinship terms refer to relatives whom we consider different, this indicated ancient marriage systems where people had actually once married a very close relative. So if the term for grandmother was the same as that used for wife, he explained the duplication by saying that the natives had married their grandmothers in the past. Genealogies were thus a way to discover history.

However, kin terms often refer to entire groups of people, not to specific individuals, and some members of those groups are not close relatives of the speaker. Today we would explain the set of terms that equate "grandmother" and "wife" *functionally*, saying it suggests that a young man would seek a spouse in the same clan from which his grandmother came. Indeed, every other generation, one particular group of tribesmen gave a bride to another particular group.

The Functionalist Reaction

By the nineteenth century, the same "primitive man" who had been a model of human virtue to philosophers of the seventeenth and eighteenth centuries became a sort of "missing link" between the apes and the

---

[1] For a modern edition with commentaries, see W. H. R. Rivers, *Kinship and Social Organization* (London: University of London, 1968); Lemuel Shattuck, "Illustrations of Genealogy, Names and Definitions of the Different Degrees of Kindred," *The New England Historical and Genealogical Register* 1 (1847): 355-59.

Victorians. The theory of cultural evolution was the anthropologists' response to the need to connect the past to the present despite a lack of historical documents. To discover the past, scholars identified "survivals" from earlier stages to the present; Rivers's kinship equations are examples. Similar customs must have had similar histories, the theory went, and thus one could reasonably impute a history to all groups with a given custom once the history of one was found.

The result was a string of cultures arranged in stages of development. The culmination of civilization, not surprisingly, was Victorian England, the culture that had devised the history in the first place. However, the theory left certain other peoples still hopelessly "stuck" in ancient ways of life. These gave the social anthropologist an urgently mandated research task: to describe them quickly before they perished.

When these schemes of "conjectural history" began to collapse in the early twentieth century, the British carried their distrust to an extreme point. They decided that there was nothing to be served by studying history at all since there could be no reliable evidence without writing. So the observer was enjoined to look for a different kind of causal pattern: the *simultaneous* effect of one custom on another, the so-called "functionalist" hypothesis that everything in a culture fits together and influences everything else. Cultures thus became "self-contained wholes"; and genealogies were elevated into a major conceptual tool of the functionalist mission because they enabled the anthropologist to see how the people of a small tribal village were all related to each other at the moment he pitched his tent.

Norms versus Behavior

In Malinowski's hands during the 1920s, the "concrete" genealogical method became the prototype for field investigations of everything from gardening to rituals. Thus one was advised to always touch, smell, and eat the crops, and to observe those in the culture who raise and cook them, rather than getting a list of their names or merely writing down an after-hours discussion of the work day. Only in this way might one get behind the formulaic rules and discover the "real" rules, those that actually guide behavior but are often not acknowledged explicitly even by people in the culture itself.

By adding information on residence and names, and on birth and death dates when they could be gleaned in societies without our sort of time reckoning, the genealogical method could be used for investigating the kinds of statements about ideal behavior that one is apt to get when one asks, "Where does the couple live after marriage?" or "Who inherits the position of chief?"

Oral Genealogies

Oral genealogies are notorious for being severely edited affairs, trimmed of most of the "died youngs" and "n.f.r."s of printed genealogies. Moreover, they are usually modified to build a political charter for the group who tells them. In our fieldwork among the Gitksan Indians of British Columbia, we were fortunate to be able to supplement the ones we collected with church records and census materials that several generations of missionaries and Indian agents had compiled. These flesh out the picture of fertility by including much infant mortality, and by revealing many adoptions, even occasional illegitimate children. More important, when compared with the oral genealogies, they helped reveal a political axiom of the Gitksan.

The Gitksan Family as Perpetual Corporation

The most important group among them is the "House," about twenty-five people who share rights to hunting and fishing spots, a stock of ancestral names and chiefly positions, and the right to display heraldic crests. In the old days the male members of this group lived in a single communal house, in front of which stood the House totem poles. Nowadays, however, people live in nuclear-family households, but they must know whose House they belong to in order to participate in the feasting system that is still alive and very strong today.

We began collecting genealogies from the House chiefs, but at the same time attempted to learn the House affiliations of everyone else we met. We soon noticed a striking pattern: in the larger Houses, oral genealogies provided by the chief omitted a sizeable number of people who claimed to belong to the House. When we asked how these people were related, the chief became uncomfortable and claimed he "didn't know. . . . Maybe our grandmothers were sisters." But what did this mean? Under the classificatory system all people in the House should be called by kinship terms. Were these women actual blood sisters? or were they merely cousins? or was "sister" being used from simple politeness?

As it happens, this genealogical "break" is important structurally. It comes just at the point where Gitksan family branches start to compete for chiefship of the corporate groups. How could they forget such important links? The answer is that they believe in reincarnation and believe that great-grandparents have all come back. With them present in one's living family, there is no need to remember their earlier incarnations. This amnesia has political importance.

Pruning the Family Tree

Now, people everywhere regard blood relationships as both a boon and a burden, and sometimes conveniently "forget" how they are related, even in societies that seem to place a high premium on kinship. Where does one draw the line when issuing wedding invitations, for instance?

Wachter calculated that if one were descended on both sides of one's family from English ancestors, then one would count eighty-five percent of the men and women alive there in 1066 as one's progenitors. By a similar process, an insurance actuary calculated that there are now about 120,000,000 Mayflower descendants alive in the United States, or roughly half the population. So any genealogy is potentially much larger than even the largest volumes on deposit in the Library of Congress.[2]

Therefore, most people make do with only a skeleton tree, one that explains how the people they see often and know to be kin are related. At most they may have a famous ancestor, and consider that the slender line back to such a personage is worth tracing in order to bask in the reflected light from a glorious past. "Oral" genealogies collected from Northern

---

[2]Kenneth W. Wachter, "Ancestors at the Norman Conquest," in Kenneth W. Wachter, Eugene A. Hammel, and Peter Laslett, eds., *Statistical Studies of Historical Social Structure* (New York: Academic Press, 1978); David Holt Winton, "Mayflower Descendants Today," *The Mayflower Quarterly* 44:4 (November 1978): 110-11; David R. Godofsky, "Methods Used in Evaluating the Number of Mayflower Descendants," ibid., 112-15; Robert S. Wakefield, "Mayflower Descendants Today: A Rebuttal," ibid. 45:1 (February 1979): 28; David R. Godofsky, "Further Notes and Comments on Mayflower Descendants Today," ibid., 29-30.

college undergraduates show an even more restricted knowledge of kin-ship.[3]

The Gitksan distinguish blood relations (among whom genealogical connections are traced) from those who are called by kin terms just be-cause they belong to Houses where there are also blood relatives. Since kinship terms are used for everyone in these groups, it looks to the outsider like a dense web of kinship ties, but in fact the bloodlines also stimulate feuding over succession to chiefship. Among the Gitksan, if one asks for actual blood ties, a three-generation tree, much like what our youngsters produce, is the norm. The seemingly warmer, family-oriented social sys-tem, in fact, is often lukewarm to downright chilly.

In addition, all cultures prune their genealogies to further their par-ticular conception of destiny, tidying them up in order to infuse the past with the sense of rightness and purpose necessary to uphold the values of the present. Comparing this with the more minimally edited record that can be reconstructed from written evidence reveals the lengths to which a culture must go to impose an order on natural events. Each culture has its particular embarrassments, from which one can deduce what it cares about enough to deny.

Cousin Marriage

Claude Lévi-Strauss, the anthropologist, built a general theory of how people choose marriage partners in each of two basic sorts of regimes: "el-ementary" (found only in small-scale societies) and "complex" (found in ours). His vision of an elementary system is based on ideas that Rivers had published in 1914 without, however, remembering their pedigree.[4] The basic idea is that in all societies there are people who are forbidden as spouses because they are considered "incestuous" for various reasons and

---

[3]Helen Codere, "A Genealogical Study of Kinship in the United States," *Psychiatry* 18 (February 1955): 65-79; David L. Hatch & Mary G. Hatch, "Some Observations on Social Characteristics of the Kinship System in South Carolina," *Search* 2:1 (Summer 1963); David M. Schneider, *American Kinship: A Cultural Account* (Englewood Cliffs NJ: Pren-tice-Hall, 1968).

[4]Claude Lévi-Strauss, *The Elementary Structures of Kinship*, rev. ed. (Boston: Beacon Press, 1969); W. H. R. Rivers, "Marriage (Introductory and Primitive)," in James Has-tings, ed., *Encyclopedia of Religion and Ethics*, vol. 8 (New York: Scribner's, 1916).

these incestuous choices are governed by so-called "negative" rules of prohibition; yet in some tribes one specific relative may be singled out as the
preferred, or even prescribed, choice by means of a "positive" rule.

Lévi-Strauss went on to show that such rules created an "elementary" structure of exchange that pervaded the entire society and held it
together in anticipation of women returning as brides to the original "wife-
givers." Thus we all—both primitive and modern—engage in reciprocity,
some of us in a restricted fashion, others in a more generalized way. In our
society the exchange consists of such things as phone calls, dinner invitations, or greeting cards.

An example Lévi-Strauss gave was a man's marrying his mother's
brother's daughter, a fairly common preference. In fact, the Gitksan had
this very "rule": if asked, they would say that "marriage should be to a
mother's brother's daughter," though they often mentioned other relatives as well. Whether they followed this rule is a tricky research question
because the answer depends on how many cousins were available to marry
within a convenient distance and whether the actual number of marriages
to cousins was therefore greater or less than one might suppose by chance.

Kasakoff wanted to test Lévi-Strauss's theory using statistical techniques to analyze a large number of recorded marriages. To do so, she constructed "spouse pools" of all the possible choices within a reasonable
distance and of approximately the same age range preferred by the Gitksan.
This project would have been impossible without the more minimally edited genealogies created from church records and informants' discussions.
Then she counted the number of cousins in each pool of potential spouses
and computed whether there was more or less cousin marriage *than one
would expect by chance* from the number of cousins available.

The upshot of the computer runs was that there was actually *less* marriage to mother's brother's daughters than one would expect by chance.[5]
We thought that was an odd sort of rule to have. Moreover, we know from
other research that *at best* less than half the young men actually had a cousin
of this type to marry, the exact percentage depending on whether the pop-

---

[5] Alice Bee Kasakoff, "Lévi-Strauss' Idea of the Social Unconscious: The Problem of
Elementary and Complex Structures in Gitksan Marriage Choice," in Ino Rossi, ed., *The
Unconscious in Culture* (New York: E. P. Dutton, 1974).

ulation is growing or not and, if so, how fast.[6] It is a very unusual rule indeed that requires a marriage that not everyone can do. Moreover, when we examined the few cases of couples who actually did marry the right sort of person, we discovered—because we knew their genealogies—that in every case either the boy or the girl *had been adopted*.

Fortunately a chief whom we had invited down to New York City set us straight: in families where the true chiefly line becomes extinct, it is important to take a replacement lineage into the family to provide heirs. Then by marrying a member of it off to a blood relative of the line that has died out, the children of the new line will also be descendants of the old. (This seems to be why the kings of Hawaii married their half-sisters, by the way.) It is hoped that by such a link homicidal feuding about who is the "real" heir can be avoided. The chief who visited us added, however, that "people make fun of you just the same for marrying your cousin!"

So the computer—given good genealogical data—can bring to light modes of behavior that cannot be observed without plenty of cases, and which the natives themselves will not tell you, thinking either that "everyone" knows a fact so basic to their culture, or that, quite frankly, it is nobody's business but an insider's.

Thus the rule about how it is good to marry a first cousin turned out to be "a rule for breaking a rule," while the presumed rule of "positive" preference was actually a rule of "preferential incest." It could only be understood within the context of implicit native political strategy and tactics. The rule said—not that it is a good thing to marry a blood cousin, as we first supposed—that in times of political uncertainty in one's family, it is better to commit (technical) incest with a putative cousin and expose oneself to public ridicule than it is to let the succession to chiefship give way to a feud.[7]

---

[6]Alice Bee Kasakoff, "How Many Relatives?" in Paul Ballonoff, ed., *Genealogical Mathematics* (Paris: Mouton, 1974).

[7]This material incorporates the main example from Adams's unpublished paper, "Preferential Incest: Its Structural Implications," prepared for delivery at the 75th annual meeting of the American Anthropological Association, Washington D.C., November 1976. How many other such cases lurk unrecognized in the literature for want of good genealogies is anybody's guess. It seems likely, though, that the Trobriand pattern of marrying one's *tabu*, which Malinowski reported, is such a case, given the genealogy he presents.

We see the Gitksan, then, not as the victims of impossible rules nor as the blind followers of ancient custom, but as politically calculating, rational people "just like us" —within their own framework of ground rules (or "constitution"). Thus even these "simple" societies have a familiar complexity that is, paradoxically, not often grasped.

The "culture" is not laid out publicly for all to see in a "handbook of living" that everyone sanctions. The counterpoint between behavioral patterns and explicit cultural codes leaves room for dispute among members of the culture themselves, to say nothing of the anthropologists. And genealogies serve both gods. In their pruned state, they reinforce the "rules" and explicit codes. In amplified versions—quite difficult to avoid the closer one comes to the present—they enable people to establish conflicting claims. Negotiations over which line gets to do the pruning and whether the surgery foregrounds or erases embarrassing moments—no one's genealogy is unblemished—are always open.[8]

The Old Unit of Study: The Village

Anthropologists rarely used to visit a tribe for more than a year or two, and they typically stayed in only one village, which later became "the tribe" when the report was written. Rarely could they record reasonably full genealogies back more than three generations due to a lack of written records. Those that went back further, moreover, were invariably of the descendants of a tribal hero or demigod, pruned of any links that were not necessary to tie the living into a web of nameable relationships.

The men and women in the genealogies that the British anthropologists collected in their colonies had survived some of the most far-reaching changes they, or anybody, were ever to experience. Most were about to be or had already been subjected to epidemics for which they had no immunity; migrations, forced or otherwise, predicated upon colonial

---

[8]Many friends who are doing their own genealogy have found pairs of cousins who married, and wonder if they have found "a lot" of such marriages in their families. Whether there is really a "desire" to marry cousins or whether the amount stems simply from their greater availability in the population should be approached by recreating the spouse pools, just as we did for the Gitksan. But given the high fertility and the tendency of certain New England lines—rich and poor alike—to remain in the same area, we guess that what looks like "a lot" would be explicable on purely demographic grounds.

schemes; and radical economic changes in which they were to give up subsistence economies for inclusion in a world market. The genealogies
painted pictures of great stability, continuity, structure, integration, and
sameness. The kind of genealogy collected, proceeding backwards from
living individuals, makes such a picture almost inevitable since it includes
neither truncated lines nor out-migrants. These genealogies were,
strangely, outside history; and the functionalist view of integration encouraged the ahistorical stance.

Such conditions of fieldwork led to a series of ethnographies of villages that were depicted outside of any time frame and isolated spatially.
Indeed the constraints enforced by the compulsion to do fieldwork were
even elevated to a conceptual framework—that the community was the
"natural" unit of analysis to be understood on its own terms.

A New Unit of Study: Marriage Groups

Our work on marriage preferences, founded as it was on comprehensive data from a local neighborhood of *seven* villages, not just one, made
us realize how important it is to know the boundaries of the group within
which people ordinarily married.[9] There is the problem of tracking marriage partners of the sex that moves upon marriage: when wives go to their
husbands' villages, studying only a single village reveals where men have
found their spouses but not where the women have found theirs. This is
why a *set* of villages is a better unit, but where and how does one actually
draw the line?

When we searched the literature for examples of how far away the
people of a village actually found a spouse, we found that we should think
in terms of *circles*, not villages. Often thirty percent of spouses are found
in a tribal village (if it is small), then about fifty percent within the *neighborhood* of nearby villages, and eighty percent within the local region. As
it turns out, there are very few one-hundred-percent groups (possibly
none), and many small islands, to our great surprise, are divided into *two*
eighty-percent groups, one on each side.

---

[9]The technical term for the marriage of people within the same group is *endogamy*,
first coined by a Scotsman named John Ferguson McLennan as early as 1865. Every text-
book mentions it, but few say much about it for lack of data. The group can be defined by
any sort of criterion, not necessarily a geographic one, whether it be religious, biological,
or economic. Lévi-Strauss's theory of marriage is in fact a partial theory of endogamy, though
he doesn't present it as such.

Thus the "eighty percent group," which is found in all societies whatever their size or civility, is what we must study if we want to examine marriage markets thoroughly.[10] This requires finding genealogies covering large regions, but in the ethnographic literature there are few such sets of data available.

We worked a bit with published figures on endogamy for China and Taiwan taken from marriage registers, and with data gathered on the tiny island of Tikopia.[11] New England, though, we eventually discovered, is one of the few regions of the world for which there are large numbers of genealogies covering two hundred years or more. Quantities of vital records have been published; Savage and others made exhaustive lists of the early generations. As one genealogist in South Carolina cautioned, "Don't waste your time studying New England—everything's been done."

New History, Old Anthropology

Yet when we began to acquaint ourselves with the latest New England studies, we found an extensive "new history" done in deliberate imitation of the old-style functionalist village studies of anthropology.[12] Many of them had begun as dissertations, and the candidates' desire to delimit the task may have made the idea of "closed corporate villages" seem like a convenient way to narrow down the research. But it is simply not a convincing model for Massachusetts towns.[13]

---

[10]John W. Adams and Alice Bee Kasakoff, "Factors Affecting Endogamous Group Size," in Moni Nag, ed., *Population and Social Structure* (The Hague: Mouton, 1975). (Reprinted in 1976 as ch. 6 of Carol Smith, ed., *Regional Analysis, Volume Two* [New York: Academic Press, 1976].)

[11]John W. Adams and Alice Bee Kasakoff, "Central Place Theory and Endogamy in China: A Postscript to Factors Underlying Endogamous Group Size," ch. 7 of Smith, *Regional Analysis;* idem, "Geography and Marriage: The Tikopian Case," *Man* 12:1 (April 1977): 48-64.

[12]Ronald Dale Karr, "New England Community Studies since 1960: A Bibliography," *The New England Historical and Genealogical Register* 138 (July and October 1984): 186-202, 290-308.

[13]John W. Adams, "Consensus, Community and Exoticism," *Journal of Interdisciplinary History* 12:1 (Autumn 1981): 253-65. (Reprinted as pp. 253-65 of Theodore K. Rabb and Robert I. Rotberg, eds., *The New History: The 1980s and Beyond* [Princeton: Princeton University Press, 1982].)

This project, conducted by historians, was to find the "past we have lost" and with it the transition from pre-industrial (here read "primitive") to modern society. The "fertility transition" from large to small numbers of children had become a privileged marker for this shift. So a basic goal for most town studies was information on marital fertility. This had the unfortunate effect of leading many researchers to restrict their studies further to those women who resided in one town for their entire reproductive lives. Thus here too a methodological constraint—the difficulty of following migrants—became one of the major findings: there was little migration.

Early New England then began to appear as a kind of golden age of stable communities whose pastoral calm was rudely shattered when the high birth rates forced sons out of the suddenly landless towns. New England became transformed, by contrast to what Malthus himself saw, into a grim Malthusian system. [14] The town was the community for these historians, and like the pruned genealogies that anthropologists collected, their family reconstitutions were oriented toward lifetime community residents. But we had decided to use the more fully fleshed printed genealogies and these gave us a different perspective.

New England Marriage Markets

The town studies mainly relied on the NEHGS sets of vital records, supplemented by a town history and surviving town records. [15] But since marriages in Colonial times were recorded primarily in the town of the bride, and because she then (sixty percent of the time prior to the Revolution) first set up house in her husband's village, many of the intentions

---

[14]John W. Adams and Alice Bee Kasakoff, "Ecosystems over Time: The Study of Migration in 'Long Run' Perspective," in Emilio Moran, ed., *The Ecosystem Concept in Anthropological Study* (Boulder: Westview Press, 1984).

[15]The town studies used the method of family reconstitution, which French social historians and demographers had invented to convert parish records into "families" so they could study demographic changes. American genealogists had been doing this for years, with the important difference being that they followed migrants. However, their work was largely ignored by those who studied towns. The exception was those whose towns had written histories that contained excellent genealogical appendices; these they did not hesitate to use. However, because they distrusted amateurs and assumed that "towns" were the important social unit, they didn't follow migrants, even though they comprise over half the population according to our tabulations from genealogies.

and recorded marriages are "lost" if one fails to search the neighborhood.[16] Furthermore, studies of marriage distances based on the vital records of single towns overestimated the degree of village endogamy because they assumed that entries with no town of residence listed for both husband and wife must indicate an endogamous marriage. However, the published versions of the vital records left out the village name if it was the same as the town whose records were being published in the volume; this meant there was no way to distinguish endogamous marriages from those where there was simply no information on residence.

We knew the residence of one spouse from the genealogy we were using and often the genealogist had provided information on the marrying spouse as well. If he hadn't, we tried to find genealogies of their families. Counting only marriages where we knew the residences of both the bride's and groom's family at the time of the marriage, we concluded that about sixty percent of New Englanders found a spouse in their own village, and about eighty percent found one within a sixteen-mile radius.[17] Here too a *set* of villages, not a village, was the appropriate unit of analysis.

Moreover, using published genealogies, we found a constant movement in and out of towns, with rates generally about twice those of town studies. Thus there was no sudden increase in migration to mark a transition to modernity. From the first, New Englanders moved a great deal: there was no prehistory of stability.[18]

Regions and Wealth

Like the anthropological village, the town was thought to represent an entire culture. But regions are not homogenous, and New England was differentiated economically from the very first. The shift from villages to genealogical lines underscores this question of "representativeness." The science of demography is constructed from data on specific *locations* of

---

[16]John W. Adams and Alice Bee Kasakoff, "Migration at Marriage in Colonial New England: A Comparison of Rates Derived from Vital Records," in Bennett Dyke and Warren Morrill, eds., *Genealogical Demography* (New York: Academic Press, 1980).

[17]John Waters tells us that 17 miles is the comparable radius for eighteenth-century Guilford CT.

[18]John W. Adams and Alice Bee Kasakoff, "Migration and the Family in Colonial New England: The View from Genealogies," *Journal of Family History* 9:1 (1984): 24-43.

populations; needless to say, migration in or out presents a difficulty. A genealogy sprawls over the countryside, which is why it is so useful. Nonetheless, if it clusters in certain areas, it may not represent the region. The problem unexpectedly surfaced in our attempt to test the common assumption that only the very wealthy are included in published genealogies.

We looked up the annual incomes of the family members we chose in the 1771 Massachusetts tax-valuation list.[19] Our families turned out to be slightly *poorer* than most of the others listed. The *mean* yearly income from real property of the households on the 1771 list is 1,222.85 pence; for our group it was only 971 pence, or seventy-nine percent of that figure. The reason seems to be that we lack the top five percent of the income distribution (that is, more than 4800p). The wealthy were concentrated in commercial centers: Boston, Salem, Gloucester, or Bridgewater. Only five percent of the members of the families we chose lived in these towns (though thirteen percent of the entire tax list did so). On the other hand, the *median* wealth of our group (720p) falls *above* the median of the tax list (600p) because we have fewer people with zero income. Twenty-seven percent of the list has zero-pence valuations, but only nineteen percent of our group is so valued. Most of those with no income from real property, such as sailors, were also living along the coast.

In New England, at least, the genealogies as a set are not biased towards the rich; but they bear traces of the regions where family members lived. Even high rates of migration cannot erase them. To be truly representative, families must be chosen with care to be sure locations mirror those of the general population. There is also the possibility that whole families—or at least entire branches—are rich or poor and that these distinctions were apparent early on.[20]

---

[19]Bettye Hobbs Pruitt, ed., *The Massachusetts Tax Valuation List of 1771* (Boston: G. K. Hall, 1978). The material in this section is from John W. Adams and Alice Bee Kasakoff, "Wealth and Migration in Massachusetts and Maine, 1771-1798," *Journal of Economic History* (July 1985), forthcoming.

[20]The 9 genealogies we currently use in our research are: Frank J. Bisbee, *Genealogy of the Bisbee Family* (East Sullivan, 1956); William Chaffee, *The Chaffee Genealogy* (New York, 1909); Mary Lovering Holman, *Ancestors and Descendants of John Coney of Boston, England, and Boston, Massachusetts* (Concord, 1928); J. D. Farwell, *The Farwell Family*

By the time of the 1850 Federal census, however, our group had become more wealthy than the general population, judging from the value of their real estate, which was ten percent greater than a large sample of "native born white farmers."[21] The progenitors of our families had immigrated early; this may have enabled them to accumulate more property than those whose ancestors had come later. The finding is all the more remarkable because land values in New England were below those of other areas at the time. Whatever the explanation, though, most people are surprised at how small the difference is since these families came so much earlier than others in the population. It may, in fact, be due to chance.[22]

The lines we traced are found in certain economic niches at any point in time. The clustering is both local and occupational and this in turn affects their wealth. In 1771 most were farmers living away from commercial centers. We deliberately chose to study descendants of people who had come during the Great Migration because the ancestors of most people of

---

(Orange, 1929); James Freer Faunce, *The Faunce Family History and Genealogy* (Akron, 1973); G. H. Greely, *Genealogy of the Greely-Greeley Family* (Boston, 1905); J. M. Pelton, *Genealogy of the Pelton Family in America* (Albany, 1892); Frank E. Shedd, *Daniel Shed Genealogy* (Boston, 1921); Joshua Wyman Wellman, *Descendants of Thomas Wellman of Lynn, Massachusetts* (Boston, 1918). We settled on our final selection of families because they had rare surnames.

[21]Lee Soltow, *Men and Wealth in the United States, 1850-1870* (New Haven: Yale University Press, 1975).

[22]Wealth differences between those covered in genealogies and the general population may be small, but there is evidence nonetheless that the poor tend to be covered less thoroughly. The percentage of people whose death records can be found increases with wealth: 93% of the rich on the 1771 list were followed to death along with only 75% of the poor (and 83% of the middle group). Among those lost before death, the poor are lost an average of 18 years earlier than the rich. In 1798 slightly more people are lost regardless of wealth—evidence of deterioration of the genealogies perhaps, but more probably of the vital records on which they are based—and they are lost earlier in life.

Unfortunately we can say nothing about whole lines lost from genealogies except to remark that there were few people on the 1771 list with "our" surnames who were not on the genealogies (1 Coney and a clump of Greelys in Boston). The 1850 census turned up several people with our surnames not on the genealogies, but most were born outside the USA. We do, however, begin to see the genealogist—or his correspondents—flagging: the name in the 1850 census matches someone whose birth is recorded in the genealogy the genealogist didn't follow. If these people are poorer than those he did follow, missing poor lines could explain why our people are wealthier than the population as a whole in 1850. But the pattern we notice is geographical: more family members get lost in the wilderness of Maine than any other place.

English descent in New England had come at that time, so clustering was little affected by time of arrival.

By 1850, with many new immigrants at work in the economy, our early comers may have dominated certain sectors. Moreover, we can see the effects of at least one major economic realignment and the flows between economic niches that it produced: the decline of the subsistence farm in northern New England. With the canals and development of the West there was little market for the grain produced there. Young sons either went west or into trades and industry closer to home. We can see certain "typical flows" caused by the different amounts of capital required for these choices. Since most capital was in land and land values varied at different locations, the migration history of the forebears affects their descendants by limiting their choices.

Adequacy of Migration Histories
from Genealogies

Genealogies are useful for the study of migration not only because they follow people in a line of descent no matter where they happen to live, but also because they contain the information necessary to place each move in the context of key events in the lives of individuals and their families. Still, how reliable are they?

We looked up the members of our nine families on the 1850 manuscript census, which few of the genealogists had been able to consult themselves, to see if they were located where the genealogy says they lived. Fortunately, by having our data on computer we could create a printout of all those alive in 1850, along with last-known and next-known addresses and dates.[23]

Approximately seventy percent were found in the exact same places the genealogy said they would be and an additional eight percent were found in the place the genealogist said they next went. Quite a respectable showing given such a highly mobile group: only some twenty percent spent their entire lives in a single town.

---

[23]John W. Adams and Alice Bee Kasakoff, "Migration and the Life-Cycle in the American North: Age-Specific Rates, 1700 to 1850," paper delivered at the Social Science History Association meetings, Washington D.C., October 1984.

It makes sense that the genealogy should lag behind the migrants since evidence for a move so often comes from events, vital and otherwise, that occurred after the moves themselves. How far behind are they? For the young adults, at least, we were able to obtain a fairly precise answer to this question by looking at how many youths were living away from their families. (The genealogies were essential because they told us how many sons there were.)

The proportion of young men away from home in 1850 fluctuated around twenty percent from age six to twenty, but thereafter it took a huge jump to sixty percent at age twenty-one and came close to ninety percent at age twenty-three. Judging from the published genealogy, however, migration peaked later: age twenty-five for men born before 1740 and around age thirty for men born between 1740 and 1840. Depending on a genealogy, then, meant we were really picking up the birth of a man's first child; the young men had actually left home several years before. Since men married and had their children later as time went on, the genealogies made it appear as though the peak came progressively later in life. The lack of detailed earlier censuses means we may never know whether people left home later as years passed. In any case, the genealogies surely exaggerate the extent of the change.

We anticipated that people of child-bearing age would be the best covered, while the elderly—for lack of births—would be skimped. Yet we found almost the opposite. The best-covered were those between fifty and seventy, the worst those between age thirty and fifty. Hence there must have been even more moving during adulthood than we see in the published genealogies. Literacy does its own kind of pruning. These otherwise full genealogies are constructed from legal documents; and in New England, in contrast to Scandinavia, for instance, people did not have to sign in and out when they changed towns.

The Fate of Women in Genealogies

We began with three genealogies that included descendants through both males and females, influenced no doubt by the resemblance between the careful work being done by the Society of Mayflower Descendents and the traditional anthropological genealogy where every connection is traced. But not only were such genealogies extremely hard to come by, they soon proved unuseful because the descendants of women in them were rarely followed as well as the men's. Assuming equal numbers of boys and girls who had offspring, only half those born into the second generation should bear the surname, one quarter of the third, one eighth of the fourth, and so on; but this was by no means the case in these otherwise quite exemplary records. The coverage inevitably gravitated toward those bearing the ancestral name.[24]

This difference in coverage also surfaced in another way. The eighty percent group overall lay within a twelve-mile radius, but when we looked separately at the marriage distances for men and women, we found that men traveled farther for their spouses than had their sisters. This seemed strange since there was no reason to believe that men and women were marrying different sorts of people.

It was due, of course, to pruning of females. If a woman married in her town or one nearby, the genealogist got the information and followed the family at least one generation; but if she moved farther away, she became an "n.f.r." Her husband's name might be in the genealogy—because she had been married in her hometown—but his place of residence was not. We decided to base our subsequent work on males only, and furthermore to limit ourselves to those descended in the male line.

Bias in Written Genealogies

Genealogies must be pruned to be manageable, and our culture's typical omissions tell us that the patriline is still important. Our surnames have become a focus of attention because they signal ethnicity. It is difficult to trace more than one so the rest of a person's background gets lost along with the women who provide the links to other lines. This conveniently allows us to focus on a single ethnic identity instead of the several that most of us actually have based on the full pedigree.

Like the trimmed oral genealogies of preliterate societies, these written genealogies are charters for valued social status. They do not need to be pruned quite so much because the out-group is not, in fact, closely related: this encompasses the more recent arrivals, usually from German or Irish stock. The New England Historic Genealogical Society was founded when a new wave of immigration was cresting and the "original" New En-

---

[24]The bilateral genealogies we used were those for the Farwell, Greely, and White families cited above in note 20.

glanders felt threatened. Later the first demographic studies to use genealogies lamented the passing of the high birthrates of the early generations and warned of the demise of the original stock if something were not done to counter the fertility transition.[25]

Thus written history serves some of the same functions as the oral variety; it provides an anchor, a justification, a perspective. Many find it in a golden age of premodernity to which they are genealogically linked. Our society is far larger than primitive societies, but our genealogies are nearly as provincial. Their aim is to explain why and how we got *here*, and account for the spread of the surname upon *these* shores. If there is a genealogy for the home country, it is of a different sort, severely truncated, and consigned to the prefatory chapter. The numbers or letters that mark the "real" members of the family are usually assigned only to those who lived on this continent. The glorification of this age can be measured by the amount of information provided on the first comer and the early generations. Famous descendants also get their share. Genealogies of more recent arrivals have the same formal structure, one that reflects their purpose: to link descendants to the American experience, which is viewed as a succession of male arrivals who begat. The melting pot is not only absent, it would require an entirely different sort of genealogical charter.

In preliterate societies genealogies link the living to a golden age that is known only through memory. In New England, however, it is known through written records and can be re-explored. This makes published genealogies complete enough to critique popular notions of destiny. We can make them more ample still by adding other records. Literacy and the tools of history in the hands of their compilers almost have made a fetish of accuracy. The ancestors are so far removed from the descendants who are doing the tracing that the procedure becomes a delightful game, a kind of "hide-and-seek" for grown-ups. The mere presence of the progenitor confers privileged status, so there is an attempt to list everyone who was there. Their behavior is immaterial. No matter how nondescript or roguish, the early generations are well covered. Societies that require proof of descent for membership increase their accuracy by providing a forum for open dis-

---

[25]F. S. Crum, "The Decadence of the Native American Stock: A Statistical Study," *Publications of the American Statistical Association* 14:215-22.

cussion in which false information eventually comes to light, as have many dubious descent lines to the Mayflower passengers.

Literacy has tarnished the heroic glow of these forbears compared to their counterparts in preliterate societies, even though most of the printed genealogies extol their hard work and patriotism. In fact, many include fragments of oral history that draw the familiar picture of the pioneers' hard work and hardship. But written records curb the imagination and so do the rules of the game. Most of us haven't changed our surnames, and in order to get back to that magical time, we are its victims. The primacy of the surname and the presence of written documentation means we can no longer choose our ancestors. At most, only half of us can be descended from the Mayflower. The rest of us must seek other heroes. And the written evidence reminds even those truly of Mayflower descent that even as we might want to make them into demigods, those who made that fateful voyage were human.

The Great Migration Shift

The migration histories in the published genealogies pointed towards a "rural-to-rural" pattern of migration different from, and complementary to, the present-day rural-to-urban movement, which until now was assumed to be virtually universal.[26] Nowadays people move before marriage or when their children are young, but in the families we are studying people moved more often in middle and old age than they do today.

Our explanation for it is that a middle-aged farmer would put his share of his father's estate together with proceeds from the sale of his first farm and pioneer cheaper land that he and his sons could then develop as a source of future capital gains. Here is an investment of human capital in youth in order to acquire productive skills for attaining real capital later in life. In fact, the ratio of the two undergoes a shift as people grow older. The hopes and energy of youth provide the impetus to move early in life; wealth is the motivator in middle age. But in all cases, the likeliest moments to move seem to come at those times in the life cycle when the dependency relationships change in a person's family. If there is a destiny in history, it takes shape at these moments.

---

[26]Donald Parkerson, using data from the 1855 census of New York State, found a similar pattern: "The Changing Pattern of Internal Migration of Americans," paper delivered at the 7th annual meetings of the Social Science History Association, November 1982.

Different Migration Rates
According to Class

The destiny was different, however, for different income groups. The pioneering form of rural-to-rural migration responsible for moving later in life was most common among the middling sorts. Forty-nine percent of those we found on the 1771 Valuation of Massachusetts lived in only one town in their lifetimes. This was a higher rate than in our sample overall because by 1771 people living in Massachusetts and Maine were the stay-at-homes in the families we were studying. But this is a much more common pattern for the top quartile, the wealthy, sixty-two percent of whom were rooted. The bottom twenty-five percent look rather like "roving poor" since they were in constant motion but confined within a relatively small radius. The middle two quartiles, on the other hand, contain the fewest stayers who do the most traveling beyond 100 miles. No poor person traveled that far, and the middling rate is three times that of the rich. The classes had different life-styles as well, which may have reflected their different occupations. People who left the oldest towns were more likely to retain or raise their status, but those who remained there were likely to lower it. A number of middlers who stayed behind became poor.

It was the middlers who were likely to create the major family branches, judging from those living in the longest-settled areas. Today people stress the disruptive effects of migration on the family. In these farm families, though, migration did not destroy the nuclear family because many long-distance moves seem to have been triggered only by the grandfather's death. But the timing of migration in the life cycle changed as the families came to rely less on real capital in land and more on human capital—education and apprenticeship to a trade—to make a living.

Thus cultures are actually sets of life-styles or, as we have been phrasing it for early New England, migration regimes, adapted to niches in the emerging national market. Moving need not mean cultural change: it can be a way of life, as it was for some New Englanders. People who stay put may in fact experience the most change, such as the downward mobility of many who stayed in older areas.[27]

---

[27]David Grayson Allen, *In English Ways* (Chapel Hill: University of North Carolina Press, 1981). This book traces the cultural continuity between towns settled largely by immigrants from certain regions of England and their home regions.

The Switch out of Farming

Our current project is to examine the switch our families made out of farming and into commerce and industry. In 1771 about ninety-five percent farmed, but by 1850 only sixty percent did. This frames the transition from a rural way of life to the more urbanized form of today and with it the change in timing of migration in the life and family cycle. Later families became smaller and migration rates declined.

Our preliminary work indicates that the switch depended on the location of industrial and farm opportunities in an emerging economy. The new opportunities arose first in coastal Massachusetts towns. The first people to leave farming apparently did not migrate; instead, they lived in households with their siblings and parents who did. We guess that these farms were somewhat poorer than those of people who sold out and went west. Once out of farming, very few returned. The modern pattern of migration based on human capital seems to occur first among those born in the poorer farming areas of New Hampshire and Maine. These sons were the first to leave home as young men.

By the time of the 1850 census, family branches were clustered in particular occupations; indeed, whole genealogies sometimes showed a bias towards metalwork, seafaring, carpentry. Thus the family is still the major source of capital, albeit now it is the human capital needed to learn a trade or obtain a clientele.

Decisions made early in the history of the family continue to influence the life-styles and fortunes of descendants, even in a society as mobile and as much in need of labor as America. But we want now to determine the precise intersection of family line and local/occupational niches and especially stress how the choices of the earlier generations influence the range of choices for later generations.

Stability and Change

Anthropology and history see different sides of human destiny. Where anthropology tells the story of stability, continuity, and integration, history seeks turning points and change. Where anthropology looks for shared values and outlooks, history seeks out unique individuals, its "great men," a diversity that leads to a new consensus.

The two disciplines are drawing more inspiration from each other now than ever before. Today anthropologists credit preliterate societies with history (even if they lacked the means to record it) and historians find institutions that seek to "guarantee" stability and continuity in the literate societies they study. We can no longer accept the idea that primitive societies were stable and unchanging—Lévi Strauss calls them "cold"—while modern ones are always "hot," or changing discontinuously. Preliterate societies are no more havens of conformity than literate societies are full of "individuals." The problem is not solved by making New England "primitive," nor, for that matter, by making "primitives" into moderns, nor by thinking that the modern varieties of stability—communism, fascism, pluralistic democracy—are "the same" past recovered.

Historians have inscribed great trajectories upon the record of the past: the settlement of the West, industrialization, the attainment of long life expectancy, and a high level of health and income. The fuller genealogies constructed from written records allow us to reach behind destiny and glimpse some new, and unforseen, consequences of the old. Certain people benefitted more from changes, others less, as the Tories' life histories show. Different social classes made varied use of the opportunities that arose from changes in the overall structure of the economy. So there is not *one* life-style or culture but an intersection of several. Thus the middle-class pattern of picking up stakes and moving to get new land as the older generation ages and dies is a family "life-style" (not a threat to a family), a counterpart to the rich habit of "staying" and the shaky nature of family bonds among the poor. Family members who are separated in space can nevertheless influence each other's behavior; the doings of one generation are interwoven with the next in unforseen ways.

Some Speculative Conclusions

Although genealogies provide convenient tools for studying social-science "problems," when we compare the full genealogies with their pruned counterparts, we catch a glimpse of broader social processes and of how we conceptualize them.

It is frequently assumed that cultures are carried by closely related people. Thus the twelve tribes of Israel are the putative descendants of the twelve sons of Jacob; furthermore, a genealogy of the people who share a culture should go back to a common couple such as Adam and Eve. These groups of close relatives should also share a territory—and stay there. Moving out and intermingling with descendants of other couples blur the boundaries. Like a language, a culture is best learned in youth and is very difficult to change.

This article covers the briefer genealogies; the more complete ones don't tell the same story. Membership in a particular ethnic group is not usually a fact of birth but a subject of active negotiation. As Freud put it, Moses was an Egyptian! People like to think that they belong to one clearly bounded culture, framed by an independent history and genetic unity, but this is rarely the case.

A Gitksan Example

Archaeologists studying the Gitksan have found remains of old communal houses on the same sites going back 1,000 years. What better example of stability and continuity over time could we adduce? Yet the current members do not have a single unified genealogy. We have already seen how these people conveniently forget. But beyond forgetfulness, there is abundant evidence that groups of outsiders are constantly being adopted from larger Houses into the smaller ones that are in danger of becoming extinct. Simple demographic likelihood would predict, furthermore, that in societies where the resource-holding groups are small, frequent demographic accidents will cause them to die out or one group will become so large that its resources aren't adequate for the population.

The Gitksan social system has no mechanism for changing the allocation of resources to groups. The social fiction is that all the Houses have equal amounts of resources, and that they exist in perpetuity. So people are adopted in, sometimes even from, a neighboring tribe. There is no reason to think that such demographic crises did not occur before white contact, for many of their stories record the regeneration of a House from its last surviving member. So far as anyone can tell, these stories predate white contact.

Here then is a set of stable positions—*perpetual statuses* is the anthropological term for them—through which people flow. The structure remains the same; the personnel change. Only when we have the fuller genealogy do we see the disjuncture between the ideology of perpetuity and the movement. The Gitksan themselves try to deny the process. The current holder of a chiefly name is supposed to have an unblemished genealogy going back to the first mythical person to hold it. What we think of as the structure is a fiction that people maintain as evidence of their belonging. Competing groups propose competing fictions with themselves as anchormen for the social process.[28]

Other Examples

The "men in motion" in nineteenth-century cities furnish another example. Katz found that the occupational structure of Hamilton, Ontario, stayed approximately the same throughout the middle of the nineteenth century, but the personnel changed. Our notion of class serves to manage what is really a very fluid situation.

Most cultures have ways of incorporating people who are not born into them. Yet people everywhere want to think that there is continuity, that they "belong" where they are and deserve what they have. Oral genealogies embody stability, and because they are concerned to justify ongoing social relations, those who have left the group are cut off. If groups are taken in, they are incorporated into the genealogy of their hosts a discrete number of generations back, far enough so that no one can actually check.

Sometimes the expansion of one ethnic group at the expense of another may entail wholesale incorporation of certain populations, or the acquisition of wealth may make a cultural switch inevitable. Once a threshold is crossed, ethnicity must change, as Barth has pointed out for Basseri herdsmen, who become townsmen when they become wealthy. Once started in a certain direction, people may not be able to maintain their former culture nor should they necessarily desire that.[29]

---

[28]For a fuller account of Gitksan social organization, see John W. Adams, *The Gitksan Potlatch* (Toronto: Holt, Rinehart and Winston of Canada, 1973).

[29]Michael B. Katz, *The People of Hamilton, Canada, West* (Cambridge: Harvard University Press, 1975); Frederik Barth, *Nomads of South Persia* (Boston: Little, Brown and Company, 1961). See also Peter J. Newcomer, "The Nuer Are Dinka," *Man* 7:1 (March 1972): 5-11; Deborah Gewertz, *Sepik River Societies* (New Haven: Yale University Press, 1983); Kenneth Ames, "Stable and Resilient Systems along the Skeena River: the Gitksan/Carrier Boundary," in Richard Inglis and George MacDonald, eds., *Skeena River Prehistory* (Ottawa: National Museum of Canada, 1978) 219-43.

The Production of Social Stability

Any genealogy can be situated between two poles: one of evolution and destiny and one of false starts and dashed hopes. Everywhere people think they live in bounded, rooted groups that have always existed. But this is the result of pruning. There is an active conspiracy to construct a world of people tied by history to specific life-styles in perpetuity.

Perhaps this is to be expected in a cultural animal. We need a symbolic world of tools and ideas, and above all, a purpose for living to complete our adaptation. We are a mobile species who can inhabit both the arctic and the tropics, but because of this very flexibility we need our "roots." We manufacture an artificial necessity out of our current circumstances in order to summon up the commitment required for survival. Thus do peoples create destinies out of their meandering flows through different environments of the past.

Acknowledgments

The authors are members of the Department of Anthropology, University of South Carolina, Columbia SC. Our New England research was funded by an NEH fellowship administered through the Newberry Library, a University of South Carolina Faculty Research Grant, and grants from the National Science Foundation's Geography and Regional Sciences Program (SES #8016384), their Anthropology Program (BNS #8305214), and their EPSCOR Program.

The data from the 1771 Massachusetts Tax Valuation Records were made available by the Inter-University Consortium for Political and Social Research. They were originally collected by Bettye Pruitt. Neither the original collector nor the consortium bears any responsibility for the analyses or interpretations presented here.

Chapter Four

THE PLACE OF GENEALOGY
IN THE CURRICULUM
OF THE SOCIAL SCIENCES

Robert Charles Anderson

T he discipline of genealogy exists first and foremost for itself. For centuries the practitioner of this craft has sought to elucidate biological and marital relationships between individuals, and has done this for a variety of reasons, but principally because this information has intrinsic personal importance for every member of the human race. The recent surge of interest in genealogy, occasioned by the Bicentennial and by the publication of *Roots*, highlighted the human needs that are fulfilled by knowing one's ancestry.

On the one hand, there are groups that are just attaining an awareness of their own uniqueness. This has been true in the last few decades for a number of ethnic groups in the United States with respect to genealogy, especially Jews and blacks. The Jews, of course, have long been aware of their unique place in history, but it is only recently that American Jews have demonstrated any organized interest in the genealogical particulars of their heritage. This is because most Jews in this country are the descendants of late nineteenth-century Eastern European immigrants, and it is generally not until the maturing of the third or fourth generation that any curiosity about origins and ancestry is displayed.[1]

For the Jews, of course, there is also the factor of the Holocaust, an enormous emotional barrier that has only recently been overcome to the point that some Jews in this country are trying to follow those branches of their families that disappeared in Central Europe during the 1930s and 1940s. There are now a number of Jewish genealogical societies, the first having been organized in New York City, and there is also a journal, *Toledot*, which is devoted solely to Jewish genealogy.

In the case of the black community, pride in ancestry has developed only after some separation in time from slavery. As is well known now, black interest in genealogy exploded in the mid-1970s with the publication of Alex Haley's *Roots*. Although there has been considerable criticism of the historical soundness of Haley's story, nevertheless interest among blacks in the details of their origins has remained high. There is currently a strong organization devoted to the study of black genealogy, and this organization publishes an excellent journal.[2]

The increased mobility of Americans has furnished another strong reason for interest in origins. Groups in this country that formerly had strong interest in origins are now reasserting that interest because of a sense, derived from increased mobility, that they have lost their roots—lost that sense of community that comes from staying in one place and growing up in an environment that is familiar and was so to one's parents and grandparents. Thus many Anglo-Americans, members of families that have been in this country and socially established for centuries, are now looking to their pasts to give them aid in reacquiring their roots. This is undoubtedly the principal reason for the vast amount of genealogical activity in the last two or three decades in California, the quintessential end point for the westward migrations of all Americans.[3]

---

[1]For a general discussion of the third-generation phenomenon, see Marcus Lee Hansen, *The Problem of the Third-Generation Immigrant* (Rock Island IL, 1938).

[2]Haley is taken severely to task by Gary Mills and Elizabeth Shown Mills in *Virginia Magazine of History and Biography*, January 1981. The Afro-American Historical and Genealogical Society, headquartered in Washington D.C., published the first issue of its *Journal* in the summer of 1980.

[3]These points are made in "Everybody's Search for Roots," *Newsweek*, 4 July 1977, 26-38.

For many genealogists, though, these motivations of a social or cultural origin are unimportant; they pursue it for other reasons. For some, there is the simple matter of curiosity. For others, the elucidation of genealogical relationships provides psychological satisfaction of the same sort provided by an intellectual challenge, solving a puzzle, or having done a good job as a detective. And there are other motivations, not so respectable as these, about which the less said the better, such as the tracing of ancestry in the hope of latching onto a mythical lost fortune.

In recent years a wide range of scholars, many without an interest in or knowledge of genealogy, have begun to use the vast treasure trove of genealogical literature as an aid to their research. There has been a century-old barrier of misunderstanding and mistrust between genealogists and virtually all varieties of academic researchers that has led on too many occasions to the misuse of genealogical materials by scholars not sufficiently skilled in genealogy. A brief review of the reasons for the gulf of misunderstanding between genealogists and professional scholars is in order here.[4]

In the nineteenth century there was no distinction, as there was not yet a profession of history, or of sociology, from which genealogy could be distinct. Most historians were patrician New Englanders, who ranged widely over the fields of history, biography, and genealogy, and who were constantly conscious of their pedigrees. But as the various academic disciplines took on organized form in the closing decades of the nineteenth century, the separation from genealogy began to increase. Many of the leaders of the historical community in the late nineteenth and early twentieth centuries were of the Progressive school, and their demographic background was quite different from that of the mid-nineteenth-century historians. Many of the Progressives were Midwesterners and children of recent immigrants from Europe. For these and other reasons, they had little interest in their own or other people's pedigrees.

In the meantime the genealogical community was going off in a different direction, with much of its activity antithetical to that of the professional historical community. Genealogical activity of all sorts abounded in the 1890s and early 1900s, but one of the most prominent movements was the foundation of dozens of patriotic and hereditary so-

---

[4]For a lengthier discussion of the split between historians and genealogists, see Robert Charles Anderson, "The Genealogist and the Demographer," *Genealogical Journal* 9 (1980): 182-97.

cieties. Those who founded these societies had many motivations, but high among them was the desire to put as much distance as possible between themselves and the great hordes of recent immigrants from Europe. Such actions did not endear this branch of the genealogical world to the Progressive historians.

Genealogy then became a field dominated by amateurs, who were unfamiliar for the most part with what was going on in academic circles. But by the same token, during the first half of this century, scholars were not aware of developments within the genealogical community that led to significant improvements in the methodology of genealogical research and writing. Because of this mutual unawareness, most scholars are overwhelmed by the vast quantities of material on the bookshelves of a good genealogical library (material that was published in the 1880s and 1890s, before the rise of modern standards of research), and they are therefore under the mistaken impression that genealogical publications in general are of low quality.

Owing to this century of divergence between the genealogist and the social scientist, we have witnessed also the evolution of the term *antiquarian* into one of opprobrium. In earlier centuries the pursuit of antiquarianism was perfectly respectable, but with the rise of professional scholars, antiquarians have been dismissed as mere grubbers of fact. This follows from the insistence by historians especially that the pinnacle of their craft is in producing interpretations of history, and not mere collections of fact. Given this interpretation, aspiring historians should be trained both in those forms of analysis that produce new bodies of fact, and also learn the processes necessary to encompass a large body of facts in a new synthetic mold.

These points underscore a fundamental difference between the work of the genealogist and that of the social scientist. Looked at in this way, the genealogist is more of a technician, employing specialized tools to perform a particular sort of analysis. When done properly, the end result will be a new body of facts, in the form of a set of biological and marital relations among individuals whose kinship interrelations had not previously been well illuminated. The genealogist does not engage in a synthetic activity, attempting to produce from this body of genealogical data a new historical interpretation of the given region and period.

An analogy between mathematics and genealogy may be useful here. Mathematics has been called the queen of the sciences because the various techniques of the mathematician may be utilized by all scientists, whether physicists, chemists, or biologists. Mathematics is often categorized as being pure or applied; pure mathematics is the study of the subject for its own sake—the elaboration of theorems and propositions by the application of logic to a small number of fundamental building blocks. Sometimes a branch of mathematics that has been pursued only from this theoretical perspective will be found, unexpectedly, to have practical applications. There are, of course, many branches of mathematics, some more applicable to electrical engineering, and others of more use to the celestial dynamicist. However, all the branches of mathematics deal with the relations among the basic building blocks of mathematical thought, whether these be numbers, sets, or geometric figures.

Genealogy is also a study of the relations among certain fundamental building blocks—in this case, people. People are the fundamental building blocks of society, and therefore also are the starting point for all the social sciences. The end product of genealogical research, a network of biological and marital relations for individuals, has importance for any studies of group interaction. Indeed, it is hard to imagine any human activity in which the bonds of kinship will not have some impact. Thus genealogy may be pure or applied. We have already seen earlier the reasons why people study genealogy for its own sake; in addition, genealogy may be studied for its values as applied to any of man's social endeavors. In fact, the value of genealogy extends beyond the social sciences to any aspect of the study of man, for one of genealogy's most important applications is the investigation of hereditary diseases.

Genealogy and mathematics, then, have these things in common: they concern themselves with relations among a group of basic elements; they may be studied for their own sake (pure) or for their value in studying other subjects (applied); and they range across many subject areas (all the natural sciences, or all the social sciences). There are differences as well, though. Mathematics has many branches, exploring different types of relations among various entities; and it is for this reason that mathematics is so widely applicable. Genealogy, on the other hand, studies only one type of relationship, the biological and marital relationships among individuals. There are many other ways in which individuals may relate to one another—socially, economically, or politically, for example—and each of these modes of relationship has its own body of literature and its own tools of investigation. Genealogy should more properly be seen as analogous to one of the branches of mathematics, and therefore as one of a variety of tools available to the social scientist for his study of the manifold relations among men and women. Genealogy should perhaps be designated, then, a princess of the social sciences. This is not so exalted as being a queen, but it is a great advance on being a handmaiden, a position genealogy has been relegated to by more than one nongenealogist.

All this is another way of saying that genealogy should be viewed as one of the auxiliary disciplines of history and of the social sciences. Many lists have been published that include genealogy in this category, along with numismatics, historical cartography, paleography, diplomatics, and the like. But genealogy over the years has not received the same treatment as have some of the other "auxiliary sciences." University courses are available in paleography and diplomatics; funded summer fellowships are available for the study of numismatics, and so on. Even though these fields are not recognized by the academicians to the point where they may establish independent departments of paleography or the like, and where degrees may be granted in these disciplines, there has at least been a willingness to incorporate these studies in the regular curriculum of the university. A more recent example derives from the increased use by social scientists of statistics and other mathematical means of manipulation of data. There are now large numbers of courses available in statistics for the historian and the social scientist. In fact, the Newberry Library runs a number of summer programs designed specifically to train historians in these techniques.

The question immediately arises as to why similar civilities have not been accorded to the study of genealogy. There are a number of reasons, among which are a misunderstanding of the methodology and literature of genealogy, a confusion between genealogy and family history, and the view of genealogy as "filiopietistic antiquarianism." On the first point, we have already seen that many nongenealogists, because of their unfamiliarity with the development of genealogy, have not yet distinguished the smaller and more recent group of high-quality publications from the earlier spate of poorer material around the turn of the century.

This point may be extended by analyzing comments made by some writers in discussing the sources for their interpretive studies. On more than one occasion, such an author has included "genealogies" in a long list of other sources, of the variety that are generally described as primary sources, such as diaries, letters, land and probate records, church records, and so on.[5] If the inclusion of genealogies in such lists is not simply a matter of convenience, then it displays a disturbing ignorance on the part of the historian or social scientist of the way in which genealogies are generated. To list them among other primary sources is to indicate that the genealogical compilations were found among the papers of a particular family, and were generated contemporaneously with the lives of the people included in the genealogical charts. This certainly does happen, and such "genealogies" are properly included among primary sources. For the most part, though, the genealogies actually used are secondary compilations, based on the same primary sources presented in the aforementioned lists. In earlier years genealogies as secondary sources were highly unreliable, since the techniques for interpreting records and data had not yet been highly developed. Moreover, even when a genealogist of the last century was skilled in such interpretation, he very rarely included citations to the sources, or a description of his reasoning. Since the second or third decade of this century, however, the knowledge of how to handle primary documents for the purpose of proving genealogical relationships has advanced by leaps and bounds, and the best genealogists provide proper documentation for the sources of their data. When these points are properly understood, then the social scientist will approach a modern genealogy as he would any other compiled, secondary work of reference: that is, by recognizing that techniques applied to primary sources are inappropriate.

There is then the second reason for the repression of genealogy as a properly accepted auxiliary discipline—the confusion between genealogy and family history. This may be profitably treated by looking at the field of record linkage. Record linkage has arisen in recent years as a sophisticated tool for handling large amounts of data about many individuals. Among the varieties of record linkage that social scientists should be interested in are prosopography, genealogy, family history, and family reconstitution. Genealogy and family history are here separable in that genealogy concentrates on the determination of kinship relations, while family history develops all aspects of the history of a given family. When examining a well-documented, historically important family, the mass of

[5]Robert A. Gross, *The Minutemen and Their World* (New York, 1976) viii; Laurel Thatcher Ulrich, *Good Wives: Image and Reality in the Lives of Women in Northern New England, 1650–1750* (New York, 1982) 5.

material to be covered may be so great that the time and space devoted to the relationships of biology and marriage may be insignificant.[6]

Another analogy may be helpful at this point. Genealogists are sometimes criticized for providing only a skeleton, for giving to the world only the bare bones of the lineage. What the social scientist cries out for is the flesh, the biographical detail in all its ramifications. Without this flesh on the bones, there is little useful work that the historian or social scientist can do. In the best of all possible worlds, then, the genealogist would provide both the flesh and the bones, would both research and determine the skeleton of familial relationships, and also give all the particulars of military service, education, occupation, and so on.

This goal the genealogist can attain in some instances, usually in a study of limited scope. Yet when the genealogist takes on a larger project, such as the discovery of all the agnate descendants of a seventeenth-century immigrant, just the determination of the biological and marital relations of the thousands of persons involved becomes a task that can occupy years and even decades of the genealogist's time. To ask him to provide full biographical data on all these thousands of individuals may be to ask for the impossible. The genealogist provides the essential foundation of a well-articulated skeleton. To ask for the flesh without the skeleton is to obtain a formless blob of protoplasm; to ask for the flesh to be placed on a skeleton that has been hurriedly put together is to obtain a deformed monster.

This leads to the third difficulty, "filiopietistic antiquarianism." Certainly, we must all deplore the researcher who begins his work having already decided that his only goal is to glorify his ancestors, without regard for the facts. But is there not some room for the rehabilitation of the antiquarian? The skilled genealogist may be excellent at the analysis and resolution of complicated genealogical problems, but may at the same time be incapable of, or uninterested in, producing the sort of synthetic, interpretive work that is the end product of modern historical work. Shouldn't other social scientists nevertheless recognize the value of the scholarly genealogist's work and learn how to evaluate and build upon that

---

[6]These varieties of record linkage are discussed from the genealogist's viewpoint in Robert Charles Anderson, "Genealogy and Record Linkage," *Genealogical Journal* 9 (1980): 3-8.

work, or even how to work in conjunction with the genealogist on some project of mutual interest?

When all of these barriers to including genealogy as a proper member of the auxiliary disciplines are down, then perhaps it will be possible to bring genealogy, as it has been practiced for the past half-century by the professional wing of the genealogical community, into the university. There would then be room for a handful of genealogy courses in the curriculum of the department of history or of sociology. A course in modern genealogical methodology could be used to satisfy a requirement in methodology, just as courses in statistics or computer science now do at some institutions. A course in the history of genealogy would be of interest as an upper-level course in social history, whether those taking the course had any intention of pursuing genealogical research or not. Summer institutes in genealogy for graduate students and faculty could be arranged, perhaps tied to some of the programs already being run for amateur genealogists.

To conclude, I would like to enumerate some of the areas in which the genealogist may be of assistance to the social scientist. The most important field in which the skills and results of the genealogist are of value is in the study of human migrations. In order to study these in detail, we must be able to follow many dozens and even hundreds of families and individuals from place to place. Such challenges are beyond the capacity of family reconstitution, since studies of this kind depend upon large, homogeneous bodies of records, which usually pertain to a single geographical location. Conversely, the resolution of the problem requires investigation of individuals from many places. And this is just the sort of study in which genealogy excels.

Another area where genealogy may be of assistance is in biography. As an example, it has been shown within the last few years that the maternal grandfather of President Hayes was of illegitimate birth. In his early years Hayes was deeply influenced by his mother's side of the family; here surely is grist for an interesting psychohistorical study.[7]

Beyond individual biography there is the study of collective biography. Professor David L. Greene is currently undertaking a detailed study

---

[7]Robert Charles Anderson, "The Maternal Ancestry of President Hayes," *The American Genealogist* 52 (1976): 140-41.

of the ancestry and descendants of all who were executed or died in captivity during the witchcraft delusions in Salem in 1692. He has made many new and striking discoveries, and once his studies are done, students of Salem witchcraft will have to revise their theories of that peculiar time.[8]

As noted earlier, genealogy may be applied to any activity in which human beings are involved. Every social scientist should review the work he is doing to see how the tools that have been developed by professional and scholarly genealogists in this century might be of assistance.

---

[8]This project is described in detail, including a list of articles already published, in *The American Genealogist* 59 (1983): 245-46.

Chapter Five

ETHNICITY AND THE SOUTHERN GENEALOGIST: MYTHS AND MISCONCEPTIONS, RESOURCES AND OPPORTUNITIES

Elizabeth Shown Mills

There is no aspect of American social history that has been so minutely scrutinized and yet remains so misunderstood as ethnicity and ethnic relations in the Southern United States. Social scientists, journalists, psychologists, and politicians have probed the myriad ramifications of this issue and offered their exegeses as solutions to almost every conceivable problem. Yet, in an ironic commentary on American social thought, this overwhelming focus on racial issues has seldom been directed toward the genealogist.

To a great extent this anything-but-coincidental omission is due to the intrinsically personal nature of family history and the extreme sensitivity that has existed toward racial issues. Generations of Americans have believed the old cliché that America is "the great melting pot," yet somehow have convinced themselves that melting did not occur across color lines—at least not in their own families. To a significant degree, the problem stems from a cumbersome legacy of myths and misconceptions that has distorted America's historic self-image. Finally, but no less significantly, the lack of interest that genealogists traditionally show to certain ethnic groups is due to a lack of awareness of, or exposure to, the resources other peoples have to offer. The traditional genealogist, unconscious of this self-imposed isolation, approaches the source materials at his disposal with arbitrary ethnic lines already drawn in his own mind. He handicaps himself from the onset.

This analysis of historic race relations and their applicability to genealogy focuses upon the South, but much of what is said can be applied to all quarters of America. Inherent differences do exist in the records and philosophies of Louisiana's Catholics and Philadelphia's Quakers, Virginia's Tidewater diarists, and Iowa's census-takers. Yet all societies share certain basic human traits. The flaws of fallibility, gullibility, and ethnic bias must rank high among these, and they are the classic Medusas that have created the most problems for genealogists.

The magnolia-scented South, laden with its burden of slavery that Margaret Mitchell and Alex Haley painted in such stereotyped melodrama, certainly spawned its share of America's myths and misconceptions. This limited paper can address only a few of them. For the most part, the myths chosen are so widely accepted that neither white nor black, Northerner nor Southerner, thinks to question them. Each misconception opened for discussion also represents an arbitrary barrier that has existed between the genealogist and the success he seeks as he reconstructs his own heritage.

> MYTH: *White Southerners are the personification of Anglo-Saxon*
> *America and its preoccupation with racial purity.*

To the contrary, the most recent historical scholarship argues that the South is not an Anglo-Saxon society at all. Extensive statistical analyses of immigration and migration, patronyms, life-styles, and economic patterns offer convincing evidence that whites who populated the early South were overwhelmingly *Celtic* in origin. The most recent statistics indicate that "upwards of 70 percent of those whose ethnic backgrounds can be ascertained were of Celtic extraction—mainly Welsh, Scots, Irish, and

Scotch Irish," while seventy to eighty percent of Northern householders in 1790 were predominantly English (that is, Anglo Saxon).[1]

The distinction is crucial, not only because it suggests the national origins of immigrants from whom genealogists descend, but also because it explains many peculiarities of the Southern life-style as well as the conflicts that have existed between Northern and Southern whites who heretofore were presumed to be of similar origins. The identification of the South as a dominantly Celtic culture also helps to explain the *lack of racial purity* that actually existed. The Celts of the British Isles were people who shared a common *cultural* heritage but were "clearly of different genetic mixtures,"[2] and they transplanted to the New World their emphasis on cultural compatibility and their lesser concern for superficial genetic distinctions.

> MYTH: *Indian-white marriages were common in the Latin regions of the Gulf but not in the Anglo-South.*

Again, this common misconception stems from the indiscriminate attribution of Anglo-Saxon characteristics to the whole of the white South. Such colonials as Alexander Spotswood, William Byrd, and Robert Beverly—members of the Anglo minority that controlled Virginia politics and letters—played the part of ostriches, buried their heads in the sands of the Tidewater, and ignored the life-style of backcountry Celts when they asserted that "they did not know of a single mixed marriage."[3] Historians, unwittingly, have perpetuated their racially myopic views.

---

[1]Preliminary glimpses of the newly emerging "Celtic thesis" of Southern history have appeared in Forrest McDonald and Ellen Shapiro McDonald, "The Ethnic Origins of the American People, 1790," *William and Mary Quarterly*, 3d ser., 37 (April 1980): 179-99; Forrest McDonald and Grady McWhiney, "The South from Self-Sufficiency to Peonage: An Interpretation," *American Historical Review* 85 (December 1980): 1095-1108; Grady McWhiney, "Continuity in Celtic Warfare," *Continuity: A Journal of History* 2 (Spring 1981): 1-18; and Grady McWhiney and Perry D. Jamieson, *Attack and Die: Civil War Military Tactics and the Southern Heritage* (University AL: The University of Alabama Press, 1982). A seminal monograph, by McWhiney and McDonald, is scheduled for publication in 1985.

[2]McDonald and McWhiney, "The South from Self-Sufficiency to Peonage," 1108.

[3]J. Leitch Wright, Jr., *The Only Land They Knew: The Tragic Story of the American Indians of the Old South* (New York: The Free Press, 1981) 234.

Certainly, Indian-white miscegenation existed widely in the Latin South. An analysis of the population settling northwest Louisiana between 1714 and 1803 indicates that by the close of the colonial era, *forty-nine percent of the native-born white population boasted Indian blood.*[4] Further study, by the same writer, of families migrating later into the region from Southeastern states, reveals high levels of Indian ancestry in their ranks as well. J. Leitch Wright has reported extensive evidence of white-Indian marriages in the Southeast, particularly involving Scots and Scotch-Irish, and asserts that such racial mixing existed there "perhaps on a larger scale than in New France."[5] If Wright is correct, and if the French of northwest Louisiana prove typical of New France, then the Indian heritage of the white Southeasterner is indeed strong.

> MYTH: *A single drop of Negro blood eternally doomed a Southern*
> *family to suffer racial prejudice, subservience, and even*
> *slavery.*

The "one drop rule" made famous by Edna Ferber's *Showboat* and its literary ilk is possibly the most miasmic myth to arise from the Old South. According to Carl Degler's study of American race relations, in most Southern states the Negro "was defined in law and in custom as anyone with a *certain amount* of Negro ancestry—*usually one eighth.*"[6] The legislatures of Virginia and other states lowered that definition to one quarter because the one-eighth ruling would include too many "upstanding" citizens. No antebellum Southern state labeled as Negro any citizen with less than one-eighth African blood.[7]

This blurred line between the Southern black and white is elucidated by the 1835 court decision of South Carolina Justice William Harper:

> The condition [of being Negro] is not to be determined solely by visible
> mixture . . . but by reputation . . . and it may be . . . proper that a

---

[4]Elizabeth Shown Mills, "Social and Family Patterns on the Colonial Louisiana Frontier," *Sociological Spectrum* 2 (Fall-Winter 1981): 238.

[5]Wright, *The Only Land They Knew,* 235.

[6]Carl Degler, *Neither Black nor White: Slavery and Race Relations in Brazil and the United States* (New York: Macmillan Company, 1971) 101; italics added.

[7]James Hugo Johnston, *Race Relations in Virginia and Miscegenation in the South, 1776-1860* (Amherst: University of Massachusetts Press, 1970) 192.

[Negro] man of worth . . . should have the rank of a white man, while a vagabond of the same degree of blood should be confined to the inferior caste.[8]

Even more surprising to students of history is the fact that intermarriage between white and black was legal in almost every Southern state or colony at one time or another, and at least one antebellum state never outlawed such marriage. Gary B. Mills's study of miscegenation in Alabama provides startling statistics on legal intermarriages and community-tolerated miscegenous concubinages—even between white females and nonwhite males. Examples of racial mixing and crossing abound, and there is clear evidence of laxity and unconcern by white citizens when called upon to distinguish between "coloreds" and "clear bloods."[9]

Such situations are evident across the Southern frontier. The 1826 census of the Celtic-Anglo settlers of Atascosita, Texas, reveals a minimum ten percent of the population with known Negro ancestry, yet no discriminatory designations are applied to them on the census.[10] Across the Sabine, in southwest Louisiana, fifteen of the "first families" of "white" Southeastern origins appear on pre-1860 censuses as "free nonwhite." Moreover, the ethnic origin of those families is discussed in published studies of the free Negro in every state along their migration path; yet their identity for the past century and a quarter has been white.

In short, "racial purity" was not a universal concern in the Old South; and the "white" genealogist would be naive to begin his work by *assuming* that he will find nothing but "white" ancestors. If he succeeds in tracing every ancestral line back to a European immigrant (as he may), he would still be foolish to assume that his ancestry was "pure white." Not only was Europe traveled by men of every conceivable hue, but African slavery existed there also, and blacks were assimilated into Europe's population before American colonization began.

---

[8]Marina Wikramanayake, *A World in Shadow: The Free Black in Antebellum South Carolina* (Columbia: University of South Carolina Press, 1973) 14.

[9]Gary B. Mills, "Miscegenation and the Free Negro in Antebellum 'Anglo' Alabama: A Reexamination of Southern Race Relations," *Journal of American History* 68 (June 1981): 16-34.

[10]Mirian Partlow, *Liberty, Liberty County and the Atascosita District* (Austin: Jenkins Publishing Co., 1974) 329-36.

When nonwhite ancestry is encountered in America, the genealogist may expect considerable difficulty in attempting to label, ethnically, that nonwhite element. The enslavement of Indians by whites introduced countless Native Americans into Negro life, while the Indian enslavement of Afro-Americans interjected Negro blood into the Indian nations. Indeed, countless Southern families with no Indian ancestry at all and more than a few drops of Negro blood have seen many advantages to painting these drops red instead of black when sketching their family tree.[11]

MYTH: *A genealogist who "knows" his family to be white need not expend time searching records already identified as "black" or "Indian."*

A successful reconstruction of any family—even an apparent "clear-blood" one—is almost never possible for the genealogist who thinks in terms of "white records," "black records," or "Indian records." These phenomena do not exist. The needs and problems of various ethnic groups did cause certain records to be created; and for convenience' sake, archivists, historians, and the general public have categorized these. However, in the recorded history of the South, no ethnic group has existed in isolation, and there is no body of records that deals with one race to the exclusion of others. Many of the problems genealogists experience—many that have stymied a family's pursuit of an elusive ancestor for generations even—result from a simple case of ethnic tunnel vision.

---

[11]The Montgomery County, Alabama, case of *Elmore* v. *Harris & Pickett* provides an excellent example of how public knowledge of nonwhite ancestry might follow a family through numerous generations and across several states; how a seeming majority of such a family's neighbors might consider its ancestry unimportant; and yet how the issue might continue to be raised whenever opponents saw advantage in airing the family's closetful of skeletons. In this particular case, when friends and neighbors were forced to testify, they consistently related the "public knowledge" (sometimes, personal knowledge) that the family in question descended from "a black Negro with a number of white wives." Yet the family itself repeatedly identified its dark progenitor as a full-blooded Indian.

In 1977 this writer, together with Gary B. Mills, photocopied abstracts of the case from *Records of the Chancery Court, 1830-1839*, Montgomery County Records, 668-754, while the court files were stored in the basement of the county courthouse. In 1980-1981 a portion of these files were transferred, at intervals, to the Alabama Department of Archives and History; also in 1981 Professor Mills's study of miscegenation was published, with a discussion of the *Elmore* v. *Harris & Pickett* case. Some months later this writer had occasion to search that same group of files in both its old and new location and found the cited volume missing. As of this writing, it has not been located.

The experience of the Charleville family of southeast Louisiana provides an excellent example. By the 1960s descendants had attempted for fifty-three years to identify the parents of their late-eighteenth-century Louisiana progenitor, Joseph Chauvin *dit* Charleville. Tradition identified his father as Captain Joseph Chauvin *dit* Charleville of the Kaskaskia, Illinois, post. He was, in fact, the only older Chauvin male in America known to have used that *dit*. Yet all "known" civil and church records dealing with the family, from Montreal to Mobile, had been searched; no younger Joseph was found in the family of the captain and his wife.

The problem was self-created. The needed proof existed, and always had, but researchers had erected superficial ethnic barriers they could not see beyond. Copious notes had been taken from the crucial parish registers at Kaskaskia, notes dealing with everyone identified in the marginal notations as a Chauvin or a known relative; but every researcher had skimmed past the numerous slave registrations interspersed amid white entries, presuming that the marriages and baptisms of blacks had no bearing on their own research. It was not until a researcher recognized the importance of the family's ownership of slaves, as a facet of their character, that proof was found of the existence of a Joseph, Jr. in the Illinois family. A 1756 marriage, annotated as "Louis and Geneviève, slaves," identified the couple as property of Captain Joseph Chauvin *dit* Charleville—and identified one of the official witnesses as "young Joseph, son of the master."[12]

Sacramental registers kept by Southern Catholic churches may or may not be segregated by race. Where separate registers do exist, the genealogist must recognize that even the church is not infallible in all things. On countless occasions, a new cleric who did not know the recipient of a sacrament racially misidentified the person in his records. The registers of the parish of St. François in the old Louisiana settlement of Natchitoches contain fifty such entries between 1826 and 1831, eleven more between 1831 and 1846, and forty-one between 1850 and 1871.[13] Other pastors

---

[12]Parish of Notre-Dame de l'Immaculée Conception de Kaskaskias, Microfilm C-2899, Public Archives of Canada, Ottawa. The cited researcher is Mary Helen (Mrs. George) Wilson of St. Louis.

[13]Archives of Immaculate Conception Church, Natchitoches LA. See also Gary B. Mills, "Piety and Prejudice: A Colored Catholic Community in the Antebellum South," ed. Randall M. Miller and Jon L. Wakelyn (Macon GA: Mercer University Press, 1983) 180-81, 192.

recorded the administration of sacraments to individuals whom they clearly, and properly, identified as white; yet they inadvertently picked up a "black" or "slave" register in which to record the entries.[14]

Censuses and other civil records, by contrast, are traditionally treated with a curiously discriminatory brand of skepticism. The neophyte genealogist rapidly loses his naiveté over the reliability of census detail regarding ages, birthplaces, occupations, and property values; nevertheless, the racial designations that accompany this data are treated as though they were engraved in stone atop Mt. Sinai. The "white" researcher who encounters a "black" or "mulatto" family of his surname, even if the given names are appropriate, will automatically assume this to be a "different family." Similarly, descendants of light-skinned Negroes may react similarly if they encounter records that label their ancestors "black."

Yet racial misidentifications are rampant in census records and cross all class lines. The 1860 federal enumeration of Barbour County, Alabama, identifies as "black" a young boy named Bragg Comer—a lad destined for the governor's chair of Alabama. No trace of African ancestry has been found among the Comers, and in that census year they were not only well known in their county but were among the social and economic elite. Nonetheless, they are clearly designated "black." A sample study, made by the present writer, of the 1860 census of the civil parish of Natchitoches, Louisiana, reveals a significant margin of error in racial identification. Seventy-six of the 1,614 families that year were misidentified: four percent of the population! In twenty-three cases, a well-known family of color was identified as white by the newcomer who took the census, while fifty-three white families whose ancestry was European with no African admixture were labeled "mulatto." Clearly, the thorough genealogist cannot afford to ignore records on individuals whose names are "right" but whose racial designations are "wrong."

Local civil records present a host of opportunities for the genealogist to expand his lineage work by reprogramming responses to race-related data. The case of Thomas Brandon, an early official in Huntsville, Ala-

---

[14]See, for example, Elizabeth Shown Mills, *Natchitoches, 1800-1826: Translated Abstracts of Register Number Five of the Catholic Church Parish of Natchitoches in Louisiana*, Cane River Creole Series, 4 (New Orleans: Polyanthos, 1980); idem, "Burials & Baptisms, 1807-1859, Parish of St. François des Natchitoches," *Natchitoches Genealogist* 5 (April 1981): 11-20.

bama, provides an excellent example. When family researchers reported that conventional research had failed to identify Brandon's origins, the federal censuses were reconsulted by the professional whom they employed—with the resulting "discovery" that in 1830 Brandon's household included a free man of color. The family had omitted him from their notes on the presumption that he was a "hired servant or something" whose presence was inconsequential. Research in the county records was then extended beyond the routine examination of entries indexed under the name Brandon. In other words, conveyance books for the period were combed for all "free papers" filed by Huntsville's free black population—and the family's problem soon was solved with the discovery of the following:

> MARVILLE SMITH—CERTIFICATE OF FREEDOM
> 8 January 1830
> Personally appeared before me, Wm. Barker, an acting Justice of the Peace of said County, Thomas Brandon, a citizen of said County and made oath in due form of law that Marville Smith . . . is a free man and that deponent was well acquainted with the father of the said boy before he was born. . . . Marville was born in the *State of North Carolina Burke County* where he [Brandon] lived. [15]

Similar records abound throughout the South with information on white associates of blacks. Mrs. Ann Bayless of Natchez, Mississippi, wife of Platt Bayless, testified in 1812 that the "yellow man" Uriah Jones, who first came to Natchez three years before, had been her acquaintance in Mason County, Kentucky, where he was bound to her fellow Quakers, the Samuel Canbys. In 1842 James W. Stewart and George S. Armistead, both whites of Lauderdale County, Alabama, swore they had first known the free black Jacob Lusk in Loudoun County, Virginia. In the Madison County, Alabama, free paper of Nancy Mayo, filed that same year, Abraham Bransford, a white, testified that Nancy was bound to him shortly after her 1811 birth in Cumberland County, Virginia, whence he brought her to "the said County of Madison . . . in the month of December 1817." [16]

---

[15]*Deed Book M* (orig. vol.) 549, Madison County Records, Old Law Library, Huntsville AL.

[16]*Deed Record A*, 89-91, and *Deed Record W*, 102, Madison County Records. *Deed Record 10*, 428, Lauderdale County Records, Florence AL.

An awareness of the friendly, and often close, relations between free blacks and whites of the Old South is equally useful to the black genealogist in search of elusive roots. Free Southern blacks, like Southern whites, seldom migrated alone. When a free black ancestor is found in a state and county without apparent relations, and when those desirable but often nonexistent "free papers" cannot be found in local records, the black migrant's origins can often be traced by identifying and backtracking his white neighbors and associates.

The copious records of the Bureau of Refugees, Freedmen, and Abandoned Lands, and the more widely available WPA "Slave Testimonies" are other examples of record groups invaluable to both blacks and whites. Again, because of their racial labels, both are seriously underutilized. White genealogists searching for Southern ancestors are seemingly unaware that WPA interviewers instructed ex-slaves to "tell about your master, mistress, their children, the house they lived in, the overseer or driver, poor white neighbors, or when some of the master's family married or died." Indeed, a closer investigation of the Alabama collection labeled "Ex-Slave Tales & Life Histories/Stories" reveals that at least half are recollections given by elderly *whites* whom WPA workers also interviewed; yet the white genealogist who suffers from racial myopia reads the first two words on the collection's label and passes it by. [17]

Almost equally neglected by white patrons of Southern libraries are the microfilmed documents of the United States Bureau of Indian Affairs. Genealogists who have not yet found Indian ancestry assume these files have nothing for them, but the loss they suffer as a consequence is great. For example, a single roll of filmed letterbooks relating to Cherokee Indians along the Tennessee-Georgia-Alabama borders for the years 1801-1802 contains data on 118 frontier whites, while the 1808-1809 letterbooks discuss some 400 whites and only one-quarter that number of Indians. Included in these files are recommendations for agency jobs, giving relationships and places of origin for the frontier applicants. There are Indian complaints against specific whites who encroached upon their lands, stole their food stores, and destroyed their crops and homes, as well as white

---

[17]Works Progress Administration, Writers' Project of Alabama, Folklore Section, *Ex-Slave & Life Histories/Stories,* Alabama Department of Archives and History, Montgomery. See also George P. Rawick, *The American Slave: A Composite Autobiography,* 31 vols. (Westport CT: Greenwood Press, 1972-1977).

accounts of Indians attacking homesteads, throwing children into blazing fireplaces, splitting open the heads of womenfolk, and other similar atrocities that white-family traditions often relate, but which genealogists seldom verify due to a supposed "lack of records."[18] In such cases, the problem often is not so much a *lack* of records as it is a failure to utilize the material that does exist.

MYTH: *Black genealogists must depend more on oral history since their families can rarely be traced through the conventional means that white genealogists use.*

This misconception, commonly believed by blacks and whites alike, is yet another example of ethnic naiveté. The traditional, historical portrayal of Afro-American life as a promiscuous, matriarchal society with weak family ties resulting from frequent sales and sexual exploitation has been seriously questioned by recent scholarship; and the rich breadth of the latest studies in black history reflects at last the broad scope of available records.[19] Unfortunately, the public is far more likely to have "learned history" from Frank Yerby's *Foxes of Harrow* or Kyle Onstott's *Mandingo* than from the scholarship of Herbert Gutman or John Blassingame. Even more damaging is the credence given this myth with the publication of Alex Haley's undocumented *Roots*, accompanied by his self-acclaimed status as "probably . . . the person most knowledgeable about black genealogy."[20] There was also his misleading but widely publicized advice that "records [do not] reflect things like children born from unions between white masters and black women so to expect these records to provide an accurate account is pure naiveté. When it comes to black genealogy, well-kept oral history is without question the best source."[21]

---

[18]Reels 1 and 4, Microcopy 208, U.S. Bureau of Indian Affairs, National Archives and Records Service, Washington D.C.

[19]Excellent rectifications of these points appear in Herbert C. Gutman, *The Black Family in Slavery and Freedom, 1750-1925* (New York: Pantheon Books, 1976); John W. Blassingame, *The Slave Community: Plantation Life in the Antebellum South,* rev. ed. (New York: Oxford University Press, 1979); and Robert William Fogel and Stanley L. Engerman, *Time on the Cross: The Economics of American Negro Slavery,* 2 vols. (Boston: Little, Brown and Company, 1974).

[20]Quoted in Peggy J. Murrell, "Black Genealogy," *The Genealogical Helper* 26 (September 1972): 417.

[21]"*Roots:* The Saga Continues," *Family Weekly,* 2 August 1981, 18.

To the contrary, legitimate historians and genealogists of recent years have proven that records do document even illicit miscegenation. Gary B. Mills's *The Forgotten People: Cane River's Creoles of Color*[22] is an excellent example of how a mixed-family's traditional descent from a black female slave and her white master can be documented thoroughly, and how the family's social, economic, religious, and political experiences, both in slavery and freedom, can be traced to an African progenitor ten generations removed—with the support of literally thousands of the same type of documents that white genealogists use.

The traditions that black or Indian families (or those of any race) have preserved are invaluable clues in reconstructing a family's heritage; however, there is inherent danger in the current fad that elevates oral history to the status of a sacred relic. As was pointed out in an interdisciplinary study of *Roots*, there is no such thing as "The Gospel According to Aunt Lizzie."[23] All humanity, regardless of race, is fallible, gullible, and biased. Any traditional story passed through successive generations will be altered by fading memories, by misinterpretation of details, and by the very human desire to present one's self or one's family in the best possible light. Generations of white genealogists rooted family trees in a mountain of mistakes and earned for themselves the scorn of serious historians before they learned (and admitted) that Aunt Lizzie's gospel was not divinely inspired. Now, a growing popular belief that oral tradition is sanctified by its association with minorities threatens to catapult black genealogy into the academic dark ages from which white family history already has emerged.

The advantages and limitations of oral history know no racial bounds, and there is a striking universality of substance within the family traditions of all people—as shown by Donald R. Wright's work with Gambian

---

[22](Baton Rouge: Louisiana State University Press, 1977). See also Elizabeth Shown Mills and Gary B. Mills, "Slaves and Masters: The Louisiana Metoyers," *National Genealogical Society Quarterly* 70 (September 1982): 163-89; and Elizabeth Shown Mills, "Mézières, Grappe, Trichel: A Study of Tri-Caste Lineages in the Old South," *The Genealogist* (forthcoming, 1985).

[23]Gary B. Mills and Elizabeth Shown Mills, "*Roots* and the New 'Faction': A Legitimate Tool for Clio?" *The Virginia Magazine of History and Biography* 89 (January 1981): 3-26.

griots and family elders.[24] Assertions that oral accounts are of more value to Afro-Americans because of their traditional lack of educational opportunities ignore the legion of white Americans who were equally deprived. The state of scholarship currently enjoyed by all ethnic groups in America mandates that the legends of each be subjected to academic standards. Whatever his heritage, the genealogist who is scholarly in his methodology and interpretation, who anticipates (and accepts) the deviances that will invariably be found between legend and fact, can utilize his family's traditions to reconstruct a meaningful and poignant heritage.

Mills's experience in tracing the "forgotten people" provides a model of good genealogical practice. One oral account of the family's life centers on a white dentist who resided on the family's isle during the Civil War. While "drilling" one of the family members, the dentist allegedly was shot by his patient for an inexplicable reason. The dentist died, and the patient fled the parish. Mills could find no supporting evidence for the story in any records known to deal with the family. By analyzing and investigating the components of the traditional account, he identified several white medical doctors living on the isle, but no dentists. As he began to reconstruct the demise of each doctor, the actual story surfaced, with all the supporting detail that a careful genealogist or historian could desire. As expected, the basic truth differed somewhat from the tradition because, at some point, a storyteller had misunderstood details he had been told. More important, while the original family tale was interesting, it lacked reason or purpose. By contrast, the actual story told much about the problems this family faced in those strained years of war.

Free and wealthy despite their African heritage, this family supported the war effort. Its members volunteered for military duty and were rejected by the Confederacy. White friends encouraged them to form militia units for homeguard duty and they did so; but the discriminatory laws of the Confederacy required them to appoint white officers. Eventually the white friends whom they chose to command their units were either drafted into regular service or died. They accepted as drillmaster another who volunteered, Dr. Jean Napoleon Burdin (a medical doctor, not a dentist as

---

[24]Donald R. Wright, *Oral Traditions from the Gambia,* Papers in International Studies, Africa Series, no. 38, 2 vols. (Athens OH: Ohio University Center for International Studies, 1980); and Wright, "Uprooting Kunta Kinte: On the Perils of Relying on Encyclopedic Informants," *History of Africa* 8 (1981): 205-17.

had been erroneously assumed from his association with the word "drill"). Burdin's prejudices proved intolerable, and the militia disbanded. Ultimately, Union troops invaded the isle and confiscated all weapons they could find; the doctor attempted to force his former militiamen to attack this army of forty thousand, even though his men were armed only with "pitchforks and sticks." The men refused; an argument ensued. The doctor fired on one recalcitrant, and another whose weapon also had escaped confiscation returned the fire. The doctor died that night, and the man responsible for his death quietly left the parish to avoid arrest in the event that public sentiment might be aroused over the incident. When no negative reactions materialized, he returned.[25]

Clearly, oral traditions can be invaluable *as clues to find the documentary evidence that should exist, that must exist before any tradition can be accepted as fact.* The black genealogist who refuses to reconcile tradition with evidence, who lets himself be daunted by obstacles all genealogists face, and then falls back on the platitude that "oral tradition is the best source" for oppressed races, does so at the expense of genealogical scholarship and compromises the academic integrity of the black American experience.

MYTH: *Much of the difficulty in tracing black roots stems from the fact that slaves used the surnames of their masters—and this changed every time a slave was sold.*

Black historiography currently offers no consensus on this point. John W. Blassingame, a more cautious authority, reports that forced name-changes were not uncommon, but concludes that "the slave used his *actual* name in conversation in the quarters and adopted it officially when he was freed." Unfortunately, he hedges the question of how a slave acquired or determined an *actual* surname. Ira Berlin has been quoted as more emphatically stating, "Slaves *rarely* took their master's name."[26] A sample study made by the present writer, from 696 ex-slave testimonies given before the three Civil War reparations commissions, indicates that in seventy-one percent of the cases, the ex-slave used the surname of the man

---

[25]Gary B. Mills, "Patriotism Frustrated: The Native Guards of Confederate Natchitoches," *Louisiana History* 18 (Fall 1977): 437-51.

[26]Blassingame, *The Slave Community*, 181-83. Berlin is quoted in a United Press International news release, "Freedmen's Files Studied," *Shreveport Times*, 18 February 1976; italics added.

whom he identified as his last master; two percent reverted to using the name of an earlier master; and twenty-five percent did not use the name of any identifiable owner. In a small number of cases (two percent), no names of former masters could be determined and the origins of those slaves' names were unquantifiable.[27]

The question of slave-naming practices is an important one to both black and white genealogists. Obviously, whether a freed slave took the name of a former master is crucial to any descendant who might search for premanumission records. Less obviously, an awareness of slave-naming customs can open new vistas for the descendants of slaveowners who place no racial bounds on their research. Included in the papers of the Southern Claims Commission, for example, are a number of files created by ex-slaves who sometimes used and sometimes did not use the surname of a former master. The efficient white genealogist who goes beyond a search for claims filed by his own ancestors and studies the claims of area blacks with the same name may well find data that augments his own work.

Examples are numerous: ex-slave Frederick Calhoun of Madison County, Alabama, testified that he was the former property of Meredith Calhoun, whose son "was afflicted [so] I stayed with him nearly all the time. *He broke his back when he was a boy."* In the claim of David Vincent, ex-slave of Stephen Willis Harris of that same county, the claimant's friend, Anderson Watson, testified: "My master was Bob Watkins. His plantation was about fifty miles from the Harris place. *My master was a brother to Mrs. Harris."* In the suit of ex-slave Quinn Grey of Lawrence County, Alabama, George W. Grey, a white, testified he had been born in 1828 and was *the son of Quinn's old master, Jonathan Grey.* In the Limestone County, Alabama, case of John Richardson, ex-slave of William Richardson, a fellow slave testified that she well knew one Colonel Phillips of the 9th Illinois, U.S. Army, since *"he married Miss Jennie Davis, sister to my master's wife."*[28] Similar testimony regarding white owners, to be found

---

[27]The three claims commissions from which these statistics are drawn are the Southern Claims Commission, RG 56, 217 and 233; Mixed Commission of British and American Claims, RG 76; and French and American Claims Commission, RG 76, National Archives.

[28]Files 18667 (Cong. No. 10146), Frederick Calhoun; 18686 (Cong. No. 9448), David Vincent; 19679, John Richardson; 4197, Estate of Quinn Grey—Southern Claims Commission.

in these claims of blacks, reports earlier places of residence, death dates, and a host of events in their masters' lives—all of which the white genealogist may not find through traditional genealogical sources.

MYTH: *Family research is more disheartening for blacks since they have inherited a legacy of oppression and tribulation, with few of the positive experiences that make ancestral research exhilarating for white (that is, free) American families.*

Carl Degler sums up this problem in pointing out that traditional American history treats the black "primarily as a problem, not as a contributor to the making of society."[29] The publishers of *Roots* capitalized upon this myth by proclaiming on its cover that the trials of this fictionalized family of slaves was "the story of 25,000,000 Americans of African descent." On the contrary, the rich legacy left by America's antebellum blacks is far more complex, far more dramatic, far more troubling, and far more rewarding for their descendants who pursue the truth.

Among the many facets of Southern antebellum race relations that popular history has obscured, the black genealogist will quite likely find a very positive heritage of achievement. On the eve of the Civil War, almost half a million black Americans—approximately one out of every eight—were *free*. (If the legions of other Americans of African descent who had crossed the color line already were included in this tabulation, the numbers would be even greater.) A middle-aged American black of the 1980s, who begins to trace his ancestry, may statistically expect to find some twenty-four direct ancestors living on the eve of the Civil War, and he may also expect that three of these ancestors were not slaves at all.

Public awareness of free blacks does exist. Movies and novels have sensationalized the "underground railroad" that took Southern slaves to freedom after slavery gradually was abolished in the North. Yet, few contemporary Americans are aware of the actual numbers of blacks who did gain freedom, nor do they realize that *half this number, almost a quarter of a million in 1860, were living in the South* where they very often were contributors to and builders of Southern life. By comparison, the number of

---

[29]Degler, *Neither Black nor White,* 7.

passengers on the fabled "underground railroad" has been estimated at only 50,000.[30]

The black genealogist may also find that his Afro-American ancestors were not only the victims of slavery, but perpetrators of the system as well. Pioneer black historian Carter G. Woodson catalogued 3,765 blacks in 1830 who were actually slaveowners,[31] but in the half-century since Woodson's study was published, popular history has tread lightly on the subject. Like Spotswood, Byrd, and Beverly of eighteenth-century Virginia, who did not want to admit the existence of miscegenation in their ranks, a twentieth-century black America that idealizes the historically nonexistent concept of "black brotherhood" overlooks the reality that black Americans enslaved other black Americans. This particular strain of historic myopia has been encouraged as well by white supremacists who are more comfortable with the image of blacks as nonachievers and are disturbed by those who dare to admit antebellum blacks to the master class.

Afro-Americans who stepped into the slave market to buy or sell, and not to be auctioned, were motivated by a variety of reasons. Every Southern state had nonwhite capitalists who enjoyed varying degrees of success. Mistress L. Horry of Colleton District, South Carolina, was enumerated in 1830 with eighty-four slaves. Martin Donato, a *creole de couleur* of Opelousas, Louisiana, was the owner that year of seventy-five blacks. The Metoyer family, planters and merchants *de couleur* of Isle Brevelle, Louisiana, owned 287 bondsmen in 1830—a stupendous number that continued to swell until, in 1850, the family collectively owned 436 other Afro-Americans.[32]

At the other extreme, there existed a still-unquantifiable number whose slave property consisted of relatives or friends. In such cases the owner may have manumitted the relative, if law permitted. Sometimes the law was more generous than the owner, and the black kinsman remained

---

[30]Johni Cerny, "Black Ancestral Research," in *The Source: A Guidebook of American Genealogy,* ed. Arlene Eakle and Johni Cerny (Salt Lake City: Ancestry Publishing Company, 1984) 592.

[31]Carter G. Woodson, "Documents: Free Negro Owners of Slaves in the United States in 1830," *Journal of Negro History* 9 (January 1924): 41-85.

[32]Ibid.; Mills, *The Forgotten People,* 108-11. The estate grounds of one of the Metoyer plantations have survived and in 1975 the site (Melrose) was declared a National Historic Landmark.

in bondage. At least one black who held title to his own children is known
to have offered them at public auction to pay off debts he had accumulated.[33]

> MYTH: *Tracing Southern ancestry is particularly gratifying to*
> *whites in search of illustrious ancestry since the plantation*
> *regime of the Old South produced so much wealth*
> *and so many already-documented, noble pedigrees.*

Historians have long since debunked the magnolia-scented and mint-
julip-soused image of the white Southerner as a slaveowning planter loll-
ing on the veranda of his mansion. Still, the myth persists. Among Southern householders enumerated in 1860, only one of every twenty-seven met
the Census Bureau's criteria for the elite status of "planter." Three-fourths
of all white Southerners owned no slaves at all, and half of those who did
had less than five. In reality, the "typical" slave quarters contained no more
than a man or woman, possibly both, and perhaps a child or two. The
"typical" owner, that one man in four prosperous enough to own a slave,
was a yeoman farmer who worked in the fields beside his bondsman. More
than three-quarters of a century have passed since the Vanderbilt professor Gustavus W. Dyer first began to incorporate these census figures into
his lectures, and generations of historians have repeated them. Still, the
moonlight-and-magnolia aura remains draped, like charming but parasitic
moss, on too many Southern family trees.

The white genealogist tracing Southern roots possibly has more sur-
prises in store. Few expect, but some do find, the chains of slavery on their
own non-African ancestors. The American colonists who first brought
Negroes to the New World as indentured servants, and then saw the economic advantages of enslaving them, developed other innovations. When
colonial leaders attempted to discourage miscegenation by legislating the
enslavement of white females who bore part-Negro children, unconscion-
able masters forced unwary white bonded girls to marry blacks and thereby
gained for life the services of the female and all her offspring. The abused
law was repealed ultimately, but throughout the antebellum era cases appeared before the courts in which whites were found to be holding other

---

[33]Interview with Angie Garrett, Gainesville, *Ex-Slave Tales & Life Histories/Stories*.
The free black who auctioned his sons in front of the local post office was George Wright,
a mill owner of Choctaw County, Alabama.

whites in slavery on the pretense that the oppressed one was a light-skinned, slave-born mulatto.[34]

To a greater degree, white American roots are manacled to slavery through the Indian roots that many families, until recently, tried to forget. A study conducted in northwest Louisiana, focusing on the white families who settled the area prior to 1803, revealed that at the close of the era a startling *23.8 percent of the white population had slave ancestry* through one or more Indian lines.[35] In all cases, the situation resulted from the enslavement of, impregnation of, and eventually the manumission of Indian females by European settlers under the same circumstances that existed in Afro-American slavery. This is but one of the many facets of the American heritage that social historians and demographers have not yet explored. It reveals one of the many ways in which the genealogist who is scholarly in his methodology and candid with his results can help achieve a better understanding of America's ethnic history.

Popular opinion notwithstanding, the Old South the genealogist encounters was an extremely homogeneous and highly integrated society. Segregation was as unworkable in the seventeenth to nineteenth centuries as in the twentieth. The attempts at segregation so commonly known today stem not as much from customs of the slave South as from reactionary experiments of a frightened, perplexed, postwar society in which Jim Crow measures were used to counter the social and political upheaval wrought by the Civil War and Reconstruction. This distinction between attitudes of the antebellum South and those of the postwar South is an important one for genealogists to remember since it affected the attitudes, activities, and associates of their ancestors.

Integrated housing, integrated churches and, occasionally, integrated schools were a fact of life in the Old South, one that produced equally integrated records for the benefit of the modern genealogist. Laws against intermarriage often did not exist. The legendary "one drop rule" is nothing but a myth. The peculiar institution of slavery did not force all blacks onto one side of a social, economic, and political line and array all whites on the other, while the Native American stood unconcerned and

---

[34]Carter G. Woodson, "The Beginnings of Miscegenation of the Whites and Blacks," *Journal of Negro History* 3 (October 1918): 340.

[35]Mills, "Social and Family Patterns," 238.

uninvolved at a remote distance. The Old South was, literally, the proverbial melting pot, a *soupe de jour* in which all social elements on hand from the Old World were mixed with the leftovers from the new. On this basis, the genealogist may well expect difficulty in separating the cream of Europe from the blood of the Native American or the hearty broth of the transplanted black.

"Ethnic awareness" and "respect for ethnic identity" are emotional catchwords, even political battle flags, in twentieth-century America. Their accompanying emphasis on the contributions of minority groups is a positive good, especially for the genealogist. It has paved the way for open admission, and frank study, of any and all ancestral elements that a genealogist may find. It has expanded the availability of records heretofore believed to be of limited interest to members of certain groups only. The genealogist now has at his disposal unprecedented resources and revolutionary computer technology to expedite his utilization of these masses of data. It is time, as well, that outmoded ethnic misconceptions be set aside and the genealogist approach these resources with the open inquisitiveness and judicious discretion that produces success in scholarship.

Part II

GENEALOGICAL APPROACHES TO COMMUNITY AND FAMILY RESEARCH

Chapter Six

RECONSTRUCTING CATHOLIC FAMILY HISTORY

James M. O'Toole

The study of the history of the family has come increasingly to oc-cupy the attention of professional scholars and amateur researchers alike. Once the exclusive preserve of genealogists, the life of this most basic unit of society is now being studied by a greater number and a wider variety of people. The interest of these students of the family goes well beyond a simple inventory of the trees of individual relatives and seeks instead to see the forest of historical context and understanding. Without intending to give offense to genealogists who have labored devotedly over the years, one might say that these new researchers seem more intent on following the advice St. Paul gave to Timothy against busying oneself "with myths and interminable genealogies which promote idle speculations rather than that training in faith which God requires" (1 Timothy 1:4).

This interest in family history cuts across all lines of social and reli-gious opinion, and is today especially vigorous among students of Roman Catholicism in America. Since the study of the Catholic Church in this country began almost a century ago, most attention has been focused on the Church's leadership elite. The lives of pioneering bishops and notable missionaries were described in minute detail. Adopting a view of church history that proceeded from the top down, historians narrowed their attention to a small number of individuals who, while surely important, represented only a small proportion of the total Catholic population, which throughout the nineteenth and early twentieth centuries was growing at a truly phenomenal rate. Today, led by such scholars as Jay Dolan of the University of Notre Dame, James Hennesey of Boston College, and others, Catholic historians are more interested in an approach that works from the bottom up.[1] The lives of ordinary Catholic lay people, most of whom did not leave large collections of written diaries and letters, are now the primary object of study. The role of religious sisters, who were far more numerous and had a greater impact on daily Catholic life than the clergy, is being investigated. An American Catholicism that existed not in the minds of bishops but in the beliefs and practices of Catholic individuals and families is beginning to emerge.

Fortunately, the archival resources that will support this more broadly based research are now receiving careful and sustained attention. Led by the Leadership Conference of Women Religious, archival activity among American nuns is particularly lively. Religious community archivists have been participating in professional training programs in large numbers, and a published guide to women's religious-order records has recently appeared. The records this guide describes can be used to shed substantial light on the history of women, of education, of social-welfare agencies, and of the family itself. Diocesan archives too are being organized on a more professional basis. Nearly one-half of the more than 170 dioceses in the United States have recently participated in a series of meetings that are designed not only to promote the preservation of church records but also to encourage their use in research. Similarly, a number of Catholic colleges and universities (especially Notre Dame and Marquette) have begun to collect the records of such lay organizations as the Catholic Family Movement, the Catholic Rural Life Conference, and the Catholic Worker Movement. These records will document lay activity at the local level and

---

[1]See, for example, Jay P. Dolan, *The Immigrant Church: New York's Irish and German Catholics, 1815-1865* (Baltimore: Johns Hopkins University Press, 1975) and James Hennesey, *American Catholics: History of the Roman Catholic Community in the United States* (New York: Oxford University Press, 1981).

will therefore prove helpful to a wide variety of researchers with many different interests.[2]

Since the concern of this conference is the history of the family,
however, we should concentrate our attention on those Catholic Church
records that will help us understand this institution's past. Perhaps the most
graphic way of doing this is to follow a "typical" Catholic through life and
observe the records he leaves behind. Archivists never tire of pointing out
that historical records grow organically out of life, and that each one of us
leaves a "trail" of records behind us waiting to be discovered by historians
and genealogists of the future. All of us here have recently participated in
that records-creation process by responding to the 1980 federal census. By
following a Catholic of the last century through life, we can come to a
better understanding of church records and what they tell us about family
history.

We begin, of course, at birth. Shortly after a child is born, his parents present him at their parish church for initiation into the Catholic
Church through the sacrament of baptism. This baptism is recorded by the
parish in a special volume, called a sacramental register, set aside for this
purpose. As a general rule, these registers are the only place in which baptisms are recorded; there are no central indexes or lists of names kept at
the diocesan chancery office or elsewhere. Baptisms are recorded one after
another as they occur. Thus the researcher needs two important pieces of
information if these records are to be searched successfully: the parish and
an approximate date. Some dioceses have collected registers prior to a certain date in their central diocesan archives. In the Archives of the Archdiocese of Boston, for example, we have issued a general call for baptismal
and marriage books prior to 1900 and most, though not all, parishes have
complied. Other dioceses have microfilmed these records and keep the
complete collections of these films, although there is some variation in
the availability of these microfilms for research.

Baptismal records contain the following standardized information: the
name of the child; the names of the parents, usually providing the maiden
name of the mother; the names of the sponsors or godparents; the date of

---

[2]See James M. O'Toole, "Catholic Diocesan Archives: A Renaissance in Progress,"
American Archivist 43 (1980): 284-93; idem, "Archives Revival and the Future of Catholic
History," *U.S. Catholic Historian* 3 (1983): 87-102. See also *Women Religious History Sources*,
ed. Evangeline Thomas (New York: R. R. Bowker, 1983).

baptism and usually, though not always, the date of birth; and finally the signature of the priest performing the rite. Perhaps equally important to the researcher is the kind of information that is not included as part of the baptismal record. The precise address of the family is in most cases not given; however, since parishes usually encompass a specific geographic territory, the area in which the family lived can at least be approximated. The relationship to one another of the various people mentioned is not specified, although the appearance of the same surnames can be strong circumstantial evidence of a familial relation. If the same individuals appear repeatedly as godparents, for instance, one can make reasonably sound guesses about aunts and uncles, since the practice of the nineteenth century was similar to that of today in calling on members of the extended family to fill these roles. Finally, baptismal records never provide information on the place or country of origin of any of the parties involved. On reflection, this is not surprising. While the present generation of this century may be anxious to discover where their ancestors originated (in Ireland, for example), for the members of the immigrant generation, the "old country" was a place filled with hardship, starvation, and bad memories—a place, in short, that they were trying very deliberately to forget once they had arrived in the New World.

The baptismal record is the starting point in reconstructing the history of Catholic individuals and families. A number of special features of this record should be noted. Although one might expect all Catholic records to be written in Latin, the vast majority of records in this country appear either in English or in the language of the particular ethnic group served by the parish. Even when the record does appear in Latin, it follows a standard formula and so it is easy to decipher and extract the pertinent information. Second, the precise content of the record is subject to some change over time. When the New Code of Canon Law was promulgated by Pope Benedict XV in 1917—the first uniform, systematic compilation of church law ever attempted in Roman Catholicism—parish priests were required to keep extensive notes on an individual's future sacramental activity (the first reception of the eucharist, the administration of confirmation and marriage) with his baptismal record. This practice is adhered to today, while nineteenth-century records, to which most researchers will have access, will not possess such extensive information. Finally, special family situations such as illegitimacy may be observed or inferred from baptismal records. Although canon law strictly forbade making special notations in cases of illegitimacy, parish priests in this country seem uniformly to have made such notations, a practice that may give rise to some interesting speculations. Notations such as "pater ignotus" (father unknown) or simply "illegit" will occasionally appear. The question of the protection of privacy rights of both individuals and their descendants naturally becomes important here, and researchers should not be surprised to encounter reluctance on the part of church record keepers in making such records readily available.

Our typical Catholic, then, is born and baptized, and the trail of records we seek to follow has begun. Almost immediately, however, it divides and becomes somewhat confused. First of all, the baptismal record stands practically alone, and if for some reason it cannot be located, it is difficult to replace. The formal parish census, for example, is a relatively late development in American Catholic history and often cannot be used to take the place of missing baptismal registers. The census, an outgrowth of Catholic institutional consolidation in the late nineteenth and early twentieth centuries,[3] was based on door-to-door surveying by parish priests, but as a general rule only aggregate statistical information survives. The working documents of the parish census (comparable to the federal manuscript census schedules) were apparently destroyed as soon as their immediate usefulness was over. It does not happen often, but researchers must sometimes accept that the records which should have been made at baptism were, for whatever reason, simply not made. In such cases, more extensive detective work is required, including a search of public and other records.[4]

---

[3]John Tracy Ellis, *American Catholicism* (Chicago: University of Chicago Press, 1969) 124-62, for an overview of this transition from the small, missionary Church of the earlier period to the massive Church of the immigrants, who had taken over the country's urban centers in 1920.

[4]An interesting substitute for actual parish census data can be the "sacramental index" developed by Francois Houtart in his pioneering study, *Aspects Sociologiques du Catholicisme Americain* (Paris: Editions Ouvriers, 1957), which is unfortunately available only in French but has been recently reprinted by Arno Press. Father Houtart, in studying the formation and functioning of foreign-language parishes in nineteenth- and twentieth-century Chicago, uses this index as a way of estimating relative parish sizes. Working from sacramental records, it is possible to determine the total number of people who were born, married, and died in a given parish. These figures for several parishes can then be compared with one another and with civil-population data to estimate the size of parishes and the concentration of Catholics in large urban areas. See especially the chapter on what Houtart calls "Religious Ecology," 217-89.

Unusual family circumstances can also obscure the trail. If a child is orphaned, for example, the researcher should shift attention away from parish records and in the direction of the records of the social-service agencies and institutions that have always been a significant part of the mission of the Catholic Church in the United States.[5] Orphanage records were not as regularly or carefully kept as parish sacramental records, but they can nonetheless be of invaluable assistance in identifying apparently missing individuals. These records offer no standard formulas for recording information. Entrance and discharge records of orphanages and homes will usually contain the child's name and age, the name of the person placing the child there, and information about when and to whom the child was released. It was customary, for example, to find farm work or other manual labor for boys and to place girls in domestic service after they had reached a certain age; records of these arrangements may still exist and say something about later careers. In the nineteenth century, it must be remembered, orphanages were not used exclusively for children who were left completely without families. If a parent was unable to support a child, whether through unemployment or because jobs required constant relocation, it was not unusual for a child to be placed in a home for a certain period of time, with the parent or other relative contributing to his support. The details of such arrangements are frequently specified in orphanage financial records, which should not be overlooked as a supplementary source to formal entrance and discharge records. Significant insights into the nature of family structure and the ways in which that structure responded to economic and social pressures can be gained from a careful use of orphanage records.

As our typical Catholic matures through childhood, parish sacramental records again become important. In addition to baptismal records, records are also kept when a child receives Holy Communion for the first time and when he is confirmed. Both kinds of records are less informative than those for baptisms. It was customary for a child to receive both these sacraments as part of a large class or group, and the records contain only

---

[5]Timothy Walch, "Catholic Social Institutions and Urban Development: The View from Nineteenth Century Chicago and Milwaukee," *Catholic Historical Review* 64 (1978): 16-32, is an excellent study of these institutions in their larger context.

the date and a listing of the children's names.[6] No information about the parents or where the family lived is usually included, but these records can nevertheless point the way to other data. In the first place, they can be used to determine an approximate age for a child. In the twentieth century, as a part of the liturgical reforms instituted by Pope Pius X (1903-1914), children usually receive their first communion at about the age of seven, but throughout most of the nineteenth century this age was much higher. It was not uncommon for a child to receive his first communion at roughly the same time as he received the sacrament of confirmation, around the age of twelve or thirteen. A child's name on a first-communion list may not, therefore, seem to say much at first glance, but it can be a vital clue in narrowing the search for other data. Second, it was common (especially with confirmation records) to divide the names into those children attending the parish school and those enrolled in the local public school. This too can assist in the location of other records that may have a higher information content.

Unfortunately, school records as such are difficult to locate. Enrollment records, student transcripts, and other documentation serve a particular purpose when they are created, but with the passage of time, their bulk and low level of administrative usefulness make them prime candidates for mistreatment and eventual destruction. Student grade books, where they do survive, can help in approximating the age of children, but other information about the child's family will be less likely to appear. When a school closes, it commonly transfers its records to another school staffed by the same religious order of nuns or brothers. While this can help in the preservation of records, it also scatters the material widely, making the search for it difficult and usually unrewarding. Studies of the Catholic school system, certainly a unique aspect of education in America, have been undertaken with greater frequency in recent years,[7] but these studies have concentrated on the larger administrative and sociological aspects of

---

[6]As part of the confirmation ceremony, each child takes on an additional saint's name, and it is that new name, rather than a middle name given at baptism, which is included in confirmation records. Researchers should not be alarmed, therefore, if John Joseph Murphy suddenly appears as John Francis Murphy; if the other information (age, place, etc.) remains the same, it is in all likelihood the same person.

[7]The best of these is James W. Sanders, *The Education of an Urban Minority: Catholics in Chicago, 1833-1965* (New York: Oxford University Press, 1977).

parochial schools. Although the family researcher will not find particular information about families or individuals in these works of scholarship, they are important in establishing the context for one key aspect of Catholic family life.

When our typical Catholic reaches adulthood, parish sacramental records (which are the religious equivalents of the vital records maintained by towns, cities, and states) again become the starting point for reconstruction of the family. Equally voluminous as baptismal records are marriage records, which are carefully maintained in every parish. These marriage records contain the date, the names of the two people being married, the names of the two official witnesses, and the signature of the officiating priest. In the very early years of Catholicism in this country, it was not uncommon for all the witnesses to a marriage to sign the register themselves, but this practice had died out by about 1800. Marriage records, like their baptismal counterparts, are made only in the parish where the sacrament is administered, so access is again first by parish name and then by date. These also do not contain information about residential addresses, family relationships, or places of origin, but they may be taken as circumstantial evidence where certain suspicions already exist.

Two special features of marriage records deserve attention. The first involves the issuance of marriage dispensations. Canon law specifies that certain impediments to the validity of marriage must be removed or "dispensed" before the marriage can take place. Second or third cousins may marry, for example, but the impediment caused by their familial relationship must be resolved before they do so. Very careful dispensation records are kept in every diocesan chancery, specifying the names of the parties and the nature of the impediment. Precise family relationships can therefore be established by researchers from dispensation records and, of course, the assistance of a good canon lawyer.

Marriage records can also be helpful if one of the parties to the marriage was not a Catholic. Although the practice was abandoned as a part of the ecumenical movement of the 1950s and 1960s, until about fifteen years ago the Church required the non-Catholic party to sign an oath before the wedding ceremony, promising not to interfere with the Catholic's religious practice and to raise all children as Catholics. This signed oath usually appears in the sacramental register immediately before the marriage to which it applies. Knowing that one of the partners was not a Catholic not only assists in the location of other records about that person; it can also be used in an aggregate way to observe patterns of inter-marriage, with all the attendant implications for family structure, mobility, and immigrant acculturation.

It is at this point in the life of our typical Catholic that the orderliness and predictability of his trail of records breaks down somewhat. We will return to sacramental registers at the time of death, but through the years of adulthood a number of other sources must be identified and used. The parish is still, however, the best starting place; indeed, a number of more informal parish records can be used to tell us much about family life. In the days before printed parish bulletins or diocesan newspapers, every parish maintained pulpit announcement books, and a great many of these have survived both in parish and diocesan archives. The pastor would record in these volumes a wide variety of parish activities of which the laity needed to be aware, and these announcements would be read from the pulpit every Sunday, immediately before the preaching of the sermon. They would begin with the banns of marriages, weekly announcements of future weddings that were made in the month before the wedding day. Also included was news of the activities of parish societies, the parochial and Sunday schools, special collections for religious or charitable purposes, pastoral letters from the bishop on particular subjects or occasions, unusual liturgical programs such as missions, and a host of other topics. The full diversity of parish life is clearly evident in these pulpit-announcement books, which are invaluable sources for discovering how life was actually lived and experienced by the man and woman in the pew.

A number of parish activities will be of special interest to the historian of the family. Primary among these are the lay organizations that existed in each parish under the spiritual direction of the clergy. The men were usually organized into a Holy Name Society. The women too had their societies, usually a Sodality of the Virgin or an altar or rosary society. A number of organizations existed for Catholic children. In all cases the working of these societies followed the same pattern: regular (biweekly or monthly) meetings that would combine educational or social activity with specific devotional exercises. These groups would frequently attend Sunday mass as a body and hold a "communion breakfast" afterwards. Annual picnics or fairs were common springtime rituals. By reaching out to every individual family member, the Church became a more potent and regular force in daily life. It is easy to trace the high degree to which family life was bound up with the life of the parish.

Other parish-based organizations were designed to accomplish charitable goals. Immigrant-aid societies, common in parishes of Eastern seaboard cities, would raise funds to provide food and shelter for newly arrived immigrants. Organizations such as the St. Vincent de Paul societies collected money, clothing, and household items for distribution to destitute families. Their activities especially revolved around religious holidays. Social-service agencies, commonly known as "Catholic Charities," had appeared in nearly every diocese by the first decades of the twentieth century, and these agencies engaged in similar activities. Most religious-social organizations such as the Knights of Columbus and the Catholic Order of Forresters likewise undertook charitable work. A study of the efforts of these organizations both through pulpit-announcement books and any records they themselves may have left behind will clearly document the interaction of all the Catholic families of a parish.

Certain special religious records may also be found in parishes. Priests affiliated with religious orders (Jesuits, Redemptorists, Paulists, for example) regularly visited parishes for brief periods to preach missions. The purpose of the mission, a two- or three-week period of particular devotions, was to reawaken and intensify religious feeling in the parish and to encourage large numbers of confessions and communions among parishioners who might have been away from these sacraments for some time. Long sermons designed particularly for separate groups of men, women, children, and for entire families were a key feature of these missions. Temperance pledges were frequently made. Mission records—including sermons, temperance pledges, and generalized conversion statements—can provide an extraordinarily clear picture of the nature of early Catholic piety and devotional life.[8]

The researcher working in the nineteenth century should also be on the lookout for certain parish records relating to an activity that has now entirely disappeared from Catholic practice: records of lay trustees. Faced with state laws that frequently made it impossible for priests or bishops to hold church property in their own names and to bequeath it to their ecclesiastical successors at death, Catholics in many places resorted to the system that came to be called "trusteeism." Boards of laymen would be

---

[8]Jay P. Dolan has written an excellent study of the parish entitled *Catholic Revivalism: The American Experience, 1830-1900* (Notre Dame: University of Notre Dame Press, 1978).

elected by the parishioners, and the title to church property would be held in their name. Not surprisingly, many of these lay boards began to assume other powers at the expense of the clergy, including the appointment and dismissal of pastors, thus taking on the characteristics of a kind of Catholic Congregationalism and causing inevitable conflict with the bishops who had traditionally exercised these powers.[9] The ecclesiology of this dispute, which for all practical purposes was resolved in favor of the Church hierarchy by the time of the Civil War, need not concern us here. What is important for the study of family history are the records left behind by this movement. Trustees were usually men of some property and social standing in the community. Records about them may therefore tell us much about the socioeconomic status of particular families or groups of families.

Beyond records that are generated as the result of actual church activities, the historian of the family should not overlook the more traditional private manuscript sources used in other fields of history. When dealing with immigrant families, of course, one cannot expect to find the large collections of letters and diaries so common among better-established native groups. Even the keeping of family Bible records, such a regular practice among Protestants, was more of a rarity among Catholics, who seemed content to let the Church maintain this information, thereby making it somehow more "official." Parish priests were not, as a rule, great diarists, but where these diaries do exist they can be unusually valuable. The regular rounds of masses, confessions, and sick calls are supplemented with information on an unlimited number of other subjects, including personal counseling of individual family members. These diaries can help bring the daily activities of the people to life. A priest's diary in the possession of the Archives of the Archdiocese of Boston, for example, reports sadly on the case of a woman who came to the rectory door in 1899 to take the temperance pledge "with the assistance of two bottles of beer." To no one's surprise, this woman's backsliding was reported two days later. This is the kind of source that diminishes history as a remote, analytical study and reminds us that we are dealing with real people.

---

[9]No single history of this fascinating aspect of early American Catholic history exists. See, however, Patrick J. Dignan, *A History of the Legal Incorporation of Catholic Church Property in the United States, 1784-1932* (New York: P. J. Kenedy, 1935) and Patrick Carey, "The Laity's Understanding of the Trustee System, 1785-1855," *Catholic Historical Review* 64 (1978): 357-76.

All real people weaken and die, of course, and it is at this point that the trail of records we have been following for our typical Catholic comes to an end. Many parishes maintain registers of sick calls made by the priests, recording visits to the homes of sick and dying parishioners. Unfortunately, these books do not always survive in large numbers; but where they do, they can provide information on age and place of residence. More common are registers of deaths and burials, which include the date of burial, the name of the deceased, the date of death, the person's age at death, and the signature of the officiating priest. Some notation was also usually made if the dying Catholic had the opportunity to make a confession and receive the eucharist before death. The cause of death was generally not indicated, although I have seen it in some cases (most notably in the records of a German ethnic parish in Boston); cases of sudden or accidental death are likely to receive special mention.

Most Catholic cemeteries are affiliated with specific parishes and their records are therefore maintained with the other parish records. Cemetery records most often consist of lot sales and burials, usually kept in distinct series of volumes. These records do not provide much detailed information about the next of kin of the deceased, but matching lot sales in particular cemeteries may be of assistance in reconstructing large and complex families. Catholic gravestones throughout the nineteenth century generally contained less information than their Protestant counterparts, making them a rather unreliable source of data. Cemetery records are also more likely to be subject to loss or misplacement than baptismal and marriage records, since these latter two will probably have an ongoing administrative and pastoral use in the parish. Cemetery records may, therefore, require a more careful search on the part of the family historian. Once found, though, they can help complete what we know of the lives of those who went before us.

Catholic Church records do not, of course, exist in a vacuum, and the wise researcher will use them in conjunction with other kinds of records to add details to the story of the past. Public records of all kinds, the genealogist's traditional source, are especially helpful. Beyond the basics of vital records, census, tax, and other public records can be compared with church records to study such topics as family size and birth rate, patterns of urban settlement, internal migration, and socioeconomic status. A fine example of a study that uses both church and civil records to good advantage is Francois Houtart's 1957 sociological study of Catholicism in Chicago, which draws some tentative conclusions about parish size and immigrant acculturation. An unpublished study of the diocesan clergy in Boston has also employed this method to reconstruct the family life and home circumstances that impelled young men into the priesthood.[10] The imagination of the researcher is the only limitation on the potential uses to which church and civil records can be combined to enlighten the past.

The current upsurge of interest in social history generally and family history in particular is coming along at an auspicious time. Church officials are becoming increasingly aware of the value of the archival resources in their custody and are interested in promoting the use of those resources to contribute to an understanding of the Church's role in the past. The cooperation of Church leaders, researchers, and archivists can do much to advance that understanding of the common heritage of this country's communities and families.

[10]Houtart, *Aspects Sociologiques;* Joseph B. Fuller, "At the Very Center of Things: The Catholic Secular Clergy and the Redirection of Catholic Boston" (honors thesis, Department of History, Harvard University, 1979).

Chapter Seven

Genealogies as Evidence in Historical Kinship Studies: A German Example*

Andrejs Plakans

During a conference in Garmisch-Partenkirchen in October 1980, I happened to glance at the obituary page of the local newspaper and read there the following announcements, each signed by a group of relatives of the decedent:

> On October 3rd God the Almighty called to eternal rest my dear husband, our dear father, grandfather, great-grandfather, and brother.
>
> We express our gratitude to all those who attended the funeral of my

*An earlier version of this paper was presented at the annual meeting of the Social Science History Association, Vanderbilt University, October 1981. The paper describes research being carried out by Professor Arthur Imhof, Free University of Berlin, West Berlin, and the author, with support from National Science Foundation Grant BNS-7926704, which is hereby gratefully acknowledged. The author also thanks the Iowa State University Statistical Laboratory for programming assistance.

deceased wife, our dear mother, mother-in-law, grandmother, daughter, sister, sister-in-law, aunt, and godmother.

The Lord of life and death has called to Himself our dear husband, our dear father, grandfather, father-in-law, brother, brother-in-law, and uncle.

These stylized announcements with their mixture of individual and collective grief were sufficiently different from obituary notices in American newspapers to immediately raise the question of why in this Bavarian town death should occasion an announcement that spells out kin roles in so precise a manner. This question could be answered only after extensive comparative field research on the meaning of death and kinship in contemporary cultures.[1] But to those of us for whom the meaning of kinship is a problem not only of contemporary society but also of historical social structure, the specificity of the German obituaries also raises a question of a somewhat different kind: namely, are these kinship networks of 1980 different in form and size than they used to be a century or two ago? Moreover, this question leads to another: Is it possible to discuss the changes that have taken place in terms of a continuous story rather than simply in terms of two widely separated moments in historical time?

In the Garmisch example, contemporary newspaper evidence about kinship ties underlines our ignorance of certain aspects of the social-structural past. It is possible, however, to posit the components of the problem in reverse order as well. In his valuable study of eighteenth-century Frankfurt politics, the historian Gerald L. Soliday presented a remarkable chart that demonstrated the family relationships in 1713 among the upper-bench councilmen of the city.[2] The chart was used by burghers excluded from the council to prove to the Imperial government that a small circle of closely related families completely controlled the important benches. Only one of the twenty-eight listed individuals appeared to be completely unrelated to the others, while the rest seem to have been connected by multiple kin ties arising from marriage and descent.[3] Yet Frankfurt politics, as

---

[1]The recent work by Phillipe Aries, *The Hour of Our Death* (New York: Random House, 1972), represents a step in this direction.

[2]Gerald L. Soliday, *A Community in Conflict: Frankfurt Society in the Seventeenth and Early Eighteenth Centuries* (Hanover NH: University Press of New England, 1974) 110-11.

[3]Ibid., 108.

Soliday explained, were not simply a matter of a clash between a close-knit elite and an opposition group in which each member stood alone. In the burgher militia, which "provided the institutional framework within which opposition [to the city council] developed its cohesive strength," something like half of the members enjoyed close family relationships.[4] The story of early eighteenth-century Frankfurt thus immediately raises the questions of how long kinship continued to be a bond within the various groups of adversaries, and to what extent kin relations continue to be used for political recruitment even in our ostensibly meritocratic world. As with the personal kin networks in the Garmisch obituaries, there is also the further question of how we could go about relating changes in the Frankfurt kinship ties as a continuous story over long stretches of the historical past.

These examples of twentieth-century obituaries and eighteenth-century urban politics indicate how far we are from a history of European kinship, especially for the centuries in which sources are no longer full of references to blood feuds and wergild and do not employ the legal terminology appropriate to societies in which corporate kin groups play a part. At the same time these examples, as well as much of current research concerning the history of European domestic groups in recent centuries, continue to present empirical evidence of kin-based links between families and between households that would doubtlessly need to be used in an integrated history of European kinship were such a history to be written.[5] Taking cues from social anthropology about what empirical evidence concerning kinship consists of, one can conclude that the obituaries permit a researcher to identify the kinship terminology in use in Garmisch-Partenkirchen (if not elsewhere in German-speaking areas); in fact, the German-language versions of the four cited obituaries contain no less than eighteen kin terms, including both terms of address (*Oma, Opa*) and terms of reference (*Gatten, Patin*). Further, when the information in each obituary is converted into an ego-centered kinship diagram, with the decedent as ego, the result is a small but measurable network of kin ties which

---

[4]Ibid., 121.

[5]A review of the existing literature, and of many of the problems pertaining to the writing of kinship history, is to be found in Andrejs Plakans, *Kinship in the Past: An Anthropology of European Family Life, 1500-1900* (Oxford and New York: Basil Blackwell, 1984).

indicate where that ego stood at the moment of his death.[6] Were a systematic collection of similar obituaries made for a period of two or three years, the resulting data file might include not only a complete terminological inventory but also sufficient evidence for making reliable statements about personal kinship networks over the entire life cycle of individuals in this community. The next step would then be to find sources in the past that allow analyses with similar results.

Even though the Frankfurt chart, by comparison with the obituaries, would appear to be evidence of a very different order, it is still not very far removed from what fieldwork anthropologists frequently seek as proof about kinship: an event that provides information simultaneously not only about kin ties but also about their use. As the anthropologist Meyer Fortes observes,

> Social relations are abstractions, since they are not directly visible and tangible, as individuals and activities are, but have to be established by inference. This does not mean that social relations are not real. It is only that they are implicit and general, wrapped up, as it were, in the particular occasions in which they emerge.[7]

Whereas a fieldwork anthropologist might have at his disposal only prosaic events such as meals and gift exchanges as examples of the social occasions in which kinship ties are "wrapped up," historians can depict a constitutional struggle with the same purposes in mind. Instead of focusing on the original distribution of offices and powers, and on the redistribution of them as a result of the conflict, such an inquiry would deal instead with the kin relations among the participants, thus using the political facts of the situation for access into the world of microstructural relationships. Soliday's monograph provides ample evidence about how difficult such an undertaking would be, in other German cities and elsewhere. But the same evidence also suggests that the task would not be an impossibility.

Another aspect of these examples needs to be mentioned. The fact that this evidence lays out three possible lines of investigation—termi-

---

[6]For an introduction to the use of the network concept, see Jeremy Boissevain and J. Clyde Mitchell, eds., *Network Analysis: Studies in Human Interaction* (The Hague: Mouton, 1973).

[7]Meyer Fortes, *Kinship and the Social Order: The Legacy of Lewis Henry Morgan* (Chicago: Aldine, 1976) 60.

nological inventories, ego-centered personal networks, and political conflicts—underlines what fieldwork anthropologists have learned in their century-long experience with the subject of kinship among living populations: namely, that there is no single type of evidence that will provide all we wish to know about this domain of social structure. A terminological inventory will not tell the researcher how the "rules of kinship" implied in it were actually made use of; nor will the close study of a particular social conflict, in which only the used ties are identifiable, lead to an understanding of the full complement of kinship roles that each participant possessed. The study of personal kin networks will not lead to an understanding of the architecture of corporate groups; nor will kin ties among the coresidents of particular households lead us to conclusions about kinship ties throughout an entire community. Anthropological researches of kinship seek order for these facts by pursuing the rules of behavior that underlie all the different types of data. There are many different kinds of behavior, but few basic rules. According to S. H. Nadel's formulation,

> We are here speaking of ways of acting governed by rules and hence in some measure stereotyped. . . . And of the ways of acting so understood it is true to say that they are finite and always less numerous than the possible combinations of people: which means that the same ways of acting are repetitive in the population. We need only to add that these ways of acting are repetitive also in the sense that they apply to changing or successive populations.[8]

The final sentence of Nadel's theoretical statement captures very nicely what historians have to think about when they deal with kinship as a historical phenomenon. For them, analysis of kinship structure at one moment in the past time will be only the first step. They will have to take Nadel's theoretical proposition as a working hypothesis and look for evidence that would permit statements about kinship in a "succession of populations."

It is far from clear at this moment which among all the possible types of evidence is best for this purpose. In this matter social-anthropological theory and practice is suggestive but far less specific than evidentiary problems would require. In the first half of the twentieth century, anthropologists sought to distinguish their current work from that of the evolutionary

---

[8]S. F. Nadel, *The Theory of Social Structures* (London: Cohen and West, 1967) 8.

theorists of the nineteenth; and they concluded, quite correctly as far as social structure was concerned, that the kind of evidence they normally employed was insufficient as a basis for statements about historical change. These data led to "conjectural history," declared A. R. Radcliffe-Brown. Others then joined him in the belief that anthropological (and kinship) research should be conducted in a strictly synchronic fashion.[9] This position, however, was very difficult to maintain, as retrospective accounts of the development of anthropology have shown.[10] Moreover, this turn away from historical concerns left unanswered the question that social historians inevitably had to take up; that is, what kind of evidence is necessary to produce a "non-conjectural" history of kinship, even in a single community? It may, of course, turn out that only cross-sectional data will prove to be sufficiently precise to deal with these questions. This is what the anthropologist Jack Goody seems to suggest.[11] But before this position (which I would characterize as a fallback position) is accepted, we should try to explore the potential for kinship analysis in genealogical reconstructions, which are the only kind of microlevel historical data that link components in a stepwise fashion for a time period sometimes encompassing several hundreds of years.

Genealogies have been used widely in anthropological fieldwork as a kind of neutral record (or map) on which to locate the ties informants mention.[12] They are created records of an individual informant's connections with other living and deceased persons as far back in time as memory extends, and their starting point is always the living informant. These remembered genealogies can be put to a wide variety of uses, including the evaluation of memory itself if the remembered record can be compared to

---

[9]A. R. Radcliffe-Brown, *Structure and Function in Primitive Society* (New York: Free Press, 1965) 50; Adam Kuper, *Anthropologists and Anthropology: The British School, 1922-1972* (New York: Pica Press, 1973).

[10]I. M. Lewis, ed., *History and Social Anthropology* (London: Tavistock Publications, 1968) ix-xxviii.

[11]Jack Goody, *Production and Reproduction: A Comparative Study of the Domestic Domain* (Cambridge: Cambridge University Press, 1976) 23-30.

[12]J. A. Barnes, "Genealogies," in A. L. Epstein, ed., *The Craft of Social Anthropology* (Oxford: Pergamon Press, 1979) 102-28.

a written one.[13] In the course of a normal period of fieldwork, anthropologists might collect several dozens of such individualized genealogical records, and then use them, together with data from observations, to make inferences about kinship terminology and relationships. Since the collection of genealogies is a time-consuming task, the anthropological fieldworker usually does not aim to have a complete record for everyone in the community. It must have occurred to some anthropologists, nonetheless, that such genealogical maps for all members of the living community, linked to each other over four or five generations or longer, could provide a much greater time depth than is normally used for kinship study. Yet because anthropologists frequently do not concern themselves with the *history* of kinship in their communities, the compilation of records in this manner has generally had low priority.[14]

Anthropologists have naturally made use of various kinds of historical sources. But, in general, they are seldom concerned with documentary records from the *distant* past unless they bear directly on explanations being offered of a living community. It is true to a great extent that if the *only* surviving records of a community in the distant past are genealogical ones, researchers are bound to feel that the kinship analysis is taking place wholly in the abstract. The relationships teased out of such genealogical records might appear to be only among names, rather than among flesh-and-blood individuals living in a concrete historical community. Still, as the experience with household lists has shown, valuable points about the history of social structure can be made even if the records seem at first glance to show no information beyond the relationships among names on a listing.

The ideal *basic* source, to which other kinds of sources could be referred for meaning, should take the form of a continuous, running record

---

[13]Barbara K. Halpern, Joel M. Halpern, and John M. Foley, "Traditional Recall and Family Histories: A Commentary on Mode and Method," in Barbara K. Halpern and Joel M. Halpern, eds., "Selected Papers on a Serbian Village: Social Structure as Reflected by History, Demography and Oral Tradition" (Amherst MA: Department of Anthropology, University of Massachusetts, Research Report No. 17, 1977) 165-98.

[14]For several exceptions, see Joel M. Halpern and Barbara K. Halpern, *A Serbian Village in Historical Perspective* (New York: Holt, Rinehart and Winston, 1972), and Robert McC. Netting, *Balancing on an Alp: Ecological Change and Continuity in a Swiss Mountain Community* (Cambridge: Cambridge University Press, 1981).

in which "successive" populations are linked. The historical records in which kinship information is "embedded" comprise a wide variety of different types; and unfortunately, they are more than likely to appear sporadically throughout the history of a community. At best, the history of kinship in such a community could consist of a succession of studies of relationships at different points in time. Since very few studies of this kind exist, a substantial number of them would definitely be a gain, but studies of this sort may not be the only kind that are possible. In genealogical reconstructions, as I suggested, there frequently exist continuous linkages among individuals (and therefore among their families) that stretch backward and forward in time for many generations. Therefore, a collection of interwoven genealogies for an entire community might very well provide a historical "map" of relationships with considerable time depth. Something like such a historical "map" exists in a remarkable data collection from the Schwalm area of Hesse in Western Germany. The collection was created by genealogists in the 1930s and 1940s on the basis of parish registers for eight villages of the Schwalm area. It has already been used for a series of biogenetic and historical-demographic studies; but at this time I would like to review its characteristics in line with the questions about kinship study outlined above.[15]

The quickest way to characterize the Schwalm collection is to say that it consists of the same kinds of materials that have gone into the preparation of a better-known type of historical source in Germany: the *Ortssippenbücher*, or village genealogical books.[16] To create such books local genealogists undertook to link the birth, marriage, and death information from parish registers in order to reconstruct both conjugal family units as well as patrilines (*Stämme*), using as the basis for the latter the surnames found in the local records. Information obtained from the Schwalm reg-

---

[15]See the studies by Heinrich Schade, "Ergebnisse einer Bevölkerungsuntersuchung in der Schwalm," *Akademie der Wissenschaften und der Literatur in Mainz* (1950) 419-91; "Neue statistiche Ergebnisse einer Bevölkerungshebung in der Schwalm," *Homo* 9 (1958): 13-20; "Sozial-anthropologische Ergebnisse einer Zensusuntersuchung (Schwalm)," *Homo* 11 (1960): 53-60. See also Arthur E. Imhof, "Génèalogie et démographie historique en Allemagne," *Annales de démographie historique* (1976): 77-113.

[16]For a description of the *Ortssippenbücher*, see John Knodel, "Ortssippenbücher als Quelle für historische Demographie," *Geschichte und Gesellschaft* 1 (1975): 288-324, and John Knodel and Edward Shorter, "The Reliability of Family Reconstitution Data in German Village Genealogies," *Annales de démographie historique* (1976): 115-53.

isters, however, was not gathered between the covers of an *Ortssippen-buch*; it was used for lineage tables (*Stammtafeln*), in which the connections within familial units and among individuals are shown via the conventional symbols for lineal descent and lateral relatedness. Thus in the context of each patriline (*Stamm*), all individuals can be studied as members of their families during birth and marriages as well as in their capacity as members of the larger configurations that had considerable time depth to them. The longest patriline tables in the Schwalm cover a period of some 300 or more years. Females originating in one patriline and marrying into another are shown in both; remarriages are recorded in a detailed fashion; and all collateral lines within a patriline are traced from their initial appearance to their latest representatives in the first half of the twentieth century, when this genealogical project was initiated. The entire "file" for the eight villages of the Schwalm area contains some 51,000 records of individuals, organized into some 7,500 family units and 758 patrilineages. The earliest birth record for an individual in this "file" is the year 1479; the most recent births fall in the 1930s.

All of the questions that pertain to reliability and accuracy in historical linkage projects of this kind are appropriate also for the Schwalm file.[17] Without assuming that these questions have been answered, however, I would like to forgo dwelling on them to consider some characteristics of the file that suggest its possibilities as a base for historical kinship research. First, this extensive collection of local genealogies differs from one a fieldwork anthropologist would gather in that each patriline (*Stamm*) is not an oral recitation of remembered ancestors, or a "line" reconstructed forward in time from a "founder," but a collection of individual names scattered throughout the pages of ecclesiastical registers of birth, death, and marriage. The genealogists chose the patrilineal principle as a basis for organizing these disparate data, and the surnames from the entire historical period are used for classifying individuals according to these patrilines. Evidently, when a surname first appeared in the original record, it immediately was considered a category for which a *Stammtafel* (lineage table) might eventually have to be prepared. A *Tafel* was therefore started and held open for other people bearing that surname. This procedure had

---

[17]As, for example, those discussed in E. A. Wrigley, ed., *Identifying People in the Past* (London: Edward Arnold, 1973).

two important consequences as far as the organization of the data is concerned. In the earliest appearance of a particular surname, there frequently are several contemporaries who have the same surname but are unrelated. Hence a number of the *Stammtafeln* begin *in medias res*, with subsequent generations of names having to be attached to two or more collateral lines that are not themselves connected. Second, because of migration and mortality numerous surnames, though still classified as *Stämme* in the file, remained unrealized as such. Out of the 758 *Stammtafeln* only 395 have configurations on them that have any time depth at all; the rest consist of a single individual, a handful of unconnected individuals, a single family unit, or a handful of them. These two characteristics of the data should be seen, however, as strengths and not as weaknesses. They suggest that the genealogists were concerned principally with transferring onto the lineage tables *all* the persons appearing in the original sources and not only with producing neatly packaged records of the persisting lines or of those for which the record was complete in the time period surveyed. In any analysis of local kinship, the researcher can have some control over those members of the local population whose stay in the community, for whatever reason, was short and who therefore did not succeed in establishing a persisting lineage. To be able to include such "negative cases" in the historical analysis is an advantage since there is evidence that in traditional European villages a persisting population core is likely to have been surrounded by subpopulations in which turnover was considerable.[18]

By using the patriline organization of these data, one can make a rough quantitative assessment of what social-structural continuity may have meant in the Schwalm population. Table 1 summarizes the number and proportional distribution of the local patrilineages in terms of their "age," that is, the numerical difference between the year of the first and last marriages recorded in a particular lineage. An important statistic in this table pertains to the method of classifying all surnames as *Stämme*: the consequence is that almost half (47.8%) of the patrilines have no time depth at all. Still, if one considers only those lineages that had an "age" of fifty years or more (that is, at least three lineally linked marriages separated from

---

[18]For a discussion of the value of "negative cases," see Allen W. Johnson, *Qualification in Cultural Anthropology* (Stanford: Stanford University Press, 1978) 43-46; and for comparative figures on village turnover, see Peter Laslett, *Family Life and Illicit Love in Earlier Generations* (Cambridge: Cambridge University Press, 1977) 50-101.

TABLE 1

"AGE" OF SCHWALM PATRILINEAGES			
		PERCENT OF PATRILINEAGES	
TIME SPAN IN YEARS	NUMBER OF PATRILINEAGES	OF ALL	OF THOSE "AGED" 50 YEARS OR MORE
349-300	21	2.7	7.7
299-250	26	3.4	9.5
249-200	51	6.7	18.7
199-150	52	6.8	19.1
149-100	64	8.4	23.5
99-50	58	7.6	21.3
49-1	123	16.2	
Less than 1 year	363	47.8	
TOTALS	758	99.6	99.8

TABLE 2

EXTINCTION AND PERSISTENCE OF SCHWALM LINEAGES						
LINEAGES ORIGINATING IN:	LINEAGES EXTINGUISHED IN:				LINEAGES SURVIVING TO 1930s	TOTALS
	16th c.	17th c.	18th c.	19th c.		
16th c. (n-48)	1 (2.0%)	17 (35.4%)	8 (16.6%)	19 (39.5%)	3 (6.2%)	48 (99.7%)
17th c. (n-208)		21 (10.1%)	60 (28.8%)	95 (45.6%)	32 (15.3%)	208 (99.8%)
18th c. (n-111)			21 (18.9%)	76 (68.4%)	14 (12.6%)	111 (99.9%)
19th c. (n-28)				25 (89.2%)	3 (10.7%)	28 (99.9%)

Total number of marriages examined: 395.
Only lineages of an "age" of more than one year counted.

each other by twenty-five years), the result is that something like half of these (150 or 55.0%) were in the community for a period of more than 150 years but less than 350. When only the lineages whose time depth was fifty years or more are averaged, the mean lineage "age" is 179.4 years.

Continuity, therefore, meant that a relatively small proportion of the total number of lineages in existence was present throughout the entire documented period, while the rest began and ended within the period. How this worked out in the centuries under observation for the lineages with an "age" of one year or more can be seen in Table 2, each line of which shows the number of lineages that ended during the century in the column heading. In the course of the 400 years prior to 1900, altogether 395 lineages had come into being in the Schwalm villages, more than half of them in the seventeenth century. By 1800, of the 367 that had appeared, 128 (34.8%) had already become extinct. It was the nineteenth century that saw a very sharp increase in the disappearance of lineages; and by the year 1900, of the 395 that had appeared, a total of 343 (86.8%) no longer had representatives in the Schwalm. It may be that the great *Auswanderung* (emigration) played a role, because something like 8-10 percent of the entire German population emigrating in the nineteenth century came from the western regions, which included the Hessian lands. [19]

It is also clear from Table 2 that, in any given century, as one lineage disappeared, others were founded, and this lineage "turnover" lasted throughout the whole period under observation. Though the mean "age" of lineages in the Schwalm was impressive (almost 180 years), no study of historical kinship in this area could afford to ignore that, repeatedly, entire lines of people simply ceased to exist. These social structures can be thought of as being of "long duration," but they cannot be thought of as eternal. [20] Keeping this in mind, I now turn to the third and final quantitative assessment of the Schwalm lineage file. The statistics in Table 3 are also "size" measures, but they pertain to marriages, or, from a different perspective, to the number of times a lineage had an opportunity to establish connections with other lineages in the community. The figures in the table are a preliminary measure of such contacts, until more telling measures can be worked out.

One sees repeated in this table the effect of using lineages to classify parish-register data: namely, the larger number of "lineages" that are represented by unmarried individuals or unconnected conjugal family units. Still, the table shows that about eight of every ten marriages belonged to lineages that had considerable marital activity in them. If the number of marriages in all lineages is averaged with the total marriages, the result is a mean of thirteen marriages, some portion of which would have estab-

---

[19] Robert Lee, "Germany," in W. R. Lee, *European Demography and Economic Growth* (London, 1979).

[20] Fernard Braudel, "History and the Social Sciences," in Peter Burke, ed., *Economy and Society in Early Modern Europe: Essays from Annales* (New York, 1972) 18.

TABLE 3

MARRIAGES IN THE SCHWALM LINEAGES				
NUMBER OF MARRIAGES PER LINEAGE	NUMBER OF LINEAGES	PERCENT OF LINEAGES	TOTAL NUMBER OF MARRIAGES IN CATEGORY	PERCENT OF MARRIAGES IN CATEGORY
-0-	193	27.9	-0-	-0-
1-9	371	47.3	1251	16.9
10-30	126	16.0	2163	29.2
31-60	44	5.6	1959	25.6
61-90	16	2.0	1141	15.4
91-120	7	.8	736	9.9
135	1	.1	135	1.8
TOTALS	758	99.7	7530	99.8

lished the average time depth of 180 years mentioned earlier. The most interesting consequence of these marriages cannot be analyzed in the table: it is that each marriage in a given lineage was a connection between that lineage and either another Schwalm lineage, the world outside, or itself. For example, the *Stammtafel* for the Roth family (no. 402) records eighty-three marriages for males distributed over two-and-a-half centuries. One of these involved as partners a male and a female from the Roth lineage (first cousins, in fact); in eleven cases the wives came, presumably, from outside the Schwalm area; but in seventy-two cases wives can be identified as having come from one of the other Schwalm lineages. The highest frequency of these contact points with another lineage was four; in most cases the other lineages "contributed" only one female to the Roth line. The history of the Roth lineage, analyzed with respect to in-marrying females only, thus reveals connections with altogether fifty other of these Schwalm configurations, over a period of 250 years. Whether this is a high rate of communal endogamy remains to be seen. What is more important is the possibility that such a high number of contact points existed among all of the Schwalm lineages. The search for the exact personnel of local kin groups—defined as ego-centered networks, kindreds, lineal kin, etc.—would therefore always have to include more than a single organizational unit (*Stamm*). Moreover, the patterns of lineage contact can be examined with data displayed as temporal sequences, and with genealogical connections among the components.

It is necessary to keep in mind, however, that genealogical reconstructions of even this complexity do not, as they stand, provide historical data about *kinship* connections. The precise relationship between *genealogy* and *kinship* remains an open matter, ranging from the assertion that kinship terms have no meaning to those who are connected except by reference to a genealogical substratum of links, to the belief that the classification involved in kinship calculation is an activity far removed from this substratum.[21] Needless to say, this disagreement on fundamentals among experts is not very helpful when the researcher is confronted with a genealogical reconstruction such as the Schwalm file, in which the need to define boundaries between kin and nonkin is of utmost importance.

For some headway to be made, two courses are open. One can adopt a generalized procedure for distinguishing between socially relevant and irrelevant genealogical ties and, simultaneously, one can use other historical sources in which the importance of particular ties is documented. In the first of these, one can draw on the distinctions made by G. P. Murdock between primary kin (who stand one degree of distance away from a given ego; e.g., father), secondary kin (who stand two degrees away; e.g., brother's son), tertiary kin (three degrees; e.g., wife's brother's wife), quaternary kin (four degrees; e.g., father's brother's wife's father), and so forth.[22] The first category in this formal system contains eight positions (calculating from an ego) that can be examined for personnel; the second contains thirty-three different positions; the third offers 151 positions, and so forth. It should be obvious that up to a certain point the identification of genealogical positions will be at the same time the identification of kinship positions, if carried out in terms of what is generally known about kinship systems and classification in German-language areas.[23] It is safe to consider the positions of parents, grandparents, in-laws, aunts, uncles, and

---

[21]For an introduction to this problem, see Ladislav Holy, "Kin Groups: Structural Analysis and the Study of Behavior," *Annual Review of Anthropology* 4 (1976): 107-31; and Plakans, *Kinship in the Past,* 76-96.

[22]For Murdock's classification scheme, see G. P. Murdock, *Social Structure* (New York: Free Press, 1949) 94-97.

[23]Stephen B. Barlau, "An Outline of Germanic Kinship," *Journal of Indo-European Studies* 4 (1976): 97-130.

cousins as having had social relevance. By using this procedure in analyzing the Schwalm file, one can give a good accounting in a quantitative manner of how the personnel of groupings delineated in such a way changed over the period under observation. The numerous lines of investigation that can be followed by this means together constitute one of the ways in which the kinship history of the Schwalm can be described.

It is equally obvious, however, that by adopting an extraneous system of classifying the nominal-level genealogical data in the Schwalm file, the researcher could not attempt to answer the important question of whether, over the long period in question, kinship classification indigenous to the Schwalm area changed in important respects; nor could he pursue to any length the equally important point concerning the involvement of kin in different kinds of social activities, transactions, and common pursuits. A complete history of kinship involves not only the personnel of groups but also activities in which kinship relations play a part. Essential information about some significant activities—such as marriage—is already a part of even so static a configuration as a *Stammtafel*, or a set of linked *Stammtafeln*. But there are numerous other activities that do not appear in genealogical reconstructions—the obituaries and political documents cited at the beginning being two examples. If there were a genealogical record of the Schwalm type for Garmisch-Partenkirchen or for Frankfurt, we could examine who was included in and excluded from public expressions of bereavement in the one case, and the ways in which kin connections were used for political recruitment in the other—and we could do this for a changing population (or successive populations) on the basis of a record that was continuous. In both cases the nongenealogical sources would be used to identify the relevance of some ties and the irrelevance of others.

It should be mentioned, in closing, that a considerable amount of insight into the nature of premodern European social structure can be gained by examining the patrilineages as such. The reference points in such a study would need to be the work of the anthropologists Robert McC. Netting, who has painstakingly reconstructed numerous such lineage formations in the Swiss mountain village of Törbel, and Joel M. Halpern, who is currently finishing such a reconstruction project, on the basis of some thirty-four different sources, for the Serbian village of Orasac.[24] There is as well

---

[24]See n. 14.

the mathematics for calculating lineage extinction rates worked out by
Kenneth Wachter and Peter Laslett on the basis of information about bar-
onetcies in England.[25] At this point of the Schwalm project, however, it
would be unwarranted to think about the identified and measured patrilines as being more than a way to organize a complex body of individual-
level data for further analysis. We cannot even make a statement for the
Schwalm comparable to the observation by Netting about Törbel, that
"though the patrilines of Törbel are not classic unilineal descent groups,
they do act as kinship units conferring distinctive and exclusive rights
within a closed corporate community."[26] Still, by examining some of the
characteristics of the identified lineages in the Schwalm, expectations have
been sharpened as research continues. This is not an area of the West in
which turnover was so great as to prevent any continuity whatsoever in
the local population. At the same time, as research continues, it is incor-
rect to see all the people who ever lived in the Schwalm villages as locked
into "structures of long duration" that were established in some primeval
period. What precisely these overall characteristics of the Schwalm population meant for the history of kinship in the area will be revealed by examining the links between individuals, the networks such links created,
and the changes such networks underwent in the course of time.

---

[25]Kenneth A. Wachter and Peter Laslett, "Measuring Patriline Extinction for Mod-
eling Social Mobility in the Past," in Kenneth A. Wachter, Eugene A. Hammel, and Peter Laslett, *Statistical Studies of Historical Social Structure* (New York: Academic Press, 1978).
For a pioneering article dealing with the quantitative analysis of genealogies in a non-Eu-
ropean area, see John C. H. Fei and Ts'ui-jung Liu, "The Growth and Decline of Chinese
Family Clans," *Journal of Interdisciplinary History* 12 (1982): 375-408.

[26]Netting, *Balancing on an Alp,* 79.

Chapter Eight

THE STABILITY RATIO:
AN INDEX
OF COMMUNITY COHESIVENESS
IN NINETEENTH-CENTURY
MORMON TOWNS*

Dean L. May
Lee L. Bean
Mark H. Skolnick

Mormon towns have been an object of scholarly interest and study since the last quarter of the nineteenth century. Edward Bellamy is reported to have visited the northern Utah town of Brigham City to observe its cooperative industrial system before writing *Looking Backward*. Geographer Lucien Gallois was struck by the distinctive qualities of Mormon

*This study is supported by National Institute of Health Records Grant HD-10267 on a data file constructed under National Institute of Health Research Grant CA-16573 Public Health Services, DHEW. An early version was delivered at the annual meeting of the Social Science History Association, November 1978.

towns, reporting his observations in "Quelques Notes sur l'Utah" in 1913. Sociologists Clyde Kluckhohn and Talcott Parsons have turned their attention at times to the study of Mormon town life, sponsoring together the "Study of Values in Five Cultures" project, which compared Mormon, Zuni, Spanish-American, Navajo, and Texan-settled towns in the Ramah Valley of New Mexico in the early 1950s. These and other scholars have commented on two particular aspects of Mormon towns: the nuclear-village settlement pattern, and the unusually high development of communal values within the towns.[1]

These observations have elicited considerable interest in the broader questions they raise. How, in an indifferent, even hostile, environment did the polyglot Mormon people manage to establish viable communities? What is the relationship of economic opportunity to stability, and how is that relationship affected by common religious values as a stabilizing element in community life?

In exploring these broader questions, we have chosen to study one variable strongly related to community cohesiveness, that of population stability, or the degree to which inhabitants of a community choose to remain within that locality over a relatively long period of time. This essential issue has been viewed as important in a variety of other studies. Typically, such studies have utilized some form of the persistence rate to measure a community's retention of population over time. The persistence rate, however, is limited in a number of respects. It is normally developed through the study of census data or other census-type listings of population, such as city directories. Calculations are made of the number of individuals recorded in one census and efforts are then made to identify which of these individuals appear in one or more subsequent censuses. It is extremely difficult, however, to determine if an individual who fails to be identified at a second time period moved from the community or died. Moreover, because names change from one census to another—female

---

[1]For an extensive listing of studies dealing with the Mormon village and community, see Dean L. May, "The Making of Saints: The Mormon Town as Setting for the Study of Cultural Change," *Utah Historical Quarterly* 45 (Winter 1977): 78. Especially pertinent to this study are Lucien Gallois, "Quelques Notes Sur L'Utah," *Annales de Géographie* 22 (1913): 185-96; Lowry Nelson, *The Mormon Village: A Pattern and Technique of Land Settlement* (Salt Lake City: The University of Utah Press, 1952); Evon Z. Vogt and Ethel M. Albert, eds., *People of Rimrock: A Study of Values in Five Cultures* (Cambridge MA: Harvard University Press, 1966).

children marry, although they may remain in the community, or recent widows remarry and may also remain in the community—persistence-rate studies are most often restricted to heads of households, "non-dependent" persons, or "employable" persons.

Another limitation in utilizing the persistence rate is that because it is usually based on the analysis of two censuses, the index is subject to the bias arising from censoring of data. Stopping observations at a particular point in time means that individuals are observed at various points in the life cycle. This may introduce a particularly significant bias in rapidly growing or rapidly declining communities because it is evident from the literature on migration that age is perhaps the most crucial variable in the analysis of migration trends.

Resolution of the potential problems and biases arising from the use of the persistence rate is not simple. First, improvement requires using data sets other than censuses that permit the study of community populations over several generations, since this is what is needed to encompass life-cycle-related variations. Second, given such alternate data resources, one is forced to maximize the availability of life-cycle data through the development of other types of indices. Having access to a data set that provides for the analysis of life-cycle data, we have developed an alternate set of indices—"stability ratios"—which we introduce and use in this paper.

Briefly, then, this study differs from previous investigations of community persistence in two ways. First, we utilize a distinctive data set consisting of family genealogies, which enable us to track several generations of individuals from birth through marriage, bearing of children, and finally to death. Second, given this longitudinal set of data, we suggest a series of indices that cover the life cycle of individuals.

This data set has been generated primarily for studies of the genetic transmission of diseases. It is also used for a variety of studies of demographic change. Its core consists of approximately 170,000 family group sheets selected from the Utah Genealogical Society, which at the time of the initial selection contained about seven million family group sheets listing information on three generations: the head of the household, parents of the head and spouse, and data on the children. These family group sheets use a sophisticated record-linkage system to provide continuous records of descending and ascending pedigrees. For our purposes, the important feature of this file is that it consists of those families in which the head of the household was born in 1800 or later, and in which the head

or a member of the family listed on the group sheet experienced a demographic event on the Mormon pioneer trail (covering the movement from
the Midwest to Utah) or in Utah. The listing does not comprehend all of
the population resident in various communities, but other research conducted by the senior author indicates that for specific communities, these
genealogical records include the majority of the population. Further details on the data set and the analytical significance of the file have been
provided in a variety of other publications; therefore, we shall provide no
further details here.[2]

The indices we have employed in this study constitute a simple device permitting comparison of stability from town to town and from region
to region. As noted, we have termed this the "stability ratio." It is defined
as "all members of a population experiencing a specific primary or secondary vital event in a given locality divided by all members of the population experiencing only the initial event in the locality, standardized to
a base of 1,000."

A specific example might clarify the procedure. In the case of lifetime stability, the computer is directed to search the entire file for persons
whose first child was born in the town of Lehi during a specified decade
(1850-1859 and subsequently by decade to 1900) and for whom the birthplace of their last child is known. The decadal cohort thus becomes persons whose first child is born within the town during the decade. Their
last child could be born at any time, in some cases well beyond 1900. The
persons meeting these criteria are then counted and the figure thus ob-

---

[2]A description of the overall project is provided in Lee L. Bean, Dean L. May, and
Mark Skolnick, "The Mormon Historical Demography Project," *Historical Methods* 11
(1978): 45-53. Additional details on the file structure, which makes longitudinal studies
over several generations possible, are presented in Mark Skolnick, Lee L. Bean, Sue M.
Dintelman, and Geraldine Mineau, "A Computerized Family History Data Base System,"
Sociology and Social Research 63 (April 1979): 506-22. Utilization of the data set for his-
torical population studies is reported in the following: Mark Skolnick, Lee L. Bean, Dean
L. May, Val Arbon, Klancy de Nevers, and Peter Cartwright, "Mormon Demographic
History 1: Nuptiality and Fertility of Once-Married Couples," *Population Studies* 32 (1978):
5-19; Geraldine P. Mineau, Lee L. Bean, and Mark Skolnick, "Mormon Demographic
History 2: The Family Life Cycle and Natural History," *Population Studies* 33 (1979): 429-
66; J. P. Bardet, K. A. Lynch, G. P. Mineau, M. Hainsworth, and M. Skolnick, "La Mor-
talité Maternelle d'Autrefois: Une Étude Comparee (De La France de L'Ouest a L'Utah),"
Annales de Demographie Historique, 1981, 31-49. The latter publication demonstrates the
comparative historical validity of this particular data set.

tained becomes the denominator in calculating the persistence rate. This same list is then reexamined to determine the birthplaces of last children or persons appearing on the list, and a record is kept of those whose last child's birthplace is the same as that of their first child. The total of these individuals then becomes the numerator in calculating persistence. The numerator is then divided by the denominator and the ratio thus obtained is multiplied by 1,000 to provide a standard base.

It is perhaps worth noting that this procedure was followed for men and women separately to make certain that persistence was not influenced by women traveling to a parental home to bear children. There was little variation between persistence rates for men and women and what variance there was followed no consistent pattern. Numerators and denominators from the male and female groups were combined to produce the ratios used in this study, and decadal rates were combined in calculating aggregate 1850 to 1900 ratios.

We have used the stability ratio to determine lifetime stability, where the vital events were the person's own birth and death; continuous lifetime stability, where all intervening vital events occurred in the same locality as the person's birth and death; youth stability, where the vital events are the subjects' own birth and the birth of their first child; adult stability, where birth of first and last child and own death are the events of concern. In the present study, however, we will be reporting only on adult stability, because it is most readily comparable to the commonly used "persistence rate" and because it is the index for which our data file is most complete.

Nine communities are the principal objects of our interest in the present study—four agrarian towns, four regional capitals, and one city: Lehi in northcentral Utah; Fairview in central Utah; Hyrum, in northern Utah; four southern towns taken as a unit, Toquerville, Glendale, Rockville, and Kanab; the regional capitals of Provo, Manti, Logan, and St. George; and Salt Lake City. As noted, our study covers the period from 1850 to 1900. We have considered the population as a period aggregate and in 10-year cohorts. Except for Salt Lake City, we have, where possible, chosen towns of roughly equal size with similar social and religious structures. The towns selected lie in regions quite distinct from one another in climate, resources, topography, and distance from major markets, and the regions themselves are units of analysis in the study.

Lehi is in the Wasatch Front—Utah's fertile crescent—a broad strip of rich arable land lying west of the Wasatch Mountains and extending

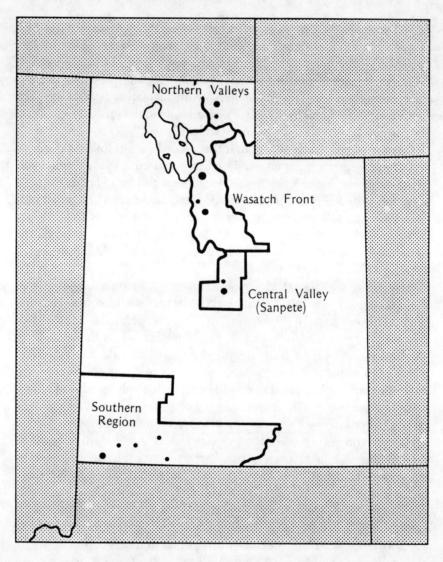

• Towns
• Regional Capitals

MAP 1
MAP OF SELECTED UTAH REGIONS, CAPITALS, AND TOWNS

from Brigham City in the north to Payson in the south. The most vital single resource of the region is the Wasatch Mountains, which provide timber and some minerals. More important, though, they trap and store precipitation during the winter and release it gradually during the summer through a series of evenly spaced canyons and streams, a situation ideal for the irrigated agriculture necessary to successful farming in the arid West. Lehi is in the north end of Utah Valley, thirty miles south of Salt Lake City and fifteen miles northwest of Provo—both of which were important markets for the wheat, barley, oats, corn, molasses, and potatoes that in the nineteenth century were the main products of the town. The average annual rainfall is fourteen inches and temperature about fifty-one degrees. Lehi was founded in 1850, had grown to 1,058 by 1870, 2,719 by 1890, and reached 3,344 by 1910. The town was connected to Salt Lake City by rail in 1872, bringing nearby urban centers even closer. The per capita value of products from farming and manufacturing for the region was generally higher than for other regions. Those censuses that produced such data on a county basis show the Wasatch Front residents producing $41.01 of goods per person in 1870, $53.55 in 1880, and then booming to $158.28 per capita by 1900. Possessed of an abundance of economic advantages over other towns in the study, Lehi and the Wasatch Front region should demonstrate substantially greater stability than the other towns in our study.

Hyrum is at the south end of Cache Valley, eighty miles northeast of Salt Lake City. Founded in the spring of 1860, the town had grown to 708 by the next census, to 1,423 by 1890, and 1,833 by 1910. Hyrum has a higher average annual rainfall than Lehi, 15.19 inches, but a lower average temperature of 48.3 degrees. Moreover, the region is subject to killing frosts in the late spring and early fall. Oats, corn, potatoes, hay, butter, and cheese were the main products of the region in the nineteenth century. The value of products per capita in the northern valleys was $18.40 in 1870; $36.26 in 1880; and $112.69 in 1900. Hyrum, we anticipated, would be next to Lehi in stability, while the northern valley region in which Hyrum is located should be second to the Wasatch Front.

Fairview is in the north end of the Sanpete valley, a narrow stretch of farmland flanked by the Wasatch and the San Pitch mountains on the west and the Wasatch Plateau mountains on the east. The town was settled in 1859 as populations moved up the valley from the regional capital of Manti, some thirty miles to the south. Fairview is ninety-eight miles from Salt Lake City and was not served by a railroad until about 1890.

Like the region in which it is situated, the town is primarily agricultural. The mean annual temperature of the area is 47.6, considerably lower than along the Wasatch Front, and rainfall is notably less as well—about twelve inches annually. Consequently the region, like the northern valleys, is not well adapted to row-crop agriculture and so produces mainly grain, hay, and livestock. The per capita production of farms and manufacturing was estimated by U.S. census marshalls to be $72.48 in 1870; it had dropped by 1880 to $41.88, but rose dramatically by 1900 to $87.55. There were 531 inhabitants of Fairview by 1870, and double that amount in 1880. The town reached 1,530 in 1900 and grew slowly thereafter, reaching 1,654 by 1910. Distant from markets and lacking efficient transportation networks until the 1890s, Fairview and the Central Valley region should be slightly less stable than Hyrum and the northern valleys in the nineteenth century.

To find a rural farming populace in southern Utah of a size comparable to Lehi and Hyrum, it was necessary to consider four towns, Rockville, Toquerville, Glendale, and Kanab as one. The main support for settlement of the area came from Brigham Young's "cotton mission"—an attempt in the early 1860s to assure Utah's self-sufficiency by promoting the cultivation of cotton in the relatively mild (average temperature, sixty-one degrees) climate. Farmlands were in very narrow strips on either side of rivers and streams. Without these sources of water, in an area with eight inches annual rainfall, no farm crop could have grown. Watercourses in the south were fed by more remote mountains than in the Wasatch Front, and were much less constant and reliable in flow. Spring freshets and flash floods washed out whole irrigation systems with depressing regularity. Rivers that overflowed their banks in the spring would commonly dwindle to a trickle by fall. Markets for whatever surplus could be managed were remote. The towns were between 300 and 347 miles south of Salt Lake City. Subsistence agriculture characterized the region through the 1860s and 1870s, with some cotton being raised for export and for manufacture in a textile mill established by Brigham Young in Washington in the late 1860s. Sorghum molasses was also exported, but the economy remained unstable until livestock provided a reliable staple in the 1880s and 1890s. The population of all the towns was 800 in 1870; 984 in 1890; and 1,491 in 1910. Per capita production of farm and manufactured products for the region was $70.49 in 1880 and only $64.20 in 1900. Remote from markets, and clinging to tiny, inelastic oases, the southern colonies should be substantially less stable in population than those in the north.

The regional capital of Provo lay some seventeen miles southwest of Lehi and forty-five miles south of Salt Lake City. Provo was the oldest town in Utah valley (founded in 1849) and had remained both the ecclesiastical and administrative center of the region. Regional church and county headquarters were located there starting in the 1850s. The town had 2,030 inhabitants in 1860; 2,384 in 1870; 6,185 in 1900; and 8,925 in 1910. The Provo Woolen Mills began operations in 1872 with 3,240 spindles. The next year the Utah Southern Railroad was completed to the town. In 1875 Brigham Young University was established. Only Salt Lake City, of all Utah towns, would seem to have had better economic advantages. Thus Provo, we hypothesized, should have the most stable population of our regional capitals.

Logan is some eighty miles northeast of Salt Lake City. It is situated near the center of the Cache Valley, at the mouth of Logan Canyon, which provides a substantial flow of water in addition to timber, quarries, and other resources. The town was settled in 1861 as Mormon movement into the Cache Valley began in earnest. It became the ecclesiastical center of the territory in 1877 with the organization of the Cache Stake (diocese) in 1877, a role confirmed by the completion of a Mormon temple there in 1884. The town also became an educational center with the founding of Brigham Young College in 1878 and the later establishment of Utah State Agricultural College. At various times there were small sawmills and other light manufacturing enterprises operated in Logan, and dairies of significant size were established in the area during the nineteenth century, manufacturing butter and cheese. But the town's economy was integrated for the most part into the grain, hay, and dairy production of the surrounding agricultural area. The Utah Northern Railroad reached Logan in 1873 and soon connected the town to settlements extending into Idaho and, by 1880, to Montana's mining areas. Logan's rapid, steady pattern of growth is consistent with the solid economy and advantages of the town. The first census report for Logan was in 1870, when there were 1,757 inhabitants. The town had grown to 3,396 by 1880; 4,620 by 1890; and 7,522 by 1910, making it second only to Provo among our regional capitals.

Manti, the regional capital of the Sanpete Valley, was founded in 1849 (the same year as Provo), but was located much farther from the urban center of Salt Lake City, which was about 125 miles to the south. The

Sanpete Valley was colder in climate than Utah Valley, with an average annual temperature of 47.6 degrees. It was thus less suited to row-crop agriculture, but had abundant water and excellent soils, making the region ideal for hay, grain, and dairy enterprises. A Denver and Rio Grande Railroad line reached Manti in 1891, but the town failed to develop manufacturing on a significant scale. The completion of a Mormon temple in 1888 and the establishment of the county seat made Manti the administrative and religious center of the region, but the town was always challenged economically by Ephraim, seven miles to the north. Manti had 916 residents in 1860, grew rapidly to 2,022 by 1880, and then stabilized at 2,425 in 1900. We estimated that the town would be third in economic advantage among the regional capitals, ranking behind Provo and Cache Valley's Logan, and that the population would accordingly be less stable.

We predicted that St. George, some 315 miles south and west of Salt Lake City, would be the least stable of the regional capitals. It was founded in 1861 as part of a church-sponsored "cotton mission" to help make Utah self-sufficient by raising cotton in a semitropical southwestern corner of the state. Greatly limited in agricultural potential by lack of water, the surrounding country did not prosper. As the century wore on, stock raising became the major product of southern Utah, though farmers in the area continued to produce fruits, grapes, nuts, and other semitropical crops. As with Logan and Manti, St. George was the site of a Mormon temple, completed in 1877, which made the town an ecclesiastical center. It later became the county seat of Washington County, making it a center of civil administration as well. St. George did not attract a railroad, however, and it remained a small provincial capital throughout the nineteenth century. There were 1,142 inhabitants in its first census report (1870) and 1,377 in 1890. By 1910 the town had grown to 1,769.[3]

Thus, of our four regions, the Wasatch Front and southern Utah represent the two extremes—the former area being fertile, well watered, close

---

[3]Data on the towns and regions is from appropriate volumes of the U.S. census. Production figures are taken from the agricultural and manufacturing censuses for the appropriate years. Climatological data is from Richard D. Poll, ed., *Utah's History* (Provo UT: Brigham Young University Press, 1978) 720. Other information is from Andrew Jenson, *Encyclopedic History of the Church of Jesus Christ of Latter-day Saints* (Salt Lake City: Deseret News Publishing Company, 1941), under the appropriate entries, and from Leonard Arrington, *Great Basin Kingdom* (Cambridge MA: Harvard University Press, 1958).

to markets of considerable size, and likely to have been very stable. The southern area lacked all of those advantages and, we estimate, would have been the least stable. The northern and central valleys were between the others in economic advantage and similar to one another. However, we would have considered the northern valleys to be somewhat more stable because of a better transportation system and reasonably steady markets for farm products in Wyoming and Montana.

What, then, do our data show? We are considering initially only adult stability—persons whose first and whose last child were born in the same town or region. Such persons may have moved at some point during their childbearing years, but their return to the original homesite by the time their last child was born indicates, in our judgment, considerable attachment to the locality. Our file contains 86,851 persons (men and women) who between 1850 and 1900 were a parent of a first child born in the territory and a last child whose birthplace is known. Of these, 75,261 last children were born in the territory. Using the first figure as denominator and the second as numerator, the adult-stability ratio computes to 866.66—that is 867 of each thousand persons whose first child was born in the territory were still in the territory when their last child was born. When one considers that Mormon colonies were founded in Arizona, New Mexico, Colorado, Canada, Wyoming, Idaho, and Mexico during this period, the figure seems remarkably high. This planned and deliberate overflow of native sons and daughters, together with others migrating elsewhere as individuals, drew off only thirteen percent of the population in roughly the twenty-to-forty age category during the period 1850-1900. All others remained within the boundaries of present-day Utah during their childbearing years.

We would expect the regions to be less stable, since they are geographically smaller units and a migrating family could disappear from a region with a much shorter move than would be needed to take them into another state or territory. If we think of migrants in the aggregate as a swarm of molecules in constant, seemingly random motion, more would achieve escape velocity from a confined area than from a larger one. Such is the case with our nineteenth-century Utah population. Regional adult-stability ratios range from 607 to 696, about 200 per 1,000 less than the territory-wide ratio. The regional pattern does not, however, follow precisely our predictions based on a general evaluation of relative economic advantage. The central Sanpete Valley is the most stable, with an adult-stability

TABLE 1

UTAH ADULT STABILITY RATIOS
BY SELECTED REGIONS, REGIONAL CAPITALS, AND TOWNS
1850–1900

		1850	R	1860	R	1870	R	1880	R	1890	R	1900	R	TOTAL	R
UTAH	N	4808	942	7674	894	11356	855	14478	835	16082	850	20863	882	75261	867
	D	5104		8588		13288		17342		18918		23661		86851	
SALT LAKE CITY	N	528	417	672	525	950	620	1312	664	1624	725	2168	730	7254	643
	D	1266		1280		1532		1976		2240		2972		11278	
WASATCH FRONT	N	1914	480	2724	627	4290	700	5546	719	6242	737	8043	734	28759	691
	D	3986		4346		6128		7712		8468		10953		41593	
NORTHERN VALLEYS	N			648	722	954	686	1266	636	1212	659	1610	692	5710	675
	D			898		1390		1990		1838		2326		8462	
CENTRAL VALLEY†	N	176	682	724	739	772	687	938	680	1100	693	1048	697	4758	696
	D	258		980		1124		1380		1588		1504		6834	
SOUTHERN REGION	N	134	465	336	600	586	521	650	581	690	683	682	705	3078	607
	D	288		560		1124		1118		1010		968		5068	
PROVO	N	134	406	124	484	228	713	338	710	374	703	466	608	1864	696
	D	330		256		320		476		532		766		2680	
LOGAN	N			144	637	178	669	274	548	248	620	368	573	1212	596
	D			226		266		500		400		642		2034	
MANTI	N	76	535	126	741	98	557	120	583	152	613	146	640	718	614
	D	142		170		176		206		248		228		1170	
ST. GEORGE	N			40	426	88	468	94	560	106	680	102	671	430	566
	D			94		188		168		156		152		760	
LEHI	N	44	324	86	632	128	753	168	700	180	604	216	603	822	614
	D	136		136		170		240		298		358		1338	
HYRUM	N			76	745	114	803	100	714	100	602	76	481	466	717
	D			102		142		140		166		158		650	
FAIRVIEW	N			50	625	58	604	88	647	102	654	94	516	392	603
	D			80		96		136		156		182		650	
SOUTHERN TOWNS	N			24	333	70	398	74	394	90	536	80	588	338	457
	D			72		176		188		168		136		740	

†(Sanpete)
N = Total persons with first and last child born in locality.
D = Total persons with first child born in locality and last child's birthplace known.
R = $\frac{N}{D} \times 1000$.

ratio of 696. The Wasatch Front, which we predicted to be most stable, was a close second at 691; the northern valleys were 675; and the southern region, as predicted, was least stable at 607.

In other words, stability for adults in the two decades of their child-bearing years ranged between sixty and seventy percent for the four regions of Utah for persons whose first child was born between 1850 and 1900. Comparing this with the analogous persistence rate, we again find the Utah population to be remarkably stable. The highest persistence rate observed thus far in the several studies treating regional or county populations in the last half of the nineteenth century is fifty-one percent of farm operators, in eastern and east-central Kansas, for the decade 1895-1905.[4] The lowest rate is twenty-one percent for Grant County, Wisconsin, from 1885 to 1895. Overall, rates of twenty-five, twenty-nine, and thirty percent are common.[5] Most such studies measure persistence only over a single decade, and though the ten-year persistors are more likely to stay another decade than is the entire initial population, the likelihood of persons remaining for a twenty-year period is clearly substantially less than for a ten-year period. One study of Dayton township, Iowa, does provide data for computing persistence over two decades, from 1860 to 1880. This study shows a one-decade persistence for the 1860 population of thirty-four percent and a two-decade persistence of twenty percent.[6] Malin also provides two-decade rates, which reach as high as forty-three percent for 1865-1885 in west-central Kansas. Of course, the farm operators he is studying would be likely to be more stable than the populations studied by others.[7]

The regional capitals of Provo, Logan, Manti, and St. George range in stability from 696 to 566. Provo's stability ratio of 696 is slightly more than the Wasatch Front ratio of 691. It is significantly higher than the next most stable capital, Manti, which had a stability ratio of 614. The northern capital of Logan was a close third with 596 and St. George, the southern capital, as predicted, was last at 566. Of other studies that have considered localities similar in size and function to our regional capitals, the most well known are Don H. Doyle's work on Jacksonville, Illinois,

[4]James C. Malin, "The Turnover of Farm Population in Kansas," *Kansas Historical Quarterly* 4 (November 1935): 339-72, esp. 366.

[5]Peter J. Coleman, "Restless Grant Country: Americans on the Move," *Wisconsin Magazine of History* 46 (1962): 16-20. See also a listing of persistence studies of rural areas in Stephen Thernstrom, *The Other Bostonians* (Cambridge MA: Harvard University Press, 1973) 226.

[6]Rodney O. Davies, "Prairie Emporium: Clarence, Iowa, 1860-1880," *Mid-America* 51 (1969): 130-39.

[7]Malin, "Farm Population in Kansas," 366.

and William G. Robbins's work on Roseburg, Oregon. Twenty-seven percent of Jacksonville's "non-dependent" population persisted from 1850 to
1860 and twenty-one percent from 1860 to 1870.[8] In Roseburg thirty-two
percent of "employable" people persisted from 1860 to 1870, and twenty-
three percent of the 1860 group were still present two decades later, in
1880.[9] Thus the Utah regional capitals, like the regions themselves, show
a stability in the nineteenth century some forty percent higher than that
indicated by persistence rates for other American towns during the period.

Now we turn to the towns themselves—Lehi, Hyrum, Fairview, and
the southern towns of Kanab, Glendale, Rockville, and Toquerville, considered as a unit. Here we are speaking of small agricultural villages, ranging in size during our period of study from approximately 1,500 to 3,000
inhabitants. These were not primarily commercial and industrial populations, serving a hinterland of farmers living in the country. In the Mormon town most farmers themselves lived in the settlement and worked
fields outside. These were thus unlike almost all other small towns in the
American West, notably lacking in the commercial drive, boosterism, and
extravagant aspirations characterizing other towns of the period. Taken
as a set, their adult stability was nearly as high as that of the regional capitals; they do not follow the predicted pattern precisely. Lehi at 614 was
second to Hyrum at 658. Fairview was third at 603, and the southern towns
were a low 457. One town, Hyrum, was significantly more stable than its
regional capital, Logan (596). This opposes a clear tendency of units of
larger size to be more stable than those of smaller size. We would tenta-
tively attribute the unusual stability of Hyrum to the large number of
Scandinavian-born in the town. A very high thirty-seven percent of the
whole population of Hyrum in 1880 were of Scandinavian birth, much
higher than most towns in the Cache Valley. Scandinavians comprised
eighty-eight percent of the foreign-born, compared to eleven percent for
the British. It would seem that the communal ties of Hyrum's Danes and
Swedes were strengthened by the high proportion of countrymen in the

---

[8]Don H. Doyle, *The Social Order of a Frontier Community: Jacksonville, Illinois, 1825-
1870* (Urbana: University of Illinois Press, 1978) 261-62.

[9]William G. Robbins, "Opportunity and Persistence in the Pacific Northwest: A
Quantitative Study of Early Roseburg, Oregon," *Pacific Historical Review* 39 (1970): 279-
96. Robbins's "employable" population includes men and women aged sixteen and older.

town. In addition, one suspects they were not always made to feel welcome by the predominantly British- and American-born populations in other nearby towns of Cache Valley.[10]

The southern towns were considerably less stable than was the regional capital of St. George, a consequence of the unreliability of water supplies and of the proximity of southern Utah to more promising settlement sites in Arizona. It was about these settlements that George Hicks, a reluctant colonist from the relatively lush Cottonwood area of the Salt Lake Valley, wrote perhaps the best, and certainly the most poignant, of early Mormon folksongs:

> Oh, once I lived in Cottonwood and owned a little farm,
> But I was called to Dixie, which gave me much alarm,
> To raise the cane and cotton I right away must go,
> But the reason why they sent me, I'm sure I do not know.

> The hot winds whirl around me and take away my breath,
> I've had the chills and fever till I'm nearly shook to death.
> "All earthly tribulations are but a moment here,"
> And oh, if I prove faithful a righteous crown shall wear.[11]

If "proving faithful" meant staying on their farms and peopling the towns of Utah's Dixie, fewer than half managed to do so. Yet, if persistence rates of other rural towns and counties in America are a fair comparison, even the people of remote southern Utah towns were twice as likely to stay put than were their counterparts in more fertile and well-watered parts of the United States.

In the present paper we can offer only a cursory view of stability ratios by decade, but the exercise is still most revealing: much is masked by the aggregate data. Whereas Hyrum's aggregate figures suggest that it was substantially more stable over the whole period than Kanab, in fact the town began to decline in stability at the end of its first decade, and continued to be increasingly unstable through the rest of the century. Lehi followed a similar pattern, while the southern towns, beginning at a very low stability of 333, experienced steady gains until those first children born in

---

[10]Charles M. Hatch, Dean L. May, and Fon R. Brown, "The People of Cache Valley's Jensen Farm Area in the 19th Century" (1979) 15.

[11]Tom Carter, Jan Brunvaand, and H. Reynolds Cannon, comps. and eds., *The New Beehive Songster* 1 (Salt Lake City: Okehdokee Records, 1975) 27.

the 1890-1900 cohort actually had a higher likelihood of staying in the town until their last child was born than did residents of Lehi and Hyrum at the same time. It may be that the diverse grain, vegetable, and dairy economies of the northern and Wasatch settlements suffered from Utah's postrailroad integration into the national economy, whereas the southern region, unable to compete in subsistence and row-crop farming, quickly gave up the effort and moved toward speculation in one commodity (livestock), which came to be in relatively greater demand nationwide. Wheat prices fell, nationally, from $2.06 per bushel in 1860 to a low of $.62 a bushel in 1900. Cattle prices reached a low point of $16.95 a head in 1890, but rose sharply thereafter to $26.50 in 1900. Prices for sheep, of major importance in southern Utah, rose steadily from $1.87 a head in 1870 to $4.06 a head by 1910.[12] The regions followed the same pattern. By the end of the century urban and ranching areas were more stable than row-crop and dairy-farming areas.

The trend in Salt Lake City is instructive as well. During the early period Salt Lake City served as a temporary stopping place for immigrants who later moved to remote farming communities. The preference of many immigrants for the city over the farm is not evident until the 1860-1870 decade, when adult stability rises very sharply to 620. Growth in stability during the next two decades was equally remarkable, moving for the 1870-1880 cohort to an adult-stability ratio of more than 650. A leveling in stability began by 1890, however, at 725 and remained fairly constant until the turn of the century. The state would enjoy a brief period of prosperity through World War I, and then lapse into a prolonged depression lasting until World War II. These trends, we suspect, will be reflected in falling stability ratios as added data make it possible to move further into the twentieth century.

What, then, can we conclude about the Mormon towns from the data we have studied thus far? First of all, the regions, the capitals, and the towns of Utah were surprisingly stable, favoring development of close ties with coresidents and strongly cohesive communal relationships. Even in the southern towns, 457 of 1,000 residents did not move away during their childbearing years. The populations of Lehi and Hyrum were considerably

---

[12]U.S. Bureau of the Census, *Historical Statistics of the United States: Colonial Times to 1957* (Washington: U.S. Government Printing Office, 1960) 289-90, 297-98.

more stable, and more than two-thirds of those with a first child born in Salt Lake City remained until their last child's birth. Whereas two-thirds of those with first children born in Hyrum between 1850 and 1900 were present in the town two decades later when their last child was born, only twenty-one percent of these present in Jacksonville in 1860 were there a decade later. The difference is impressive.

Our observation that Mormon towns were unusually stable offers one response to the questions about Utah's towns raised at the beginning of this study. How, in an arid environment with inelastic supplies of basic resources, was such stability possible? We estimate that the same pressures on available land—which Philip Greven saw destroying family and community solidarity during 100 years of settled life in Andover—were at work in some Utah towns by the end of the first decade of settlement. Yet descriptions of Mormon towns in the late nineteenth and early twentieth centuries are strongly reminiscent of those Greven used to describe Andover in her halcyon years.[13] Did Mormon towns achieve, in the absence of the paternal whip of land control that made Andover so tranquil, a similarly stable and cohesive society? If so, then could it be that Greven's stabilizing mechanism is altogether too simplistic and that there were more important factors operant in Andover and Utah that have not yet been identified? We suspect that this may indeed be the case.

Though we cannot speak for Andover's Puritans, it would seem likely that in the case of the Mormons, homogeneity in religious belief overrode disjunctive forces such as differing national origins, lack of experience in farming, and paucity of resources. The effect of these latter circumstances is still evident in regional variation, particularly of the economic variables. But the overall high level of stability, even in the least propitious environments, says much for the power of religious commitment as a unifying and stabilizing force in the lives of the settlers. Church leaders used their influence on the faithful not only to establish new colonies, by "calling" families to participate in such a venture, but to maintain the colonies by considering the venture a "mission" from which the settlers could not withdraw without formal release from the church. Called in 1850 to

---

[13]Philip J. Greven, Jr., *Four Generations: Population, Land, and Family in Colonial Andover, Massachusetts* (Ithaca NY: Cornell University Press, 1970); see also Dean L. May, "The Making of Saints," 84-92.

help settle the first colony in southern Utah, Joseph G. Hovey confided
to his diary sentiments that must have been widespread.

> The President Called out some Hundred to go and make a Settlement
> in Iron County on the Little Salt Lake. I Joseph, being Called to go also
> not with standing my harde labours since I have been in the valley. I
> am willing to forsake all and go build up the Kingdom of God. I have
> laboured with all my might and god has bless me with helth and strength
> and my family. I had my mind made up this winter to rest a littl and
> enjoy my labours hence there seams to be no stoping place for a man
> but he must do the wil of God.[14]

Like George Hicks, he did go, and once there, like many of the faithful, he stayed. Levi M. Savage, called to settle on the Little Colorado River
in Arizona in 1876, was still laboring there almost forty years later, at the
age of seventy, when his son Parley requested and received permission from
church officials in Salt Lake City for his father to be released and return
to Utah.[15]

Such external restraints on migration were present in the Mormon
colonization effort and were of considerable importance at critical junc-
tures, especially in opening new areas. Most people, however, did not migrate in response to calls, and most towns were spontaneously settled rather
than called. Even then, however, our data suggests that there was a general tendency to follow Brigham Young's admonition to remain in the
Mormon domain and not be tempted by Eastern comforts or California's
rich lands. Perhaps most important, Mormons, derided from New York to
California as clannish and alien, seemed to prefer the company of other
Mormons. Utah towns offered a refuge from the distrust and animosity they
had encountered almost everywhere they had been. It would take much
to shake them loose.

---

[14]Diary of Joseph G. Hovey, Latter-day Saints Church Archives, Salt Lake City, Utah.

[15]Cited in Charles S. Peterson, *Take up Your Mission: Mormon Colonizing along the
Little Colorado River, 1870-1900* (Tucson: University of Arizona Press, 1973) 60.

Chapter Nine

THE MASSACHUSETTS TOWNS AND THE LEGISLATURE, 1691-1776: CONTRIBUTIONS OF GENEALOGY TO COLLECTIVE BIOGRAPHY

John A. Schutz

Genealogists regularly cite membership in the Massachusetts colonial legislature as a standard of leadership and renown when they are identifying a subject. Membership becomes the standard, sometimes without checking if there were multiple terms of service, if the person actually came to Boston and took the oaths of office, and if he performed any services in office. Election to the legislature, nonetheless, set apart townsmen from other residents and was often an indicator of personality, principles, and ability; equally often, it was reflective of wealth, free time, and family condition. Membership was a standard of judgment that could easily distinguish New England men of the eighteenth century from others in their town.

One may ask, then, what it meant to be elected a Massachusetts legislator. Surely, there was no group of men anywhere in the American colonies that was more determined to defend the rights of the people than those men sitting in the General Court. And there were nowhere in America lawmakers who insisted upon their prerogatives with greater fervor than those New Englanders. In the eighty-five years from 1691 to the Revolution, they won the dubious reputation of being contentious and hardheaded in their relations with royal officials. These legislators regarded liberty for the colony to depend upon the passage, even the execution, of laws by them—the elected representatives of the people—and they thus condemned pugnaciously the British exercise of veto power over legislation.[1] According to one governor, they claimed the veto "to be contrary to their Charter and destructive of all their privileges."[2]

At the same time the legislators of the interior towns were nearly as hostile to their colleagues from Boston and the other ports. By looking upon the capital with suspicion, they were peculiarly local in their attitudes concerning trade and luxury. For them the legislature was a last resort when all other means locally had failed to resolve an issue. Service in the legislature they regarded as burdensome; living in Boston as strange and corrupting; and officials as knaves and cheats who were "capable of finding the weak side of mankind." These curious attitudes toward people and service in Boston were carried to such lengths that some towns ignored the elections altogether, a few sent no representatives until the Revolution, and others sought to bind their representatives through instructions and limit any independent action. Once aroused, however, the country towns sent representatives in such numbers to Boston that they disturbed the ordinary working of the House.[3] Their power was potentially so great that

---

[1]In 1691 the English government presented the colony with a charter, and the result was the introduction of royal government. The legislature was opened to all landowners who qualified by taking the oath of allegiance. The governor became a royal official with a flexible term of office. Religious dominance of politics was weakened, but only Protestants were able to participate.

[2]William Shirley to the Duke of Newcastle, 17 October 1741, in Charles Henry Lincoln, ed., *Correspondence of William Shirley*, 2 vols. (New York, 1912) 1:76. Thomas Hutchinson regarded them as having narrow minds and tight purses when taxes were an issue (see Hutchinson to William Bollan, 4 March 1765, Massachusetts Archives, Boston, 26:130-31).

[3]Governor Hutchinson describes well this situation in a letter of December 1770 to Lord Hillsborough (Hutchinson Papers, Massachusetts Archives, 27:74-75): "It seems

William Shirley successfully sought in the 1740s a British instruction that prohibited the legislature from enfranchising new towns.[4]

As a body of deputies, the General Court was not large: twenty-eight in the upper house, or Council, and slightly over a hundred on average in the lower house, or House of Representatives. But size was no measure of legislative vigor and determination, nor a deterrent in taking on the powerful British ministry when members felt the Charter was endangered. Leaders would arise to meet the challenge, and the ordinary way of handling business by committee gave way to floor debates, speeches to inform visitors in the gallery, and tactics by talented leaders who could arouse an audience.[5] Long before the younger James Otis and Samuel Adams gained notoriety as agitators, Elisha Cooke (1678-1737) and James Allen (1697-1755) had dared speak their minds. Some of their best moments, however, were spent in the taverns where they seemed to have greater freedom of expression and debate than on the House floor. With a glass of ale in one hand and a finger from the other pointing in the direction of the governor's mansion, Cooke fiercely argued and contested issues, while listeners tactfully excused his show of audacity by claiming he was drunk.[6] Allen also had his tactics, but he once spoke from the floor and was sum-

---

necessary that limits should be set to the number of House of Representatives. . . . If every town would use its privilege, the number would exceed 300 and in a few years as the Law stands for settling the number it may amount to 500. At present it does not exceed 130—the small towns not being willing to pay for their members attendance will not choose any and they have not inhabitants able to bear their own charges." See also *The Massachusetts Spy*, no. 16, 6 September 1770.

[4]In 1754 the town of Lincoln was the first to be granted incorporation after ten years' prohibition of new representatives. Chambers Russell presented the petition on behalf of the inhabitants and his own family interests. See *An Account of the Celebration by the Town of Lincoln, Mass[achuse]tts April 23rd, 1904 . . .* (Lincoln MA, 1905) 39-41.

[5]The spirited proceedings often brought forth great oratory. These few lines from Joseph Warren to Josiah Quincy, 14 November 1774, Quincy MA, Massachusetts Historical Society, are illustrative: "You would have thought yourself in an Assembly of Spartans or ancient Romans, had you been a witness to the Order which inspired those who spoke upon the important business."

[6]Cooke's heroic encounter with Governor Belcher and others is well described by Clifford K. Shipton, *Sibley's Harvard Graduates: Biographical Sketches of Those Who Attended Harvard College* (Cambridge MA, 1873-) 4:354-55.

marily ousted from the House when it bowed to protests from the governor.[7]

Few of these great occasions for debate are now remembered, though most people then knew the activities of their representatives. For those eighty-five years more than two thousand men actually served the towns in Boston, working from a few days to a decade or more. No complete list of them has been hitherto available, and many have remained misty figures even when they are identified by name, because not much more can be found about their lives or activities than a service record of a few positions in their towns or membership in the local church.[8] Their obscurity, though, should arouse curiosity to know more about them and to ponder what was in their spirit and background that made them as a group such persistent spokesmen of home rule and liberty in legislative halls.

To illuminate the lives of such large numbers of obscure men requires a far different method of research and documentation than has been familiar to most historians. Collective biography requires a massive examination of family histories, genealogies, vital records, and documents of all kinds—like deeds and wills—often with very little useable information as the reward. Until recently most historians have been wary of genealogical findings and of biography, and have been equally suspicious of using a computer, which is particularly valuable for sorting large amounts of data. Genealogists, too, have not been interested in legislators, except to fit them into a family study, often by listing starkly the years of service, honors, and any other details of a career incidental to the recording of family data. Nonetheless, membership in the General Court carries a certain kind of luster that is attractive to historians and genealogists alike, but neither has known the exact meaning of this prominence—for the legislator himself and for society.

---

[7]*Journals of the House of Representatives of Massachusetts,* vol. 25 (Washington, 1748-1749; rpt., Boston, 1950) 116-19, 137, 148, 150-51. See also Shipton, *Sibley's Harvard Graduates,* 6:162-63.

[8]The National Endowment for the Humanities awarded me and Dean Tipps, who was then a senior graduate student at the University of California, Berkeley, three research grants to experiment and study the operations of the General Court by using methods of hard-data research, including the computer. We employed various time periods in our research, but, in general, studied the period from 1691 to 1780 when Massachusetts was governed under its second charter.

Research for this paper, which is part of a larger project, was possible through the use of very many genealogies and family biographies. Without these accounts, often lovingly done by a family member, it would be impossible to know as much of these representatives as has been found. The research requires much more than the information obtained from books; it requires an understanding of indices, magazines, and the habits of recording genealogical data. It is unfortunate that this lore is frequently preserved for the insider and associates. The best general places to do research on New England materials are the New England Historic Genealogical Society, the Essex Institute, the American Antiquarian Society, and the Library of Congress in Washington, D.C. But many times the best place to go is the library where a genealogist lodged his notes in a desperate attempt to preserve a lifetime of hard work.[9]

The Massachusetts Charter of 1691 provided for a two-house legislature of unequal size and prestige. The resident landowners of the towns ordinarily chose the representatives each May unless there was a special legislative election. Most towns could choose one or two delegates, depending upon the size of their population. Boston could elect four, and almost always did; Salem usually chose two, with some consistency. In order to select delegates, the towns needed to be incorporated by an act of the legislature, to secure the approval of the governor, and to receive the consent of the British government. Once permitted to hold elections, the towns had to choose resident landowners. The issue of residency had been settled early in the 1690s, but that requirement put a heavy burden on the township to find someone able and willing to take on yearly the onerous obligations of the House of Representatives. Some towns could not find anyone and were unrepresented for long periods. Others undoubtedly regretted the expense but did send a delegate, often taking the precaution to instruct him because they feared his independence. Representation for the whole colony reached seventy-nine percent of the towns in 1776; over the years it varied from fifty-five to sixty percent.

In place of the representative, an agent was often employed to handle any pending town affairs in the capital; he was not bound by the rules

---

[9]Fortunately for researchers, only the truly large libraries are able to handle massive collections so that the Massachusetts Historical Society, the New England Historic Genealogical Society, and the Forbes Library at Northampton receive more of these gifts than the smaller libraries.

of the legislature, especially by the requirement of residency. However, the town was less concerned about the burden to be shouldered by an inhabitant than it was about the expense and necessity of representation.[10] The agent could be instructed to handle any serious problem, thus relieving the town of heavy expense. Sometimes the problem was sufficiently complex or important for the town to send a representative and engage an agent to help him.

For members of the Council, the burden of service on its committees was heavier than for representatives. The Council met several times a week, often as many as five. It was chosen yearly by a joint vote of the House and retiring Council after a great deal of debate, but with most of the old councilors being returned to office for another year. Since a quorum of the Council could conduct business, not all members were compelled to be present in Boston, though the members were expected to be available most of the year. The members generally maintained two residencies and did not ordinarily rent rooms in boarding houses as some representatives who remained in the city for only a few weeks.[11] The councilors often owned considerable property and a business. They were far wealthier than the representatives, often with relatives in Boston, and absences from home were not as burdensome to them. They seemed, moreover, to be committed to long service on the Council and a life outside the town.

In legislative business, the representatives, even more than members of the Council, spent massive amounts of time adjudicating local disputes. They heard petitions by the hundreds in ad hoc committees, and these deliberations frequently resulted in fact-finding trips, reports, and bills. The numbers of committees during such sessions as 1755, 1756, and 1757 were extraordinarily heavy, mounting to 750, 973, and 804, respectively. There

---

[10]Lynn's town records reveal much anxiety about the expense of representation. When William Collins was chosen in May 1748, he agreed to account in writing for the days he sat in the House. In 1752 the townsmen voted that the representative must account for his "attendance on the General Court and for the time expended in . . . Journeying to and from hence and at the end of every last session in each year successively shall give an account in writing to the Selectmen" (*Records of Ye Towne Meetings of Lynn, 1742-1759*, pt. 5 [Lynn MA, 1966] 47). The town voted three shillings per day for expenses.

[11]Many representatives, with the approval of their colleagues, charged the per diem fee for the entire session of the House. The townsmen of Lynn wanted to be charged only for the actual days of service. See ibid., 47, 65. They expected an overpayment ("overplush") to be returned to the town treasurer.

were years when standing committees also processed petitions. Issues for the committees often involved the selection of ministers, town boundaries, probate, and family disputes; in fact, nearly any issue not resolved in the towns became a matter for legislative inquiry. The representatives seemed more vitally concerned with these petitions than with the inevitable tax bill or salary allowance for the governor. Both followed a formula that was debatable but generally predictable. The presence of the representatives in Boston continued often until the particular petition was processed. Then they might take advantage of an early completion of business and leave for home.

Other times they might be involved outside of Boston with business matters in towns neighboring theirs. They could be called upon to survey a disputed boundary, preside over the first town meeting of a newly established township, or act as referees in a division of family property. Further, the business of the legislature included surveying land, laying out towns, looking after defense, and dealing with the Indians. If the town was exposed to frontier hazards, one would expect the legislator and his constituents to be vitally interested in defense. Indeed, any hearing in Boston on this subject should have been a priority item in the legislator's schedule. In such cases the representative might be the son, relative, or client of the land developer who founded the town.

The average representative was a family man of approximately fifty years of age, then married, and father of eight children. A few unlucky souls were single or widowers, but most passed quickly through those stages of life and were joined soon in a second or third marriage. Over the years from 1691 the average age remained relatively stable, even though the House of Representatives grew larger with the decades. While the spread of ages included some men in their sixties and a few in their seventies and eighties, younger men, in their twenties and thirties, were also present. In times of intense public distress, older legislators often consented to election. Their presence seemed rather special and might be limited to service on a committee or two. It included, perhaps, some weeks in Boston as observers and advisors and, most likely, some military duty if a frontier crisis was threatening. These temporary councilors were generally older than those who did day-to-day legislative work. Sessions in 1763, 1767, and 1773 reflected concern for the colony's welfare; thus seasoned people from the towns stood for election. The average age in 1763 for these members was sixty years. Undoubtedly, the depression conditions during that year which formally ended the Seven Years' War affected many people, and their concern for trade, politics, and naval search and seizure was sufficiently disturbing to want able representation.

Though public restlessness drew older men into colonywide affairs, the active people in the legislature were usually younger by four or five years below the annual averages. Unlike the rank and file, they were considerably younger as a group, even during the critical decade prior to the American Revolution. In 1763 when the legislature was much older as a body, the work force in House affairs was about eleven years younger than the average.[12]

Under ordinary circumstances this working group seems to have been unstable, changing annually in personnel. They may not have been the actual leaders of the House, but they did the committee service. It is possible that people with a longer tenure were unwilling to serve or had businesses in Boston and refused to spend much time in routine committee matters when defense or budget problems were pending. Of course, there were always personal matters that may have claimed importance. It is clear, nonetheless, that the representatives were broadly composed of two groups who were divided in their opinions of legislative work. Those living near the coast were likely to serve regularly in the legislature,[13] and some of these men made themselves available for committee service. Those living farther from the coast regarded the House as a chamber of occasional and extraordinary appeal, rather than as an agency that was part of everyday life. In short, they looked to the House primarily for help. In any year one-fourth or less of the members performed committee tasks; this was especially true in the calmer years before the revolutionary struggle. Even in 1773 and 1774, however, few members did extensive committee work. An insight into work distribution can be seen in Table 1.

Since most business was done in ad hoc committees, the nonactive member was on hand to represent his township when a special issue was being discussed. Otherwise, he seems to have had little to do in the sessions and probably welcomed the opportunity to take care of his personal

---

[12]The range of ages in 1763 was 24 to 74, with the mean at 50.16 and the mode at 60. Only in 1764 were the ages somewhat older at 50.87 and 61, respectively. In contrast, in 1771 the range of ages was 29 to 82, with the mean at 53.52 and the mode at 47.

[13]Such terms as "near the coast" and "farther from the coast" might be defined as a day's ride from the seacoast—in short, about twenty miles.

TABLE 1

MEMBERSHIP AND HIGH PARTICIPATION IN THE HOUSE OF REPRESENTATIVES		
YEAR	MEMBERSHIP[14]	HIGH PARTICIPATION
1767	122	35
1768	128	42
1769	132	33
1770	124	37
1771	121	39
1772	135	40
1773	132	31
1774	143	36
1775	217	75

affairs. The most active people thus were not necessarily the most experienced members, the oldest in service, or the most influential. Experience for many had little to do with their service; more important was the willingness to serve or the location of the township. A significant number of the active members of each session had only one to five years' service, and most had ten years or less. The impression one gets of the membership is that it came and went, with a large turnover yearly, and that most business was conducted by representatives who volunteered for a session or two and did the daily chores.[15] They then withdrew from the activity. In the 1765 legislature 121 men took the oath to be members. Of that number thirty-eight were first- and second-year members, fifty-eight were in their first five years of service, and fifty-one had served longer than five years. In the final analysis, thirty-six members did most of the work; seventeen of these active people had served five or fewer years.

---

[14]High-participation members were those men who ranked roughly in committee assignments as doing 75 percent of the work. In 1767 the range of assignments was thus: Sheafe had 56 and Hobson had 13.

[15]Among the 37 high-participation people in 1770, only 3 served more than 10 terms—Joseph Gerrish, John Murray, and John Worthington. Thirteen were serving in their first or second term.

Obviously years of service and experience do not touch the meaning of participation in legislative business. Maybe leadership in the House should not be calculated simply by the number of committees on which a member sat. Perhaps a quality consideration should also be raised. Certainly some committees may have been more important than others, especially those that were primarily financial appropriation or defense committees, or involved holding the speakership. It is possible that presence in the House as a debater or voter had its advantages if the legislator was a Boston member. Perhaps, too, election could offer tangible rewards through bringing a representative's name and opinions to the attention of the governor and Council. For most members, it seems, an election brought appointments as justice of the peace, military commissions, and recognition in the county government in the form of a commission in the militia or a berth on the bench. Something more, then, was looked for than prominence on the floor of the House.

Other tangible benefits of service most certainly were associated with securing frontier land. "A fondness for Land jobbing," Thomas Hutchinson once observed, was a characteristic of many members.[16] The colony over its entire history had abundant frontier land, especially in the District of Maine, and representatives used their positions to form companies and exploit any grant. Then they organized townships, collected settlers, and provided defenses—frequently at the cost of the colony and to their own profit. Land companies like the Kennebeck Proprietors presented opportunities for speculation, investment, and employment, and few members could resist the advantages of joining in these ventures. At the same time as areas of Maine were divided into counties and townships, positions of honor and profit in the courts, in law enforcement, and in the registry of deeds and wills were made available.

The Kennebeck Proprietors, for example, was incorporated as a land company in 1752. A list of its major proprietors reads like a blue book of the Council and House of Representatives: certainly the great families of the day shared in the speculative profits.[17] These men included James and

---

[16]Thomas Hutchinson to Lord Hillsborough, 24 May 1770, Massachusetts Archives, 26:493-94. See William Cushing to John Cushing, 12 March 1766, Cushing Papers 1, Massachusetts Historical Society; *Boston Evening-Post*, 29 January 1750.

[17]See Gordon E. Kershaw, *The Kennebeck Proprietors, 1749-1775* (Portland, 1975) esp. 75, 79-92.

William Bowdoin, Thomas Hancock, Silvester Gardner, Jacob Wendell, and the Temples, John and Robert. They founded Frankfurt, Maine, in 1752, and through their contacts in Boston kept their hands on the town's development, building a sawmill and equipping a fort. Settlers for their project were recruited in Germany and England, and supplies from such Bostonians as James Pitts and Charles Apthorp, who were also proprietors, were sold to the settlers.[18]

So valuable did the land activities of the companies become that important people from other parts of Massachusetts shifted their residences to Maine to benefit from the developments. The companies in 1760 succeeded in getting two new counties created in Maine, with Frankfurt designated as the seat of Lincoln County and the court house contracted by a proprietor. Indeed, William (1732-1810) and Charles (1744-1810) Cushing, sons of Judge John Cushing (1695-1778) of Scituate, won such coveted places in the new bureaucracy that they were well along in their efforts to be numbered among the elite of Maine at the Revolution. Great fortunes may not have been made by the proprietors, who were often wealthy men already, but good money and livings for their relatives were created for those seeking opportunities.[19]

Neither Cushing entered legislative politics until the outbreak of revolution. But they depended upon their father, relatives, and friends to keep them remembered in high places. For others not so well favored, town politics was preferred to service elsewhere. They faced the reality, however, that most honors were gained by having connections with the legislature.[20] Hence service in the House of Representatives and Council, even though distasteful because of travel and absence from home, was a necessity if one wanted to live contented at home.

---

[18]Pitts was also a member of the Muscongus or Broadbay Proprietors. A partial listing of proprietors on 21 July 1766 revealed a fine cross-section of the Boston merchant community. Such proprietors were listed as James Bowdoin, John Jeffries, Andrew Oliver, Robert Treat Paine, and Nathaniel Appleton.

[19]The activities of William and Charles Cushing are well described by Shipton in *Sibley's Harvard Graduates*, 13:26-39, 563-69.

[20]William Cushing to John Cushing, 12 March 1766, Cushing Papers 1; Charles Cushing to William Cushing, 16 February 1772, Robert Treat Paine Papers, Massachusetts Historical Society.

In a society conscious of honors, election to the House could lead to an appointment as justice of the peace or the title of esquire. The resultant prestige usually spurred recognition in the town, and election as moderator of the annual and periodic meetings of the town usually followed—an honorific sign of personal importance. For those militarily inclined, Boston connections were influential with the governor, who could commission for the ranks above captain in the militia.[21] For the courts all major positions were filled by nominations of the governor, though the recommendations of Boston politicians were important. While the legislature was not the sole route to these honors, it was a proven road and a direct one. Sometimes the path was rocky, too, as the gossip of Thomas Cushing indicates: "You ask how your Representative conducts [himself]. Why truly it is a difficult time with him, he does not well know how to conduct [himself]. The G-V-N on one side and the People on the other press him pretty severely—I pity him, poor Man."[22]

Membership in the legislature seemed a means to many ends: in a family-conscious society like Massachusetts, it was the way for fathers and sons, nephews and cousins, in-laws of all degrees, and friends to gain recognition. Almost every town had its dynasties of families who served year after year in its offices as selectmen, moderators, surveyors, deacons, captains, and committeemen. Many families were not obvious as officeholders because they held only a position or two. But again, their prestige might appear in the seating arrangement at church, in the ownership of land, or in the education of their children. They might deign to serve a term or two in the House of Representatives, do duty on a county or provincial court bench, or accept appointment to the Council. The fathers of the town may not have been the office-holders, but instead the weighty citizens who joined in the debates, offered advice, or served on a committee.

Obscurity and prominence seemed to be handmaidens. Some families were ever present in public affairs, while others only volunteered in times of public distress or family need. They seemed to come out of nowhere to serve and then to retreat into obscurity when the need was satisfied. Others were visible by family name, so that sons followed fathers

---

[21]Governor Hutchinson gave Israel Williams blank commissions so that he could favor friends and relatives in his regiment. See Hutchinson to Williams, 22 February 1771, Israel Williams Papers 2, Massachusetts Historical Society.

[22]Thomas Cushing to John Cushing, 28 January 1766, Cushing Papers 1, Massachusetts Historical Society.

or sons-in-law followed fathers-in-law. Older members usually dropped out as the younger ones came of age. Such were the Minots of Concord, whose family will serve as the first example of life patterns for members of the House of Representatives and Council. The elder James Minot (1653-1735) was born in Dorchester to a merchant family. After taking degrees at Harvard College, the young man traveled to towns neighboring Boston as a preacher, settling finally in Concord in the 1680s. Marrying a local girl, Rebecca Wheeler, he also secured some modest property and was able to provide eventually for his wife and family of ten children. He became justice of the peace in the 1690s, a captain of the militia, and an occasional preacher and teacher. In 1700 and 1701 he was elected member of the House of Representatives when Jonathan Prescott tired of the yearly duty and spent the remaining years of a long life as a captain and physician. From time to time, until 1716, the town called upon Minot to be moderator of the annual meeting, but then his son James (1695-1759) became visible in town government along with another son, Timothy, a minister and teacher.[23]

James, Jr. served as selectman in 1727 while still in his thirties and town moderator in 1736 when he already was a commissioned major of the county regiment. Rapid advances brought him the rank of lieutenant colonel and election to the House of Representatives in 1737, 1738, and from 1741 to 1744. The color of his politics in 1741 earned from Governor Jonathan Belcher a rare veto of a member of the Council.[24] But in 1746 he won his first term in the Council and remained in that body as a supporter of the colonial governors until his death. When he became occupied in provincial politics in the 1740s and 1750s, Jonas, Samuel, and George Minot, his grandsons, represented family interests as did the Wheeler relatives who never rivaled the Minots in local honors but did enjoy some prestige.[25]

---

[23]James Minot was the son of the immigrant John (1626-1669) who spent all of his life in Dorchester. A modest genealogy traces the family into the nineteenth century; see Joseph Grafton, *A Genealogical Record of the Minot Family* (Boston, 1897).

[24]Minot was not alone in 1741 when Governor Belcher negatived him. Twelve nominees to the Council were likewise removed. The issue was the governor's opposition to the Land Bank. See William H. Whitmore, ed., *The Massachusetts Civil List. . .* (Baltimore, 1969) 65 (notes under year 1741).

[25]For a few years after James Minot's death, no member of the family served regularly as selectman or moderator, but in 1767 Jonas began his three years as selectman, and in 1779 George was first elected selectman and remained for a long period of service.

While both James Minots amassed only moderate wealth, apparently James, Sr. took advantage of his Harvard College education to make his way in the county village of Concord. His son built upon that prestige (though not with a Harvard degree) by being a justice of the peace and captain of the militia at an early age. The son's years in the House of Representatives undoubtedly advanced his military career and qualified him politically as a potential councilor. Possibly the wars of the 1740s and 1750s were the chief attraction for him in provincial politics because he maintained his home base in Concord throughout his life. Almost every annual meeting of the town chose the "Honourable" Minot to preside as moderator. [26]

Another family of considerable importance—but differing from the Minots—is the Dwights of Hatfield, Springfield, Western, Northampton, and Brookfield. They are related to the Puritan settlers of Dedham and to Captain Timothy Dwight (1629-1718), who served in the House of Representatives in 1692, 1693, and 1694. [27] Captain Dwight, the father of fourteen children and a prosperous farmer, sent his sons, Henry and Nathaniel, west in search of fortunes that he apparently sensed were possible from land grants. When son Henry Dwight (1676-1732) left his family home in Dedham to speculate in land, trade, and agriculture, Henry probably never dreamed that his blood in two generations would be mixed with the blood of most leading families of the upper Connecticut Valley and that he would die a very wealthy man. In 1702 he married Lydia Hawley and over the years had ten children. His many sons and daughters in time married well and had large families. Henry served in most local offices at Hatfield, was a militia captain, and judge of the county court. His townsmen elected him also for five terms as a representative. Land and politics were part of the same cloth for Henry, who managed to improve his position as a speculator by maintaining good relations in Boston.

His three sons, Joseph (1703-1765), Josiah (1715-1768), and Simeon (1720-1776) improved upon their father's estate. Joseph and Josiah

---

[26]In 1737 Minot served on no committees, but then was chosen to sit on two in 1738. He was undoubtedly busy with Land Bank politics and advancing his career as a military man who rose during these years from major to colonel. In 1742, 1743, and 1744 he was among the most active members of the legislature.

[27]The Dwight family has an excellent genealogy; see Benjamin W. Dwight, *The History of the Descendants of John Dwight of Dedham, Massachusetts*, 2 vols. (New York, 1874).

were sent to college, and both married Pynchon girls. Joseph served twelve terms in the House of Representatives and five terms in the Council. Over the years he established himself as a lawyer and as an expert on Western defense. In the Louisbourg mobilization of 1745 he improved upon his military position by being commissioned brigadier general, and his prominence in the war won him a county court appointment in 1753. Through many of these years he also served Brookfield as selectman and moderator and as justice of the peace.[28] His brother Josiah also served many years in the House of Representatives, but spent more of his time at home in Springfield where he was a merchant, landowner, and proprietor of an iron foundry. Josiah's years as selectman and moderator equalled those of his brother, as did his service in the county courts. Josiah, however, was deacon of the local church from 1743 to 1768 rather than a military man. Their brother Simeon devoted almost his entire life to farming in Western (now Warren) and only moved out of town affairs when the American Revolution upset the routines of life. For more than two decades he was elected town clerk, regularly chosen as selectman, and a few times voted moderator of the annual town meeting. In county affairs he rose to be appointed colonel of the militia and sheriff, and he accepted election three terms as representative, in 1772, 1774, and 1775. His good luck was also evident in his marriage to Sibyl Lyman in 1743. The couple had thirteen children.

Timothy's son, Nathaniel (1666-1711), speculated in land like his brother Henry, and made his home eventually in Northampton. His son, Timothy (1694-1771), followed in his footsteps as a land speculator and merchant. Like father and uncles, the son served the town well as a selectman and town clerk. He was both justice of the peace and quorum as well as the judge in the county courts. In the critical 1760s he served four terms in the House of Representatives and retreated apparently to Northampton when violence in Boston became unsettling.

Joseph's son and grandson, both named Timothy, carried on family tradition. The son (1726-1777) farmed in Northampton and had a store, but spent most of his time as justice of the peace and quorum, county judge, and town clerk. He was first elected in 1762 to four terms in the House of

---

[28]Shipton, *Sibley's Harvard Graduates*, 7:56-66; Chester Dewey, *History of the County of Berkshire* (Pittsfield MA, 1829) 234: "No man in the county, in civil life, was more esteemed [than Joseph Dwight]."

Representatives and was only moderately active. At his death he owned three thousand acres of land and much personal property. His son (1752-1817) served in the constitutional convention of 1779-1780 and in the 1780 House of Representatives. Most of his life, however, was given to Yale College, where he reigned as president for many years.

The Dwights were primarily land speculators, sometimes lawyers, office holders, military men, and preachers. They were unusually successful over the years in securing tract after tract of land, many of which were obtained due to their involvement in the legislature. They were equally sensitive about gaining high offices and controlled the distribution of commissions through their Boston connections. Needless to add, they were very wealthy and influential, especially in county affairs.

The striking behavior of the Dwights is revealed in their repeated but limited service in the legislature, while similar families on the coast had longer, more consistent service. Such families as the Olivers, Hutchinsons, Wendells, and Wattses expended themselves in provincial chores. Undoubtedly the difference between Joseph Dwight and Samuel Watts (1698-1770) is in the nature of what each was getting from the service.[29] Watts was first elected to the House of Representatives in 1739 and moved to the Council after the 1742 election. He was repeatedly elected until 1763. In his town of Chelsea, he was moderator of most annual meetings from 1739 until a year before his death, and acted as a selectman and treasurer for a few terms. For the county, he served as judge of the county court and a justice of the peace. His main interest, however, was as a landowner; perhaps one-third of modern Chelsea was owned by him. In addition, he had a store, inn, ferry, wharves, and warehouses. In his day he was known, some say notoriously, as a director of the famous Land Bank and thought to be interested in a colonywide coinage system based upon land. Like Joseph Dwight, he owned a few slaves who were probably used in the household and to drive the chaise. Unlike Dwight, Watts was constantly in Boston to look after his town's affairs and, most particularly, after his own financial interests.[30]

---

[29]A good genealogical note on the Watts family is in Mellen Chamberlain, A Documentary History of Chelsea, 2 vols. (Boston, 1908) 1:338-62.

[30]Ibid., 1:338-39. During the four sessions of the House in which Watts served (1739-1741), he was conspicuous for his membership on committees handling tax and economic issues. He ranked among the most active members. In 1741 he served on 46 committees.

A colleague of Watts on the Council was Jacob Wendell (1691-1761), who came to Boston as a young man, married Sara, the daughter of Dr. James Oliver, and had a family of twelve children. His sons also married well—Oliver into the Jackson-Quincy families and John Mico into the Brattle-Saltonstall families.[31] His Dutch relatives in Albany were lifelong business associates, and he developed in Boston an extensive mercantile operation that included wharves, warehouses, a manufacturing establishment, and wagons for transport. From 1734 to 1760 Wendell was a member of the Council, justice of the peace, and colonel of the Boston regiment. Elsewhere in the colony he had interests also as a landholder, land developer, and Indian trader.[32] As one of the very wealthy merchants of Boston, he opposed Watts's Land Bank and joined a rival group that put forward the Silver Bank. Jacob was succeeded by his sons Oliver and John Mico in the 1750s, and they added substantially to their father's business. Oliver served several times in the legislature during the revolutionary crisis and helped write the Massachusetts Constitution of 1779-1780. As a Harvard College graduate, lawyer, merchant, and businessman, he gave Boston the benefit of his wisdom as selectman and the state his support as legislator in both houses.

Unlike his father, Oliver Wendell was no legislator. His father served twenty-six years in the Council and was a visible supporter of hard money, sturdy defense, and massive land sales. Oliver spent little time in Boston government, though he was colonel of the regiment for eighteen years. The legislature, for Jacob, was the governing arm of the colony along with the governor and courts. For Oliver, business was most important, and Boston affairs occupied his spare time.[33]

Probably no family group had a greater part in the legislature than the Hutchinson-Oliver family. In any year of the pre-Revolution decades, there were Hutchinsons and Olivers almost everywhere in Suffolk county gov-

---

[31]Shipton, *Sibley's Harvard Graduates*, 12:218-19, 13:367-74.

[32]S. V. Talcott, *Genealogical Notes of New York and New England Families* (Baltimore, 1973) 385-86, 394.

[33]*Boston Town Records, 1770 through 1777: A Report of the Record Commissioners*, vol. 18 (Boston, 1887). See Whitmore, *The Massachusetts Civil List*, esp. 55 to 60.

ernment, in the courts, and in the legislature.[34] As young men out of Harvard College, Thomas Hutchinson (1711-1780) and Andrew Oliver (1706-1774) married the Sanford sisters of Rhode Island. While their fathers were members of the Council, Andrew's uncle was the governor and Thomas's uncle was a councilor and judge. Both had extensive and prosperous businesses; perhaps Thomas was more successful than Andrew because of his wide-ranging contacts in Massachusetts and Rhode Island, the West Indies and England. Yet Andrew also had impressive wharves and docks in Boston and the means to transport merchandise from the colony for his international trade. In the 1730s he and brother Peter (1713-1791), together with Thomas Hubbard, engaged successfully in the textile trade until Peter moved to Middleborough to establish an iron foundry.[35] The brothers, nonetheless, remained partners in politics with Thomas Hutchinson.

After being very successful in the family business, Thomas Hutchinson entered the House of Representatives in 1737 and served, except for 1739, 1741, and 1742, until he was elected to the Council in 1749. Over those nine years he ranked among the most active members of the House. Governor Shirley praised him as the prime mover of the administration.[36] Andrew Oliver joined his brother-in-law in 1743 and served until 1746 when he was elected to the Council. Those three years were busy ones for both men; they were among the half-dozen men who did the most work. Hutchinson spent his time on legislative issues, tax measures, defense, and manpower problems, while Oliver scattered his efforts to include a wide assortment of legislative issues. Like his brother-in-law, he too concentrated some effort on defense and manpower problems.

By way of comparison, Joseph Dwight of Northampton in those years served mainly on defense and manpower committees, Indian affairs, and land matters. His services were extensive, but he did not concentrate on any major type of activity. Dwight seemed to be available for service and

---

[34]See Shipton, *Sibley's Harvard Graduates*, 8:149-214, 7:383-412; John J. Waters and John A. Schutz, "Patterns of Massachusetts Colonial Politics. . . . Rivalry between the Otis and Hutchinson Families," *William and Mary Quarterly* 24 (October 1967): 543-67.

[35]*Peter Oliver's Origin & Progress of the American Rebellion*, ed. Douglass Adair and John A. Schutz (Stanford, 1967) pref.

[36]Nathaniel Sparhawk to Samuel Waldo, 8 March 1750, Massachusetts Archives, 13:117-19. See also my *William Shirley: King's Governor of Massachusetts* (Chapel Hill, 1961) 151.

gave freely of his time, while Hutchinson handled only certain types of governmental matters. This degree of concentration may be the difference between coast and county members.

When Hutchinson left the House of Representatives in 1748, he joined Oliver on the Council, where both served until 1776. Both were ousted that year as a result of the popular emotion against the Stamp Act. By that time Hutchinson was also lieutenant governor and Oliver was secretary of the colony. They had spent most of their careers supporting hard currency and measures to increase the cooperation between the British Isles and the colonies, with the result that in the 1770s, they were accused of being enemies of colonial rights. Hutchinson commented in 1762 on the situation that eventually unseated him in 1766: "We have violent parties in our little mock Parliament and sometimes the public interest gives way to private picques and prejudicies."[37]

Public service for both Hutchinson and Oliver was a matter of citizenship. Neither of them needed money or influence; they may have sacrificed fortune and peace of mind by serving the king. However, they feared that if they didn't serve, others of lesser worth would do so in their places. They contributed, too, to the welfare of the family in providing positions of honor and trust; and, of course, they stirred business in the form of new contracts. Their sons succeeded to their wealth, with Andrew (1731-1799) establishing a business in Salem as a result of his marriage with Mary Lynde, and Thomas III (1740-1780) taking over his father's business and marrying Andrew Oliver's daughter Sarah, who was his first cousin.

These prominent families who were visible in colonial affairs for nearly forty years contrast with obscure families whose service in the House was barely known. Such was the obscurity of the Folger family of Sherburne, Nantucket, that Abishai (1700-1778) was known only to a few people outside the legislature.[38] He served in every legislature from 1745 to 1765, except in 1753 when he was presumably ill. He married into the Mayhews and Starbucks, both good families, and had ten children. His presence each year in Boston was undoubtedly for business reasons, perhaps as a mer-

---

[37]Thomas Hutchinson to Richard Jackson, 15 November 1762, Massachusetts Archives, 25:28-29.

[38]See genealogical notice in Alexander Starbuck, *The History of Nantucket* (Rutland VT, 1969) 749.

chant or agent. His presence in the legislature was usually limited to service on a single, obscure committee, often one dealing with taxes and other matters of economic regulation.

The inactivity of Abishai Folger raises questions about his long tenure in the House, but his occasional service on committees reveals that he was there to look after tax matters. His activity was selective but limited, and of some value to the town. The Bancrofts of Reading, by comparison, served altogether more years in the House than Folger, but their inactivity is even more pronounced.[39] Thomas (1673-1731) was first elected in 1725 and served until 1731, getting reelected in 1727 and 1731 to partial terms when there were special elections. Over those years he served on only three committees. Thomas's younger brother, Samuel (1693-1772), and nephew, Samuel (1715-1782), were cordwainers who did their duty in Boston with little enthusiasm. The senior Bancroft served between 1740 and 1745; but unlike Thomas, during one of his terms he interested himself in defense matters. Otherwise, he was inactive. The younger Bancroft was first elected in 1769 and showed some interest in Indian affairs and defense in the years 1770-1774.

All of these Bancrofts had been selectmen of their towns and had served in other town positions. Samuel Sr. was a deacon of his church and a captain of the militia, while his son became justice of the peace in 1774 and provided service for years as captain of the militia. The fundamental question of motivation, however, is not answered conclusively by any information about their tenure in the House of Representatives.

Some legislators, it seems, were chosen because they were willing to go to Boston and the town could relieve itself of the legal obligation to have representation. Many had few stakes in their towns, and sometime after their duty in Boston, they would leave for New York, Rhode Island, or New Hampshire and disappear into the countryside where they presumably became farmers again. Such is the career of Harmon Briggs, who served in the 1777 legislature for Windsor and lived in the town until 1800, when he left for New York. Little is known about him except that he had qualified for the House of Representatives. Almost as elusive is Joseph Packard of Pelham, whose birth and death dates are unknown, but who served three

---

[39]John Kermott Allen, "Thomas Bancroft of Dedham and Reading, Mass., and Some of His Descendants," *The New England Historical and Genealogical Register* 94 (July 1940): 215-24; (October 1940): 311-21.

terms as a selectman and as a committeeman. His term in the constitutional convention of 1779-1780 apparently was an act of patriotism. In
Pelham he owned the inn and some land.

For most towns, the election of a representative raised questions of
cost and necessity. If life in the township was placid, then the town would
debate the need for sending anyone to Boston and pay a modest fine for
nonparticipation. To be sure, the availability of a candidate was a major
consideration in sending a representative.[40] An unresolved grievance might
be another motivation. Location of the township also had much to do with
the town's decision. The coastal areas were more likely to be interested in
questions of trade, defense, and British politics than in the problems of a
rural township. Otherwise the town paid its fine and let a year pass until
it asked the question: will we send a representative to Boston?

One may still ask why the legislature could be the center of great oratory and emotion when most affairs of day-to-day importance were settled in the towns. The location may be the explanation. Emotional issues,
transferred from selectmen to the representatives in Boston, were already
fanned by controversy before coming to the capital. The high visibility of
many of these issues made the legislators pay extraordinary attention to
their deliberations. Still, the House was a divided body, partly frontier and
partly coastal in sympathy, and therefore issues had different impacts on
the members. Partial attendance at debates as evidence of legislative conduct may not always correctly indicate the feeling of members; perhaps it
indicates instead where the impact was being felt.

The houses reacted as they did to issues because they were dominated
by local interests. Most local issues could be settled by them if the towns
permitted solutions to be found there. The preference was regularly a local
one for most towns, but the people were often divided to such a point that
only impartial mediators could be effectual. Many times the burden of tax-
ation affected more than one town, and the legislature, by the choice of
the towns, thus became the center of mediation. Such was the dispute over
a stamp tax in the 1750s that towns and legislature joined to argue soundly

---

[40]Often men were elected to the House and then requested the town to choose someone else, offering as an excuse family business, health, or some other private reason.

its need. Heeding the flood of petitions being sent to Boston, representatives in good number were there to show their attitude by voting.[41]

In those days of crisis, almost the whole membership of the houses was present in Boston. A call probably went out to the members, the excitement of a great issue was debated everywhere, and men of counties or regions gathered as groups to unify their positions. Governor Shirley hated these waves of emotion because the usual direction of the House of Representatives gave way to other men. During these tense days the House was not so deliberative as it was responsive; it became a popular vent for feelings and actions. Since there were few other ways to register emotion against a British governor, or the military forces, or the cutters of the royal timber, the floor of the House of Representatives was the place for protest. These extraordinary moments rarely occurred, except for the late 1760s and the early 1770s, but anxious times were experienced in nearly every decade when popular issues pressed themselves to Boston. The legislature for a time then threw off the ordinary role of processing petitions and passing the usual taxes and became briefly a center of political fire and excitement. These days, more than any others, gave the legislature its reputation as a fiery center of liberty.

I should add several concluding observations for the genealogist. To cite service as a representative for a townsman, one should indicate if the person actually served and was active; if his service was intended to obtain a special project for the town; and if he was in Boston looking out for family interests. Certainly all kinds of motivations were legitimate, but the service may reflect on the kind of man the representative was. Most of the representatives, except some who lived in the coastal towns, were actually in Boston on special missions, and election to the House could have public or private benefits of varying degrees of importance. To list years of service in the House of Representatives will likely not be informative without an explanation.

[41]Mack Thompson, "Massachusetts and New York Stamp Acts," *William and Mary Quarterly* 26 (April 1969): 253-58.

Chapter Ten

"BELOVID WIFE" AND "INVEIGLED AFFECTIONS": MARRIAGE PATTERNS IN EARLY ROWLEY, MASSACHUSETTS

Patricia Trainor O'Malley

In 1655 the Essex County (Massachusetts) Quarterly Court fined Jonathan Platts of Rowley for "inveigling the affections of Mr. Rogers' maid."[1] Platts's crime was to persuade Elizabeth Johnson, an orphan serving the home of the Reverend Ezekiel Rogers, to marry him. He had won her hand without the intercession of a parent, or a surrogate parent such as Mr. Rogers, and society in the form of the colonial court was aggrieved. Despite the court's intervention at the beginning, the Platts' marriage survived for a quarter of a century, ending only with Jonathan's death in 1680.

---

[1] *Records and Files of the Quarterly Courts of Essex County, Massachusetts* (Salem, 1921) 1:340.

In his will he directed a specific bequest to his "belovid wife."[2] Elizabeth did not remarry, though she was to live another forty-one years as a widow.

This specific case is unusual in the court records of that time, but it illustrates many of the challenges to traditional marriage patterns that are encountered in a study of colonial life. Recent studies of family patterns in colonial towns have made it clear that the new world of New England produced marked demographic changes from that of the old. Environment, food, and space had a direct impact on family size and length of life.

The shift from the structured, limiting, peasant world of Europe can be especially well noted in studying the data related to marriage in the colonial era. Evidence is accumulating that those aspects of marriage which imply "choice"—that is, the possibility of romance—appear with regularity in colonial records far in advance of similar records in Europe. Such evidence of choice has been defined as characteristic of "modern" marriage, as opposed to "traditional" marriage.[3]

Research on marriage offers an excellent use of genealogical sources. The many volumes devoted to listing the descendants of first settlers provide a cache of material that is easily mined and capable of uncomplicated transfer to the statistical graphs and tables used by social historians, demographers, and other students of life-styles.

Of the three major statistical sources used in studying the family—birth, death, and marriage records—the last is the most reliable because marriage was the most likely act to be recorded. Marriage, in Puritan New England, was a civil ceremony. There would be no church records in which to file a substitute record, as would happen with baptismal and burial records. And, unlike records for births and deaths, there were no mitigating circumstances such as distance or abnormal situations—infant death, death in battle, drowning at sea—that might prevent a record from being filed by the town clerk. Marriage, as an action of adults, and as a purely legal ceremony, always received a public recording. Also, should the couple have come from two different locations, there was the added possibility of duplicate recordings in the spouses' hometowns.

The study of marriage patterns in a colonial town, then, offers opportunities for exactitude and hypothesizing that are not as available in the study of family size and length of life. The records for the town of Row-

---

[2]*The Probate Records of Essex County, 1635-1681* (Salem, 1916) 3:390.

[3]Edward Shorter, *The Making of the Modern Family* (New York, 1977) 148 passim.

ley, Massachusetts, are particularly useful for conducting such a survey. The town was, and remained, small; thus the total numbers involved are easily managed. The town records are complete and available. In addition, an extensive genealogical study has been published that supplements the public local record with sources listed outside the town, such as county and province probate records and property records. The value of such complete resource tools to the researcher is the opportunity to study all children of a family, not just the males who carry on a family name.

Rowley, Massachusetts, was established in 1639. The original fifty-nine families were primarily Yorkshiremen under the leadership of the famed Puritan minister, Ezekiel Rogers. The site of the settlement was on the Atlantic coast between the earlier settlements of Ipswich and New-bury. The original center of the town, with meeting house and tightly clustered home sites, was a limited three-mile-wide strip of land squeezed in between the two older settlements. The tract given to Rowley extended eight miles westward, far beyond the limits of its immediate neighbors, permitting the town's central and western sections to "balloon" from three miles in length at its eastern end to more than eighteen miles in length as it filled in the space between its neighbor's western boundaries and the Merrimack River. Later pockets of settlement in the town tended to be in the far corners of this trapezoidal-shaped figure, rather than part of a con-tiguous growth from the original center. The size and shape of the town and its residents' movements from one section to another has a bearing on certain developments in this study.

What follows is a profile of marriage patterns among the first three generations to live in Rowley, including both those children who contin-ued to be residents in town as well as those who migrated. Also included were those newcomers who became part of the permanent population.

More than 700 families have been studied, a total of almost 4,000 individuals. Data acquired about each family were transferred to family-reconstitution forms. These forms are similar to traditional genealogical charts, but they also allow space for inclusion of such quantitative findings as length of marriage, length of widowhood, intervals between births, age at marriage, age at death, and other such information that can be com-puted manually or by machine.[4]

---

[4]A full explanation of the methodology and complete tables on Rowley demography in the seventeenth and early eighteenth centuries can be found in Patricia Trainor O'-Malley, "Rowley, Massachusetts, 1639-1730: Dissent, Division and Delimitation in a Co-lonial Town" (dissertation, Boston College, 1975).

Families were counted as residents when there was evidence of a marriage record and/or records of the births or deaths of their children, thus indicating some measurable stay in the community. Each family was placed into an appropriate generation by using the first settlers and any additional newcomers up to 1660 as the base, or first, generation. Their children and other newcomers to the town from 1661-1690 constitute the second generation. Children of the second generation and newcomers to town from 1691-1720 form the third generation. Some computations were also carried out on the children of the third-generation families, but no additional heads of families were researched beyond the 1720 cutoff date.

Questions were asked of each generation which could touch upon any aspect of marriage that required a public record, or that could be calculated from the public record: who married whom, when, at what age, and for how long? How did the marriage end, who was widowed, for how long? Did remarriage occur? What was the age differential between spouses? What was the length of time between marriage and the birth of the first child?

Comparisons were made among and within three generations of Rowley families. Because each form contains information on both parents and children, it was also possible to compare the experiences of parents—permanent residents of the town—with their children, only some of whom remained in Rowley to lead the next generation, while their siblings migrated to other areas. The data collected about this latter group make it possible to raise questions about the impact of local economic and social conditions on marriage ages and choices. In addition, comparisons between this group and their siblings who remained in Rowley provide a key to the question of "tradition or choice" in colonial marriages.

What was learned, after analyzing the 700 Rowley marriages of the seventeenth and early eighteenth centuries, can be summarized briefly. Marriage in colonial Rowley was an almost universal adult experience, first undertaken by men and women in their early to mid-twenties, with a ceremony in the winter months. Marriages lasted for many years, generally ended with the husband's death rather than the wife's, and only occasionally would occur two or more times in a person's life. Each of these conclusions is valid for each generation of Rowley families and there is no marked variation between generations.

Universality of Marriage

Question: who did marry among the Rowley residents? Answer: almost every child who reached adulthood. This conclusion was reached by considering every child in each of the first three generations who is known to have lived for at least twenty years, even though an exact birth date may not be available. The percentage of the group known to have been married—again, with or without an exact date of marriage—was computed. The findings indicate the high premium placed on the married state: ninety-one percent of the first-generation children, eighty-nine percent of the second-generation children, and eighty-seven percent of the third-generation offspring were married at least once. Only four percentage points separate the children of the first group from their grandchildren more than fifty years later.

What do we know of those who did not marry? The family-reconstitution forms show that they were young adults who died in their twenties and hence not a permanent single order within the society. There were twenty-seven young adults among the children of the first generation who did not marry. Of these, twenty-three were young men; fifteen of them had died before the age of thirty. Twelve men of the twenty-three were soldiers or mariners, and their average age at death was 27.6 years, or about the age when their contemporaries were marrying.[5] Three others among this generation were more than thirty when they died, but their ages are not easily determined. Only one man appears to qualify as a true old bachelor. Richard Hazen, ninth of the eleven children of Edward Hazen, died in Haverhill, Massachusetts, at the age of sixty-four, in 1733.

Only four of the first-generation daughters did not wed. Two were less than thirty years of age at death (twenty-three, twenty-seven), a third was forty-four, and the age of the fourth cannot be learned. The same disproportion between sons and daughters is repeated for the next two generations with one marked variation: the increasing number of older, married adults.

Twenty-nine second-generation male children did not marry and sixteen of them were less than thirty at their deaths. The average age at

---

[5] John Harriman, 25, died at Bloody Brook in 1675. William Browne, 39, and his brother Samuel, 35, died on the ill-fated expedition to Canada in 1690.

death for the entire group of bachelors was 32.9 years, but five sons of this generation were more than fifty at death, including two who died in their seventies.

Known ages at death are available for fifteen of the nineteen unwed females of the second generation. One-third of these were less than thirty at death, but six were more than fifty, including one spinster who survived to the venerable age of ninety. Some of these women were singled out for comment in the church record with labels such as "defective mine" and "cancer." The average age at death for all these nonmarried females—a figure that is skewed by the presence of the ninety year old—was 44.5 years.

We know the ages of twenty-six of the thirty-two unmarried sons of the third generation and, with six men dying unmarried beyond the age of fifty (including a ninety-one year old), the evidence attests to a growing single population. This is underscored by evidence that, of the twenty-nine unwed females of this generation, more than half (fifteen) lived to be more than fifty; indeed, eight of these were more than seventy years old at death. Though the average age at death for the men remained less than forty (38.7), that of the women soared to a high of 54.5 years. Clearly, by the middle of the eighteenth century, Rowley had a small but persistent group of single, older adults, probably without homes of their own, and dependent on others for their livelihood and board.

Two conclusions are quite clear: first, marriage was the accepted way of life for the overwhelming majority. Second, the increasing minority of single adults that appeared in the early eighteenth century raises questions related to both economic life and the role of parental authority in controlling their children's status.

Source of Spouses

With marriage being the clear destiny for the overwhelming portion of Rowley youth, where did they find their spouses? Marriage in a traditional society implies the existence of prior contacts between the families of the bridal couple or among friends of the couple. "Parental consent was required by law for a first marriage, and parental consent usually depended on the attainment of a satisfactory bargain with the parents of the other party, each side endeavoring to persuade the other to give a large portion to the young couple."[6]

---

[6]Edmund Morgan, *The Puritan Family* (New York, 1966) 57.

When both partners came from the same town, years of interrelationships and familiarity between the families existed and was buttressed by contacts in church, town, and field. The relationship may have been reinforced at an earlier time through the intermarriage of aunts, uncles, cousins, and older siblings of the couple. Such endogamous marriages may be expected and seem to increase in a small town or isolated community.

But residents of New England towns, even in as small a community as Rowley, were not tied completely to their new locales. Mobility was a constant fact of emigrant life. Extended families often split up upon arrival in America, settling in a number of different towns. Neighbors from Old and New England similarly moved apart to varying locations. Thus it was possible for every family to have social contacts that extended beyond their immediate locale to include those of relatives and friends in distant areas. This was certainly true of the Rowley families, and it created specific patterns in determining the choice of spouses for their children.

From the beginning of the settlement, the affections of Rowley residents were extended to outsiders. Though residential information on the first settlers is sparse, more than fifty percent of all first marriages from the 1660s on were with nonresidents of the town. For nine decades (the second and third generations and their children) the percentage of marriages in which both partners came from Rowley—an endogamous marriage—was a consistent thirty to forty percent, for an average of 34.8 percent over ninety years.[7] Essentially, marriages within Rowley by two Rowley inhabitants were the exception and not the rule.

The majority of exogamous marriages—those with at least one partner from outside the town—demonstrate a clear, repeated pattern: the preponderance of outsiders were men, husbands for Rowley women. Only for the last group, the children of the third generation, did the proportion shift with more wives than husbands coming from outside the town.[8]

Exogamous marriages resulted when a Rowley native found work in another town or moved there permanently. Other outside marriages stemmed from contacts with relatives in other towns. A move by a num-

---

[7]O'Malley, "Rowley, Massachusetts," 124.

[8]The evidence also shows that when a Rowley woman married a nonresident male, she moved from the town. Only in a small number of instances did such a marriage result in the couple's residing in Rowley. Ibid., 126.

TABLE 1

ORIGINS OF ROWLEY MARRIAGE PARTNERS				
GENERATION	NUMBER	BOTH FROM ROWLEY	ONE/BOTH OUTSIDERS	UNKNOWN
First	53	37.8%	36.4%	25.9%
Second	168	32.5%	61.5%	6.0%
Third	238	35.2%	62.1%	2.7%
Fourth	131	34.4%	56.5%	15.1%
Averages		34.98%	54.13%	12.43%

ber of Rowley families to a new area invariably was followed by a series of marriages between their new and former neighbors. Also, certain family names from neighboring towns are repeated over and again among those marrying into Rowley families, which indicates yet another pattern. The Doles and Thurstons of Newbury, the Hardys and Haseltines of Bradford, the Pingrys and Bradstreets of Ipswich provided innumerable matches in decade after decade.

That more women than men had to seek a spouse outside the town might indicate a lack of available men at home. That some men also chose their spouses from other areas may suggest that the problem was as much one of status for both men and women as it was of numbers.

Age at First Marriage

Rowley men, and their fathers before them, were generally married before their thirtieth birthday. Their wives, like their mothers, were wed before they were twenty-five. The plainness of this statement belies the overwhelming consistency of the facts. Excluding the parents of the first generation (about whom not enough information is known), at least seventy-five percent of all males with known marriage ages, in each generation studied, had married by their twenty-ninth birthday. And three of the six groups surveyed—the sons of the second generation, and the fathers and sons of the third generation—had close to ninety percent of under-thirty marriages.

These high rates of youthful marriages are reinforced by the average ages: a high of 27.7 years for the handful of settler-fathers to a low of 24.5 years for the sons of the third generation. The overall average marrying

TABLE 2

KNOWN AGES OF FATHERS AND SONS AT MARRIAGE				
GENERATION	NUMBER	% UNDER 25	% UNDER 30	AVERAGE AGE
First: Fathers	22	21.7%	56.7%	27.7
Sons	125	31.8%	74.8%	26.6
Second: Fathers	93	37.4%	79.4%	26.3
Sons	200	49.4%	88.0%	26.5
Third: Fathers	178	49.7%	89.2%	25.3
Sons	189	60.3%	90.3%	24.5
			Total Average	26.2

age for all men in Rowley in the colonial era is 26.2 years. The youngest in the fathers' group was nineteen; the oldest, Andrew Stickney, was forty-five. Among the children's group, Joseph Wheeler, of the third generation, wed at eighteen, while a number of Rowley sons, including Stickney and two of his brothers, waited until their forties to wed. Joseph Duty, at 49, claimed a prize as the oldest groom of all men—resident and emigrant—who were surveyed.

The decision to marry in the seventeenth and early eighteenth centuries depended on many factors, with economic opportunity carrying the major weight. Oldest sons might inherit a double share of their father's estate. Youngest sons might be given the family homestead in exchange for the care of an elderly parent. Lack of economic opportunity might delay marriage or encourage migration. Much depended on a father's status. Joseph and Maximilian, immigrant clothiers, had been men of status in the original settlement. Their sons were all married between twenty-one and twenty-six years of age. Thomas Wood, a carpenter, had six sons and all were married before their twenty-sixth birthdays. Conversely, the four sons of Thomas Tenney, a small farmer and original settler, married at or above the average for their peers at thirty-four, thirty-two, thirty-four, and twenty-seven years.

Some of the factors affecting age at marriage can be seen in the lives of the sons of pioneer William Stickney. Stickney's first two sons had married at twenty and twenty-eight respectively. But each of the next three males were aging men, past forty, at their weddings—one of the few instances over four generations studied where so many in one family were so much above the average age.

The first two Stickneys had married while their father was alive. The latter three wed fifteen to twenty-five years after his passing. The elder Stickney's will offers some explanation. The oldest lads had been taken care of, and the father was none too happy with the outcome.

> [A]s for my son Samuell stickney I haveing bene at certane Cost towar his settlein therfor I will and give unto him but ten pounds more out of my estate and that to his full portion and I will him to be satisfied there-with. As for my son Amos stickney he haveing at noe time bene any way beneficiall to my estat and I haveing procured him a trade and given him some part of estat toward his settleing I therefor will and give unto him but five pounds more out of my estat and that to be his full portion and I will him to be satisfied therewith.

The remaining six Stickney children were to divide the balance of the estate evenly with particular parcels of land specifically given to the males and movables to the females.

John, the third son, was to inherit the family homestead after his mother's death. She was still alive some fifteen years later, and John was still unmarried. The farm, and its approximately thirty acres of scattered fields, was valued at almost one hundred pounds. The fourth son, Andrew, was given the "Merrimack lands" at the western end of Rowley. These forty acres were valued at only twenty pounds, and were most likely not developed. The fifth son, Thomas, was given the "village lands" in Rowley's southwestern section. Seven-score acres of land were listed in the inventory for that parcel, but the valuation was only thirty-five pounds, again indicating undeveloped lands. The inequity of the allotments had been recognized by the elder Stickney, so each son was told to evaluate his inheritance and distribute to his brothers and sisters whatever was above his one-sixth share of the total estate.

> Unto my Son Thomas stickney I will and give my village land for his inheritance of my lands and if in its valuation it amounteth to more than his equall share with the rest of his brothers and sisters then it [is] to be made up unto him soe as they be equall as for my three daughters I will that they have ther portions out of my estat in moveables or if they fall short to be made up out of the overplus of ther three brothers land soe as that they may be made all equall alike and that they have ther por-tions payed unto them as they come of age or at marriage.[9]

---

[9]*Probate Records*, 2:6, 7.

Sister Mary, then twenty-eight and single, married two years later and received her portion. But sister Faith, twenty-three at her father's death, waited another ten years for her nuptials. Sister Mercy died at the age of twenty-seven, unwed, some eleven years after her father. Andrew, John, and Thomas were still not married when Mercy's portion was redistributed, and they would remain unmarried for a number of years to come.

Time does not say much about the personal appeal of the Stickney children and the part that their appearance might have played in their extended bachelorhoods, though cultural historians insist that physical attraction played small part in the choice of a spouse. Indeed, among contemporaries of the Stickneys who did marry were a woman described in court records as having a "crooked hunchback" and a man "dumb and deaf from birth." Yet the experiences of these three brothers and their sisters is at such variance with those of their neighbors that speculation cannot be resisted.

And what of the brides of the young Rowley grooms? The data for all three generations match the information for their husbands. Women who would mother new Rowley families were youthful when wed—far more so than their contemporaries in England and the Continent, yet without the extreme examples of very young brides that local lore insists upon maintaining.

More than seventy percent of the sixty-five second-generation brides were less than twenty-five at their weddings, and almost a third of them were less than twenty years of age. No bride in that group was more than thirty-five years old. The third-generation figures were even higher, with almost eighty percent under twenty-five at marriage. In neither generation were more than a few brides beyond age thirty; and only one bride in each generation was as young as fifteen.

The females followed suit with the males in this study. More than two-thirds of each generation's daughters were married by twenty-five, thus following the patterns set by their mothers. Yet one contrast between the sexes is noticeable and does influence another matter—the choice of partner. The percent of youthful grooms *increases* with each generation (fifty-seven, eighty-eight, and ninety percent). The same finding is so for their sons (seventy-five, eighty-eight, and ninety). Rowley brides, though consistently young, show a decreasing incidence of marrying before the age of twenty-five both for mothers (ninety, seventy-two, and seventy-six per-

TABLE 3

KNOWN AGES OF MOTHERS AND DAUGHTERS AT MARRIAGE				
GENERATION	NUMBER	% UNDER 25	% UNDER 30	AVERAGE AGE
First: Mothers	10	90.0%	100.0%	20.5
Daughters	102	77.5%	92.2%	22
Second: Mothers	65	72.3%	89.2%	22
Daughters	207	69.6%	84.5%	24.1
Third: Mothers	97	76.3%	93.8%	22.2
Daughters	219	68.4%	90.0%	23.5
			Total Average	22.4

cent), and for daughters (77.5, 69.6, and 68.4 percent). The impact on choice of partners is clear. The ratio of eligible males to females was increasingly in favor of the males. It was taking longer to find suitable mates for the girls of Rowley from the last quarter of the seventeenth century on into the eighteenth century.

Such characteristics as early marriage age and limited nonmarriage patterns often provide insight into parental influence over their children. Certainly economic dependence played a very significant role in determining marriage patterns, and in an agricultural society, which Rowley was, control of family land could be a decisive element in encouraging or discouraging marriage. The alternative was to leave the community, an option more and more young men appear to have taken.

A factor that might demonstrate the influence of parents is the marriage order of children. Seventeenth-century society could still show the influence of a European hierarchical ethos. Each child should have a place in the family and dominance belonged to the oldest. Children were expected to marry in chronological order in a traditional society.

A survey of Rowley marriages in families with at least two children of the same sex indicates that the majority adhered to tradition, though other signs of parental authority were waning. The children of the second generation, a group with a high emigration rate, showed a marked tendency to deviate from the norm with close to forty percent of males and females marrying out of order. First- and third-generation children averaged close to a seventy-five percent adherence rate in following the established norms, but the existence of even a twenty-five percent deviation from established form suggests strongly a softening of yet another tradition.

Duration

One of the most persistent myths about colonial life is the assumption that marriages were brief and remarriage frequent. Most casual observers would also add that it was the husband who most often played the role of the chief mourner, and not his wife. The number of Rowley marriages of less than ten years' duration that were terminated by death would seem to reinforce this belief. Almost one-fifth of all marriages during the first three generations lasted less than ten years (19, 17.1, and 18.6 percent).

But a complete analysis of all Rowley marriages demonstrates that lengthy marriages were by far the more normal occurrence. A lengthy marriage, in this study, is one that survives long enough for most of a couple's children to attain possible independence—that is, age twenty, or marriage. Over half of the marriages of first- and second-generation parents, with known marriage and death dates, lasted more than thirty years. Another twenty-two (out of forty-two) marriages with unknown dates were thought to be of such length based on the couples' stay in town. Here extended duration suggested marital stability.

The second generation, with more exact statistics, reveals an even higher percentage of long marriages. Forty-six of eighty-two marriages lasted more than thirty years (52.6 percent). The tenacity of these early marriages is underscored by the finding that 71.7 percent of first-generation couples and 67.1 percent of second-generation pairs were wed more than twenty years. Only in the third generation do the favorable averages diminish. Less than half of these early-eighteenth-century marriages survived for thirty years (45 percent), although a high 64.5 percent of the 118 marriages lasted at least two decades. This generation suffered far more than their parents and grandparents from such epidemic diseases as smallpox and diphtheria.

Each generation witnessed early marriages terminated by death, though there is no evidence of divorce. The frequency per generation is limited. Marriages lasting less than five years include five in the first generation, six in the second, and nine in the third (12, 7.3, and 7.6 percent). Very few of the young wives' deaths appear to have been related to

childbirth. From 1640 to 1730, only twenty women out of the many Rowley wives died soon enough after childbirth to even suggest that it was the
cause—an average of only 6.1 percent for all marriages.[10] What was far
more likely to bring a marriage to an early end was a husband's untimely
death from accident, illness, or military action.

Such brief marriages were more than offset by those of extraordinary
length, by any century's standards. A surprising number of them lasted fifty
years or longer—more than twenty percent of the second-generation marriages, for example. Jeremiah Ellsworth and his wife, Hannah, survived
sixty-seven years of wedlock (1712-1779), only to die within two days of
each other. They outlived all nine of their children. Edward and Jane Hazen reached their sixty-fourth anniversary (1684-1748). Their eight children had all grown to adulthood and the majority were still alive and
imitating their parents' longevity at the end of their parents' marriage.

Disease, deprivation, hardship, crop failure, Indian wars. All of this
was the lot of the colonial settler, yet time and again sturdy couples survived. To illustrate, William Acy and his wife Margaret were married in
England in 1620, a marriage that lasted more than fifty-five years. Thomas
Crosby and his bride, Jane Sothern, both born in the late sixteenth century, were married more than sixty years. They, too, outlived all of their
children. The Crosbys were in their sixties when they migrated to Rowley
to join the newly established settlement in the 1640s. Later couples would
face many hardships, but the Acys and Crosbys would also endure the
challenge of trans-Atlantic migration and settlement in a wilderness. If
only the vital records could tell us how they endured so long, or how well
they endured.

Remarriage

The other half of the diptych, which has traditionally portrayed colonial marriage, generally suggests a grieving widower—deprived by the
death of his young wife, left with young children to raise, and in search of
yet another wife, who will probably also die young and leave him with yet
more young children to raise. Accumulated data indicate that many men
were widowed early in their marriage, but the same data are clear that it

---

[10]O'Malley, "Rowley, Massachusetts," 230.

was far more likely that the wife was the grieving survivor, and she was in no rush to bind herself to a second husband.

Of 275 marriages studied, the male spouse survived in 116 of them, but the female did so in 38 more, or 154 instances. Almost seventy percent of the men remarried eventually, but only thirty-nine percent of the females did so. The great majority of second marriages were undertaken by men and women who had been married less than thirty years. With few exceptions, remarriage occurred most often when children under the age of fifteen were among the survivors of the deceased.

Not only were men more likely to remarry than women, they did so after a briefer interval of widowhood. With little variation from generation to generation, widowers acquired a second wife within twenty months of the death of the first. Widows, by contrast, were without mates an average of almost thirty-two months. The first two generations of widows survived about twenty-six months alone, but a high average of 42.4 months for the third generation draws the average up to more than thirty months.

Some second marriages for men may appear to have been undertaken with unseemly haste, until one notes the ages of the children left motherless. John Palmer of the first generation was left with a nine-month-old child at his wife's death; he had a second wife nine months later. His contemporaries, Thomas Tenney and Thomas Burpee, waited only five and ten months respectively to wed again. The former's youngest child was four; the latter's was a year old.

Those first-generation wives who remarried displayed similar situations. Nine of the ten widows who did remarry, and had previously been married less than twenty-five years, all had children under six years of age. The same parallels between men and women can be seen in the second-generation families. Three men whose wives appear to have died in childbirth were left to care for infants ranging from five days to a month in age. Francis Palmer remarried within eleven months; Samuel Pickard within a year; and his brother, John, father of the five-day-old baby and three other children, waited only eighteen months to wed again.

Joanna Bennett, married sixteen years, mother of eight children, was widowed when she was thirty-eight. Her ninth child was born one week after her husband's death. She remarried within ten months. Edna Lambert, also married for sixteen years, had borne six children. Three were still alive when, at the age of thirty-six, she delivered her seventh child. Three days later, her husband, Thomas, was dead at the age of forty. Edna's oldest child was only fourteen. Forty months later she separated Andrew Stickney from his long bachelorhood.

The pattern repeats for the third generation. An equal number of widows and widowers remarried (twenty-four). More than three-fourths of each group had children under the age of six (seventy-five percent of the men, ninety-two percent of the women). Yet the men remarried sooner than the women—19.4 months compared to 42.4 months. The men endured widowhoods that went from three months (Joseph Nelson) to sixty-one months (Jonathan Bailey); the women's widowhoods ranged from seven months (Sarah Prime) to eighty months (Rebecca Burpee).

Certainly a prime impetus toward remarriage must have been the great difficulty of raising a family alone in an agricultural milieu. The care of infants and young children, the tending of fields and livestock, the daily chores and handicrafts incumbent upon any preindustrial household placed heavy demands on parents. To carry such burdens without a spouse meant the necessity of hiring help, if family assistance were not available, or, conversely, of struggling on alone for many years.

With such powerful forces encouraging a second marriage, it is striking to discover how many of the widowed never did enter into a second union. For instance, there were how many women, for whom single parenting would seem particularly burdensome, who remained widows for spans of time up to twenty-plus years? For every two widows who remarried, three did not. Like their sisters, widowed after marriages of less than thirty years, they too all had children less than fifteen years of age. Yet this latter group chose not to remarry or did not have the opportunity to do so.

Six first-generation widows, all with children, were in this category. They would remain widows until their deaths, an average of 23.5 years later. Two of the widows should have been considered most desirable woman. Ann Reyner Hobson, daughter of one of Rowley's most prominent founders, Elder Humphrey Reyner, had been married only six years to early settler William Hobson. Her third child—all her children were males—was an infant when her husband died. As her father's only surviving child, she had inherited his sizeable estate. Combined with her husband's property, this estate made her one of the richest property owners in town. Her widowhood lasted thirty-four years. She outlived two of her sons. There are no indications of how many land-hungry men attempted to join her acres to theirs, but it takes little imagination to assume that they were not few in number.

Jane Lambert, wife of Francis, another well-placed first settler, was widowed after more than fifteen years of marriage. Her youngest child was only two years old. Jane, too, had a sizeable estate to inherit. In addition, she had the security of a wealthy, childless brother in town, Thomas Barker. He appears to have assisted in the rearing of her sons. She died, still a widow, eleven years after her husband.

Widows were also among the original land grantees of Rowley. Two of them were wealthy enough to be included among the proprietors of the town with special privileges in the use of the town commons. All of these widows had young families when they migrated from England; there was no child in the three families beyond the age of fifteen. Each widow lived to a great old age, deeding parts of her property to sons and sons-in-law at marriage, yet not one of these women ever remarried. Constance Crosby lived in Rowley as a widow for forty-one years, Jane Brocklebank for forty-eight years, and Jane Grant for fifty-six years, dying at ninety-four in 1696.

Few men chose the alternative of extended widowhood. Over three generations eighty widowers remarried; only thirty-six did not. Twenty-six of that latter group had been married more than thirty years. In the hundred years of Rowley marriages included in this study, only ten widowed men who had been married less than thirty years did not seek second wives. Six of them had children less than fifteen years of age.

By contrast, twenty-eight women who had been married less than thirty years remained permanent widows during that same hundred-year period. Twenty-five of the twenty-eight had young children at home when their husbands died.

The disparity between marriage patterns for men and women raises numerous questions. From this distance in time, only hypotheses can be offered. Possible explanations for the greater tendency to remarry may depend on psychological needs for companionship, economic demands for domestic help, or the demographic factor that there were more eligible women than men in the society.

A comparison of women who remarried with those who did not offers a possible answer for the contrast in their actions. Permanent widows, from marriages of less than thirty years, were an average of ten years older at their husbands' deaths than widows who remarried (44.2 years versus 34.9). Almost the same difference marked the ages of older widows. Those married more than thirty years, who wed a second time, averaged 58.6 years of age at their first husband's death compared to 67.9 years for those never remarrying. Perhaps younger widows were considered more desirable or more in need.

The age differential is consistent for both categories—those married less than and more than thirty years—through three generations. The older the widow, the more mature her children. Testamentary evidence suggests that husbands tended to will estates for life to young wives, while older wives were only given the use of quarters in their homes, which had since been inherited by a grown child. Francis Lambert, before his death in 1647, set the following will.

> I give unto my wife my house and land joyneinge thereunto with six acers of land lately bought of Joseph Juitt as alsoe all the meadowes and gates which doth belonge unto the sayd house all which I give unto hir dureing hir naturall life. Item: I give unto my eldest sonne all the aforesayd house and land with gates and meadowes after the death of Jane my wife.

In 1672 John Dresser, who had grown children, granted to his son Samuell half of his land, and

> also I will and give unto him my house, orchard barne and house lot excepting the west end of it: which I give unto my welbeloved wife dureing her natturall life and then to be his wholy.

Eight years later, when Jonathan Platts made out his will, his property went directly to his sons.

> First my will is that my tou sons John and Jonathan dou provid well fore my belovid wife and that they let hire want nothing that is needfull for hire self so long as she Remaneth my wedow and in petickler I give unto my wife the euse of the parler which is that end of my hous nexst the barne.[11]

For those who did not inherit such a dependent position as the Widow Platts, it was probably preferable to have hired help, or to rent out family lands—as John Brocklebank's young widow did—rather than yield their independent position, no matter how trying, to another husband's control. Finally, as longevity tables demonstrate, there were more women in

---

[11]*Probate Records*, 1:94; 3:262, 390.

the upper age brackets in Rowley than men.[12] Hence most men could re-marry, if they chose to do so. The same choice did not exist for women because the proportion of the sexes did not aid such action, regardless of the personal inclination of the woman.

This might particularly explain the contrast among the older widows between the few (eight) who remarried and the great many (sixty-six) who did not (an eight-to-one differential). Most of the widows were well into their sixties when they lost their husbands. What is extraordinary is not just that they lived singly after the event but that they endured in that state for great lengths of time.

Dorcas Pearson had been married for about fifty-seven years to miller John Pearson. The youngest of their eleven children was twenty-seven when John died. We don't know Dorcas's age, but she had to have been in her mid-to-late seventies at the time. She lived nine more years. More astonishing was the widowhood of Sarah Hidden. A widow at seventy-six after forty-eight years of marriage, Sarah survived another twenty-seven years to die at a venerable 103 years of age.

The opposite can also be found: widows who joined their husbands in death after the briefest of intervals. Hannah Pearson, seventy-two, died two months after her husband of fifty-one years. Twelve of her thirteen children were alive. Hannah Johnson Palmer, seventy-six, lasted just one week after her husband. They had been married for fifty-four years. Her sister-in-law, Frances Johnson, died five days after her spouse. He was seventy-nine, she was seventy-five. They wed fifty-six years previously.

When, as in the case of Jeremiah and Hannah Ellsworth, there were no living children, we must assume that the aged couple either cared for themselves or came under the responsibility of the town. The church record does note Hannah's death on 2 August 1731 with a personal comment: "Hannah Ellsworth, with a cancer."[13]

I should make one final note in this discussion of widowhood and re-marriage: there is a very clear connection between a widow's remarriage and the age at which her unmarried sons decide to marry. In each generation fatherless sons, whose mothers remarried before they were wed,

---

[12]O'Malley, "Rowley, Massachusetts," 218. Rowley wives had a 51.9 percent likelihood of attaining age seventy; their husbands a 45 percent chance.

[13]"Second Book of Records," First Church in Rowley, 1720-1775.

married at a younger age than those whose mothers remained widows. Significantly, the sons of the second and third generation who come under this heading married at a markedly younger age than either those with fathers who were alive or those with dead fathers and mothers who remained widowed.

Summary

The discussion above, of the impact of a father's death on a son's marriage age, recalls the preliminary theme, the significance of the Rowley marriage data. Do the findings suggest that the move from a traditional to a modern society was well underway in the colonial settlement during its earliest years?

Edward Shorter notes that two characteristics of a traditional society can be seen in the group's methods of choosing marriage partners. A true traditional society utilizes parental control as completely as possible with the result that most marriages occur within the community. Second, spouses are chosen without regard to age compatibility. Thus the appearance of older wife/younger husband marriages is more likely in a traditional than in a modern society. In a society where the couple has some say in the choice—that is, a romantic marriage—there is more apt to be a closeness of age and a sharing of interests that may not include those of the parents but rather those of their peers.

At first reading, Rowley marriages might appear to be traditional. Most marriages were not endogamous, suggesting the possibility of arranged marriages. But eighty percent of all such exogamous marriages— those with one outside spouse—involved a partner from one of Rowley's contiguous neighbors (Ipswich or Newbury), or from its two daughter communities, Bradford, carved from its western section, and Boxford, from

TABLE 4

	AGE DIFFERENTIAL / SOURCE OF SPOUSE					
	ENDOGAMOUS MARRIAGE			EXOGAMOUS MARRIAGE		
GENERATION	OLDER HUSBAND	YOUNGER HUSBAND	SAME AGE	OLDER HUSBAND	YOUNGER HUSBAND	SAME AGE
Second #	43	9	3	15	2	1
%	78.2%	16.4%	5.5%	82.3%	11.1%	5.6%
Third #	62	22	7	22	9	2
%	68.1%	17.9%	5.7%	26.8%	7.3%	1.6%

its southwestern portion. Not once in eight decades, from 1660 to 1730, does the percentage drop beneath seventy percent of outside spouses from these towns. And of the 336 nonresidents involved in Rowley marriages, a clear majority (61.3 percent) were from the established neighbors, Ipswich and Newbury.[14] Contacts with all of these four areas would have been regular, which strongly suggests that relationships could have been initiated between males and females without parental or other adult intervention.

As for the second characteristic—the age differential between spouses—the weakening of controls over choice is even more apparent. In this study the wife was older than the husband in less than sixteen percent of the marriages, and even then there was an eighty-seven-percent chance that the age differential was less than five years. This is not strong evidence of an arranged marriage. In the large proportion of marriages where the husband was the older spouse, forty-nine percent of the matches involved a male less than five years older than his wife, and in just five percent of the marriages was there more than a ten-year difference in ages.

As further evidence that the colonial experience tempered the traditional control mechanisms, it should be noted that even in those occasional marriages where the wife was older than the husband, seventy-one percent of them occurred between neighbors only one to four years apart in age.

Jonathan Platts may have run into trouble with the courts for arranging his own marriage, but the figures above suggest strongly that the youthful brides and grooms of colonial Rowley had "inveigled" their affections for each other with or without their parents' assistance. The sporadic signs of independent choice that marked the end of life for so many Rowley widows also appear to have made an appearance at the beginning of marriage.[15]

---

[14]O'Malley, "Rowley, Massachusetts," 128.

[15]Rowley did retain one very clear link with tradition: no marriage took place as a result of premarital pregnancy. Comparing the date of marriage with that of the birth of the first child reveals about two dozen infants born nine months after the parents' nuptials, eleven born in the eighth month (within range of full term), and only seven, over three generations of families, born less than eight months after marriage. And one of those, a child of minister Edward Payson, is clearly labeled "premature" in the town records.

Chapter Eleven

THE FERTILITY TRANSITION IN NEW ENGLAND: THE CASE OF HAMPTON, NEW HAMPSHIRE, 1655-1840*

Lawrence J. Kilbourne

One familiar characteristic of modernization is a shift from high to relatively low levels of fertility. Throughout most of Western Europe this transition occurred in the late nineteenth century. In the United States it apparently happened much earlier. Yasukici Yasuba's pioneering work in American demography demonstrated that the refined white birthrate in older areas of settlement was already quite low by 1800, while Coale and Zelnick confirmed that a downward trend in U.S. fertility had begun well before 1850.[1] But precisely when the decline began remains in doubt.

*This paper was written while I was a research assistant to Professor David H. Fischer of Brandeis, whose encouragement and advice I would like to acknowledge gratefully.

[1]Yasukici Yasuba, *Birth Rates of the White Population in the United States, 1800-1860* (Baltimore: Johns Hopkins University Press, 1962) 50-72; Ansley Coale and Melvin Zelnick, *New Estimates of Fertility and Population in the United States* (Princeton: Princeton University Press, 1963).

R. V. Wells, using techniques of family-reconstitution analysis, discovered a group of mid-Atlantic Quakers whose fertility fell sharply in the late eighteenth century and continued to fall thereafter.[2] Although Wells makes no claims that his Quakers were typical—rather, he suggests that they merely foreshadowed tendencies subsequently generalized throughout society—the possibility nevertheless arises that a shift toward reduced fertility may have occurred in many late colonial communities.[3]

Efforts to date the transition inevitably raise questions of method and motive. Most population historians credit changes in early-modern natality to variations in marriage age. Wells ascribes the diminished size of his Quaker families to intramarital fertility control. Discussions of motive usually associate reduced fertility with the emergence of an urban-industrial society. Such a society, so theory holds, lowers the economic value of children while creating consumption patterns that compete with them as sources of satisfaction. Since the consumption patterns and life-style of the urban middle class are affected first, this group is considered most likely to initiate efforts at birth control.

Despite its plausibility, the urban-industrial explanation of fertility decline has not lacked critics. Yasuba stressed the importance in America of population density and availability of farmland. More recently, Maris Vinovskis has attempted to move beyond urban-rural dichotomies, emphasizing instead the pervasive influence of an increasingly commercialized, market-oriented society.[4] Following Vinovskis's lead, Nancy Osterhud and John Fulton see the spread of family-limitation practices at Sturbridge, Massachusetts, during the early nineteenth century as the combined result of land pressure, which provided motivation, and a

---

[2]R. V. Wells, "Family Size and Fertility Control in Eighteenth-Century America: A Study of Quaker Families," *Population Studies* 25 (1971): 73-82.

[3]One recent study of a Massachusetts township found evidence of family limitation in the middle decades of the eighteenth century. A family-reconstitution analysis of Philadelphia's social elite, however, found no evidence of intramarital fertility control prior to 1825. See Edward Byers, "Fertility Transition in a New England Commercial Center: Nantucket, Massachusetts, 1680-1840," *Journal of Interdisciplinary History* 13 (Summer 1982): 17-40; Louise Kantrow, "Philadelphia Gentry: Fertility and Family Limitation among an American Aristocracy," *Population Studies* 34 (1980): 21-33.

[4]Maris Vinovskis, "A Multi-Variate Regression Analysis of Fertility Differentials among Massachusetts Townships and Regions in 1860," in *Historical Studies in Changing Fertility*, ed. Charles Tilly (Princeton: Princeton University Press, 1978) 225-57.

"commercial revolution," which fundamentally altered familial attitudes, inducing habits of rational planning and allocation.[5]

This essay deals with Hampton, New Hampshire, between the mid-seventeenth and mid-nineteenth centuries, and is an effort to shed further light on the origin and causes of fertility decline in early America. Although much work on Hampton's economic and social history is still undone, the rough outlines are known. Founded in 1638 on a sandy strip of the Atlantic coast, Hampton remained a predominantly agricultural community until well into the nineteenth century. The growth of Portsmouth, however, exerted a strong influence on all the towns in its hinterland, and by the mid-eighteenth century farming at Hampton had long been market-oriented. While the early industrialization of southern New Hampshire affected the town indirectly, Hampton itself never became an industrial center. Nonetheless, between 1815 and 1850 the town did undergo a modest commercial revolution. Due to its excellent beach, it became a popular summer resort—a development reflected in the increasing number of nonresidents paying property taxes, and in the establishment of several hotels such as the Eagle House, founded in 1820, and the Boar's Head, first opened in 1826. Further evidence of commercial expansion during these years is the construction of two new roads (one joining town and beach) and the completion in 1840 of a railroad linking the community to Boston.[6]

The genealogical section of Josiah Dow's *History of Hampton*, supplemented by local and family histories, furnished the data for this essay. Though the genealogy contained information on more than 1,200 families, only 281 completed unions that met Henri and Gautier's Type 1 criteria were selected for analysis.[7] These families were then divided into

---

[5]Nancy Osterhud and John Fulton, "Family Limitation and Age at Marriage: Fertility Decline in Sturbridge, Massachusetts, 1730-1840," *Population Studies* 30 (1976): 481-94.

[6]Our chief source for the social, economic, and political history of Hampton is Joseph Dow's *History of the Town of Hampton, New Hampshire*, vol. 2 (Salem MA, 1893).

[7]Ibid.; Type 1 families are those in which both the marriage date and end-union date as well as the wife's birth date are known. Completed unions are defined as those unions that lasted into the wife's forty-fifth year. For a fuller discussion of the techniques of family reconstitution, see Louis Henri's *Manuelle de Demographie Historique* (Geneve: Droz, 1967), or E. A. Wrigley, *An Introduction to Historical Demography* (London, 1966) 91-159. Type 1 families are discussed in the opening chapter of Louis Henri and E. Gautier's model study, *La Population de Crulai, Paroisse Normande* (Paris: Presse Universitaire de France, 1958).

seven marriage cohorts. Material on pre-1700 families was relatively scarce; therefore, those unions that I was able to reconstruct were combined into a single cohort covering the second half of the seventeenth century. The other cohorts range over periods of twenty to thirty years.

Since genealogical data is often regarded as suspect, a preliminary defense of my source is required. A random check of material found in Dow against vital records preserved by the town clerk at Hampton revealed an insignificant margin of error (between two and three percent). In addition, I examined surviving tax records both to determine Dow's comprehensiveness and as a test for economic bias. The percentage of households on tax lists for 1647, 1709, 1800, and 1820 omitted by Dow varied from a low of 1.4 (1647) to a high of 9.3 (1820) with an overall omission rate of 6.3 percent. Virtually all of these households belonged to the poorer half of the population. The genealogy is consequently biased somewhat in favor of more prosperous members of the community, but not sufficiently to distort seriously my statistics. In the absence of reliable colonial censuses, the proportion of indigent nontaxpayers left out of the genealogy cannot be estimated accurately. I must assume that at Hampton, as elsewhere in New England, extreme poverty was rare and that those indigents who may have been omitted were not numerous enough to jeopardize my conclusions. In any case, my checks indicate that Dow's level of comprehensiveness is remarkably high, comparable to the most complete vital records.

With these methodological problems put aside, I can now turn to the population trends that emerge from the data. The most notable feature of fertility in completed families is the decrease over time in the mean number of children born. Between the first and last cohort (Table 1), family size dropped by 3.4 births. Abrupt decreases occurred in the mid-eighteenth and early nineteenth centuries, dividing Hampton's demographic history into three distinct phases. An extremely high rate of reproduction characterized the first three cohorts—roughly eight children per union. A slight downward fluctuation occurred just after 1700, but rapid recovery ensued. Not until 1760 did a permanent decline commence. While still high, natality in cohorts married in the late eighteenth century was markedly lower than during preceding periods. In the final phase, covering 1800 to 1840, this falling trend descended to five children per marriage.

The mean number of births per union, therefore, was already in decline by the mid-eighteenth century. A steady increase in female marriage

age offers the simplest explanation for such a trend and, as Table 2 indicates, marriage age for women did go up. Between 1655 and 1840, mean age at first union rose by slightly more than three years. But assuming an average birth interval of 24 months, an increase of 3.02 years would result in a loss of only 1.5 births, less than half of the actual decrease. The increase in marriage of 1.58 years between the mid-seventeenth and mid-eighteenth century could have reduced family size by at most only one child, rather than the actual reduction of more than two. A more sophisticated test for the effects of changes in marriage age is to multiply the difference in decimal years by the 20-24 age-specific fertility rate of the cohort in question. Doing this, it is evident that changes in female marriage age accounted for sixty-three percent of the decline in births for women married during the first half of the nineteenth century; however, only a third of the decrease in family size between 1760 and 1799 stems from this source. A full explanation must consequently take into consideration changes in intramarital fertility.

Table 3 shows age-specific fertility—the best indicator of intramarital fertility—for each of our seven cohorts. A careful comparison reveals that 1760-1779 marks a boundary between a period of fluctuating but high fertility, and a period of falling fertility. A clearer picture emerges by combining the data into larger groupings (Table 4). Once again, Hampton's demographic history divides into three distinct phases. Marriages begun during the town's first hundred years were extremely fecund. In contrast to this initial phase, fertility in unions begun after 1800 was quite low. The late eighteenth century formed a transition. While rates, particularly in the later age groups, were lower than in the preceding era, they remained significantly higher than they would be during the first half of the nineteenth century.

These statistics link decreases in family size firmly to changes in marital fertility. They do not establish, prior to 1800, that deliberate practices designed to limit births caused these changes. Populations in which family-limitation practices are widespread usually have a convex fertility curve. This typical shape results from an abrupt decline in age-specific rates between the wife's late twenties and early thirties as couples, having produced a desired number of children, make efforts to avoid further pregnancies. When graphed, the rates for 1655-1759 form a concave curve, showing no sign of fertility control (Figure 1). The graph for the combined post-1800 cohorts has the convexity associated with contraception. But the graph for unions begun during the latter half of the eighteenth century is neither convex nor concave; rather, it descends smoothly from the high plateau of age groups twenty to twenty-nine.

When applied to the 1760-1799 cohorts, other standard tests to determine fertility control also prove negative or inconclusive. Fertility rates for women wedded before and after age twenty-five differed little; telltale jumps in the interval between penultimate and last births did not occur; and mothers at the birth of their last child were only one year younger at the close of the eighteenth century than they had been at the close of the seventeenth.

Of course, biological factors can also reduce a population's fertility. Unfortunately, current research renders this hypothesis an unlikely explanation for the eighteenth-century fertility decline in Hampton. Biologically induced lower fecundity results from a deterioration in nutrition, or from genetic damage caused by excessive intermarriage. Although data on early American nutrition remains rare, New England diets in the late colonial period seem to have improved. Starting around 1740, inventories left among the probate records of Middlesex County, Massachusetts, reveal a steady rise in both the quantity and quality of food.[8] As to the possibility of genetic debility, a study of endogamy patterns at Hampton, terminating with males born before 1720, concluded that husbands, in general, picked their spouses from a fairly broad cross-section of the geographic, economic, and social spectrums.[9]

Deliberate family limitation accounts best for the early decline in the town's fertility. The ambiguity in the 1760-1799 statistics probably reflects a lack of consensus regarding ideal family size. Table 5 gives a percentile distribution by cohort of births per union. The modal number of children born to women in the first three cohorts fell between eight and nine. After 1800 the mode pay is in the range of two to five as extremely large families became unusual. Typically, couples married in the late eighteenth century had from six to seven offspring. The next most common frequencies, however, were four to five births and eight to nine. The ag-

---

[8]Sally McMahon, " 'Provisions Laid up for the Family': Toward a History of Diet in New England, 1650-1850" (Brandeis University).

[9]James M. Gallman, "Small Words and Large Worlds: Barriers and Bonds in Colonial New Hampshire" (Brandeis University).

gregate effect of statistical measures that superimpose such diverse fertility behavior would be to obscure traces of a significant minority practicing birth control within a community whose fertility is still largely unregulated. Highs and lows would cancel each other out, and age-specific rates for the population as a whole would, when graphed, slope smoothly rather than turning convex.

The data, therefore, allows me to draw three conclusions with reasonable certainty: (1) Like Well's Quakers, the number of births per union at Hampton started to decline in the latter half of the eighteenth century; (2) while a rising marriage age played a role, changes in marital fertility were more important; (3) reduced fertility resulted from voluntary choice rather than biological debility.

Is it possible to determine which groups initiated fertility control? The small size of the samples on which family-reconstitution studies are based hinders attempts to measure the impact of economic variables. Nevertheless, by using what information is available on the economic status of a few of the families in Dow's genealogy, some light can be shed on this question. Taking the state tax for 1800, I divided all couples in which the wife was born between 1750 and 1774 into three groups and computed age-specific fertility rates for each (Table 6). The town's richest citizens had the highest reproductive rates; the poorest had the lowest. Low fertility among Hampton's less prosperous taxpayers is unsurprising and easily explained. Due to nutritional deficiencies the poor in early-modern communities usually had the lowest fecundity. Of more interest are the age-specific rates for couples in the middle range ($1.00 to $3.00). In these unions fertility fell precipitously after the wife's twenty-fifth year, precisely the expected pattern among couples practicing birth control.

A simple analysis of the demographic mechanisms by which fertility is lowered leaves aside larger issues of social causation. Obviously hypotheses stressing urbanization or industrialization do not fit conditions at Hampton. Though one of the smallest of Rockingham County's townships, Hampton commenced a long-term decline in its fertility a full half-century before New England experienced even the first stirrings of industrialization.

As it would at Sturbridge Village a few years later, land pressure provided Hamptonians with the strongest motivation for smaller families. On the whole, Hampton's demographic history conforms to what James Henretta has called the "morphology" of a New England town: there is a growth phase during which the earliest settlers, graced with an abundance of land, multiply prodigiously, followed by a period of contraction as the favorable land-people ratio reverses.[10] Probably Hampton first felt the pangs of population pressure quite early, perhaps just after 1700, but solved the problem through out-migration, sending its surplus inhabitants to settle the newly opened territories of inland New Hampshire. Local and family histories mention numerous offspring who in the middle decades of the eighteenth century pioneered homesteads in Maine and along the Merrimack and Connecticut valleys.

Yet unlike Sturbridge, the origins of the specific *mentalité* that persuaded Hampton's citizens to choose intramarital fertility control (as opposed to more traditional methods of reducing population pressure) cannot be traced to a concurrent commercial revolution. Chronic depression characterized the three decades extending from the mid-1760s to the mid-1790s. The struggle for independence and its aftermath disrupted trade, while monetary retrenchment in the 1780s created further hardship. Even wartime inflation, which stimulated so many sectors of the colonial economy, helped New Hampshire farmers very little since the cost of labor outstripped rising food prices.[11]

At Hampton, the evolution of a rationalistic, risk-calculating *mentalité,* which Osterhud and Fulton see as a psychological precondition for the spread of family-limitation practices, preceded the town's demographic crisis. By the early eighteenth century, Portsmouth had already woven Hampton, along with the other towns of its Piscataqua hinterland, into an aggressive, market-oriented, entrepreneurial economy. The economic adversities of the late eighteenth century acted as a catalyst, triggering a demographic response for which the requisite *mentalité* already existed.

---

[10]James Henretta, "The Morphology of New England Society in the Colonial Period," in *The Family in History,* ed. Theodore Rabb and Robert I. Rotberg (New York: Harper and Row, 1971) 171-78. See also Kenneth Lockridge, "Land, Population and the Evolution of New England Society, 1630-1790," *Past and Present* 39 (1968): 62-80.

[11]For the economic plight of New Hampshire during these years, see James H. Flannagan, *Trying Times: Economic Depression in New Hampshire* (dissertation, Georgetown University, 1972); Richard Francis Upton, *Revolutionary New Hampshire: An Account of the Social and Political Forces Underlying the Transition from Royal Province to American Commonwealth* (Hanover NH: Dartmouth College Publications, 1936).

Most likely, land scarcity also motivated the second sharp decrease in fertility that occurred after 1800. Here, however, other factors must be considered. Diversification of the local economy as Hampton began its slow transformation into a summer resort, combined with new consumption patterns and labor options created by the industrialization of nearby communities, may have lessened both the economic value and emotional satisfaction conferred by a numerous progeny. The many distinguished private schools founded in New Hampshire toward the turn of the nineteenth century—Hampton Academy among them—suggest that the "quality" of children had become important. Moderately prosperous couples, unable to afford both a higher standard of living and a large family, would be the first to feel the influence of these forces and to respond by attempting to avoid unwanted pregnancies.

Whatever the proximate causes behind the fertility transition, psychological changes are of greatest importance. In a wide-ranging theoretical article, R. V. Wells has argued that family planning rests on an assumption that life chances are subject to rational manipulation. The spread of birth control reflects a society's enhanced sense of mastery over its fate.[12] Doubtlessly the increasingly commercialized nature of the late colonial economy tended to induce the type of *mentalité* that Wells describes, but political upheaval also played a role. The collapse of colonial oligarchies and the spread of egalitarian ideas during the Revolution powerfully reinforced feelings of individual identity and personal autonomy. The data from Hampton suggest that in the closing decades of the eighteenth century many Americans seized control of their reproductive as well as their political destinies.[13]

---

[12]R. V. Wells, "Family History and Demographic Transition," *Journal of Social History* 9 (Fall 1975): 1-19.

[13]For an account of the evolution of politics and political ideas in late eighteenth-century New Hampshire, see Jere R. Daniel, *Experiment in Republicanism: New Hampshire Politics and the American Revolution, 1742-1794* (Cambridge: Harvard University Press, 1970).

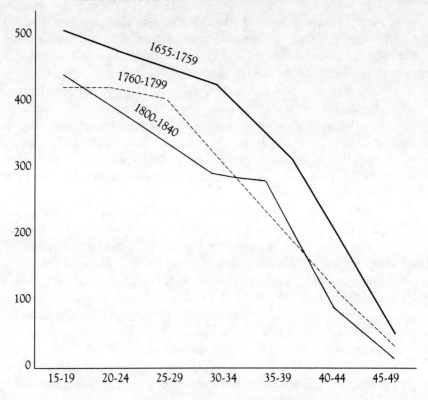

FIGURE 1

AGE-SPECIFIC FERTILITY RATES: COMPLETED UNIONS

TABLE 1

COMPLETED FAMILY SIZE: NUMBER OF RECORDED BIRTHS		
	MEAN	N
1655-1699	8.44	35
1700-1729	7.17	52
1730-1759	8.05	52
1760-1779	6.12	27
1780-1799	6.20	45
1800-1819	5.32	49
1820-1840	5.00	21

TABLE 2

MEAN AGE OF WOMEN AT FIRST UNION: COMPLETED FAMILIES ONLY		
	AGE	N
1655-1699	21.48	35
1700-1729	23.31	52
1730-1759	22.90	52
1760-1779	23.06	27
1780-1799	22.67	45
1800-1819	23.17	49
1820-1839	24.50	21

TABLE 3

AGE-SPECIFIC FERTILITY: COMPLETED UNIONS							
	15-19	20-24	25-29	30-34	35-39	40-44	45-49
1655-1699	514 (17.5)	435 (108)	438 (159.5)	394 (170)	265 (170)	224 (170)	052 (170)
1700-1729	364 (11)	443 (144.5)	424 (233)	393 (249.5)	300 (255.5)	138 (260)	028 (252.5)
1730-1759	500 (26.5)	478 (140)	424 (228.5)	402 (243.5)	341 (246.5)	182 (253.5)	036 (249.5)
1760-1779	600 (05.0)	417 (58)	381 (114)	344 (125)	201 (129.5)	123 (130)	024 (126.5)
1780-1799	407 (27.0)	436 (128.5)	356 (196.5)	274 (225.5)	220 (277.5)	153 (230)	013 (228)
1800-1819	496 (26.5)	415 (144.5)	307 (210)	251 (235)	208 (240)	071 (242.5)	004 (232)
1820-1839	500 (05.0)	415 (26.5)	387 (75)	268 (97)	276 (105)	076 (105)	001 (100.5)

TABLE 4

COMBINED AGE-SPECIFIC FERTILITY: COMPLETED UNIONS							
	15-19	20-24	25-29	30-34	35-39	40-44	45-49
1655-1759	484 (55)	456 (392.5)	420 (621)	384 (663.0)	313 (672.5)	175 (683.5)	036 (672)
1760-1799	437 (32)	434 (186.5)	364 (310.5)	299 (350.5)	213 (357)	142 (360)	017 (354.5)
1800-1839	444 (31.5)	415 (171)	333 (285)	256 (332)	229 (345)	079 (347.5)	006 (332.5)

TABLE 5

PERCENTILE DISTRIBUTION OF FAMILY SIZE BY COHORT: COMPLETED UNIONS ONLY						
	0-1	2-3	4-5	6-7	8-9	10-11	12 OR OVER
1655-1699	-----	3.64	3.64	22.39	28.64	25.51	16.14
1700-1729	5.56	7.41	12.96	24.07	29.63	14.81	5.56
1730-1759	1.92	1.92	15.39	17.31	38.46	17.31	7.69
1760-1799	-----	8.44	27.62	31.52	23.83	8.44	-----
1780-1799	6.67	15.56	20.00	26.67	17.78	6.67	6.67
1800-1819	6.12	28.57	16.33	18.37	18.37	12.25	-----
1820-1840	4.55	18.18	50.00	18.18	-----	4.55	4.55

TABLE 6

AGE-SPECIFIC FERTILITY RATES BY ECONOMIC STATUS OF WOMEN BORN 1750 TO 1774: BASED ON 1800 TAX LIST						
	20-24	25-29	30-34	35-39	40-44	45-49
$ 0–1.00	354 (14.5)	311 (22.5)	267 (30)	200 (30)	92 (32.5)	0-0 (35)
$ 1.00–2.99	463 (28.0)	333 (54.0)	267 (60)	217 (60)	167 (60)	17 (60)
OVER $ 3.00	596 (23.5)	400 (47.5)	355 (53.5)	244 (57.5)	183 (60)	17 (60)

Chapter Twelve

FORENAMES AND THE FAMILY IN NEW ENGLAND: AN EXERCISE IN HISTORICAL ONOMASTICS

David Hackett Fischer

Leah, Alpheus . . . 'tis good to impose such names. . . . A good name is as a thread tyed about the finger, to make us mindful of the errand we came into the world to do for our master.
> —seventeenth-century Puritan minister William Jenkin, who favored the name of Hannah for a daughter

Good Bye, Ruby Tuesday,
Who could hang a name on you,
When you change with every new day. . .
> —twentieth-century rock musician Mick Jagger, whose daughter was named Jade Jagger

Onomastics, the study of names, has long been a hobby of anti-quarians, genealogists, and literary men and women. Today it is also of interest to social scientists as well. A geographer argues that given names are the "ideal cultural metric . . . the most nearly ideal measure for analyzing spatial and temporal variation in total cultural systems." A sociologist has shown that the descent of names is important evidence of family structure. Anthropologists concern themselves with naming customs as clues to cultural values. Psychologists have discovered that names make a difference in how others regard us. A psychiatrist concludes from clinical practice that the "wrong" names are powerful "pathogens" that bring pain to those who bear them.[1]

For a historian of the family, a special opportunity lies at the intersection of those approaches. There is an epistemic problem about the family: scholars call it the silent institution, for its purposes are frequently unspoken, its rules are tacit, its inner workings are hidden from outsiders, and its ordinary occurrences commonly leave no traces behind. As a consequence, our knowledge of the family tends to be vague, uncertain, impressionistic. More than any other social institution, it lacks an exact and rigorous chronology, which is a major deficiency in historical knowledge; for not knowing when and where things happened, we cannot understand how and why.

It is precisely here that onomastics may help. "The naming of children is culturally never a trivial act," Daniel Scott Smith observes, in a seminal essay on the subject. As empirical indicators of family values and relationships, names have many things to tell us about the timing and direction of change in the structure of a "silent institution."[2] To that end, this essay examines naming practices among 1,000 families who lived in Concord, Massachusetts, from the seventeenth to the nineteenth century. It seeks to answer a set of descriptive questions: What names did parents choose for their children? Who did the choosing? What values and social purposes were embedded in their choices? In what manner and pro-

---

[1]Wilbur Zelinsky, "Cultural Variation in Personal Name Patterns in the Eastern United States," *Annals of the Association of American Geographers* 60 (1970): 743-69; Claude Lévi-Strauss, *The Savage Mind* (Chicago, 1966); Alice Rossi, "Naming Children in Middle-Class Families," *American Sociological Review* 30 (1965): 499-513; John W. McDavid and Herbert Harari, "Stereotyping of Names and Popularity in Grade School Children," *Child Development* 37 (1966): 453-59; William F. Murphy, "A Note on the Significance of Names," *Psychoanalytic Quarterly* 26 (1957): 91-106.

[2]Daniel Scott Smith, "Child-Naming Patterns and Family Structure Change: Hingham, Massachusetts, 1640-1880," unpublished paper prepared for the April, 1972, Clark University Conference on the Family and Social Structure. I am very much obliged to Professor Smith for allowing me to see this pathbreaking essay.

portion did names descend from one generation to another? How did all these things change during the past four centuries?[3] From the Concord data and other studies, it is possible to sketch the main lines of change in at least a preliminary way. In brief, the evidence suggests that the naming system was always dynamic. The existence of change itself was the only unchanging historical fact. But the pattern of change was not constant in its rhythm, direction, pace, or timing. At three particular points in time, there were revolutions that might be understood as moments of "deep change," when one change-regime yielded to another. All of those revolutions in the dynamics of naming practices probably reflected major transformations in the trend of family relationships. None of them, in New England at least, coincided with urbanization, industrialization, or immigration—the three great processes that have been used to organize our conceptual understanding of the history of the family in the modern world. It may be safely predicted that other empirical tests will show precisely the same result.

Revolution, 1580-1630

The first deep change came at the very beginning. The founders of New England introduced a distinctly Puritan naming pattern that differed radically from old English customs. Those differences may be observed in a comparison of given names at Roanoke (1587) and Plymouth (1620). In the first Virginia settlement, feminine names included *Agnes, Audrey, Emma, Elyoner, Margery,* and *Winifred*—a selection from the Saints' Calendar and traditional English favorites. Among Roanoke males, most of the common names were Teutonic—*William, Robert, Richard, Roger, Henry, George.*[4]

---

[3]The Concord data were drawn from a family-reconstitution project by a team of Brandeis undergraduates including Joanne Early, Marc Harris, James Kimenker, Susan Kurland, and Richard Weintraub under the supervision of the author. After they finished, the worksheets were passed on to Professor Robert Gross of Amherst College, who checked the results of their research, and extended it to genealogical materials. I am grateful to Professor Gross for generously sharing his findings with me. This small project would not have been possible without his help.

[4]Among the founders of those colonies, the most common forenames were the following:

Plymouth names, on the other hand, had a strong scriptural flavor. *John* and *Mary* were odds-on favorites, together with a profusion of obscure Old Testament choices. Pilgrim parents also made heavy use of grace names and hortatory names. The Brewster family named two of its sons *Love Brewster* and *Wrestling Brewster*, and two daughters *Patience* and *Fear*. Also among the *Mayflower* passengers were *Remember* Allerton, *Humility* Cooper, and *Desire* Minter. Later, in the larger Massachusetts Bay Colony, there were more bizarre inventions of the same sort, such as *Hate-evil* Nutter and *Faint-not* Wines. Hortatory names were used in non-Puritan colonies, but not so often nor in the same way. On a Virginia shiplist in 1623 we found *Fortune* Taylor; in Barbados, there was a Madame *Joye* Sparks.[5]

Other seventeenth-century naming fads had little to do with Puritanism, but much to do with New England. Shakespeare makes Pericles speak of "my gentle babe *Marina*, whom, for she was born at sea, I have named her so." In Anglo-America there was *Oceanus* Hopkins, born on board the *Mayflower*, along with *Seaborne* Egginton and the Puritan pun *Sea-mercy* Adams, and *Increase* Mather and *Peregrine* ("belonging to another country") White.[6]

ROANOKE, 1587		PLYMOUTH, 1620	
MALE	FEMALE	MALE	FEMALE
1. John	Jane	John	Mary
2. Thomas	Elizabeth	William	Elizabeth
3. William	Agnes	Edward	Sarah
4. Richard	Margery	Richard	Catherine
5. Henry	Audrey	Thomas	Anne
6. Robert	Joyce	Francis	Ellen
7. George	Alice	Joseph	Alice
8. Michael	Joan	Samuel	Demaris
9. Roger	Rose	Elias	Rose
10. Ambrose	Emma	Isaac	Dorothy
Hugh (tied)	Elyoner (tied)	Peter and	Priscilla
James (tied)	Margaret (tied)	twenty	and six
	Winifred (tied)	singles	singles

In Roanoke, 28% of names were biblical; in Plymouth, 64%. Compiled from ship lists in D. B. Quinn, ed., *The Roanoke Voyages, 1584-1590*, 2 vols. (London, 1955) 1:539-43; and William Bradford, *Of Plymouth Plantation*, ed. S. E. Morison (New York, 1952) 441-48.

[5]Charles Wareing Bardsley, *Curiosities of Puritan Nomenclature* (London, 1897) 69, 201-12.

[6]William Shakespeare, *Pericles*, 3.3.12-13.

In short, New England naming practices were extraordinarily diverse during the first generation of settlement. There are biblical names, often very obscure; hortatory names, sometimes very bizarre; grace names in great variety; and names to commemorate an occasion. At the same time, traditional English naming practices coexisted with these inventions. This diversity was created by a great naming revolution that took place generally throughout the English-speaking world during the late sixteenth and early seventeenth centuries.[7]

Involution, 1630-1770

By the mid-seventeenth century, New England naming practices settled into a pattern that persisted for the better part of two centuries. Old English favorites such as *Agnes, Catherine, William,* and *Robert* faded away, as did the more contrived hortatory names such as *Search-the-scriptures,* and the more bizarre grace names such as *Wrestling,* and occasional names such as *Peregrine.* For a very long period, New England parents drew their names from a single source. In Concord, to the mid-eighteenth century and beyond, ninety percent of forenames were biblical, a proportion that seems to have been normal throughout New England.[8] Few bible names failed to be used in some family or other. There is evidence that perplexed parents sometimes shut their eyes, opened the Good Book, and chose a word at random—with results such as *Notwithstanding* Griswold or *Maybe* Barnes, both in Connecticut. Other parents consciously cultivated a spirit of scriptural uniqueness. One unfortunate citizen of Newport, Rhode Island, was named *Mahershalalhashbaz,* the longest in the Bible.[9] But such eccentricities were rare. A remarkably small number of biblical names ac-

---

[7]The full sweep of this revolution, which began in Elizabethan England, lies beyond the scope of the present paper. An Anglican student of Puritan onomastics dates the "Hebrew invasion" of "Font names" from the year 1560, when the Geneva Bible was published in a compact quarto English-language edition. See Bardsley, *Puritan Nomenclature,* 38-108; and Lloyd E. Berry, ed., *The Geneva Bible: A Facsimile of the 1560 Edition* (Madison WI, 1969) 1-28.

[8]See n. 24; in Hingham, the proportion of biblical names was nearly the same. Smith, "Child-Naming Patterns," table 16.

[9]Still-longer compounds were created in New England, as by Samuel Pond, who in 1721 named a son *Mene Mene Tekel Upharsin Pond;* Donald Lines Jacobus, "Early New England Nomenclature," *New England Historic & Genealogical Register* 77 (1923):11-12. N. I. Bowditch, *Suffolk Surnames* (London, 1861) 5-27, 473-79. *Maher-shalal-hash-baz* was often used by English Puritans; see Bardsley, *Puritan Nomenclature,* 41 passim.

counted for the larger part of New England choices. In Massachusetts Bay Colony as a whole, fifty-three percent of all females were named either *Mary*, *Elizabeth*, or *Sarah*. The concentration of male names was almost as great. In Concord before 1710, one-third of all boys were called *John*, *Joseph*, or *Samuel*.[10]

Clearly, scriptural forenames were not selected at random. From a broad array of possibilities, Puritan parents made their choices with care. Biblical names common in other cultures were never used in New England. No Concord child was named *Jesus* (a strong Catholic favorite), or *Emmanuel* or *Christian* or even *Christopher*. A Puritan minister, Thomas Adams, expressed the common belief that "*Emmanuel* is too bold. The name is properly to Christ, and therefore not to be communicated to any Creature." Adams also thought it "not fit for Christian humility to call a man *Gabriel* or *Michael*, giving the names of angels to the sons of mortality." The archangels were common namesakes in Anglican Virginia, but Puritan parents carefully matched biblical names to their mortal condition within the great chain of being.[11]

In the same spirit, New England parents also chose names appropriate to their social rank. *Hezekiah* the great king of Judah and *Amos* the simple herdsman were both favored in New England—but not by the same families. On Connecticut muster rolls, *Hezekiah* appeared ten times as often for officers as for enlisted men. *Amos* was more common among the rank and file. Naming choices in early New England expressed an almost fatalistic acceptance of social status.[12]

By and large, though, New Englanders of all conditions did not choose their names primarily in terms of rank or power or wealth or even wisdom. The names of great patriarchs and lawgivers were rarely used. *Moses* was exceedingly uncommon. *Adam* was virtually unknown. Comparatively few children were named *Abraham* or *Solomon* or *David*. A striking omission

---

[10]George R. Stewart, *American Given Names: Their Origin and History in the Context of the English Language* (New York, 1979) 15; other names in the top ten were *Hannah*, *Abigail*, *Rebecca*, *Ruth*, *Lydia*, *Anne*, and *Martha*.

[11]Thomas Adams, *Meditations upon the Creed* (1629; reissued, London, 1872) 3:213.

[12]Stewart, *American Given Names*, 26. The status ascriptions of *Hezekiah* and *Amos* are particularly vivid in the Geneva Bible, 173 verso, 175 recto; 370-72.

from New England naming lists was *Paul,* despite the fact that New England Puritanism lay squarely within the Pauline tradition.

New England's favored names were chosen primarily for their associated moral qualities—for character, virtue, decency, integrity, and inner strength. The leading male namesake was *John,* the most Christlike of the apostles, the "disciple whom Jesus loved" for goodness of spirit. Other favorites were *Joseph,* whom the Puritans particularly respected for strength of character; *Samuel* the upright judge; *Josiah* the just ruler; *Benjamin* the beloved; honest *Jonathan;* and good old reliable *Nathan.*[13]

A similar pattern appeared in feminine names. The leading choice was *Mary,* humble and devoted, but also thoughtful, sensitive, and serious. Close behind was *Elizabeth,* wife of Zecharias and mother of John the Baptist. Third was *Sarah,* wife of Abraham, mother of Isaac, "mother of nations." Also popular was *Rebecca,* wife of Isaac, mother of two nations, who appears in the Bible with a pitcher upon her shoulder. And many a daughter of New England was named for *Ruth,* industrious and obedient, who gleaned the field and beat out her gleanings, and lay down her head at the foot of her husband Boaz.[14]

---

[13]In Concord, families married between 1691 and 1770. In each period the five names most frequently chosen for males were as follows. Underlined names were chosen equally.

	1st	2nd	3rd	4th	5th
1691-1700	John	Joseph	Samuel	Thomas	David
1701-1710	Joseph	John	Samuel	Timothy	Ephraim
1711-1720	John	Joseph	Thomas	Jonathan	Josiah
1721-1730	John	Samuel	Joseph	Thomas	Jonathan
1731-1740	John	Samuel	Joseph	Ephraim	Daniel
1741-1750	John	<u>Joseph</u>	Jonathan	<u>Nathan</u>	<u>Samuel</u>
1751-1760	John	Samuel	<u>Joseph</u>	<u>David</u>	<u>Reuben</u>
1761-1770	John	<u>Joseph</u>	<u>James</u>	Abel	Daniel

[14]For females, the most popular names were:

	1st	2nd	3rd	4th
1691-1700	Mary	Elizabeth	Sarah	Abigail
1701-1710	Mary	Elizabeth	Sarah	Abigail
1711-1720	Mary	<u>Elizabeth</u>	<u>Sarah</u>	Hannah
1721-1730	Mary	Elizabeth	Sarah	Hannah
1731-1740	Mary	Sarah	Elizabeth	Rebecca
1741-1750	Mary	Elizabeth	Sarah	Hannah
1751-1760	Mary	Elizabeth	Hannah	Sarah
1761-1770	Elizabeth	<u>Mary</u>	<u>Sarah</u>	Rebecca

The favored feminine namesakes of New England were all firmly an-
chored in a domestic role. But at the same time, they were also notable
for intellect, courage, spirit, and strength of character. The few female
prophets—*Anne, Hannah, Deborah,* and *Huldah*—were often honored in
New England. The Puritans were also partial to *Abigail,* who bravely de-
fended her husband against a monarch's wrath, and to *Rachel* who stood
for her husband and the right even against her own father. They did not
admire independence for its own sake. No Concord child was named *Eve,*
and comparatively few were called *Judith* or *Miriam.* Nevertheless, Puritan
parents chose their feminine models for a combination of intellect, character, strength, spirit, piety, and dutiful domesticity. The feminist movement has taught us to think disjunctively of those qualities; but in early
New England they were one.

In the naming system of New England, these scriptural criteria coexisted with a second set of purposes that were mainly a matter of family
identity. In eighty percent of Concord families, the forenames of both father and mother were given to at least one child, and most grandparents'
names were kept alive as well. A major goal was the maintenance of a
strong sense of family unity through as many generations as possible.
Scriptural names not rooted in a family's past tended not to be repeated,
and family names not sanctioned by Scripture also faded away. In early
New England those two sets of naming criteria were commonly combined.
When, for example, a daughter arrived in Samuel Sewall's household, a
friend suggested that Sewall should "call her *Sarah* and make a Madam of
her," for *Sarah* in Hebrew meant a woman of high rank. The father hesitated for a moment: "I was struggling whether to call her *Sarah* or *Mehit-
able,*" he wrote in his diary, "but when I saw *Sarah's* standing in the
scripture, viz: Peter, Galatians, Hebrews, Romans, I resolved on that side.
Also, Mother Sewall had a sister *Sarah.*"[15]

Sometimes the biblical criterion was uppermost, as for the son whom
Sewall named *Joseph,* "in hopes of the accomplishment of the Prophecy,
Ezek 37th and such like, and not out of respect to any relation except the
first *Joseph.*" In other decisions, family came first. When Sewall's last child
was born he noted, "I have named this little daughter *Judith,* in remem-

---

[15]Milton Halsey Thomas, ed., *The Diary of Samuel Sewall, 1674-1729,* 2 vols. (New
York, 1973) 1:324.

brance of her honoured and beloved Grandmother Mrs. *Judith* Hull." The same mix of motives appeared in other New England diaries.[16]

By and large, names appear to have been chosen by the father, without even consulting his wife. Other male friends were mentioned as being involved in the decision more than the mother. In Concord, paternal relatives were honored more often than those on the other side. By these nominal connections, families tied themselves more closely to the paternal line.

Once chosen, the survival of forenames was important to New England families—so much so that when a child died, its name was used again in a way that startles a modern observer. A case in point was the Concord family of Ephraim and Elizabeth Hartwell. After their marriage in 1732, five children arrived in swift succession, and they were given the biblical names of both parents and three grandparents. In the autumn of 1740, the "throat distemper" came to Concord, and Elizabeth and Ephraim Hartwell watched helplessly as all the children sickened and died in less than a month. But the parents survived, and nine more children were born, and every name was used again. Those children lived to adulthood, and the family forenames survived to reach another generation.[17]

---

[16]Ibid., 1:175, 460; the same pattern appears in *The Diary of Ebenezer Parkman, 1703-1782* (Worcester, 1974) 1:27, 35, 150. When Parkman's first son was born, he wrote, "God gave me a son, which I have set up for my Ebenezer, for hitherto the Lord hath helped me." Two years later, he had cause to write, "The salvation of God was seen, and my wife brought forth a second son, and upon consideration of God repeating his Blessing in this kind, as well as my having an ancestor of this name, I call'd him Thomas."

[17]Ephraim Hartwell (1707-1793), son of Samuel and Abigail (Stearns), married Elizabeth Heywood (1714-1808), daughter of Samuel and Elizabeth (Hubbard), on 7 November 1732. Their issue:

Ephraim	1733-1740	Oct. 9
Samuel	1735-1740	Oct. 11
John	1736-1740	Oct. 7
Elizabeth	1737-1740	Oct. 27
Isaac	1739-1740	Oct. 5
Elizabeth	1741-1823	
Samuel	1742-1829	
Abigail	1744-1809	
Ephraim	1746-1816	
John	1747-1820	
Mary	1749-1813	
Sarah	1750-1773	
Isaac	1752-1831	
Jonas	1754-1765	

The sad history of the Hartwell family was unusual only in the scale of its suffering. Most families lost at least one child, and when another was born of the same gender, the dead child's name was used again seventy to eighty percent of the time. The custom existed equally for boys and girls, no matter if they died in infancy or as old as fifteen. For 150 years, necronyms were a normal part of New England's naming system.[18]

From the early seventeenth century to the mid-eighteenth, that system was never static. As time passed, the descent of family forenames to the third generation became somewhat more common, while the use of parental names became a little less so. Necronyms increased as the death rate rose in New England. The proportion of scriptural names diminished, and the criteria for assigning them became more specific and precise. *Benoni,* for example, came to be reserved for boys whose mothers died in childbirth; *Ichabod* was assigned to posthumous sons. Some names became associated with a particular birth order; others reflected social rank. Individual towns and clans developed their own special refinements. Altogether, that complex pattern of change was a classical case of cultural involution. From 1640 to 1780, the system changed mainly by becoming more elaborately the same.[19]

Revolution, 1770-1820

In the late eighteenth century, a revolution occurred in New England's naming system. The first harbingers of that event appeared in the turbulent years before the American Revolution, but it happened mostly between 1780 and 1820. Within four decades one dynamic change-regime that had existed for 150 years yielded to another that would prove to be equally durable.

That pattern of deep change clearly appears in the naming customs of Concord families, which were simultaneously transformed in seven ways at once. First, as noted, before 1770 roughly eighty percent of Concord fathers and mothers gave their first names to their children. That practice was abandoned so rapidly that by 1810 the proportions were nearly reversed; between seventy to eighty percent of Concord parents did not pass

[18]See n. 19.

[19]Jacobus, "New England Nomenclature," 11-20.

on their forenames to the next generation. The trend weakened in 1811 and briefly ran in reverse, but its effect endured from the early nineteenth century to the late twentieth.[20]

Second, a similar tendency also appeared in the use of grandparents' names. Before the mid-eighteenth century, most of those names (52 percent) were used again. That custom was abandoned by Concord couples who married between 1750 and 1811. Thereafter, only twenty percent of grandparents' names survived to the third generation. That new pattern also proved permanent.[21]

---

[20]The descent of names from Concord parents to children occurrred in the following proportions:

	PROPORTION OF FAMILIES IN WHICH AT LEAST	
	ONE SON IS GIVEN	ONE DAUGHTER IS GIVEN
MARRIAGE COHORT	FATHER'S NAME	MOTHER'S NAME
1601-1700	73.3% (15)	86.7% (15)
1701-1710	84.2% (19)	75.2% (18)
1711-1720	85.7% (35)	80.0% (35)
1721-1730	77.7% (45)	76.2% (42)
1731-1740	81.3% (64)	83.3% (66)
1741-1750	70.6% (102)	87.3% (110)
1751-1760	80.2% (91)	65.9% (88)
1761-1770	68.6% (67)	63.3% (71)
1771-1780	73.8% (65)	61.8% (67)
1781-1790	66.2% (77)	56.9% (72)
1791-1800	48.6% (74)	34.8% (69)
1801-1810	49.1% (53)	43.4% (53)
1811-1820	14.7% (68)	10.4% (67)
1821-1830	26.1% (69)	18.5% (54)
1831-1840	53.1% (32)	32.4% (34)
1841-1850	30.3% (43)	21.1% (38)

These calculations include in column two only families in which at least one son was born, and in column three only families in which at least one daughter was born. There were few families with children of a single gender in the seventeenth and eighteenth centuries, but many in the nineteenth century, as family size fell rapidly. The inclusion of all families would, therefore, increase the magnitude of the transformation by diminishing the numbers for the nineteenth century.

[21]The descent of names from grandparents to grandchildren may be observed in the following table. Columns one through four give the proportion of cases in which each grandparent's name was passed on to the third generation. Column five is the mean of columns one through four, a general index of the persistence of names through three generations. Column six tests the relative influence of maternal and paternal grandparents. It

Third, Concord parents also stopped tying themselves more closely to the father's side of the family. The patrilineal pattern disappeared circa 1800; in the nineteenth century, the mother's parents were more often honored, and the mother's mother more than all other grandparents combined. Diaries and autobiographies suggest that the primary (but not the sole) responsibility for naming children passed from the father to the mother.[22]

Fourth, necronyms were rapidly abandoned in New England. The proportion of dead children's names being reused fell from eighty percent in families of the later eighteenth century to less than twenty percent in those of the early nineteenth. Once gone, necronyms never returned. When a child died, its individual identity remained alive in the collective

---

is a ratio in the form of FF + FM divided by MF + MM. The last column gives the number of families, which were restricted to those in which names of all grandparents were known, and in which both male and female children were born.

MARRIAGE COHORT	PERCENT OF NAMES DESCENDING FROM GRANDPARENTS FF	FM	MF	MM	MEAN	FF + FM / MF + MM	N
TO 1700	44.4	66.7	55.5	44.4	52.8	1.11	9
1701-1710	57.1	57.1	42.9	42.9	50.0	1.33	7
1711-1720	60.9	56.5	52.2	52.2	52.2	1.12	23
1721-1730	50.0	45.8	45.8	50.0	47.9	1.00	24
1731-1740	46.3	63.4	46.3	65.8	55.5	0.98	41
1741-1750	47.5	47.5	34.4	57.3	46.7	1.04	61
1751-1760	41.7	30.0	28.3	48.3	39.1	0.94	60
1761-1770	40.8	38.8	38.8	40.8	39.8	1.00	50
1771-1780	47.1	52.9	35.3	58.8	48.5	1.06	34
1781-1790	47.6	28.6	31.0	50.0	39.4	0.94	42
1791-1800	51.2	29.3	31.7	31.7	36.0	1.27	41
1801-1810	40.0	25.0	12.0	44.0	30.3	1.16	25
1811-1820	7.1	10.7	21.4	21.4	15.2	0.42	28
1821-1830	40.9	27.3	27.3	40.9	34.1	1.00	22
1831-1840	10.0	00.0	00.0	50.0	15.0	0.20	10
1841-1850	10.0	10.0	10.0	50.0	20.0	0.33	10

[22]See column 7 in n. 21.

memory of the family: its name was not used again.[23]

Fifth, the same generations also turned away from biblical names. In Concord families, the proportion of forenames drawn from Scripture fell from more than eighty percent in the marriage cohort 1751-1760 to less than forty percent after 1820.[24] For males, in the period 1770-1820, the

---

[23]The decline of necronyms appears in the following statistics for Concord families:

NECRONYMS AS A PERCENTAGE OF OPPORTUNITIES

MARRIAGE COHORT	MALE	FEMALE	TOTAL	MOVING AVERAGE
TO 1700	50.0% (2)	100.0% (3)	80.0% (5)	-----
1701-1710	100.0% (2)	100.0% (1)	100.0% (3)	83.5
1711-1720	80.0% (10)	57.1% (7)	70.6% (17)	74.3
1721-1730	42.9% (14)	66.7% (9)	52.2% (23)	64.2
1731-1740	68.1% (22)	72.7% (11)	69.7% (33)	64.6
1741-1750	76.0% (25)	68.0% (25)	72.0% (50)	70.6
1751-1760	75.0% (12)	66.7% (15)	70.0% (27)	72.0
1761-1770	69.2% (13)	78.6% (14)	74.1% (27)	74.7
1771-1780	80.0% (10)	80.0% (10)	80.0% (20)	73.2
1781-1790	50.0% (2)	63.6% (11)	65.5% (13)	60.2
1791-1800	23.1% (13)	57.1% (7)	35.0% (20)	39.3
1801-1810	18.1% (11)	16.6% (12)	17.4% (23)	28.6
1811-1820	27.3% (11)	42.8% (7)	33.3% (18)	30.2
1821-1830	35.7% (14)	50.0% (6)	40.0% (20)	26.7
1831-1840	00.0% (5)	10.0% (10)	6.7% (15)	19.3
1841-1850	14.0% (7)	00.0% (2)	11.1% (9)	-----

These numbers estimate the frequency of necronyms in proportion to "opportunities," which are defined as a death of a child followed by the birth of another child of the same sex. The quality of the data is not good. Many (perhaps most) infant deaths were unrecorded in the seventeenth century. Further, the small number of cases allows an instability in the result, from random fluctuations that may be damped down by a moving average. Nevertheless, the trend is clear.

[24]In Concord, the proportion of names drawn from the Bible changed as follows from the seventeenth to the nineteenth century:

MARRIAGE COHORT	PERCENT OF NAMES FROM THE BIBLE		
	MALE	FEMALE	TOTAL
TO 1700	91.2% (68)	90.6% (53)	90.9% (121)
1701-1710	90.2% (82)	91.7% (60)	90.8% (142)
1711-1720	84.9% (146)	85.4% (130)	85.1% (276)
1721-1730	89.7% (156)	81.1% (143)	85.6% (209)
1731-1740	92.0% (224)	82.9% (252)	87.2% (476)

old favorites *John, Joseph,* and *Samuel* gave way to a new set of nonbiblical choices such as *Charles, William, Frank, George, Henry, Frederick, Richard, Walter,* and *Albert.* By the marriage cohort 1841-1850, only one biblical names, *James,* remained among the top ten in Concord. Feminine choices changed in much the same manner, though not in the same degree. *Mary* preserved its popularity; *Sarah* and *Elizabeth* stayed in the top ten. But other scriptural names were replaced by nonbiblical choices such as *Ellen, Frances, Harriet, Caroline,* and *Charlotte.*[25]

1741-1750	87.1% (348)	80.8% (370)	83.8% (718)
1751-1760	88.0% (309)	79.6% (304)	83.8% (613)
1761-1770	88.0% (209)	75.7% (227)	81.6% (436)
1771-1780	80.7% (192)	74.7% (222)	77.5% (414)
1781-1790	78.4% (218)	72.6% (205)	75.6% (423)
1791-1800	71.0% (228)	60.1% (193)	66.0% (421)
1801-1810	62.9% (151)	59.5% (131)	61.3% (282)
1811-1820	41.9% (186)	47.5% (181)	44.6% (367)
1821-1830	33.5% (167)	51.9% (152)	42.3% (319)
1831-1840	37.5% (72)	39.2% (74)	38.3% (146)
1841-1850	34.9% (86)	45.9% (61)	39.4% (147)

Total population, 5,600. James Hastings, ed., *Dictionary of the Bible* (Edinburgh, 1936), was used to determine whether a name appears in the Bible. I am grateful to my colleague, Professor Nahum Sarna, for his advice in this matter.

[25]In Concord, families married between 1771 and 1850. In each period the five names most frequently chosen for males were as follows. Underlined names were chosen equally.

	FIRST	SECOND	THIRD	FOURTH	FIFTH
1771-1780	John	Samuel	William	Joseph	Isaac
1781-1790	John	James	Thomas	Samuel	Jonas
1791-1800	George	William	John	Nathan	Samuel
1801-1810	William	John	James	George	Samuel
1811-1820	Charles	George	William	John	Henry
1821-1830	Charles	George	John	William	Henry
1831-1840	Charles	William	James	Henry	John
1841-1850	Charles	William	Frank	George	James

For females, the most popular names were:

1771-1780	Mary	Sarah	Elizabeth	Lucy	Hannah
1781-1790	Mary	Elizabeth	Sarah	Lucy	Hannah
1791-1800	Mary	Sarah	Lucy	Elizabeth	Ann
1801-1810	Mary	Sarah	Elizabeth	Harriet	Eliza
1811-1820	Mary	Sarah	Lucy	Eliza	Louisa
1821-1830	Mary	Sarah	Martha	Caroline	Harriet
1831-1840	Mary	Ellen	Sarah	Lucy	Abby
1841-1850	Mary	Frances	Sarah	Martha	Anne

Sixth, naming practices became more eclectic. As in the English naming revolution of the late sixteenth and early seventeenth centuries, the range of choices expanded during the transformation, partly because parents drew both from the old and new naming systems, and partly because of a tendency for eccentric names to become more common. The top ten masculine names had accounted for nearly two-thirds of all choices in the seventeenth and early eighteenth centuries. By the marriage cohort 1711-1780, they were reduced to about one-third. A similar trend also appeared in female names, but it was slower and weaker in its development.[26]

Seventh, middle names suddenly made their appearance. Conservatives such as Theodore Dwight had warned darkly that the "spirit of democracy" would end in the "abolition of surnames."[27] But New England names grew longer rather than shorter. Before 1770 middle names had been so very rare that ninety percent of Concord children did not bear them.

---

[26]One simple measure of concentration is the percent of total names accounted for by the leading choices:

MARRIAGE COHORT	MALE NAMES			FEMALE NAMES		
	TOP NAME	TOP FIVE	TOP TEN	TOP NAME	TOP FIVE	TOP TEN
TO 1700	10.3%	42.6%	63.2%	28.3%	60.4%	79.3%
1701-1710	11.0%	37.8%	58.5%	23.3%	61.6%	78.3%
1711-1720	14.4%	35.6%	62.1%	13.8%	54.6%	77.7%
1721-1730	10.3%	30.8%	50.6%	16.1%	48.3%	70.6%
1731-1740	13.4%	34.8%	50.4%	16.7%	51.9%	71.0%
1741-1750	10.0%	26.5%	43.7%	14.9%	47.6%	69.2%
1751-1760	10.0%	29.6%	47.8%	13.8%	49.7%	73.4%
1761-1770	10.0%	29.7%	47.8%	12.3%	50.2%	67.8%
1771-1780	5.8%	23.4%	36.0%	13.1%	46.8%	71.7%
1781-1790	9.2%	26.6%	42.6%	14.6%	44.8%	64.3%
1791-1800	6.1%	27.2%	43.4%	15.5%	40.9%	59.6%
1801-1810	8.6%	30.4%	47.0%	17.5%	42.7%	62.5%
1811-1820	9.6%	42.5%	56.5%	14.9%	40.8%	58.1%
1821-1830	11.3%	42.5%	55.6%	17.8%	46.1%	64.5%
1831-1840	11.1%	43.1%	63.8%	14.9%	44.6%	63.5%
1841-1850	9.3%	32.6%	46.5%	19.7%	42.6%	55.7%

[27]Theodore Dwight, *Oration Delivered at Hartford* (Hartford, 1801).

By 1820 they had become normal and even universal.[28] The town's elite families were among the first to adopt the new custom, which they used to celebrate their kin connections with one another. The minister William Emerson named his daughters *Mary Moody* Emerson (b. 1770) and *Hannah Bliss* Emerson (b. 1774), both for grandmothers. In the next forty years, middle names spread so swiftly through the entire community that by 1820 eighty percent of all Concord children received them. Families of high status tended to give their children two surnames and one forename (e.g., *John Brooks* Wheeler). Families of lesser rank assigned two first names and one surname (e.g., *John Thomas* Smith). This distinction was often made for both boys and girls: for example, *Anne Mary* White. Once third names had become normal, a fourth and fifth sometimes followed. Boston's Dr. *Osee* Dutton, circa 1800, enthusiastically named one son *Sebastian Maria Ximenes Petruchio* Dutton and another *Thomas Albert Bonaparte Jefferson* Dutton.[29]

Within a remarkably short time, the naming system of Concord was radically transformed. A similar revolution has been found in Hingham

---

[28]Middle names appeared in Concord families with the following frequency.

CHILDREN OF MARRIAGE COHORT	PERCENT WITHOUT MIDDLE NAMES			PERCENT WITH MIDDLE NAMES		
	MALE	FEMALE	TOTAL	MALE	FEMALE	TOTAL
TO 1700	100.0%	100.0%	100.0%	0.0%	0.0%	0.0%
1701-1710	100.0%	100.0%	100.0%	0.0%	0.0%	0.0%
1711-1720	100.0%	100.0%	100.0%	0.0%	0.0%	0.0%
1721-1730	99.9%	100.0%	100.0%	0.1%	0.0%	0.0%
1731-1740	97.8%	99.6%	98.7%	2.2%	0.4%	1.3%
1741-1750	99.2%	99.8%	99.5%	0.8%	0.2%	0.5%
1751-1760	95.8%	99.4%	97.6%	4.2%	0.6%	2.4%
1761-1770	94.3%	98.7%	96.6%	5.7%	1.3%	3.4%
1771-1780	91.7%	94.2%	93.0%	8.3%	5.8%	7.0%
1781-1790	93.6%	88.3%	91.2%	6.4%	11.7%	8.8%
1791-1800	74.1%	69.1%	72.3%	25.9%	30.1%	27.7%
1801-1810	56.1%	42.0%	49.7%	43.9%	58.0%	50.3%
1811-1820	51.1%	32.6%	40.1%	48.9%	67.4%	59.9%
1821-1830	25.3%	21.1%	23.6%	74.7%	78.9%	76.4%
1831-1840	16.7%	17.6%	17.4%	83.3%	82.4%	82.6%
1841-1850	23.3%	16.4%	20.4%	76.7%	83.6%	79.6%

The size of each cohort is the same as that given in note 24, above.

[29]Jacobus, "Early New England Nomenclature," 13.

during the same period, and also among students enrolled at Harvard and Yale. It appears to have been general throughout New England.[30] Behind that change in naming practices is a strong current of secularization, and also of modernization in the special sense of a turning away from tradition. At the same time, there was a radical break in ideas of the family that those naming choices implied. It was not a loss of family consciousness, but the growth of a new ideal that was less patriarchal and more matrifocal, less hierarchical and more egalitarian, less holistic and more individuated. Middle names were particularly useful in all those various ways, as mediating devices that allowed a strong sense of family to coexist with an equally strong sense of individuality. The disappearance of necronyms was another important sign.[31]

Such a reading of the naming revolution in New England is consistent with interpretations drawn from other sources as to the direction of change. But it dates the transformation primarily within the period 1770-1820, and locates it in a small country town with a homogeneous population and an agrarian economy. It is evidence that the revolution in Concord occurred before urbanization, industrialization, or the new immigration. One of the few rules of historical causality is that if event B came before event A, it cannot have been caused by it. *Post hoc* is a fallacy; *pre hoc* is an absurdity. If the Concord evidence is generally representative (and other tests find it to be so), and if onomastic indicators accurately reflect changes in family relationships, then the urbanization-industrialization synthesis of family history must be rejected out of hand, and with it any tendency to conceptualize family history into periods that are primarily "preindustrial" and "postindustrial."

---

[30]For names at Yale and Harvard, see George Philip Krapp, *The English Language in America* (New York, 1925) 1:215-18; see also Smith, "Hingham," 15, where the timing is similar.

[31]It should be stressed that this chronology refers *only* to New England. Work in progress by Professor Allan Kulikoff of Bryn Mawr College finds a very different history in the Southern colonies; and in Europe, even greater differences existed. A third name became common in Florence during the fourteenth and fifteenth centuries; in the south of France during the sixteenth, and in the north of France during the seventeenth century. See Christiane Klapisch-Zuber, "Le Nom 'Refait': La transmission des prenoms a Florence (XIVe—XVIe siècles)," *L'Homme* 20 (1980): 77-104, n. 7. I am grateful to my colleague Professor Samuel Cohn for bringing this essay to my attention.

Involution, 1820-1950

From the early nineteenth century to the mid-twentieth, the naming system of New England, and of the United States as well, appears to have been remarkably stable in its complex dynamics. Throughout that long period, middle names grew more common and necronyms much less so. A study of the descent of names in American families from 1910 to 1960 found the same pattern that had appeared in Concord and Hingham from 1820 to 1900: trendless fluctuations within the same fixed range.[32] The proportion of biblical names remained roughly constant, and the whirl of fashion caused nonbiblical favorites to rotate like the colors of a kaleideo-scope—ever changing and yet always the same in their etymology and tex-ture. Once again, one finds a process of involution in which things changed mainly by becoming more elaborately the same.

That involutionary tendency also appeared in another aspect of the modern American naming system—in the fantastic ingenuity parents used to express a spirit of individuality in the names they gave their children. European visitors to America in the nineteenth and twentieth centuries never wearied of expressing a mixture of horror and amusement at the wild proliferation of American names. Americans in Europe, on the other hand, were equally appalled to discover that the naming of children was elabo-rately regulated by the state. In France a revolutionary decree restricted choices to forenames in the Saint's Calendar, and those of ancient he-roes.[33] Until the mid-twentieth century, French bureaucrats solemnly

---

[32]Alice Rossi's research in Chicago produced the following result:

	PERCENTAGE OF CHILDREN NAMED AFTER RELATIVES			
	MALE		FEMALE	
	FATHER	PATERNAL GRANDPARENTS	MOTHER	MATERNAL GRANDPARENTS
1900-1929	48	18	18	30
1930-1939	50	16	22	30
1940-1949	48	18	19	28
1950-1959	38	20	17	21

Rossi, "Naming Children in Middle Class Families," *American Sociological Review* 30 (1965): 511; cf. notes 20, 21, above; and Smith, "Hingham," 16. Direct comparisons between the Hingham and Chicago data are not possible because of differences in research design.

[33]Decree of 11 Germinal, Year 11.

compiled lists of authorized names, and children without them could not be legally registered. Similar state controls existed in Germany and other European nations. The unfettered freedom to name one's child in one's own way, which Americans take for granted, is not normal in the world.

The existence of that freedom allowed American parents to convert child-naming into an individualistic art form. However, Tocqueville's irony took full effect. The more free Americans became, the more they behaved in the same way. One example was the tendency of Americans in the nineteenth and twentieth centuries to invent names of extravagant femininity for their daughters. In Oklahoma City, during the 1940s, a woman named *Hoyette* White named her daughters *Hoyette, Norvetta, Yerdith, Arthetta, Marlynne,* and *Wilbarine* White. To an inquiring reporter, Mrs. White explained, "When my mother saw I looked so much like my father, she made a girl's name out of the family name Hoyt and called me *Hoyette*. That started the names. When I named my own girls, I wanted names no one had ever had and names that nobody would ever want. So I made them up."[34]

That custom was not created in the Oklahoma Bible Belt, as some onomasts seem to believe. In Concord, Massachusetts, during the early nineteenth century, many such names were invented. We find *Mirann, Marinda, Marsena, Elzina, Augusta, Elna Ann,* and *Alma America.* And in the Boston birth register before 1860, one finds *Adelia, Azalia, Delicia, Diantha, Izannah, Izora, Lowella, Luceba, Mahala, Malvina, Silvira, Syphronia, Zeda, Zoa*—and most extravagant of all, a Boston lady named *Aldebarontiphoscofornia,* after which even Cabot became an anticlimax.[35]

That curious custom established itself in Concord and Boston in the early nineteenth century, and during the twentieth century spread south and west to the outer rim of the Republic, where name collectors found *Aprienne, Bevelene, Chlorine, Dathel, Ezella, Freedis, Gala,* and the sisters *Ivaleen* and *Kartaleen.*[36] Curiously, there was a suffocating sameness in these inventions; a great blur of novelty created a sense of weary repetition. The

---

[34]Oklahoma City *Oklahoman,* 19 May 1947; as quoted in Thomas Pyles, "Bible Belt Onomastics; or, Some Curiosities of Antipedobaptist Nomenclature," in *Selected Essays on English Usage* (Gainesville, 1979) 152.

[35]Bowditch, *Suffolk Surnames,* 5-7.

[36]Pyles, "Onomastic Individualism in Oklahoma," in *Essays,* 144-49.

names were different, but their origins, rhythm, and texture were very much the same.

A second example was the tendency of American parents to invent names in matched sets that expressed a strong sense of individuated family consciousness. Many examples have been recorded in the twentieth century. In Concord the first stirrings of this custom occurred during the late eighteenth and early nineteenth centuries. A case in point was *William Wheeler* (married 1790), who had a particular attachment to the letter W. His sons were named *Wareham, William, Woodham, Warren, Willard, Winthrop,* and *Webster*. With a curious sense of sexual consistency, his daughters were given names beginning with the letter M—*Mehitabel, Mitty, Mary*[37]—which is the letter W lying on its back. In the twentieth century eccentric set-naming spread to the Southern and Western states. Aldous Huxley, a social observer without a sense of history, studied Southern California through his bifocals and imagined that he was observing something new. But its dynamics were already a century old.

A third expression of individuality in naming practices was the appalling American custom of playing onomastic pranks upon offspring. The most familiar example is, of course, the eminent Hogg family of Texas, with its daughters named *Ima* Hogg, *Ura* Hogg, and *Etta* Hogg. Again, that naming practice appeared in New England a century earlier. In Boston during the early Republic, a Mr. Robert New named his unlucky children *Something* New and *Nothing* New. A family called Ball christened its children *Cannon* Ball, *Pistol* Ball, and *Gun* Ball. New England city directories recorded as many of these monstrosities in the nineteenth century as do Texas telephone books in the twentieth.[38]

Still another tendency in nineteenth- and early-twentieth-century America was the conversion of last names of famous individuals into forenames. In seventeenth- and eighteenth-century New England, there had been a scattering of single instances, mostly of Protestant theologians such as *Calvin* and *Luther, Ames* and *Perkins, Bulkeley* and *Cotton*. In the late eighteenth century, the custom became more common. Many a Concord

---

[37]Wheeler's father was named Wareham Wheeler. The children were born between 1792 and 1812. As in the Oklahoma White family, the naming pattern was begun by the grandparents and extended by the second generation.

[38]Bowditch, *Suffolk Surnames,* 7.

family named a son *Emerson,* not after Ralph Waldo but after his grand-father William Emerson, a much larger figure in the town. After the American Revolution, the names *Franklin, Washington,* and *Otis* were often used. The party battles of the 1790s produced the names *Rufus King* and *John Jay* and *Harrison Gray Otis* in abundance. And the election of Jeffer-sonian Governor Gerry briefly made *Elbridge* one of the ten most-popular names in Concord between 1809 and 1813. That pattern continued through the nineteenth and early twentieth centuries. The two Northern heroes of the Civil War inspired many forenames in the manner of *Lincoln* Steffens and *Grant* Wood. During the twentieth century film stars became common namesakes, both for girls and boys.

Victorian parents also chose names for their children which ex-pressed a spirit of social striving that contrasted with the hierarchical at-titudes of the Puritans. Children were deliberately given names above their station, sometimes so much above that the effect was the reverse. In the Boston marriage register during the mid-nineteenth century, there was a Miss *Queen Victoria* Brown, and a carpenter was christened *Marquis Fay-ette* Josselyn. Other forenames included *Earl, Duke, Baron, Dean, Wealthy, Major,* and *Admiral.* Forenames and surnames that were associated with legitimately high status were more common. In the late 1790s Massachu-setts citizens also began to exchange their last names for new ones with more éclat. The classical example was a Jew named Kabotchnick who sent a thrill of horror through Brahmin Boston by trying (unsuccessfully) to change his name to Cabot. With this new attitude toward naming, Amer-icans in increasing numbers deliberately broke a tie to their parents and grandparents in order to advance themselves as individuals.[39]

One might multiply at length these expressions of individuality. Suf-fice it to say that few were common in New England before 1770; most appeared during the great transition of 1770-1820, and all persisted from the early nineteenth century to the mid-twentieth in a classical instance of involutionary change.[40]

---

[39]Ibid. For a chronology of name changes in New England, see Massachusetts, Sec-retary of the Commonwealth, *List of Persons Whose Names Have Been Changed in Massa-chusetts* (Boston, 1885).

[40]For a helpful conceptualization of varieties of individualism, see George Simmel, "Individual and Society," in *The Sociology of George Simmel,* trans. Kurt Wolff (Glencoe IL, 1950) 78-83. In New England names there are elements of both *einzigheit* and *einzelheit:* both the individualism of uniqueness and the individualism of singleness.

Revolution, 1950-1980

In our own time, onomasts agree that another great transformation is taking place in American naming practices. "Some kind of revolution has struck the name pattern," George Stewart wrote. "In all the lists the continuity of tradition seems to have been destroyed. New names have risen far upward and centuries' old leaders have fallen backward into obscurity."[41] During the 1960s and 1970s, many new names suddenly appeared. For girls, the new favorites are *Nicole, Melissa, Michelle, Jennifer, Jessica,* and *Erica;* for boys, *Jason, Brian, Anthony, Christopher, Michael,* and *David.* Many of these names were uncommon in America before the mid-twentieth century; some were unknown. At the same time, traditional names have acquired a sleek new look. *Catherine* is becoming *Kathryn; Deborah* is abridged to *Debra; Elizabeth* to *Lisa; Lavinia* to *Lee.*[42] Perennial

---

[41]Stewart, *American Given Names,* 42.

[42]The New York City Bureau of Health Statistics has made an occasional count of naming preferences with the following result.

	1898	1964	1973	1974	1976
1.	Mary	Lisa	Jennifer	Jennifer	Jennifer
2.	Catherine	Deborah	Michelle	Michelle	Jessica
3.	Margaret	Mary	Lisa	Christine	Nicole
4.	Annie	Susan	Elizabeth	Lisa	Michelle
5.	Rose	Maria	Christine	Maria	Melissa
6.	Marie	Elizabeth	Maria	Melissa	Maria
7.	Esther	Donna	Nicole	Nicole	Lisa
8.	Sarah	Barbara	Kimberly	Elizabeth	Elizabeth
9.	Frances	Patricia	Denise	Jessica	Danielle
10.	Ida	Anne	Amy	Erica	Christine

And Males:

	1898	1964	1973	1974	1976
1.	John	Michael	Michael	Michael	Michael
2.	William	John	David	John	David
3.	Charles	Robert	Christopher	Robert	John
4.	George	David	John	David	Christopher
5.	Joseph	Steven	Robert	Christopher	Joseph
6.	Edward	Anthony	James	Anthony	Anthony
7.	James	William	Joseph	Joseph	Robert
8.	Louis	Joseph	Anthony	Jason	Jason
9.	Francis	Thomas	Richard	James	James
10.	Samuel	Richard	Brian	Jose	Daniel

favorites from the Scriptures such as Mary and Sarah have faded away, as did Teutonic names such as *Charles, William,* and *Albert.* Plain *Tom, Dick,* and *Harry* rarely appear in the top five names today.

Hero-namesakes such as *Grant* and *Lincoln* also have disappeared in the past two decades. *Wilson, Roosevelt,* and *Truman* were the last of that long line. *Eisenhower,* as a forename, was perhaps more than the tradition could bear, and even loyal Republicans were understandably reluctant to inflict the name of *Nixon* on their sons. Hollywood names are also out of fashion. One observer, Robert Appel, comments that "the days of naming a baby after a movie star . . . seem to be over."[43]

Clearly, George Stewart's "some kind of revolution" is more than merely a matter of new names. It is a new naming process. We appear to be living through a third period of deep change in the dynamics of the naming system—a transformation as profound as those that began in Old England during the sixteenth century, and in New England during the eighteenth. Further, the transformation seems to exist throughout America. It has been observed in every region, from Massachusetts to California; in every social rank from the slums of Harlem to the eating clubs of Princeton; and among many ethnic groups.[44]

One important part of the revolution is a rise in the relative importance of forenames and nicknames. That trend was evident as early as the 1950s, perhaps earlier. A case in point was the speaker of the House of Representatives from 1940 to 1961, who insisted on being called Mr. Sam. "I was named *Sam,* not *Samuel,*" he solemnly lied to a journalist in 1955. "We don't believe in putting on airs in our family." In actual fact, he had been christened *Samuel Taliaferro* Rayburn and sent into the world with the usual onomastic equipment of an upper-middle-class Southerner, including in his case one of the more pretentious Tidewater middle names, which by its unimaginable pronunciation (Tolliver) served in still another

---

The 1898 birth cohort is very close to New England patterns that took form in the early nineteenth century. The new names of the 1960s and 1970s had been very rare before that decade. Of the 1976 list, only one female name (Elizabeth) had been common in earlier decades. Male names were not quite so radically transformed. These lists, it must be stressed, are from New York City and reflect the ethnic composition of that city, with Hispanic families accounting for the popularity of Maria and Jose.

[43]Quoted in Christopher Anderson, *The Name Game* (New York, 1977) 69.

[44]For a review of the evidence, see Stewart, *American Given Names,* 28, 42.

way to sort out the sheep from the Southern goats. That was how the world
was meant to be when *Samuel Taliaferro* Rayburn entered it in 1882. But
by 1955 it had changed so radically that the speaker felt compelled to revise his onomastic past and to become Mr. *Sam*.[45]

During the 1960s and 1970s, a predilection for first names and nicknames became almost compulsory in American politics. In 1977, a sign of
the times was a new president, James Earl Carter, who officially insisted
that suppliants should know him as *Jimmy*. In that act he converted an
informal custom into a new formalism, which was speedily adopted
throughout the Republic.

In these affectations, politicians reflected the prevailing mood of the
Republic. A poll of the Woodstock generation found many who assented
to a proposition that "last names were bullshit."[46] The 1970s generation,
which increasingly thought of itself as conservative and business-minded,
was busily conserving an onomastic attitude that was recent and radically
new. In Boston, telephone operators were instructed to answer callers by
giving their first names: "*Michelle*. May I help you?" The weatherman in
Suffolk County began by reporting his first name, and then the weather:
"This is *Jason*. The five p.m. temperature was. . ." At huge shopping malls
in Framingham and Burlington, hitherto anonymous clerks wore plastic
forenames on their uniforms, so that total strangers could greet them as
David or *Lisa*. And on a billboard near the place where the Puritans had
hanged their witches, travelers were enticed by an abundant young woman
who said, "I'm *Wanda*! Fly me!"

At the same time, forenames became more important to Americans
in still another way. During the 1960s and 1970s, writers rushed into print
with best-selling advice books. Some were addressed primarily to young
parents. Others sought a larger audience. Christopher Anderson's *The
Name Game*, for example, breathlessly informed its readers that "your name
can make you a winner or a loser. Your health, longevity, business and
personal success are determined by your name." The book summarized academic research on the right names and offered legal advice on how to be
rid of the wrong ones. Each forename was shown to possess in the popular

---

[45]Interview in the Jacksonville FL *Times Union*, 16 April 1955; quoted in Thomas
Pyles, *Essays*, 153.

[46]Rex Weiner and Deanne Stillman, *Woodstock Census* (New York, 1979) 238.

mind tacit connotations that indelibly attached themselves to the bearer. *Joseph* meant "earnest but dull" without regard to biblical associations. *William* was "kind not aggressive," and never mind 1066, 1688, or 1914. *John* was "trustworthy" but "passive." *Sarah* was "selfish"; *Mary*, merely "wholesome"; *Hannah*, "dull and unloved"; *Abigail*, "proper and staid." More highly recommended were *Kimberly* ("very, very popular!"), *Laura* ("sexy, mysterious, like the song"), *Linda* ("utterly feminine, extremely popular"), *Cynthia* ("aggressively sexy"), *Jacqueline* ("a bombshell . . . very popular"), and *Natalie* ("dynamic—tops in all categories"). For boys, *Jason* was recommended ("hugely popular"), *Craig* ("a winner—exceedingly masculine"), *Brian* ("a superstar, macho-dynamic"), and *Michael* ("very, very popular, extremely manly").[47]

To the uninitiated, the rules of the "name game" are more than a little mysterious. Why should *Anne* with an "e" be "beautiful but trustworthy," while *Ann* without an "e" is "honest but pretty"? How can *Bill* be "super macho" and *William* "not aggressive"? But never mind. The annual "top ten" lists and opinion surveys suggest that the onomastic attitudes of Mr. Anderson are not his stereotypes alone. The book is based on elaborate polls and the literature in learned journals, where social scientists give solemn warnings against "socially undesirable" names. In 1966, for example, two psychologists wrote that "a parent might appropriately think twice before naming his offspring for Great Aunt *Sophronia*,"[48] for their researches showed that children named *Sophronia* are apt to be unpopular among their peers.

In short, the evidence of the name books and the learned journals, in league with naming choices, strongly suggests that forenames are increasingly chosen today primarily for their probable effect upon intimate relationships. Will a given name make a child well liked by other children? Will it make a young adult attractive to the opposite sex? In the naming manuals the "right" names are called "sexy," "macho," "dynamite," "bombshell." The wrong names are "proper," "dull," "prim," "sedentary," and "unpopular." In place of the Puritans' concern for virtue and religion, and the Victorians' interest in individuality and status striving,

---

[47]Anderson, *The Name Game*, 147-72.

[48]John W. McDavid and Herbert Harari, "Stereotyping of Names and Popularity in Grade-School Children," *Child Development* 37 (1966): 454-59, 458.

one finds today a new set of naming criteria expressed in a language that not even Puritans and Victorians could have understood. It is a language of image-building, peer approval, sexual harmony, personal adjustment. These are the considerations that the naming handbooks urge upon us, and the evidence of survey-research shows that most young American parents share them.

In operation, the new naming system tends to be highly unstable. How can a parent know which name is "dynamite . . . hugely popular"? Much depends on the vagaries of popular taste, which change rapidly and without warning. Media and mass-culture events exert a major influence, more so today than in any previous period. The success of *Michelle* owed much to the Beatles' song of the same name. Another song by Donovan, together with a popular love story, created a vogue for an obscure variant of *Guinevere—Jennifer*—which suddenly became the most popular name in America during the early 1970s. The naming system had become so volatile in the mid- and late-twentieth century that an onomast could identify the age of many Americans merely from their forenames.

Implicit in this concern for "sexy," "popular," "dynamite" names is a new idea of the family, which appears as merely one of many relationships, and not the strongest or most important—certainly not as important as peer relations, or the intimate pairings of friends and lovers. Ethnic traditions, family connections, religious ideas, and class identities all have been subordinated to another set of considerations.

Conclusion

In the absence of a continuous time-series for the twentieth century, such as those earlier constructed for Concord, it is not possible to make strong statements about the timing and cause of social transformations in our time. Nevertheless, the main lines of change are clear in a descriptive way during the past four centuries: an alternate rhythm of revolution in which stable change-regimes were punctuated by periods of deep change. In the history of New England, there are three great naming systems: Puritan, Victorian, and another that is emerging today. In the Puritan system, the primary criteria for choosing names were religious and moral. The Victorians were more interested in individuality and social status. The naming system of our own time is oriented more toward peer acceptance and personality adjustment. We also find embedded in those systems three distinct ideas of the family. By comparison, the Puritan family was patriarchal, patrilineal, patrifocal, hierarchical, and holistic. The Victorian family was a strong and intimate connection of distinct individuals. In our time, the family appears to be increasingly understood as a voluntary association that is merely one of many evanescent relationships and not even the most important one.

Each of these great naming systems was dynamic in its nature. But their rhythms of change were not the same. The Puritan naming system was most stable, with the same small set of biblical favorites dominant for many decades. The Victorian system was characterized by a slow rotation of favorites from one generation to the next. In our time, new names abruptly rise and fall in popularity from one year to the next. Another set of contrasts appears in the locus of the naming system. New England names were probably very special in the seventeenth and eighteenth centuries, since it was a distinct onomastic region with its own cultural system. In the nineteenth century, the naming systems were larger and strongly ethnic in nature. Today one sees evidence of national and even international integration and stronger temporal variations. Many other inferences might be drawn from the data. Perhaps the most important is the timing of change in the first three centuries of American history. The leading conclusion is that deep change in naming practices and in implicit ideas of the family did not coincide with urbanization and industrialization. If that is so, then the synthesis that organizes family history into preindustrial and industrial stages must be discarded. Researchers must find another way of making sense of the subject.

Chapter Thirteen

"IN NOMINE AVI": CHILD-NAMING PATTERNS IN A CHESAPEAKE COUNTY, 1650-1750

Darrett B. Rutman
Anita H. Rutman

W hat's in a name? To Shakespeare's Juliet, nothing and every-thing at one and the same time. To James Joyce, a name evoked a child's quandary: "What's in a name? That is what we ask ourselves in childhood when we write the name that we are told is ours."[1] Yet names, specifically forenames, speak less of children and more of those who assign the names, and of the culture that delimits the pool of names from which they choose. It follows, therefore, that patterns found among forenames, having arisen in a particular culture, point back to the culture and reveal something about

---

[1]William Shakespeare, *The Tragedy of Romeo and Juliet*, 2.2; James Joyce, *Ulysses* (New York: Random House, 1946) 207.

it.[2] At the same time, analyses of naming patterns done for a number of cultures and at varying points in time can highlight differences and similarities, secular trends and, potentially, human constants.

Names as a clue to culture involve, moreover, a highly economic research strategy. The work is easily done, for all that is required are the names of parents and children, and knowledge of the vital events of their lives—which is the very stuff of genealogies. Still, there are rules to be followed: how many and how stringently applied will depend on the questions to be asked. The names obviously must represent the whole of a single, bounded culture or a carefully delimited part—an elite group, for example—with conclusions applied only to the part. Our interest for the past decade has been in the culture of the early Chesapeake, and our way has been to use a single Virginia county—Middlesex—as a mirror of the larger region. We have broken down the records of the county over a hundred-year period (1650 to 1750) and recompiled them on a name basis to create more than 12,000 "biographies" of Middlesex residents.[3]

The names alone, grouped by sex, race, and date of entry into or birth in the county, constitute our data. A simple frequency count established

---

[2]Daniel Scott Smith, "Child-Naming Patterns and Family Structure Change: Hingham, Massachusetts, 1640-1880," *The Newberry Papers in Family and Community History*, 76:5 (1977): 2-4, briefly reviews the theoretical basis for linking discernible naming patterns and culture. Smith's work proceeded from studies in anthropology, sociology, and geography, notably Claude Lévi-Strauss, *The Savage Mind* (Chicago, 1966); Alice S. Rossi, "Naming Children in Middle Class Families," *American Sociological Review* 30 (1965): 499-513; Wilbur Zelinski, "Cultural Variation in Personal Name Patterns in the Eastern United States," *Annals of the Association of American Geographers* 60 (1970): 743-69. Despite the fact that it has been available since first presented in 1972 at a Clark University Conference on the Family and Social Structure, Smith's study has not been systematically replicated by Americanists nor have any efforts been made to extend the analytic device or findings. Early American historians, for example, have been content to offer snippets couched in Smithian terms. Continental scholarship (but not British) is well advanced. Note that the entire issue of *L'Homme: Revue Française d'Anthropologiè* 20 (1980) is devoted to the subject of names.

[3]The construction and testing of the data base is described in Darrett B. Rutman and Anita H. Rutman, " 'More True and Perfect Lists': The Reconstruction of Censuses for Middlesex County, Virginia, 1668-1704," *Virginia Magazine of History and Biography* 88 (1980): 37-74. See also our " 'Now-Wives and Sons-in-Law': Parental Death in a Seventeenth-Century Virginia County," in *The Chesapeake in the Seventeenth Century: Essays on Anglo-American Society*, ed. Thad W. Tate and David L. Ammerman (Chapel Hill, 1979) 175-77. In what follows here, biographical information presented without specific citation has been drawn from our file of biographies.

the popularity of particular names, and also underlined the extremely small size of the pool from which white names were drawn. (We will have occasion later to consider black names.) Tables 1 and 2, for example, isolate the fifteen most-popular names among four particular groups of white males and females: those entering the county as immigrants in the seventeenth century, and those born in the county in three successive periods. Roughly eight of every ten men in a category and between eight and nine of every ten women bore one of the top fifteen, while between four and five of every ten men and women bore one of the top three: John, William, or Thomas among the males; Elizabeth, Mary, or Ann among the females. The lists compared to each other (the correlation coefficients entered on the tables) indicate the constancy of the overall pool. Names rose and fell in popularity; note the rise of Benjamin from a five-place tie for fifteenth among males born in Middlesex, 1650-1699, to fifth place among the children of 1720-1749. The pool overall did, however, remain largely unchanged. Comparisons between such lists drawn from other areas highlight cultural similarities and divergences. Our Middlesex-born pool originated with the seventeenth-century immigrants to the county, and the immigrant pool was essentially the English pool of the moment. But when the lists are compared to similar lists drawn from New England during the same period, the comparison fails. New England, rooted in the Bible, created its own unique pool. John, Thomas, Mary, and Elizabeth remained at or near the top, but for the rest it was a matter of Samuels, Josephs, Joshuas, of Hannahs, Rachels, and Jaels.[4]

To go beyond simply defining the pool of names—that is, to discover actual patterns in naming—more is required of the data. From the biographies we reconstituted families by linking women to their husbands and children, establishing the age of the mother at each cultural event (marriage, childbirth), and calculating the intervals between events. And from the set of reconstitutions, we selected those capable of bearing the weight

[4]See Leslie A. Dunkling, *First Names First* (New York, 1977) 76, for the English list; Daniel Scott Smith, "Child-Naming Practices as Cultural and Familial Indicators," forthcoming, for the New England list. We are grateful to Professor Smith for allowing us access to his count before publication. Rank-order correlations between Middlesex and the New England lists supplied by Smith are in the order of 0.01 to 0.25.

TABLE 1

WHITE MALE FORENAMES FOUND IN MIDDLESEX, 1650–1750

WHITE MALES IMMIGRATING INTO MIDDLESEX, 1650–1699			WHITE MALES BORN IN MIDDLESEX								
			1650–1699			1700–1719			1720–1749		
RANK	NAME	CUM %	RANK	NAME	CUM %	RANK	NAME	CUM %	RANK	NAME	CUM %
1	John	19.2	1	John	21.9	1	John	22.9	1	John	19.8
2	Thomas	33.0	2	William	37.2	2	William	38.5	2	William	36.6
3	William	44.7	3	Thomas	49.6	3	Thomas	48.4	3	Thomas	43.7
4	Richard	50.8	4	Richard	54.4	4	James	54.4	4	James	50.5
5	Robert	55.3	5	George	58.8	5	Robert	59.4	5	Benjamin	54.9
6	James	59.5	5	Robert	63.1	6	Henry	64.1	6	George	59.0
7	George	63.0	7	James	67.3	7	Richard	67.2	7	Robert	62.5
8	Edward	66.3	8	Henry	71.3	8	George	69.8	8	Henry	65.4
9	Henry	69.5	9	Charles	73.7	9	Joseph	72.1	9	Samuel	67.8
10	Samuel	71.2	10	Edward	75.3	10	Edward	74.2	10	Charles	70.1
11	Francis	72.5	10	Joseph	76.9	11	Charles	76.0	11	Joseph	72.0
12	Joseph	73.9	12	Peter	78.3	12	Benjamin	77.6	11	Richard	73.9
12	Peter	75.2	12	Samuel	79.3	13	Peter	79.1	13	Daniel	75.4
14	Charles	76.4	14	Francis	80.3	14	Christopher	80.4	13	Edward	76.3
15	Daniel	77.5	15	Benjamin	81.0	15	Daniel	81.3	15	Josiah	77.4
			15	Christopher	81.7	15	Samuel	82.3			
			15	Edmund	82.4						
			15	Nicholas	83.1						
			15	Philip	83.8						
			15	Ralph	84.5						
rho		0.86			0.93			0.90			0.79
r		n.a			0.98			0.98			0.97

Sources and notes: Names are drawn from the Middlesex biographies described in the text. The number of cases in the various categories are 1,883, 575, 616, and 839, respectively; total names in the pools, 127, 86, 92, 110. Duplicate rankings indicate ties. The correlation coefficients (Spearman's *rho* and Pearsonian *r*) are measures of the strength of the relationship between each column and the immediately preceding column, the first column (immigrants) being correlated with Leslie A. Dunkling, *First Names First* (New York, 1977) 76—a compilation of the fifteen most popular baptismal names from 200 English parishes in 1700. In computing *rho*, names appearing on one list and not another are counted as tying for sixteenth place on the latter. Data for computing *r*, the stronger of the two measures, were available only for Middlesex. All correlations are significant at better than 0.01 level.

of the more stringent analysis. Again, there were rules to follow. Because we need to know accurately the birth order of each child in order to define patterns, we could select only those reconstitutions that contained no intervals between births so large as to hint at a missing child. Additionally, we worked only with the reconstitutions of first marriages or marriages of

TABLE 2

WHITE FEMALE FORENAMES FOUND IN MIDDLESEX, 1650–1750											
WHITE FEMALES IMMIGRATING INTO MIDDLESEX, 1650–1699			WHITE FEMALES BORN IN MIDDLESEX								
			1650–1699			1700–1719			1720–1749		
RANK	NAME	CUM %	RANK	NAME	CUM %	RANK	NAME	CUM %	RANK	NAME	CUM %
1	Mary	20.1	1	Elizabeth	21.8	1	Mary	16.8	1	Elizabeth	16.5
2	Elizabeth	38.8	2	Mary	37.9	2	Elizabeth	32.3	2	Mary	31.7
3	Ann	52.7	3	Ann	49.8	3	Ann	45.9	3	Ann	45.2
4	Sarah	59.3	4	Sarah	58.6	4	Sarah	54.4	4	Sarah	54.8
5	Margaret	64.5	5	Catherine	64.1	5	Catherine	59.5	5	Jane	60.8
6	Jane	67.9	6	Margaret	68.4	6	Jane	64.3	6	Catherine	66.3
7	Catherine	70.6	7	Frances	72.3	7	Judith	67.9	7	Frances	70.1
8	Frances	73.1	8	Alice	75.0	8	Margaret	71.1	8	Susanna	73.4
9	Alice	75.0	8	Jane	77.7	9	Frances	74.2	9	Judith	76.5
9	Dorothy	76.9	8	Rebecca	80.4	10	Susanna	76.6	10	Margaret	79.0
9	Susanna	78.8	11	Eleanor	82.0	11	Agatha	78.2	11	Lucy	81.3
12	Joan	80.3	12	Lettice	83.4	12	Martha	79.6	12	Ruth	83.1
12	Martha	81.8	13	Hannah	84.6	13	Hannah	80.9	13	Agatha	84.5
14	Hannah	83.1	14	Agatha	85.5	13	Joanna	82.2	14	Avarilla	85.7
15	Rebecca	84.3	14	Judith	86.4	15	Avarilla	83.2	15	Hannah	86.8
			14	Martha	87.3	15	Diana	84.3	15	Rachel	87.8
			14	Mical	88.2						
			14	Winifred	89.1						
rho		0.73			0.70			0.58			0.84
r		n.a			0.96			0.94			0.98

Sources and notes: See the preceding table. The number of cases in the categories are 676, 560, 555, and 756, respectively; total names in the pools, 66, 50, 62, and 58.

individuals whose prior marriages were demonstrably barren.[5] And since we intended probing for generational patterns, we could select only those where we knew the names of the maternal and paternal grandparents. The application of these rules to the white population of Middlesex (as reflected in our biographies) gave us in the end a data set of 1,019 children,

---

[5] Our procedure was to compute for each reconstitution the mean interval between cardinal events and the statistical variance; where the variance exceeded 150—a standard set by demographers—we assumed a missing birth and dropped the reconstitution from consideration. The procedure is based upon Louis Henry, "Intervals between Confinements in the Absence of Birth Controls," *Eugenics Quarterly* 5 (1958): 200-11. A number of tests validated our assumption regarding the absence of contraception in the society.

563 males and 456 females, grouped in 222 families.[6]

With the data in hand, we asked our first question relevant to patterned behavior: how prevalent was name sharing among the children of our families, and particularly between the children of one generation and the preceding generations? Did children tend to bear unique forenames, implying that the culture saw them as unique individuals, or did they share names with parents and grandparents, uncles and aunts, implying that they were construed more as elements of an ongoing family or lineage and less as individuals? William Gray of Middlesex, in his will, reflected the latter view of children. Childless himself, he left his land to his sister Jane's son, Hugh Stewart, on condition "that the said Hugh Stewart Shall Name the first Male Child lawfully begotten of his body Gray Stewart . . . to take up my name on the land." The instances of shared names within our sample immediately suggest that Gray's attitude was general.[7]

Only with respect to their siblings were children individualized. With the exception of necronyms—the practice of deceased siblings' names being reused—no two children bore the same forename.[8] For the rest, namesharing was a common phenomenon. Of male children, seventy-seven percent shared their forename with a father, grandfather, or uncle; six percent with some other relation; three percent with a deceased brother (a necronym). A mere fourteen percent bore unique names. Of females,

---

[6]The skewed sex ratio in the sample (123 males per 100 females) is an artifact of the procedure. An "under-registration" of females (see Rutman and Rutman, " 'More True and Perfect Lists,' " 53-54) and the genetic element in sex-determination combine to create a bias against families inclined to female births and toward those inclined to males. The bias does not affect the analysis here.

[7]Middlesex County, Virginia, Will Book B, 1713-1734, 374, Virginia State Library, Richmond. In what follows, the construction of a forename from a surname has been accounted an instance of name-sharing. Middle names were all but unknown in early Middlesex. There were only four in the refined data set, and they were all male.

[8]The proscriptive rule by which children were individualized with reference to siblings extended across multiple marriages. We have noted only one clear instance in all our Middlesex data in which it was broken. Among the children of Penelope Paine by two husbands were her first son Thomas (by Thomas Warwick) and fifth son Thomas (by William Cheyney): the first son Thomas was alive at the time the second was born and subsequently named his first daughter Penelope. In another case, William Hackney, who had fourteen children by two wives, named his third and seventh daughters Sarah and Sally respectively, but this seems an early example of "Sally's" gradual emergence as a name independent of its origin.

sixty-nine percent shared a name with a mother, grandmother, or aunt; six percent with another relative; three percent with a deceased sister. Twenty-two percent had names that were their own. A more refined pattern emerged when we asked the same question of the data broken down by birth order of the children, as in Table 3. Roughly ninety percent of the first and second sons shared names with fathers, grandfathers, and uncles compared to forty percent of fifth, sixth, seventh, and eighth sons, more than a third of whom bore unique names. Among daughters the same pattern held, simply to a lesser degree. Some eighty percent of first and second daughters shared names with mothers, grandmothers, or aunts; less than half of the fifth-, sixth-, and seventh-born daughters did so.

Instances of shared names are highly suggestive of a familial rather than an individual view of children. But such a conclusion is not defini-

TABLE 3

NAME SHARING BY BIRTH ORDER IN MIDDLESEX, 1650–1750						
		PERCENT SHARING FORENAME WITH:				
BIRTH ORDER	SAMPLE SIZE	DECEASED SIBLING	PARENT OR GRANDPARENT	AUNT OR UNCLE	OTHER RELATION	NO ONE
S O N S						
1	197	0.0	71.1	17.8	4.6	6.6
2	152	1.3	63.8	26.3	2.6	5.9
3	98	8.2	33.7	30.6	6.1	21.4
4	58	1.7	25.9	36.2	10.3	25.9
5 +	58	12.1	13.8	25.9	12.1	36.2
ALL	563	3.2	52.0	25.0	5.7	14.0
D A U G H T E R S						
1	177	0.0	65.5	15.8	1.7	16.9
2	118	1.7	58.5	18.6	6.8	14.4
3	77	5.2	29.9	32.5	5.2	27.3
4	47	10.6	19.1	17.0	21.3	31.9
5 +	37	5.4	13.5	27.0	5.4	48.6
ALL	456	2.9	48.7	20.4	5.9	22.1

Sources and notes: The table is derived from the sample described in the text. The categories are exclusive from left to right, that is, if a child shares a forename with both a deceased sibling and parent, only the first category is augmented; with a parent and uncle or aunt, only the second.

tive. Consider the case of a father, Thomas, a son John, and a grandson John, with no John among the child's uncles or on his maternal side. One can presume with small chance of error that the boy was named for his father. But consider another family: A Grandfather John and his wife Mary have a son John, who marries Anne, daughter of John and Elizabeth, and sister of their son John. For whom is John, son of John and Anne, named? His father John? Paternal grandfather John? Maternal grandfather John? Or for his maternal uncle John?

There is, of course, no certain answer to such a question. In constructing Table 3, we assumed that the cultural norms dictating the naming of children gave precedence to parents and grandparents over aunts and uncles. The resulting symmetry—that is, the rough inverse correlation between the percentages of children (by birth order) sharing names with parents and grandparents as opposed to aunts and uncles—tends to validate the assumption. When the precedence is reversed, the symmetry disappears. But the problem of finding the rules of precedence between parents and grandparents, maternal and paternal, remains. Table 4 organizes a subset of the data in such a way as to make apparent a pattern that stimulates a highly probable guess. The table deals solely with first and second sons and daughters who carry the name of either their parent of the same sex or that parent's same-sex parent. Thus, in the male segment of the table, we have included first and second sons who share their forename with either their father or paternal grandfather; this amounted to fifty-four percent of all first and second sons and eighty percent of all sons bearing the name of a parent or grandparent. In the female segment are all first and second daughters who shared their forename with either their mothers or maternal grandmothers. Fifty-one percent of all first and second daughters and eighty-one percent of all daughters did bear a parent's or grandparent's name. We ignore the far right column of the table, which records instances such as John, son of John, naming his son John. Note, rather, the instances of a child bearing the name of a same-sex parent and *not* that parent's same-sex parent—"Fa" and not "FaFa," for example (column 3)—and of the child bearing the name of the same-sex parent's parent and *not* the parent—"FaFa," not "Fa" (column 4). Note particularly the reversal of the percentages in these columns between first and second sons, and that the same reversal occurs in the female segment. These reversals are improbably the result of chance. The overwhelming likelihood is that they are pointing to a pattern of behavior: parents tended to name first sons for the child's paternal grandfather, second sons for the father. Similarly, first daughters tended to be named for their maternal grandmothers, second daughters for their mothers.[9]

To isolate a central tendency in a society is obviously not to argue for the inevitability of its operation. The particular naming pattern we have identified reflects the strong family orientation of the society in question. But when we lower our gaze from the level of the whole society to that of the individual, personalities and personal situations come into view. By all rights Richard and Sarah Sandeford, both children of a "Sarah," should have named one of their daughters Sarah. They chose instead Anne (Richard's sister's name) and Priscilla (a name unknown in either family). Why? Conceivably Richard opposed the use of his mother's name; for almost immediately after the death of Richard's father, his mother had been accused before the Middlesex County Court of "Riotous liveing" and the "ill Management" of the estate left in her care.[10] Younger sons conceiv-

TABLE 4

PARENT AND GRANDPARENT NAMES SHARED BY FIRST AND SECOND SONS AND DAUGHTERS					
BIRTH ORDER	TOTAL (1)	SUBTOTAL (2)	PERCENT OF COLUMN 2 SHARING NAME WITH:		
			(3)	(4)	(5)
SONS					
1	197	111	19.8	51.4	28.8
2	152	79	54.4	17.7	27.8
DAUGHTERS					
1	177	92	29.3	63.0	7.6
2	118	57	64.9	26.3	8.8

Sources and notes: (1) Total number of children from table 3, which see for source; (2) number sharing with a same-sex parent and/or the same-sex parent of that parent; (3) same-sex parent only; (4) same-sex parent's parent only; (5) same-sex parent and same-sex parent's parent. Table values compute a chi square of 30.17, with 2 degrees of freedom significant at the .001 level—that is to say, there is a better than 999 out of 1,000 chance of being correct when we say the table is not the product of purely random factors.

[9]The significance of the grandparent in the pattern shows again in necronyms, forty-two percent of which were apparently efforts to retain the forename of a grandparent, twenty-six percent attempts to retain the forename of a parent.

[10]Middlesex County, Will Book A, 1698-1713, 179; Order Book, no. 4, 1705-1710, 27—both in Virginia State Library.

ably gauged their attachment to their family according to the portion of the family's goods that they received. Charles Wood, the third son of William Wood, is a good example. Among the children of his older brothers and sisters were three Williams, three Janes, three Samuels, and two Catherines—all names drawn from the family. Additionally, two of the Wood children married siblings, and both duplicated the siblings' parents' names among their own children. Charles, however, named his only son for himself; called his first two daughters Sarah and Mary (his wife's mother's name and wife's name respectively); and, eschewing the Catherine-Jane syndrome of his own family, named his three other daughters Elizabeth, Susanna, and Rachel. Richens Brim, another younger son, avoided his family's pool of names as well, naming one son for himself, one for the biblical Melchesedek, and his three daughters for the daughters of Job: Jemima, Kezia, and Kerenhappuch.

With that noted, we may return to the major pattern and the strength of family that it implies. When the data are disaggregated into cohorts—as in Table 5—the constancy of a concern for family is obvious. Parents who began childbearing in the early seventeenth century drew the names of their first and second sons from a pool of names defined by the parents' families of origin (their own parents and their parents' siblings) roughly ninety percent of the time. Names of their first and second daughters were culled from the same pool roughly eighty percent of the time. Parents who began childbearing in the years after 1720 acted similarly.

Only the proportions drawn from the various parts of the pool varied, and then only slightly. The clear pattern of first son named for FaFa, second for Fa (and, on the distaff side, first daughter for MoMo, second for Mo) is cloudy in the very earliest period, when parents were most often immigrants separated by an ocean from their own parents.[11] Fathers and mothers seem to have loomed larger in the image of the lineage than did grandparents. This is symptomatic, perhaps, of a feeling of a new begin-

---

[11]When Table 4 is regenerated by cohort, the seventeenth-century cohort varies sharply from the general pattern. Of seventeenth-century first sons bearing the name of Fa and/or FaFa, 50 percent are instances of Fa not FaFa, 12.5 percent of FaFa not Fa; of first daughters bearing the name of Mo and/or MoMo, 64 percent are instances of Mo not MoMo, 27 percent MoMo not Mo. Eighteenth-century cohorts are simply random variants of each other and of the pattern indicated in Table 5.

TABLE 5

		PERCENT SHARING FORENAME WITH:			
COHORT*	SAMPLE SIZE	PARENT OR GRANDPARENT	AUNT OR UNCLE	OTHER RELATION	NO ONE
FIRST AND SECOND SONS					
1650-1699	45	73.3	17.8	2.2	6.7
1700-1719	128	68.8	19.5	4.7	6.3
1720-1749	176	65.9	23.9	3.4	6.3
FIRST AND SECOND DAUGHTERS					
1650-1699	35	68.6	11.4	2.9	17.1
1700-1719	109	63.3	11.9	4.6	18.3
1720-1749	151	60.9	21.9	3.3	13.9

NAME SHARING BY COHORT
(FIRST AND SECOND MIDDLESEX SONS AND DAUGHTERS)

Source and notes: The table is derived from the sample described in the text. Cohort (*) is defined by the year of birth of the first child in the family, that is, roughly the equivalent of a marriage cohort. The categories are exclusive from left to right. The percentage rows do not sum to 100 because of the omission of necronyms.

ning for the line.[12] Over time, brothers and sisters of parents (uncles and aunts of the children) grew in importance as a source of names while parents and grandparents declined, a function perhaps of a growing awareness of the importance of lateral kin in the high-mortality situation of the Chesapeake.[13]

---

[12]Daniel Blake Smith, *Inside the Great House: Planter Family Life in Eighteenth-Century Chesapeake Society* (Ithaca NY, 1980) 229n, catches a glimpse of this phenomenon; but his analysis is too rudimentary to allow real comparison.

[13]When the basic first son for FaFa, second son for Fa rule was violated, the name given the child was more often than not one shared with one of the father's male siblings or a relative in the maternal line (MoFa, MoBr). In such instances there seems to have been a tendency, particularly in the case of first sons, to link the child to *both* lines, that is, to select a name common to both FaBr and MoFa or FaBr and MoBr. Such duplication occurred in the case of nineteen percent of first sons sharing a name with FaBr, MoBr, and/or MoFa, ten percent of second sons, and four percent of third through eighth sons; in nineteen percent of the instances of a first daughter sharing a name with MoSi, FaSi, and/or MoMo, fifteen percent of second daughters, and two percent of third through seventh daughters. Such behavior would be logical in a high-mortality situation where orphaned children were common. Notably, orphaned elder children would be more in need of kin-protection than orphaned younger children who would have elder siblings.

A complex naming pattern in the Chesapeake involving both parents and grandparents is, on the surface, a surprising finding for two reasons. First, the exaggerated mortality rate of the region can easily be
construed as having worked *against* the pattern.[14] In other words, it was
not very likely that a child would be named for a grandparent in the ex-
pectation of the grandparent's favoring the child in a will; for in over three-
quarters of the instances of a child named for a grandparent, the grandparent was dead at the time of the naming. Moreover, the complex skein
of marriage and remarriage, its extent a function of mortality, conceivably
worked against adherence to such a naming pattern. We have isolated that
pattern in terms of first marriages. If, indeed, the pattern reflected a strong
cultural trait in the society (and we think it did), then when we enlarge
the scope to encompass second and third marriages, a potential for personal disappointment looms.

John Batchelder, son of William and Sarah, is a case in point. Because he bore his grandfather's name, he might well have anticipated
naming his own sons William (for FaFa) and John (for Fa). But he married
a widow, Elizabeth (Crank) Davis, who already had among her children
a John and William. Was John disappointed when, barred by the proscriptive rule against duplicating names among siblings and half-siblings,
he could not name his first son for either his father or himself? (He ended
up naming the boy James, his brother's name.) To the extent such disappointment was general, the overall pattern might be weakened. But
perhaps not. High mortality could just as easily have strengthened the
family orientation of the society and the naming pattern itself—the du-
rability of families and lineages contrasting favorably with the fragility of
individual life. And if John Batchelder could not reproduce by his own
seed a William and John, the William and John who came to him from
Elizabeth's prior marriage might well have been all the dearer, making a
closer family unit out of the mixed bag of parents, step-parents, siblings,
and half siblings that, for a while at least, he headed.

A second surprise is the contrast between this Chesapeake pattern
and that isolated for New England by historian Daniel Scott Smith.[15] Us-

---

[14]On the high mortality in Middlesex and some of its social consequences, see Rutman and Rutman, "Of Agues and Fevers: Malaria in the Early Chesapeake," *William and
Mary Quarterly*, 3d ser., 33 (1976): 31-60, and " 'Now-Wives and Sons-in-Law,' " 167-
74.

[15]Smith, "Child-Naming Patterns," passim.

ing reconstituted families from Hingham, Massachusetts, for a roughly comparable period, Smith found a significant tendency to name firstborn sons and daughters for the same-sex parent. First sons shared their father's name in 59.7 percent of his sample, first daughters their mother's name in 58.6. (The comparable figures from Middlesex are 27.4 and 19.2 percent respectively.) The parent-grandparent syndrome involving first and second sons and daughters is nowhere in evidence in Hingham. Smith also found that a proscriptive rule applied not only to siblings but to the children of male patrilineal cousins: for example, two brothers Thomas and William (sons of Thomas) could not each have a son Thomas. Such was not the case in Middlesex. In a sample specifically drawn to test for the phenomenon—seventy-three sets of two or more brothers of a known father, each brother having sons of his own—names were shared by male cousins in sixty-three percent of the sets and by female cousins in fifty-three percent.[16] The patrilineal grandfather's name (in New England conveyed almost exclusively through the eldest son) was, in Middlesex, shared by coexisting cousins in forty-two percent of the sixty-seven sets in which it occurred at all. The difference hints at a slightly different degree of familial orientation in naming. If, as Smith argues, the extension of the proscriptive rule from siblings to patrilineal cousins indicates a greater individualization of the child, the absence of such an extension in the Chesapeake would argue for a higher degree of familialization.

The different patterns found in Middlesex and Hingham become particularly important when we remember that both emerged from still a third pattern—that (or those) prevalent in the English mother culture.[17] The paramount question then becomes the relationship among the three. Does

---

[16]The original sample contained too few brothers to make the test. The larger sample was created by dropping the rule that we must know the name of the mother and maternal grandmother of the children.

[17]To speak of an English pattern is, at this point in time, merely a convenience. It is certainly possible that there were many English patterns. It is also possible that there was an overarching Western concern (although not a single, precise pattern) to link children to the lineage by keeping alive the names of grandparents. Fairly suggestive on this point are: Christiane Klapisch-Zuber, "L'Attribution d'un Prénom a L'Enfant en Toscane a la Fin du Moyen-Age," L'Enfant au Moyen-Age, Publications du CUER MA, Universite de Provence, 9 (Aix-en-Provence, 1980) 75-84; idem, "Le Nom 'Refait': La Transmission des Prénoms à Florence (XIVᵉ-XVIᵉ Siècles)," L'Homme 20 (1980): 77-104; André Burguière, "Un Nom Pour Soi: Le Choix Nom de Babtême en France Sous l'Ancien Régime," ibid., 25-42; and Nicholas Tavuchis, "Naming Patterns and Kinship among Greeks," Ethnos 36 (1971): 152-62. The Chesapeake naming pattern clearly reflects such a concern.

Middlesex reflect more closely traditions of the old country, in which case New England's pattern is a variant? Is New England's pattern in the tradition of the homeland and the Chesapeake's a variant? Or have both overseas areas varied from the original? Assume for a moment the first question is answered affirmatively; one could then argue that, in New England, the force of a Puritan ideology and the accent within that ideology on the father as governor of the family had a direct effect upon behavior. Assume that the first is answered negatively and the second affirmatively; then the Middlesex pattern is the variant. One could argue that the variation flowed from the high mortality of the early Chesapeake.

We make no conclusive choice between these two alternatives. True, New England differed from England in the biblicism of its names, but this is not necessarily a telling point when it comes to the naming pattern itself. The choice must depend upon what pattern (or patterns) prevailed in England, and to the best of our knowledge the requisite studies have not been made. We simply offer a hint in Table 6. The table contrasts results from both our Middlesex sample and Smith's Hingham sample with those from an availability sample drawn from licenses to leave England for the colonies in the 1630s.[18] Some of these licenses—all involving departures for New England—include the names and ages of parents and their English-born and English-named children; hence they are approximate English family reconstitutions. Obviously important data are missing. We have no idea of grandparents. We can work safely only with the first sons and daughters listed, and only then when the parents' and children's ages are such as to allow an assumption that the children are indeed the first-born of their sex. Equally obvious is the potential for bias in the data. All the families were underway for Puritan New England; if they were English Puritans, they could already be naming children according to a variant pattern that would ultimately prevail in New England and be isolated by Smith. In this event, the results are startling for the similarity between English immigrants and Middlesex and for the contrast of both with Smith's Hingham findings. The table, in brief, suggests that New England's naming pattern was the variant.

---

[18]As printed in John Camden Hotten, ed., *The Original Lists of Persons . . . Who Went from Great Britain to the American Plantations, 1600-1700* (London, 1874).

TABLE 6

PERCENT OF FIRST CHILDREN SHARING NAME WITH SAME-SEX PARENT IN MIDDLESEX, HINGHAM, MASS., AND AMONG ENGLISH FAMILIES IMMIGRATING TO NEW ENGLAND				
	SONS		DAUGHTERS	
SAMPLE	N	% SHARING WITH SAME-SEX PARENT	N	% SHARING WITH SAME-SEX PARENT
MIDDLESEX 1650-1750	197	27.4	177	19.2
ENGLISH IMMIGRANT FAMILIES TO N.E.	71	28.2	61	19.7
HINGHAM 1640-1760	385	59.7	408	58.6

Source: The Middlesex data are described in the text; English immigrants to New England have been compiled from John Camden Hotten, ed., *The Original Lists of Persons . . . Who Went from Great Britain to the American Plantations, 1600-1700* (London, 1874); Hingham data, from Daniel Scott Smith, "Child-Naming Patterns and Family Structure Change: Hingham, Massachusetts, 1640-1880," *The Newberry Papers in Family and Community History*, no. 76-5 (1977).

Our look at the naming of children in Middlesex offers two other suggestions as to the nature of Chesapeake society. First, when names were not drawn from a family pool, what sorts of names were selected? Trends in such freely chosen names have long been suspected of reflecting broad cultural trends. The English Reformation, for example, brought with it a radical shift from traditional names with roots in the nonbiblical saints, such as Agatha, to biblical and particularly Old Testament names such as Sarah. These shifts are not readily caught, however. Simply counting names (as in Tables 1 and 2) and categorizing them as biblical or nonbiblical, although easy to do, is not definitive; for it fails to take into account that in a situation dominated by a family-oriented naming pattern, a freely chosen name quickly moves into the family pool and recurs not as an example of free choice but as a family pattern. In Middlesex, "Kezia" is a case in point. Kezia (or Keziah) Ball arrived in the county in 1685. This name occurs time and again in the generations descended from her, but only once, to 1750, was it noted in an unrelated individual. Clearly we cannot simply count all "Kezias" in an effort to determine the biblical orientation of the culture. By this reasoning, the rise of Benjamin in Table 1 and the appearance of Josiah in the last grouping there can only be taken as hints of an increasing biblicism in Middlesex, which will have to be confirmed or refused by a more refined procedure. We have chosen to use our more stringently derived sample to count and categorize only *unique* names, that is, names that are *not* found within the family pool associated with the parents. The penalty for this procedure is a small sample, but the benefit is a sample devoid of family bias. Table 7 depicts the results. The overall extent to which biblical names were resorted to in situations of free choice (almost sixty percent of all cases) is surprising. Smith, counting *all* Hingham names for a comparable period, found eighty-five percent of them to be biblical.[19] Even more revealing, however, is the shift over time from a secular to biblical orientation, confirming to an extent the hint offered by the rise of Benjamin.

Thus far all of our findings refer to Middlesex's white population. What of its blacks? Blacks were present from the first settlement of the county in 1650. In the 1680s and 1690s Africans began arriving in larger and larger numbers as slavery displaced white servitude. By the 1720s a majority of the county's population was black. Also, roughly a quarter of our Middlesex biographies are of blacks. What do their names tell us?

The question is particularly pertinent in light of work of the last few years. Scholars intent on reconstructing the culture of the slaves (and accentuating African elements in the doing) have tended to stress the Af-

TABLE 7

BIBLICAL AND SECULAR NAMES AMONG FREELY CHOSEN
(NON-FAMILIAL) NAMES IN MIDDLESEX, 1650-1750

YEAR OF BIRTH OF CHILD	SAMPLE SIZE	PERCENT BIBLICAL IN ORIGIN	PERCENT SECULAR IN ORIGIN
1650-1709	23	39.1	60.9
1710-1749	47	68.1	31.9
ALL	70	58.6	41.4

Sources and notes: See text for the derivation of the sample. Determination of biblical and secular have been made using George R. Stewart, *American Given Names: Their Origin and History in the Context of the English Language* (New York, 1979); E. G. Withycombe, *The Oxford Dictionary of English Christian Names*, 3d ed. (Oxford, 1977); and Leslie A. Dunkling, *First Names First* (New York, 1977). Sample size precludes dividing the sample into any finer periods or by sex.

---

[19]In the original paper as presented in 1972 (see n. 2) and cited with permission of the author. See also David W. Dumas, "The Naming of Children in New England, 1780-1850," *The New England Historical and Genealogical Register* 132 (1978): 196-210.

rican names among the slaves—the Cuffees and Jubas—and the appearance of days of the week as names, reflecting a common African practice of giving children the name of the day on which they were born. In the hands of these scholars, the naming of a newly arrived slave is made into a bargain between the white master and the black slave, the latter struggling to retain his or her own name and identity. Thus Jack is accepted (and John presumably rejected) because Jack sounds like Quaco (Wednesday); Jemmy is accepted in lieu of James because of the former's likeness to Quame (Saturday); and Abby rather than Abigail is favored because it sounds like Abba (Thursday). This then became the pool of black names that slave parents drew from in naming their children according to a pattern carried from Africa or derived within the condition of slavery.[20]

What does our Middlesex data offer? The first argument, strained at best, is simply untenable. On the one hand, we found among 3,429 slaves entering or born in Middlesex prior to 1750 only 23 day names in either an African or English form (a little over one-half of one percent) and fewer than 150 African names in all (4.4%), even when taking the liberty of construing every strange-appearing name "African." On the other hand, we found a significant correlation between the white names in common use (Tables 1 and 2) and their diminutive or, more properly, familial forms among the blacks (Tables 8 and 9). Bargains were undoubtedly struck at times: historian Peter Wood recounts one slave's narrative about a futile attempt to bargain.[21] Moreover, African names were occasionally accepted by whites. But when the aggregate is considered, it is clear that the

---

[20]See, for example, J. L. Dillard, *Black English: Its History and Usage in the United States* (New York, 1972) 123-35; Eugene Genovese, *Roll, Jordan, Roll: The World the Slaves Made* (New York, 1972) 447-50; Peter H. Wood, *Black Majority: Negroes in Colonial South Carolina from 1670 through the Stono Rebellion* (New York, 1974) 181-86; P. Robert Paustian, "The Evolution of Personal Naming Practices among American Blacks," *Names* 26 (1978): 177-91; Cheryll Ann Cody, "Naming, Kinship and Estate Dispersal: Notes on Slave Family Life on a South Carolina Plantation, 1786 to 1833," *William and Mary Quarterly*, 3rd ser., 39 (1982): 198-206. Newbell Niles Puckett's work—which is inevitably cited—supports none of this, although his "Names of American Negro Slaves," in *Studies in the Science of Society*, ed. George Peter Murdock (New Haven, 1937) 477-90, was the only analysis of a large aggregation of black names (10,954, largely from Mississippi) available when these authors were writing.

[21]Wood, *Black Majority*, 181, 182n.

initial pool of black names (at least in Middlesex) was established by whites assigning familial forms of common English names.

That such should be the case is quite understandable when one realizes the ways in which names were used in the white society. As historians we come to know, and consequently to identify, the whites solely by their formal names. This is simply a function of the way in which we gain our knowledge, for our sources almost inevitably reflect formal occasions.

TABLE 8

BLACK MALE FORENAMES FOUND IN MIDDLESEX, 1650–1750											
ENTERING OR BORN IN MIDDLESEX						BORN IN MIDDLESEX			ENTERING MIDDLESEX		
1650–1699			1700–1719			1720–1749			1720–1749		
RANK	NAME	CUM %	RANK	NAME	CUM %	RANK	NAME	CUM %	RANK	NAME	CUM %
1	Jack	10.8	1	Jack	11.8	1	Will	6.5	1	Jack	7.5
2	Will	18.7	2	Will	19.9	2	Jack	11.9	2	Harry	13.2
2	Peter	26.6	3	Tom	26.1	3	Jemmy	16.8	3	Will	18.4
4	Tom	33.1	4	Tony	31.6	3	Peter	21.6	4	Dick	23.0
5	Dick	38.8	5	Dick	36.3	5	Tom	26.3	4	Sam	27.6
5	Harry	44.6	5	Harry	40.9	6	Harry	30.7	6	Jemmy	32.0
7	James	49.6	7	Robin	44.6	7	Ben	34.6	6	Tom	36.4
7	Tony	54.7	8	Peter	48.0	8	Dick	38.4	8	Robin	40.3
9	Frank	59.0	9	Ben	51.3	9	Robin	41.7	9	Peter	43.9
10	George	62.6	10	George	54.0	10	Tony	44.9	10	George	47.1
10	Ned	66.2	11	Frank	56.4	10	Charles	48.0	11	Tony	49.6
12	Ben	69.1	12	Jemmy	58.4	12	Sam	50.9	12	Charles	51.8
12	Sambo	71.9	12	Sam	60.5	13	George	53.5	13	Ben	53.7
12	Samson	74.8	14	Cesar	62.4	14	Ned	55.6	14	Cesar	55.0
12	Robin	77.7	14	Ned	64.2	15	Mingo	57.6	14	Sawney	56.4
						15	Phil	59.5			
rho	(1)	---			0.76			0.72			0.78
	(2)	0.60			0.53			0.63			0.63
r	(1)	---			0.82			0.72			0.79
	(2)	0.74			0.86			0.70			0.70

Sources and notes: Names are drawn from the Middlesex biographies described in the text. The number of cases in the various categories are 139, 433, 662, and 456, respectively; total names in the pools, 45, 105, 132, and 135. Only the most frequent variant is listed. For example, given 19 Wills, 13 Billys, 2 Williams, and 1 Bill, we list only Will. In addition to the three formal names for which there were no diminutives (Peter, George, Charles), formal names accounted for only 4.4% of the entire sample. The percentage was highest among black males entering 1650-1699 (8.6%). See table 1 for definitions of r and rho. Correlations are computed (1) between each column and the column immediately preceding it, and (2) between each column and whites of the same sex born in Middlesex during the same period. All correlations are significant at better than 0.01 level.

TABLE 9

BLACK FEMALE FORENAMES FOUND IN MIDDLESEX, 1650–1750											
ENTERING OR BORN IN MIDDLESEX						BORN IN MIDDLESEX			ENTERING MIDDLESEX		
1650–1699			1700–1719			1720–1749			1720–1749		
RANK	NAME	CUM %	RANK	NAME	CUM %	RANK	NAME	CUM %	RANK	NAME	CUM %
1	Betty	15.3	1	Betty	8.3	1	Jenny	6.2	1	Jenny	8.5
2	Moll	26.0	2	Jenny	16.0	2	Moll	12.2	2	Kate	15.5
3	Kate	32.8	3	Moll	23.4	3	Judy	17.9	3	Bess	21.6
4	Jenny	38.9	3	Sarah	30.8	4	Frank	23.3	4	Moll	27.4
4	Nanny	45.0	5	Kate	37.8	4	Nan	28.7	5	Judy	33.1
6	Pegg	49.6	6	Frank	43.8	6	Kate	33.5	6	Beck	38.3
7	Frank	54.2	7	Judy	49.4	6	Sarah	38.3	7	Nan	42.9
8	Joan	58.0	8	Sue	54.2	8	Betty	42.7	8	Dinah	46.9
8	Sarah	61.8	9	Dinah	58.2	8	Hannah	47.1	8	Frank	50.8
10	Judith	64.9	10	Phillis	61.6	10	Lucy	50.8	8	Sarah	55.0
10	Phillis	67.9	11	Hannah	64.7	11	Dinah	54.4	11	Hannah	58.7
12	Alice	70.2	11	Nanny	67.9	12	Phillis	57.9	11	Phillis	62.2
12	Hannah	72.5	13	Letty	70.8	13	Letty	61.1	13	Peg	65.3
12	Nora	74.8	13	Rose	73.7	14	Margery	63.9	14	Lucy	67.5
12	Sue	77.1	15	Alice	76.4	15	Rose	66.3	15	Sue	70.8
rho	(1)	---			0.56			0.65			0.69
	(2)	0.65			0.62			0.61			0.63
r	(1)	---			0.62			0.61			0.54
	(2)	0.90			0.60			0.56			0.49

Sources and notes: See the preceding table. The number of cases in the categories are 131, 445, 665, and 496, respectively; total names in the pools, 39, 71, 85, and 78.

In baptismal records, legal appearances, and contracts, people's names were set down as Matthew, Francis, Henry, Mary, Susanna. Yet these same people bore familial names and now and again the records allow us to see their use on informal occasions: "Matt" Kemp, "Frank" Dodson, "Harry" Daniel, "Poll" Cole, "Molly" Byrd, "Sukey" Carter. Once in a great while, the records allow us to see the relationship between the particular form of the name being used and the relative situations of the individuals using it. Consider the following snippet of conversation recorded as part of a lawsuit. The speakers are Alice Creek and Jane Olney, women of very different social standing: the subject of their conversation is Richard Gabriel, Creek's servant. Jane speaks first.

> [I] asked, "Madam, I pray Madam, why are you in such Anger and bitterness against me?"
> "Jane, not I. But you meddle with Dick the Taylor my Servant . . . and threaten to take away his Eares."

"Truly Madam, Not I if I can help it. . . . I shall not meddle with Richard nor any that belongs to you."[22]

Their different *social* positions clearly determined the forms of address—Mistress Olney speaking upward to "Madam," Madam speaking downward to "Jane." The *familial* position of Gabriel relative to the speakers was also determinative. He was Madam's servant and seen as a dependent within the family, in effect akin to a child, hence Madam referred to "Dick"; he was also a person apart from the Olney family, hence Jane referred to "Richard." Because slavery was rationalized in familial terms—William Byrd's strolling his plantation, viewing his "family" at work comes to mind—the assignment of the familial form of English names to blacks naturally followed.[23] And since the slave had no existence apart from the family, he or she had nothing but a familial name, just as he or she had no surname. To everyone, and on every occasion, a particular slave would be simply Madam Creek's Dick.

Of the second argument—parents assigning names to black children in some patterned way—we can speak only tangentially. In order to test for the existence of such patterned behavior and have any measure of confidence in the results, we need the sort of carefully derived data that were used in discerning patterns among the whites. We simply do not have them. It is, indeed, appropriate to ask if a slave bore his father's name? his grandfather's? his paternal uncle's? But it would be irresponsible to attempt an answer when we know the names of fathers in only a handful of cases. We know more frequently the child's mother. But this suggests only a negative. Few black girls—not even enough to allow for more than a random coincidence—bore their mother's name.

Our black name lists (Tables 8 and 9) suggest another negative. The existence of a strong naming pattern in a population will inevitably tend

---

[22]Middlesex County, Deeds, 1679-1694, 31, Virginia State Library.

[23]Louis B. Wright and Marion Tinling, eds., *The Secret Diary of William Byrd of Westover, 1709-1712* (Richmond, 1941) 19, 34, 483. See also Peter Laslett, *The World We Have Lost* (New York, 1965) 1-15; Gerald W. Mullins, *Flight and Rebellion: Slave Resistance in Eighteenth-Century Virginia* (New York, 1972) 3-33. Among whites, familial names occasionally trespassed into the realm of formal names in the seventeenth century, but they did so increasingly in the eighteenth—Betty as a baptismal name, for example. Perhaps it was an ironic consequence of the fact that with slavery the familial forms were so much more publicly expressed.

to reinforce the popularity of leading names within the pool. The complex mathematics of this phenomenon can be demonstrated in a crude way by tracking the names of the male descendants of John, son of Thomas, in a culture in which the following hierarchical rules are invariant: (1) every first son is to be named for his paternal grandfather; (2) every second son for his father; (3) no two sons of a father can bear the same name; (4) wherever possible, the name of a father's brother must be used. If we assume that every male has only two sons, the pool will never grow beyond John and Thomas. If we reverse the fourth rule to make it proscriptive— the name of a father's brother is never to be used—and so force the introduction of new names, our pool in four generations will still be dominated by John and Thomas (50%). The tabulation of white names (Tables 1 and 2) demonstrates the phenomenon in reality: note the consistent strength of the top four male and female names, encompassing in every group more than fifty percent of all cases. But the top four black names, male and female, among Middlesex-born blacks, 1720-1749, account for less than half this number.[24] Note, too, that 1,595 Middlesex-born white children, 1720-1749, shared 168 names, a ratio of 9.5 to 1; 1,327 black children born in the same period shared 219 names, a ratio of 6 to 1. The mere size of the black pool argues against strongly patterned behavior.

Beyond such negative arguments, however, we can question for this early period the basic assumption that underlies the very notion of a pattern; that is, did slave parents themselves assign their children's names? Consider, for example, William Stanard's slaves. Between 1717 and 1729, in conformity with the requirements of the law, he brought ten imported black children into the Middlesex County Court to have their ages adjudged. Stanard was obviously intrigued with the classics, for the children's names were given as Pompey, Scipio, Bacchus, Caesar, Cupid, Julius, Jupiter, Mars, and—apparently momentarily at a loss—Orronoco (a variety of tobacco) and Sommerset. Between 1715 and 1728 he registered sixteen children born to his slaves: Apollo, Letty, Clarinda, Molly,

---

[24]Note, too, the diffusion of names where patterned behavior is considered weak to nonexistent. See Kenneth M. Weiss, et al., "Wherefore Art Thou, Romeo? Name Frequency Patterns and Their Use in Automated Genealogy Assembly," in *Genealogical Demography*, ed. Bennett Dyke and Warren T. Morrill (New York, 1980) 52, 57, and Dunkling, *First Names First*, 17; usage of the top four names ranges from roughly thirteen to seventeen percent, of the top ten from twenty-six to thirty-three percent.

Cyrus, Mercury, Frank, Phillis, Titan, Jerrell, Irene, London, Juno, Winny, Nimrod, and Diana.

At least in this case, it seems obvious who was choosing the names of the children born on the plantation. A more general clue lies in what we term the "Lucy Syndrome." Through 1719 only a handful of white Lucys appeared in Middlesex—four entering from England, one native-born; after 1720, however, the popularity of the name surged and it moved into eleventh place among whites. Black Lucys followed the same trend, from a sprinkling through 1719 to tenth place among native-born blacks between 1720-1749. Still another clue lies in the makeup of particular slave holdings. We found no instance of Middlesex-born blacks of the same generation bearing exactly the same name on the same plantation. In every case an apparent violation of this finding proved to be a matter of either a predeceased child of the same generation or of a black purchased or inherited who bore the name of a slave already on the plantation. In the latter instance, some sort of modifier was almost invariably added to the name of one or the other of the slaves—"Jack Rascow" (rascal?), for example, or "Barbary Jack," or "Jack Carpenter." In the same way, modifiers were used on the relatively rare occasions of intergenerational name duplication (rare because of high mortality): "Great Alice" and "Little Alice," "Old Doll" and "Doll."

None of this is meant to argue that blacks played absolutely no role in the naming of their children, only that at this time in Middlesex the need of the white owner to distinguish between hands was a sharp constraint on the development of indigenous naming. Should William Stanard send for "Young Molly," he could not countenance his messenger asking, "Which one?" In this situation the most that one might expect is that black parents put forward a name for their newborn child, and this was accepted or rejected by the white master.[25]

---

[25]There are hints that when blacks assumed a significant role in naming their children, they patterned their behavior on the whites. Mary Beth Norton, in a brief analysis of child-naming among Thomas Jefferson's slaves, 1774-1822, noted that "black youngsters who bore their grandparents' names held a marked percentage edge over their parentally named siblings (57 percent to 43 percent)" (*Liberty's Daughters: The Revolutionary Experience of American Women, 1750-1800* [Boston, 1980] 85-87). Norton's analysis does not allow a definitive statement, but it looks very much as if Jefferson's slaves were following our grandfather pattern in naming their children. Compare, however, Herbert G. Gutman, *The Black Family in Slavery and Freedom, 1750-1925* (New York, 1976) 186-99.

Neither is this to argue a unique conclusion. In an analysis of nineteenth-century black names published in the 1930s—an aggregative analysis and hence comparable to our own in a way that the recent qualitative (that is, selective) studies are not—the investigator discerned "the direct or indirect influence of the master in the naming of the slave child." Further, diminutives followed "patterns current in the white population." "Slave children," he concluded, "were often, if not usually, actually named by the master or mistress."[26]

"What's in a name?"—to return to our opening question. The historian answers, "clues"—about the ways in which children were discerned, about the strength of family and lineage. And in the case of our biracial society, there was a glimpse into the relationship between master and slave. Our exploration of the naming of children in the early Chesapeake has been brief, yet strong and surprising patterns have emerged: white children christened *in nomine avi* in a society in which, given high mortality, there were few grandfathers; a clear and growing biblicism in an area little marked for its attachment to the Gospel; the significance of white influence in the naming of black children. As noted, our ability to compare—the crux of any real understanding—has been sharply limited by the paucity of comparable work. Yet the comparisons that can be made are intriguing: variant patterns in the North and South; a "Puritan" pattern that offers a finite, empirical test of the impact of ideas (the Puritan accent on the father's role) upon behavior (the naming of sons); a white role in the naming of blacks of the same magnitude as that found by at least one scholar for the nineteenth century. The patterns found and the comparisons that intrigue both testify to the necessity for further systematic probing of child-naming patterns.

---

[26]Puckett, "Names of American Negro Slaves," 489.

Part III

GENEALOGY
IN
MIGRATION RESEARCH

MIGRATION, KINSHIP, AND THE INTEGRATION OF COLONIAL NEW ENGLAND SOCIETY: THREE GENERATIONS OF THE DANFORTH FAMILY

Virginia DeJohn Anderson

Although historians know a great deal about early New England towns, the character of New England society as a whole remains elusive. Recent studies have explored local government, population growth, settlement patterns, and inheritance practices within individual communities. From the findings of these local studies, there has begun to emerge a composite portrait of the larger society as, by the eighteenth century, a loosely bound collection of self-consciously independent towns. But this image represents more an agglomeration of discrete elements than a unified society. Was the whole of New England society merely the sum of its towns?

To some extent, this impediment to our understanding can be traced to methodological factors. Because many historians have tended to focus on single communities, they have been able to examine their subjects in considerable depth, but have not been able to investigate phenomena external to the town in similar detail.[1] Of particular interest here is the way in which geographical mobility has been portrayed in the social history of New England, for this is a topic that cannot fully be explored in a local study. Since town studies focus on the individual community and its inhabitants, migrants leaving town are perforce absent from any analysis. Mobility is often reduced to quantitative terms, expressed as the number of people who first appear on the records and then disappear. Statistics derived in this way are difficult to compare and interpret, for variations in the physical size of different towns will generate equally variable statistics. Data from towns with large land areas will indicate fewer exits and entries than will be found in smaller communities where no one lived more than a couple of miles from the border. Moreover, often-used sources, such as tax lists, deal primarily with adult males; the experiences of women, children, and other nontaxpayers are not included. Qualitative aspects of migration, such as the destinations and subsequent fortunes of migrants, are likewise absent.[2]

These methodological limitations have encouraged historians to portray mobility in two complementary ways. The first interpretation sees migration as a destabilizing force, a breach in the walls of communal integrity, which occurs only at that point when dwindling local resources

---

[1]See, for example, Kenneth A. Lockridge, *A New England Town: The First Hundred Years* (New York, 1970), and Philip J. Greven, Jr., *Four Generations: Population, Land, and Family in Colonial Andover, Massachusetts* (Ithaca NY, 1970). In his *Peaceable Kingdoms: New England Towns in the Eighteenth Century* (New York, 1970), Michael Zuckerman emphasized the localist perspective of Massachusetts towns. While this paper in no way seeks to dispute his important conclusions about the working of consensus and local autonomy in the political sphere, it does suggest that an examination of other aspects of society, such as kinship relations and migration patterns, provides a less atomistic portrait of early New England.

[2]W. R. Prest indicates some of the problems inherent in this methodology; see his "Stability and Change in Old and New England: Clayworth and Dedham," *Journal of Interdisciplinary History* 6 (1976): 359-74. See also John Patten, *Rural-Urban Migration in Pre-Industrial England*, Research Paper No. 6, School of Geography (University of Oxford, 1973).

threaten the survival of some of the inhabitants.[3] The second view, paradoxically, sees migration as a stabilizing process for the very reason that it helps rid towns of propertyless, potentially disruptive persons.[4] It is important to note that both interpretations present a negative image of migration, and suggest that most migrants had little or no alternative to movement; rather than deliberately choosing migration as a strategy for economic or social betterment, these men and women were forced by circumstances to take to the roads.[5]

A different approach to this question, however, yields different results. By tracing the patterns of family movements over a period of a few generations, the geographical limitations of town-based studies may be transcended, and new questions asked. Who were the migrants and at what point in their lives did they move? How far did they go? More important, why did some individuals choose to leave the towns of their birth in the first place? The answers to these questions suggest that migration may actually have served as an integrative mechanism in early New England, rather than as a disruptive factor. As families grew and sent members to different parts of the region, they developed extensive kin networks that transcended local boundaries and united a larger regional community. Migration within families, in short, served as one important means by which individual towns, like so many patches, were stitched together to form the quilt of provincial New England society.

The following study examines the patterns of mobility among the first three generations of the Danforth family in New England. An excellent family genealogy provided much of the information, although its usefulness was limited by the fact that, like all genealogies, its main concern is

---

[3]See, for instance, Douglas Lamar Jones, "The Strolling Poor: Transiency in Eighteenth-Century Massachusetts," *Journal of Social History* 8 (1975): 28-54; Kenneth Lockridge, "Land, Population, and the Evolution of New England Society, 1630-1790," *Past and Present* 39 (1968): 62-80. Jones has recently revised his views on the effects of migration; see his *Village and Seaport: Migration and Society in Eighteenth-Century Massachusetts* (Hanover NH, 1981).

[4]Linda Auwers Bissell, "From One Generation to Another: Mobility in Seventeenth-Century Windsor, Connecticut," *William and Mary Quarterly*, 3rd ser., 31 (1974): 79-110.

[5]One work that does portray migration in a more favorable light, as a means whereby families adapted to growth and change over time, is Christopher M. Jedrey, *The World of John Cleaveland: Family and Community in Eighteenth-Century New England* (New York, 1979) esp. ch. 3.

for the male lines of the family. Since three of the six first-generation Danforth children were daughters, surnames changed quickly; to include female lines as much as possible, other genealogical sources covering collateral families were also used. Vital records from several towns were consulted to cross-check genealogical references. In this way, nearly 85 percent of the 266 Danforths were traceable.[6]

The Danforth family, like many of those for whom a comprehensive genealogical record exists, owes this coverage to the fact that it participated in the Great Migration of the 1630s and also that it numbered among its members several prominent men. In the first three generations alone, the family included both a governor and a deputy governor of Massachusetts, along with a couple of provincial councillors and judges. Moreover, the Danforths had a strong tradition of sending sons to Harvard and then into the ministry.[7] Time, fortune, and the sheer multiplication of numbers exerted an inevitable leveling influence, however; the same generation that produced Governor Jonathan Belcher also included dozens of middling farmers, artisans, and housewives scattered in various towns throughout the province. By the first half of the eighteenth century, the Danforths on the whole were representative of the broad middle portion of New England's population.

In 1634 Nicholas Danforth and his six young children embarked on the long voyage that carried them from the Old World to the New. Within a year of his arrival in Massachusetts, Danforth acquired a considerable amount of property in the town of Cambridge, compensating for the lands

---

[6]John Joseph May, *Danforth Genealogy. Nicholas Danforth of Framlingham, England and Cambridge, N.E. (1589-1638)* . . . (Boston, 1902). The copy of this book at the New England Historic Genealogical Society in Boston contains corrections and additions made by May shortly after the book's publication. For a list of additional genealogical sources, see the Appendix.

[7]Six Danforth sons attended Harvard during the first three generations and then became ministers: Samuel Danforth (graduated 1643), John Danforth (1677), Samuel Danforth (1683), Thomas Blowers (1695), John Whiting (1700), and Thomas Foxcroft (1714). I would like to note here that the label "Danforth" is used throughout as a convenient generic term, meaning a direct descendant of Nicholas Danforth, the emigrant from England. Since by the third generation, the sample group studied included dozens of separate nuclear families with many different surnames, I do not mean to suggest that there was any strict "clan" identification (e.g., that Jonathan Belcher felt that he was a "Danforth" first). Later in this paper, I do suggest, however, that the various families were aware of their wider kin connections.

and orchards he had left behind in England.[8] But his sojourn in the New World was to be of short duration. Danforth died in 1638, and since he had arrived in Massachusetts a widower, his sons and daughters were left orphaned. In time, all six found spouses and together they produced thirty-five children whose adult careers can be traced. This second generation in turn begat 116 more surviving sons and daughters.[9] Nicholas Danforth's early death was amply redeemed as his descendants multiplied and helped to populate the colony.

The Danforths were not only a prolific clan; they were also peripatetic. Forty-three percent of a sample of 100 adults left the towns of their birth and settled elsewhere. For the first two generations, the rate was even higher—fifty percent in the first generation and fifty-two percent in the second. Parents with six or seven children could expect at least two or three of them to move away. By the time the third generation reached maturity, the migration rate had slowed somewhat, to thirty-nine percent. This may have been due in part to an expanding and diversifying economy in eastern Massachusetts as well as to the growing number of Danforths moving to and then remaining in Boston.[10]

---

[8]May, *Danforth Genealogy*, 4; Sumner Chilton Powell, *Puritan Village: The Formation of a New England Town* (Middletown CT, 1963) 67. A seventh child, a daughter, is listed as having come over from England with Nicholas and the other children. Her name is mentioned in the genealogy, but there is no other information about her.

[9]Birth cohorts were as follows:

GENERATION	N BORN	N SURVIVING TO ADULTHOOD	N OF TRACEABLE ADULTS
FIRST (1619-1628)	7	6	6
SECOND (1640-1676)	55	38	35
THIRD (1664-1718)	204	155	116
TOTALS	266	199	157

[10]Bissell discovered that Windsor's growing economy helped the town to absorb its expanding population; see Bissell, "From One Generation to Another," 94. When the statistics of migration for the Danforths were computed, the practice of new towns splitting off from older ones was taken into account in the following manner. Whenever someone showed up in a different town than the one in which he or she was born, I checked to see if that new town had once been part of the other one. If so, that change of residence was not counted as migration. The overall persistence rate for the three generations of the Danforths (57 percent, N = 100) is comparable to the rates of Dedham's adult males in the seventeenth and early eighteenth centuries and Windsor's male taxpayers in the late seventeenth century; see Table 7 in Bissell, "From One Generation to Another," 102.

For the Danforths, migration did not necessarily mean a complete severing of ties with the towns of their birth. The pattern of their movement was high frequency but short distance. Most remained within twenty miles of their native towns, a distance that could be traveled on foot in a day. Several moves involved shorter distances and thus less travel time.[11]

The Danforths could have moved farther than they did, but only a few ventured away from eastern Massachusetts. Lydia Danforth was the only member of the first generation to settle outside of the colony. In 1643 she and her husband William Beamon moved to his home in Saybrook, Connecticut. Sarah Danforth Whiting, a second-generation daughter, first journeyed with her husband, the Reverend Joseph Whiting, to Lynn. There, during the next nine years, Sarah gave birth to a succession of six sons, four of whom died in infancy. In 1682 the Whitings packed up their belongings and traveled with their remaining sons to Southampton, Long Island. Another long-distance migrant was Jonathan Belcher, one-time Massachusetts governor and a great-grandson of Nicholas Danforth, who moved to New Jersey after his appointment as that colony's governor in 1747.

Two third-generation sons left North America entirely. Daniel Foxcroft was born either in Cambridge or Boston, served in the 1711 expedition to Canada and, around 1723, sailed to Yorkshire, England. Seven years later, he died in Plaistow, Sussex. The reasons for this transatlantic migration are unknown; Foxcroft's father was born in Leeds in Yorkshire, so perhaps Daniel returned to his father's birthplace. Thomas Danforth, born in 1685, also traveled extensively, leaving his birthplace in Dorchester, Massachusetts, and becoming a merchant in Paramaribo, Surinam.

These last two examples, however, describe exceptions and not the rule. Among the Danforths, the predominant pattern of geographic mobility was short-distance movement. No literary evidence survives to explain either personal decisions to migrate or the predilection for nearby destinations; therefore, such questions must be approached indirectly.

---

[11]This pattern corresponds to studies of geographic mobility in pre-industrial England, where distances covered often amounted to a "half-day's walking distance"; see Peter Spufford, "Population Mobility in Pre-Industrial England," pt. 1, *Genealogist's Magazine* 17 (1973): 428; also, J. D. Chambers, *Population, Economy, and Society in Pre-Industrial England* (Oxford, 1972) 46.

Biographical sketches of Danforth sons and daughters provide useful tools in this context. An analysis of the factors of migration and certain characteristics of the migrants offers a means of evaluating the impact of short-distance mobility on colonial Massachusetts society as a whole.

Mobility was a much more common experience for women than for men; nearly three-fifths of all migrants were female. Expressed in a different way, of all the women for whom there is information about residence, half became migrants. For men, just over a third did so. Any particular woman simply stood a greater chance of moving away from her birthplace; one out of two women would do so, compared to one out of three men (see table below).

For the vast majority of these women, the cause of migration was marriage. Prevailing custom dictated that wives usually settled in the husband's town of residence if the two spouses did not come from the same place. This custom, combined with the fact that women proved to be more exogamous than men, produced this high rate of geographic displacement

TABLE 1

SEX DISTRIBUTION OF DANFORTH MIGRANTS					
	NUMBER OF	MEN		WOMEN	
GENERATION	MIGRANTS	N	%	N	%
FIRST	3	2	67	1	33
SECOND	12	4	33	8	67
THIRD	28	12	43	16	57
TOTALS	43	18	41	25	58

	NUMBER OF	FEMALE MIGRANTS		NUMBER OF	MALE MIGRANTS	
GENERATION	FEMALES	N	%	MALES	N	%
FIRST	3	1	33	3	2	67
SECOND	16	8	50	7	4	57
THIRD	31	16	52	40	12	30
TOTALS	50	25	50	50	18	36

among young wives.[12] Marriage migration was also likely to be short distance. Since marriage was an economic as much as a romantic arrangement, parents and children engaged in extensive negotiations with prospective in-laws over portions, dowries, and jointures. These affairs were more easily conducted when both sides had some knowledge of each other's assets; geographic proximity promoted this sort of familiarity.[13]

Most migrants ranged in age from eighteen to thirty years.[14] This figure is related to the twin factors of the predominance of women among migrants and the relationship between marriage and mobility. Women were the more mobile sex, and since marriage was the cause of most changes of residence, one could predict that the female average age at first marriage would closely correspond with the age at migration. This is exactly

---

[12]Bissell also found women to be more mobile than men; see "From One Generation to Another," 87, 94. Conversely, Susan L. Norton discovered that women were less exogamous than men and that overall exogamy rates varied with the size of the town involved. Physically smaller towns had higher rates. Since many of the Danforth women lived in relatively small towns such as Roxbury, Charlestown, and Dorchester, this could help to explain the discrepancy in these findings. See Susan L. Norton, "Marital Migration in Essex County, Massachusetts, in the Colonial and Early Federal Period," *Journal of Marriage and the Family* 35 (1973): 409-11.

[13]For a discussion of marriage negotiations, see Edmund S. Morgan, *The Puritan Family: Religion & Domestic Relations in Seventeenth-Century New England*, rev. ed. (New York, 1966) 56-59, 81-83; John Demos, *A Little Commonwealth: Family Life in Plymouth Colony* (New York, 1970) 63, 85-86, 155-58, 160-61, 167-68; Greven, *Four Generations*, 74-76, 78-82; Daniel Scott Smith, "Parental Power and Marriage Patterns: An Analysis of Historical Trends in Hingham, Massachusetts," *Journal of Marriage and the Family* 35 (1973): 419-28.

[14]Twenty-six out of thirty-two migrants of known age were in this age group. A note of clarification is needed here. English studies suggest that young people serving as apprentices or household servants were a particularly mobile part of the population. But there is little information for the Danforths during this period of their lives. First-generation son Samuel Danforth was apparently put in the care of the Reverend Thomas Shepard after his father's death; see Cotton Mather, *Magnalia Christi Americana; or, the Ecclesiastical History of New-England, from Its First Planting, in the Year 1620, unto the Year of Our Lord 1698*, vol. 1 (1702; rpt. Hartford CT, 1853) 59. The existence and function of service is not dealt with in this essay; rather, it outlines the pattern of the Danforths' permanent removal from home after they reached adulthood. For the English background on adolescent mobility, see Peter Laslett, *Family Life and Illicit Love in Earlier Generations* (Cambridge, 1977) 72-75, 98, 100; Roger Schofield, "Age-Specific Mobility in an Eighteenth-Century Rural English Parish," *Annales de Demographie Historique* (1970): 261-74; Alan Macfarlane, *The Family Life of Ralph Josselin, a Seventeenth-Century Clergyman: An Essay in Historical Anthropology* (Cambridge, 1970) 92-93, 145-48, 205-10.

what occurred: women's average marriage age was 22.8 years (N = 63) while their average age at migration was 22.4 years (N = 17). For men, the average age at migration was somewhat higher, amounting to 25.6 years (N = 10). The small sample causes some problems here, in that seven of the ten male migrants for whom ages can be determined were between twenty and twenty-five years of age at the time of migration. Daniel Foxcroft's late departure from his native town at age thirty-seven skews the figure; when he is omitted from the calculation, the average drops more than a year, to 24.3. For most men as well as for most women, then, early adulthood was the time for permanent removals from the towns of their birth.

Men did not move for the same reasons as did women. For the male Danforths, marriage was not directly related to the timing of migration or the choice of destination.[15] Key factors for them involved trades or professions, and especially the choice of a career in the ministry. The decision to become a minister almost inevitably entailed a change of residence. Unless the incumbent of his own parish either died or agreed to hire an assistant, the prospective preacher was forced to seek an appointment in another town. All but one of the Danforth men who entered the ministry settled in a new location, although they generally did not travel very far. In 1650 the town of Roxbury invited the Reverend Samuel Danforth of Cambridge to settle there and preach. Some thirty years later, his two sons entered the ministry and relocated, John moving the few miles from Roxbury to Dorchester, and Samuel undertaking a longer journey to Taunton. In 1719 another Danforth descendant, the Reverend Thomas Blowers, traveled about fifteen miles from his native Cambridge to his new parish in Beverly.

Other men migrated in order to follow more worldly pursuits. As already mentioned, Thomas Danforth voyaged to Surinam to engage in trade. Commercial interests also determined the course of travel for other members of the Danforth clan. Andrew Belcher moved from Cambridge to Boston sometime after the death of his mother, Elizabeth Danforth Belcher, in 1680. Over the next twenty years, he worked his way up from a modest trade in wholesale goods to affluence as an independent ship-

---

[15]Thus the average age at first marriage (26.4) and average age at migration (25.6) did not correspond as closely as they did for women.

master and merchant. By the beginning of the eighteenth century, Belcher was investing in more ships than anyone else in Boston.[16] His son Jonathan reaped the benefits of his father's success. Born in Cambridge, he was moved to Boston while still a child. After earning an A.M. degree at Harvard in 1704, Jonathan embarked on two visits to Europe, first for four years from 1704 to 1708, and then a shorter stay from 1715 to about 1717. Once he had returned to Boston to stay, Jonathan immersed himself both in mercantile activities and local politics. This latter interest eventually required a further change of residence, for in 1747, as a result of his appointment as governor of New Jersey, he moved to that colony and died in Elizabethtown ten years later.[17]

The pattern of migration among the Danforth mercantile families offers an interesting variant of the overall experience of mobility. In most cases, involvement in trade required a move to Boston, followed by continued residence there. Men like the merchant Andrew Belcher and the mariner Jonathan Phipps moved from outlying towns to the provincial capital; women such as Mary Danforth Bromfield, Elizabeth Danforth Lowder, and Abiel Danforth Fitch settled in Boston after their marriages into mercantile families. There was no recorded instance among the Danforths of migration out of Boston into rural areas.

The sons and daughters of these merchant families were interwoven into the existing fabric of Boston society. Three daughters of Andrew Belcher all married into prominent commercial families—the Olivers, the Noyeses, and the Stoddards—and all of the newlywed couples remained in the provincial capital. Mary Danforth's future husband, Edward Bromfield, was a Boston merchant who died leaving an estate worth over £4000[18]; three of the four surviving Bromfield children remained in Boston. Edward, Jr. became a prosperous merchant in his own right; his sister Mary wed Thomas Cushing, an eminent merchant, lawyer, and politician, while Frances Bromfield married the Reverend John Webb of Bos-

---

[16]Bernard Bailyn, *The New England Merchants in the Seventeenth Century* (paperback ed., New York, 1964) 195; Bernard Bailyn and Lotte Bailyn, *Massachusetts Shipping, 1697-1714: A Statistical Study* (Cambridge, 1959) 128.

[17]Sibley, *Biographical Sketches*, 4:434-49. (For full publication information, see the Appendix.)

[18]See n. 22.

ton's New North Church. A third sister, Sarah, married a Captain Isaac Dupee, who may also have engaged in Boston trade.

The experience of Abiel Danforth Fitch resembled that of her sister Mary Bromfield. Abiel's husband, Thomas Fitch, was another well-to-do merchant and government official. All three surviving children of that marriage maintained their residence in Boston. John Fitch married his cousin Martha Stoddard in 1732. Mary Fitch's marriage added another strand to the web of kin connections; her husband was the Boston merchant Andrew Oliver, the son of Daniel and Elizabeth Belcher Oliver, and therefore a cousin of John Fitch's wife Martha. The other Fitch daughter, another Martha, wed Boston merchant and politician James Allen.

Intermarriage was a strong social adhesive binding the leading mercantile families to one another.[19] Danforth descendants moving to or born in Boston remained in the provincial capital, forging conjugal and commercial links with members of the social and economic elite. Not all Danforths were absorbed into the Boston mercantile community, however; the careers of many other migrants were less spectacular.

Some men quit their birthplaces to seek their fortunes in port towns other than Boston. In 1696, for example, twenty-year-old Thomas Phipps left his native Charlestown to study at Harvard College. From there he went on to become first a schoolmaster and then a lawyer and government official in Portsmouth, New Hampshire. His political career was subsequently marred by persistent accusations that he had sold off timber which had been reserved for ship masts of the Royal Navy. In spite of (or perhaps because of) this scandal, Phipps died possessed of a considerable estate to bequeath to his heirs.[20]

Other men traveled less extensively. Jonathan Danforth, a first-generation son of Nicholas, set out from Cambridge to Billerica, about fifteen miles to the northwest, to become one of the original proprietors of that town.[21] Four third-generation sons likewise embarked on short-distance moves. Two shoemakers, Samuel Phipps and John Danforth, moved to new towns a few miles from their birthplaces, undoubtedly exploring new

---

[19]Bailyn, *New England Merchants,* 135-38.

[20]Sibley, *Biographical Sketches,* 4:266-69.

[21]Reverend Henry A. Hazen, *History of Billerica, Massachusetts, with a Genealogical Register* (Boston, 1883) 31.

markets in which to ply their trades and new land on which to build farms. Samuel Danforth, originally a Dorchester schoolmaster, went to Cambridge where he rose to political prominence, ultimately serving on the Governor's Council for several years in the 1760s and early 1770s. Finally, Nicholas French left his native Billerica for Hollis, New Hampshire, just over the Massachusetts border, most likely to seek a farm of his own.

The question of economic motives for migration suggests another possible sphere of inquiry; that is, the effect that inheritance might have had on the propensity to move and the choice of destination. Fifteen probate documents, including wills and inventories, survive for members of the first three generations of the Danforth family.[22] They demonstrate a close relationship between inheritance of land and persistence in one's native town. In 1730, for example, Elijah, the eldest son of John Danforth, received one-half of his father's house and most of the homestead land in Dorchester—property worth several hundred pounds. He remained in Dorchester, unmarried, working as a schoolteacher and physician until his death in 1736. Similarly, two merchants' sons, Jonathan Belcher and Edward Bromfield, received the bulk of their fathers' estates and accordingly remained in their native Boston.

In a different instance, persisting sons inherited their occupations as well as lands from their father. In 1690 Samuel Livermore died in Watertown, leaving his estate to his widow Anna to provide for raising their ten surviving children, who then ranged in age from one to twenty years. Once the two eldest sons reached their majority, they were to purchase the dwelling house and lands from their mother, at a price "so moderated as may make it a comfort & not a burthen to them" and agree to support her so long as she remained a widow. This arrangement presumably served several purposes: it allowed economic independence to young Samuel and

---

[22]The following probate documents were used in this essay. First-series wills, on microfilm, at the Middlesex County Registry of Probate, Cambridge MA include: Andrew Belcher, 1673 (docket no. 1478); Pyam Blowers, 1709 (no. 2109); Matthew Bridge, 1738 (no. 2599); Jonathan Danforth, 1712 (no. 5890); Samuel Danforth, 1742 (no. 5902); William French, 1723 (no. 8529); Benjamin Garfield, 1717 (no. 8901); Samuel Livermore, 1691 (no. 14187); Oliver Wellington, 1727 (no. 24061). Manuscript wills at the Suffolk County Court House in Boston include: Samuel Danforth, 1674 (no. 714); Andrew Belcher, 1717 (no. 3874); John Danforth, 1730 (no. 5962); Edward Bromfield, 1734 (no. 6612); Elijah Danforth, 1735 (no. 6945); Benjamin Whitney, 1737 (no. 7064). Several of these men were spouses of Danforth women.

his brother Daniel, provided for the widow's support, and created a fund from the estate's purchase price that could be divided among the remaining children. As well as splitting up their father's estate, Samuel and Daniel also divided up their father's trades. The inventory of the elder Samuel's holdings listed both a "potting office" and a "malt house," each containing the proper tools and supplies. Both sons remained in Watertown, Samuel becoming a maltster and Daniel a potter.

Inheritance was not the only means of transmitting land from one generation to the next. Several sons who persisted in their native towns received real property during their father's lifetime by deeds of gift.[23] When eighty-four-year-old Jonathan Danforth of Billerica composed his will in 1712, he first mentioned the lands, goods, and rights that would go to his widow, and then enumerated the bequests to his seven children. In making these bequests, Jonathan made sure to account for "the lands that I have given to each of them by deeds of gift as a part of their portions." An inventory listing the "valuation or prise that I have set upon the Lands and Medows that I have given to my children by deeds of gift" has survived; it shows that £339 worth of land was under the control of the seven Danforth children before their father's death. The eldest son Jonathan held property worth nearly half of this amount, including a houselot and plots of arable meadow, pine land, and swamp ranging in size from five to fifty-two acres. His only brother Samuel was deeded £62.10 worth of land, also including a houselot, meadow, pine land, and swamp. Both sons remained in Billerica.

The disposition of the estate of Matthew Bridge of Lexington echoed this procedure. His will of 1738 noted that he had "allready putt all my Sons into Possession & Title of Diverse Lands & Tenements." Since his only bequest of land to his four sons was part of a swamp, the deeds of gift to Matthew, Joseph, John, and Samuel Bridge must have included the bulk of his real estate. The third son, John, apparently received the house and surrounding lot, while the other three sons settled elsewhere in Lexington.

These probate documents do not indicate the dates at which Matthew Bridge or Jonathan Danforth deeded their land to their sons. But since

---

[23]Greven discusses deeds of gift in *Four Generations*, 79-80, 82-83, 92-93, 126, 131-33, 145-50, 158, 168.

all of these heirs remained in their native towns, it is likely that they acquired this land—which in at least three cases included a houselot—around
the time they married. Matthew Bridge was already nearly seventy years
old when his eldest son married; his advanced age undoubtedly diminished whatever reluctance he might have felt in relinquishing his control
over the family land.

Although these documents demonstrate a clear relationship between
the acquisition of family land and persistence in one's native town, that
relationship was not absolute. John Danforth of Dorchester, for instance,
bequeathed his land to his two sons, Elijah and Samuel. Elijah remained
in town, but Samuel had already moved to Cambridge. Samuel probably
knew that he would one day receive part of his father's property, but he
chose not to wait around in Dorchester until John Danforth's death. On
the whole, this was a wise decision since his father lived three-score and
ten years; Samuel would have had to wait until he was thirty-four years
old to become independent. Instead, he removed to Cambridge in 1724,
and married two years later, when he was thirty years old. In another example, both of Samuel Danforth's two surviving sons inherited shares of
their father's property; both entered the ministry, however, and settled in
Dorchester and Taunton instead of their native Roxbury.

Inheritance of land by women seems to have had no effect on their
migration or choice of destination. Most women, in fact, received bequests in the form of money or moveable property rather than land, a
practice that encouraged their geographic flexibility. Some women did receive land from their fathers, but the daughters' residences still were determined by those of their husbands. Edward Bromfield left land to his
daughters Mary and Sarah, who remained in their native Boston. Each
had married a Boston man more than a decade before her father's death,
however, and in each case persistence was a result of the marriage and not
the inheritance. Although Elizabeth Blowers received land in Cambridge
from her father's estate, she moved with her husband Thomas Symmes to
Bradford. In two cases unmarried women moved away from their native
town, but, once again, the removal was not related to inheritance. Two
sisters, Elizabeth and Martha Bridge, left Lexington after their father Matthew's death and journeyed to Boston to live with their widowed sister,
Abigail Whitney. This move did not stem from convenience or financial
necessity, for the two women had been granted the right to remain at home
according to the terms of their father's will. Rather, their purpose in mov-

ing was to assist Abigail in running her late husband's business, and no doubt to keep her company as well.

Evidence suggests that a father's landholdings in other towns than that in which he was a resident had little effect on his children's residences. The disposition of the Reverend John Danforth's land provides a good example of this. In 1706 Reverend Danforth received a grant of two hundred acres from the proprietors of the undivided land in Dorchester. He still owned the land eleven years later, for in 1717 the town allowed his two sons, Elijah and Samuel, to build a corn mill there.[24] Danforth's will indicates that he added to his initial grant by purchasing another farm in the area, which was subsequently incorporated as the town of Stoughton in 1726. All five of Reverend Danforth's surviving children received bequests of Stoughton land after their father's death in 1730, but only one daughter eventually dwelt there. Stoughton Danforth died only five years after his father and apparently never left Dorchester. The eldest son Elijah had inherited half of his father's Dorchester homestead in addition to property in Stoughton, and remained in Dorchester until his death in 1736. His brother Samuel received half a farm in Stoughton plus a portion of Elijah's share after 1736, but he had already moved to Cambridge. Elizabeth Danforth Lowder was married and living in Boston at the time of her father's death and never attempted to occupy the one hundred acres she inherited in Stoughton. Only Hannah Danforth Dunbar settled in the new town, but her residence there had nothing to do with her inheritance. Hannah's husband was the minister of Stoughton; they were married in 1729 and settled in their new home nearly a year before her father's death.

Again, the disposition of Thomas Danforth's lands reinforces this impression that inheritance of land did not always dictate residence patterns. In the 1660s the General Court granted Danforth 450 acres in what was to become the town of Framingham. Through subsequent purchases of adjoining plots, Danforth amassed a total of 15,500 acres. Instead of parceling out this territory among his children, he formulated a plan whereby suitably hard-working men and women would be enticed to settle on the undeveloped tract in return for 999-year leases. Thomas Danforth had no surviving sons, and this may help to explain his unusual scheme.

---

[24]City of Boston, *Fourth Report of the Record Commissioners of the City of Boston* [Dorchester Town Records], 2d ed. (Boston, 1883) 282, 288.

At the time of his death in 1699, however, he had eight grandsons and six granddaughters. Two of the grandsons eventually received reversions of leased estates, but none appears to have received actual grants of land or to have settled in Framingham.[25]

Ministers and merchants, husbands and wives—these were the Danforths who became migrants. They did not constitute a fluid group of luckless adventurers passing from town to town. Danforths had already achieved some degree of social respectability by the time of their decisions to leave their native towns; they were young adults moving within the framework of social and economic institutions. Newly married women traveled to their husbands' towns or perhaps elsewhere to set up households and raise another generation of children. Ministers moved to new towns to follow their calling, and merchants and their wives migrated to Boston to follow theirs.

Danforths migrated to seek a better future—in marriage, preaching, farming, or trade—and not to escape a bitter past. They generally traveled short distances, ten or twenty miles to a new town, remaining in eastern Massachusetts.[26] This pattern of limited movement must have prevented the disruption of ties with family, friends, and neighbors at the same time that the migrants were creating ties to their new communities. Historians, however, are unlikely to discover much evidence chronicling the ordinary contacts among people in the seventeenth and early eighteenth centuries. Colonial society functioned on a face-to-face basis, and family visits and communication were usually deemed too commonplace to merit recording.[27] Evidence of interaction among women is especially difficult to recover. Nonetheless, this topic can be approached with some success through indirect means. Third parties occasionally mentioned Danforths

---

[25]J. H. Temple, *History of Framingham, Massachusetts,* . . . (Framingham, 1887) 2, 89-94, 111-12, 115, 121.

[26]This pattern of short-distance movement for social or economic improvement fits the model of "betterment migration" that Peter Clark describes in his study of three Kentish communities; see "The Migrant in Kentish Towns, 1580-1640," in Peter Clark and Paul Slack, eds., *Crisis and Order in English Towns, 1500-1700: Essays in Urban History* (London, 1972) 137.

[27]Samuel Danforth did keep a diary of sorts, but it was really a part of the Roxbury church records and does not record many personal anecdotes; see William B. Trask, "Rev. Samuel Danforth's Records of the First Church in Roxbury, Mass.," *New England Historical and Genealogical Register* 34 (1880): 84-89, 162-66, 297-301, 359-63.

in their accounts. Samuel Sewall noted that even after Elizabeth Danforth Foxcroft's marriage and subsequent move from Cambridge to Boston, she visited her father Thomas in Cambridge and watched over him during his final illness.[28] Similarly, Cotton Mather recorded that Mary Danforth Bromfield of Boston was "a rich blessing and comfort" to her widowed mother, who remained across the Charles River in Cambridge.[29]

But these casual references are extremely scarce, and one is compelled to look further for evidence of continued family connections. Wills again prove to be useful in this context. Besides listing the conventional disposition of an estate among the various heirs, these documents occasionally include bequests of special items to particular individuals, favorite possessions to favorite relatives. In some cases these kin lived several miles away from the testator, and had done so for years. The inclusion of such affectionate bequests strongly suggests that the ties between these relatives had not been strained by distance, but rather had been maintained by some sort of regular communication over the years.

For instance, when Thomas Danforth of Cambridge composed his will in 1699, he stipulated that money and certain possessions were to go to several relatives located elsewhere in Massachusetts and also on Long Island. Five pounds in currency went to his "verry loving Kinsmen"—his nephews John Danforth of Dorchester and Samuel Danforth of Taunton—while the sum of ten pounds was bequeathed to his son-in-law, Joseph Whiting of Southampton, Long Island. To his brother Jonathan of Billerica, Thomas left "my best Cloake & Suit of apparel and [money] to buy him a ring." He remembered his grandsons as well: Thomas Phipps of Charlestown and John Whiting of Southampton equally shared their grandfather's books and manuscripts. Thomas Danforth's nephew and "Loving friend" Andrew Belcher was called upon to act as an executor of the will. The frequent use of affectionate terms in the wording of this document, as well as the specific nature of the bequests, strongly suggest continued family ties over distance and time. Thomas Danforth singled out important personal items—his best clothing, his books and papers—to go to certain relatives, ones with whom he was probably especially close. In-

[28]M. Halsey Thomas, ed., *The Diary of Samuel Sewall, 1674-1729*, 2 vols. (New York, 1973) 1:345, 416.

[29]Mather, *Magnalia Christi Americana*, 2:62.

deed, young Thomas Phipps apparently visited his grandfather in Cambridge; his share of the books and manuscripts to be inherited included "those that said Phipps hath already had" from Danforth.

Other examples of similar behavior reinforce this impression of communication and affectionate ties among kin. In 1674 Samuel Danforth of Roxbury desired that, if his wife and children died soon after he did, his books would go to "my Kinsman Samuel Danforth sonne of my Brother Thomas," then residing in Cambridge. Both John Danforth, who died in 1730, and his son Elijah, who died six years later, left bequests to Elizabeth Danforth, the daughter of John's second son Thomas, who had moved to Surinam and died in 1714. Although it is not clear if Elizabeth remained in Surinam, there is no evidence that she had come to live with her grandfather and uncle in Dorchester. John Danforth left his granddaughter his "Lands & Interests at Woodstock" and, as part of the bequest, released his late son from a debt of £150. Elijah gave his niece a silver spoon, marked "T. D. 85," a family heirloom that undoubtedly once belonged to her father Thomas, who had been born in 1685.

In-laws seem also to have been well integrated into the kin network. Jonathan Danforth's will, proved in 1712, directed that his six surviving children divide up his estate among themselves. After their father's funeral, Samuel Danforth and his five sisters, along with four of their husbands, met to apportion their inheritance. At this time, Samuel, Anna, and Sarah still lived in their native Billerica; Lydia and Elizabeth had moved to Concord, and Mary to Chelmsford. Together all ten of them "Joyntly agreed" to sell part of the family land, assess the value of real and moveable property, and divide it up. At this meeting, they also took the opportunity to settle up another item of family business. Edmund Wright of Concord, Lydia's husband, had become involved in a land-title dispute; as evidence of their family solidarity, his in-laws agreed to share the burden of any "debts or damages" that "our brother Wright" might incur as the result of legal action.

Certain characteristics of the Danforth migrants fall into place to form a distinctive pattern. The family regularly sent out its sons and daughters to become established in nearby towns; like the growth of new branches each spring, these families in turn sent their own offspring a little farther in the next generation. By the middle of the eighteenth century, the Danforth clan had expanded to form an intricate network of kin connections transcending the boundaries of individual towns. Multiply this pattern by hundreds to account for other prolific Massachusetts families; the picture that emerges suggests the ways in which migration served to knit together the larger society. Towns exchanged young men and women to become the spouses of their neighbors. Young adults dispersed across the countryside to fill important social and economic functions in their new homes. And overlaying all of this, kinship ties provided links between migrants and those less-mobile members of their families.

The world of colonial New Englanders was not circumscribed by the geographical limits of their individual towns. Rather, their sense of community incorporated several layers of meaning. Membership and participation in the activities of their towns and churches certainly defined an important part of their existence. But kinship ties provided another significant component of the individual's identification with a larger community, and these links ignored physical boundaries. By extending these networks throughout the countryside, by creating avenues for the transmission of skills, information, and affection—as well as property—migration acted as an important mechanism of regional integration.

APPENDIX:
GENEALOGICAL RESOURCES

Other sources used in this study include John L. Sibley, *Biographical Sketches of Those Who Attended Harvard College*, vols. 1-7 (vols. 4-7 ed. Clifford K. Shipton) (Boston, 1873-1945); the vital records of Andover, Bedford, Beverly, Billerica, Boxford, Bradford, Cambridge, Chelmsford, Concord, Lynn, Medford, Roxbury, and Taunton in Massachusetts, and Saybrook in Connecticut; and the following genealogies available at the New England Historic Genealogical Society in Boston and Widener Library, Harvard University, in Cambridge:

Lieutenant George Andrews, *Genealogy of the Andrews of Taunton and Stoughton, Mass.*, . . . (Rochester NY, 1887); John Herbert Barker, "Genealogical Mss." (dated 1946); Everett Hosmer Barney and George Murray Barney, *Jacob Barney 1634. James Hosmer 1635.* (Springfield MA, 1912); Henry Bond, *Family Memorials . . .* , 2 vols. (Boston, 1855); H. Bond, *The Garfield Family* (N.p., n.d.); Reverend William Dawson Bridge, *Genealogy of the John Bridge Family in America, 1632-1924*, rev. ed. (Cambridge MA, 1924); William Frederick Bridge, *An Account of the Descendants of John Bridge, Cambridge, 1632* (Boston, 1884); Julius B. Champney, *History of the Champney Family . . .* (Chicago, 1867); Reverend F. W. Chapman, *The Chapman Family . . .* (Hartford CT, 1854); City of Boston, *A Report of the Record Commissioners of the City of Boston Containing Boston Births from A.D. 1700 to A.D. 1800* (Boston, 1894); Edward C. B. Danforth, Jr., "Fifteen Generations of Danforths in England and America" (bound typescript in Widener Library, dated 1970); Roscoe Conkling Fitch, *History of the Fitch Family . . .* , 2 vols. (Haverhill MA, n.d.); Lieutenant J. M. French, *William French and His Descendants* (N.p., 1890);

Samuel A. Green, *Percival and Ellen Green* (N.p., 1897); Reverend David B. Hall, *The Halls of New England* . . . (Albany, 1883); George F. Hoar, *President Garfield's New England Ancestry* (Worcester MA, 1882); Almon D. Hodges, Jr., *Genealogical Record of the Hodges Family* . . . , 3rd ed. (Boston, 1896); Mary Lovering Holman, *Ancestors and Descendants of John Coney of Boston, England and Boston, Massachusetts* (Brookline MA, 1928); Charles Hudson, *History of the Town of Lexington* . . . (Boston, 1868); Asa Keyes, *Genealogy. Robert Keyes of Watertown, Mass.,* . . . (Brattleboro VT, 1880); William H. Manning, *The Genealogical and Biographical History of the Manning Families of New England* . . . (Salem, 1902); Tyler Seymour Morris, *The Tucker Genealogy* (Chicago, 1901); Colonel Henry E. Noyes and Harriette E. Noyes, *Genealogical Record of Some of the Noyes Descendants* . . . , 2 vols. (Boston, 1904); Frederick Clifton Pierce, *Whitney. The Descendants of John Whitney* . . . (Chicago, 1895); John B. Pierce, "Genealogical Notes Relating to Patrick Grant IX" (dated 1960, at the New England Historic Genealogical Society); James Savage, *A Genealogical Dictionary of the First Settlers of New England* . . . , 4 vols. (rpt. Baltimore, 1965; Boston, 1860-1862); Daniel Denison Slade, "The Bromfield Family," *New England Historical and Genealogical Register* 25 (1871): 329-35; Ezra S. Stearns, *Fitch Genealogy* . . . (Boston, 1902); Matthew Adams Stickney, *The Stickney Family* . . . (Salem, 1869); Henry F. Waters, *The Gedney and Clarke Families of Salem, Mass.* (Salem, 1880); W. H. Whitmore, *The Hall Family Settled at the Town of Medford, Mass.* (Boston, 1855); idem, *Record of the Descendants of Andrew Belcher* (Boston, 1873).

Unless otherwise noted, references to Danforths in this essay are based on the compilation of information from these sources. When material for the specific reference comes from just one source (other than May's genealogy), that source will be given a specific citation. In the context of the research, "traceable" means that at least two or three bits of information were available—for example, a birth and marriage date, a birth and death date, place of birth and place of death. Therefore, sample sizes in the calculations vary according to the particular topic (e.g., marriage age, migration). Information was available for 223 of the 266 members of the first three generations of the Danforth family. Sixty-six of those traceable died before reaching adulthood, thus leaving a total of 157 traceable adults.

Chapter Fifteen

THE WILSONS MOVE WEST: FAMILY CONTINUANCE AND STRAIN AFTER MIGRATION

Claudia L. Bushman

Hundreds of thousands of Americans moved west in the first half of the nineteenth century. What happened to the family during that break? The importance of the family in factory employment, in farm work, and in inheritance has been well described. The effect on family ties, however, in that typically American transition, the move from east to west, is not clear. Recent work describes family life along the trail, but less is known of the relationships between those who left and those who stayed behind.[1]

---

[1]Since Stephan Thernstrom's pioneering study, *Poverty and Progress: Social Mobility in a Nineteenth Century City* (Cambridge MA, 1964), the subject of transience as demonstrated through demographic means has received widespread attention. Chapter 9 of his more recent book, *The Other Bostonians: Poverty and Progress in the American Metropolis,*

Although systematic data on family ties across such distances will be hard to assemble, literary materials are plentiful. Indeed, one of the ironies of historical documentation is that we know more about families that were separated than about those that were together. The romantic love of John and Abigail Adams has been celebrated because they were so often far apart and writing across those distances. The same is true of parental relations: we know more about the child-rearing habits of parents who sent their children away to school and put their advice on paper. Migrant families likewise wrote home. These traditional sources—collected correspondence and other personal papers, along with family genealogies—enable the researcher to trace personal relationships over broad spaces, to perceive motivations and tensions, and to collect modest amounts of statistical information.

How did the family function over distance? Family networks traditionally sustain domestic economy and provide primary social relationships. Both functions are best performed when the family is together. Could they continue to operate from afar? If those primary family relationships were of necessity less functional, did the family have any value at all?

An excellent case study of a migrating family can be found in several generations of the Wilson and Corbit families of Odessa, Delaware. Successful in farming, tanning, and trade, the families built two handsome colonial brick mansions, still bearing their names, in this town that prospered as a trading and shipping center. Later some of the Wilsons moved west. Their continuing interaction with those they left behind is the subject of this narrative.

The founding father of the family came virtually from nowhere, apparently with some cash in hand, and entrenched himself as a leading member of the town. David Wilson I (1742-1820) arrived from Sussex County, Delaware, or somewhere in Maryland, about 1768 with his first wife, Margaret Empson (1737-1768), and two children, all of whom died

---

1880-1970 (Cambridge MA, 1973), summarizes subsequent findings. See A. Gordon Darroch, "Migrants in the Nineteenth Century: Fugitives or Families in Motion?" in the *Journal of Family History* 6 (1981): 257-77, for a recent essay that reviews findings and provides an extensive bibliography. But these demographic studies are of necessity general and faceless. To understand the inner dynamics of family life during migration, the vital statistics of an individual family, compiled by a genealogist, provide the required framework. A more personal study that speaks of family interaction in terms of migration is John Mack Faragher, *Women and Men on the Overland Trail* (New Haven, 1979).

shortly after his arrival. Wilson amassed considerable wealth as a merchant and storekeeper who also farmed. According to his granddaughter, he owned 800 acres at his death.[2]

The well-located little town where he settled was originally called Appoquinimink for the navigable creek that flows to the Delaware River, a major artery leading both north to Philadelphia and south to the Atlantic. The settlement was renamed Cantwell's Bridge in 1731 when a toll bridge crossed the creek and completed the cart-road connection across the peninsula to deep-water rivers flowing to the Chesapeake. The final name change to Odessa in 1855 reflected the town's identity as a shipping port where shallops gathered up grain from the fertile countryside and carried it to Philadelphia. The Wilsons bought grain and stored it in large granaries along the Appoquinimink Creek. Seven or eight such buildings rose above the creek, and in them crews loaded grain from second-story chutes. Grain made many Delawareans rich, and farmers from 1840 until about 1890 found an even more lucrative crop in peaches. Then the peach blight gradually destroyed the orchards. The gracious mansions of prosperous farmers still dot the countryside.

David Wilson's wife and children died, and in 1769 he eloped with Mary Corbit (1749-1803). In doing so, he formed an alliance with a prosperous and well-established Quaker family. David Wilson was an Episcopalian, and he knew Mary's father, Daniel Corbit, would oppose the marriage. So David persuaded Mary to climb down a ladder and run off with him.[3] That same year he began to build a handsome Georgian mansion and turned the adjoining old (possibly about 1740) house into an office and kitchen. His brick mansion—a two-story, five-bay dwelling one room deep—stood just to the west of his brick, two-story store on Main Street. Elegant domestic and business enterprises went together in the eighteenth century. At the store he engaged in a lively and varied trade, with many of the goods being carried in his own fleet of vessels. He kept a coach lined with red leather and driven by a coachman. Wilson was in all ways a country gentleman.

---

[2]Mary Corbit Warner, "Annals of Odessa, Formerly Cantwell's Bridge," 19 July 1917, 29. Manuscript copy on file at the Wilson-Warner House.

[3]Ibid., 29, 35.

David Wilson's brother-in-law, William Corbit, built an even more elaborate brick mansion in 1772 next to the Wilson house and behind the Wilson store. The Corbit mansion turned its back on the Wilson house and its side to Main Street, preferring to face the Appoquinimink Creek and the tanning yards that brought their owner success and standing in the community. Again, the proximity of those smelly tanyards to the gracious living of the Corbit House tells us something about eighteenth-century sensibility. The rise of such an elegant and stylish dwelling as "Castle William," as the house has since been dubbed by relatives, in undistinguished Cantwell's Bridge is a testimony to the interaction between rural traders and fashionable Philadelphia, where the models for the house are to be found.

Wilson was an interloper in Quaker society, and his wives, both of whom were Quakers, were disowned by the Duck Creek Monthly Meeting for marrying him. He nevertheless showed support of the sect by building the first Quaker meetinghouse in Cantwell's Bridge in 1783. Meetings of the Society of Friends still take place monthly in the diminutive brick structure. Mary was reinstated in 1775.[4] Wilson himself was admitted to the society several years after the building was erected.

Only two children of the six born to David Wilson I and Mary Corbit survived. Rachel (1775-1816) married Samuel Thomas, bore eight children, and moved into another handsome brick house built by her father. David Wilson II (1787-1870), the only surviving son, is the long-lived protagonist of this little drama. Letters show David Wilson I as a devoted father to his last son, urging him to do well in his studies at the Quaker-run Westtown Boarding School in Pennsylvania, and promising dynastic opportunities. "When thee comes to get in business if I should be alive I intend to try and do as much for thee as I have done for Sammy."[5] Sammy would be Samuel Thomas, his son-in-law. In his will David Wilson I left

---

[4]Robert L. Davis, "Genealogy of David Wilson (1742-1820)," dated 4 February 1974, revised 19 March 1976. Unpublished computer printout, 28 pp., on file at the Wilson-Warner House.

[5]David Wilson I to David Wilson II, 5 August 1800, 16 January 1805, Wilson-Warner Papers, Joseph Downs Manuscript and Microfilm Collection, Winterthur Museum Library. The Wilson-Warner Papers are identified as DMMC69x224.1-515. All references in this article, except for those otherwise specified, pertain to that collection.

his entire, unspecified estate, save for a few cash bequests, to his son David II.[6]

In 1808, when David Wilson II was twenty-one, he made a successful marriage to Ann Jefferis (1791-1822), the daughter of Deborah Hunt and James Jefferis, the captain and owner of the brig *Brothers*. Although her parents were Church of England, Ann was a staunch Hicksite Quaker, as were all the Wilsons in that doctrinal dispute.[7] In the year 1821, leaving four young children (two others had died young) and her husband at home, she set off with a friend to attend the New York Yearly Meeting of Friends. While there she nursed a dying friend, called on Elias Hicks, and participated in a number of Friends' meetings, notably for the "class of poor creatures at the penetentiary" and for a group of "people of colour." She was gone for more than a month, a rather ambitious and liberated journey for a woman of the 1820s, even for a Quaker woman who might well travel in the ministry.[8]

Ann Wilson came home from New York in 1821, but early the next year was laid to rest in the Friends' cemetery near the meetinghouse, leaving behind her five children: James, sixteen; Mary, eleven; David, seven (he died at age ten); George, five; and Jefferis, who was less than two months old and with whom she had been pregnant at the time of the New York journey. The poor motherless baby may well have been the cause of his mother's early death.

A year after Ann Wilson's death in 1822, David Wilson II took Mary Poole (1795-1863), a woman of "brilliant mind," as his second wife.[9] The daughter of Sarah Sharpless and William Poole, Jr., a silversmith turned flour miller in Christiana Village near Wilmington, Mary Poole was also a Quaker. She proceeded to raise Wilson's children, who called her

---

[6]The will of David Wilson I, dated 13 May 1818, reads in part as follows: "As to all the rest and residue of my Estates of every kind and nature whatsoever whether real, personal or mixed that is not herein before otherwise disposed of, I give devise and bequeath the same be it what it may more or less to my beloved son David Wilson and to his heirs and assigns Forever." State of Delaware, Archives, Dover, Delaware.

[7]Information from the marriage certificate of Deborah Hunt and James Jefferis. Communication with Horace Hotchkiss.

[8]Letters from Ann Jefferis Wilson to David Wilson date from 20 May 1821 to 20 June 1821.

[9]Warner, "Annals of Odessa," 37.

mother, and to produce a brood of her own. Four children were born to her: Sarah Poole (1824-1909); Ann Jefferis, who was named for the first wife and lived to be only seven; William Poole (1828-1880); and Daniel Henry (1837-?).

When David Wilson I died in 1820, his son and namesake took over the operation of the business. David Wilson II was a lively, charming, and optimistic man. His granddaughter called him "a broad thinker, wonderful in his progressive ideas and vast reading."[10] In 1828, the same year that his ninth child, William, was born, Wilson suffered a rather spectacular failure. When it became clear that he could not continue his business operations, his assets were "assigned" or transferred to others for the benefit of his creditors.

Wilson's financial activities were directly based on the soil. He bought and shipped wheat and in exchange provided goods to nearby farmers. His business may well have begun to founder as the Delaware farmlands, admirably flat and rock-free but relatively acid and poor in nutrients, lost their richness. The sandy soils leached easily, and the farmers did not return nutrients to the soil. Yields diminished, and Appoquinimink Hundred soils were almost completely ruined by the 1830s.[11]

The business affairs of the Wilson operations were necessarily complex. A merchant owed many creditors, even as his customers owed money to him. Such business reversals were not uncommon, but Wilson's crash was sudden. "The assignment of David Wilson['s assets]," wrote Edward Gilpin, a Quaker merchant from Philadelphia, to Wilson's brother-in-law, "is so unexpected to most of us, that our curiosity, as well as our interest is much excited."[12] What is notable is David Wilson's cheerful attitude during this adversity. "I am really glad to hear from thee," he wrote to an "Esteemed Friend." "*Even in the shape of a dunn* I most sincerely wish thee success I am thy friend."[13]

The Wilson family departed "dear old Cantwell's Bridge" and repaired to Philadelphia to learn a trade, either brushmaking or shoemak-

---

[10]Ibid.

[11]Joanne O. Passmore, Charles Maske, and Daniel E. Harris, *Three Centuries of Delaware Agriculture* (N.p., 1978) 16.

[12]Edwin Gilpin to Respected Friend (Samuel Thomas), 30 July 1828.

[13]David Wilson II to "Esteemed Friend," n.d.

ing. David and Mary Wilson and their seven children transferred to the Cherry Street Monthly Meeting in Philadelphia in 1830.[14] Wilson's friends urged him to stay in Cantwell's Bridge or Philadelphia, but feeling that his failure would make social relations chilly, he chose to go west.[15]

The Wilsons' Philadelphia interlude marked an important transition in the family's movement from the aristocratic to the artisan class. Family unity gave way to fragmentation. At the age of fourteen, George set sail on a whaling vessel and followed the sea for eight years. When the family turned up six years later in Indiana, their chosen Western home, the group consisted only of David and Mary Poole and two sons, James and William. The boys were received on 27 January 1836 by the Whitewater (Hicksite) Monthly Meeting in Richmond, Indiana, on certificate of transfer from the Cherry Street Monthly Meeting. Sarah, George, and Jefferis, perhaps farmed out to relatives during the transition, were received five years later on 22 September 1841.[16] It is unfortunate that many of the details of the family's life are lost from this period.

A Quaker settlement since 1807, Richmond was located near the Ohio border of Indiana on the Whitewater River, with the National (or Cumberland) Road forming the principal street from east to west. Richmond had enviable proximity to transportation by road and water: the Whitewater Canal opened in 1848, and the railroad came through in 1853. Richmond soon became a trading and manufacturing center. Tremendous timber covered the rich, black soil. In 1840 a visitor noted that Richmond was "in the midst of a fine agricultural district, and the most thriving in the State." He was "more pleased with Richmond than anyplace" that he had yet seen.[17]

Richmond, with its promised prosperity and its congenial inhabitants, seemed to be an ideal place for the Wilsons to settle. An intelligent

---

[14]Family Bible. Their daughter Ann Jeffris [sic] Wilson was noted as buried in Philadelphia on 8 February 1831.

[15]David Wilson to Mary Wilson Corbit, 1 March 1869.

[16]Davis, "Genealogy of David Wilson."

[17]Mary Poole Wilson to Mary Wilson Corbit, 20 March 1854, noted that they could travel to Philadelphia in thirty-three hours for $15. Shirley S. McCord, *Travel Accounts of Indiana, 1697-1961: A Collection of Observations by Wayfaring Foreigners, Itinerants, and Peripatetic Hoosiers* (Indianapolis, 1971) 327.

man, well educated in liberal and practical ways, with a large family to help him, David Wilson had moved west in search of opportunity and settled in a place favored by climate and circumstance. The family should have prospered, but it did not.

The Wilsons bought a farm named Hopewell, located two miles from Richmond, and began to farm while making brushes on the side. They raised corn, wheat, oats, pigs, and fowl.[18] In 1842, six years after its arrival, the Wilson family had only twenty-eight cents remaining. The business was beset with difficulties from the beginning. David had to peddle his brushes on the road; and the late and muddy springs often meant that he was delayed until merchants had already ordered their brushes from the East. Their oldest son, James, who should have been the main help, had chronic asthma and was often disabled for months at a time.

In 1847 the family "determined to give up farming altogether and go into Richmond, to reside and *make brushes* and not only make them but sell them too."[19] They rented out the farm for the value of half the produce, and moved to town to keep a store. They began the steady litany of the articulate poor. Although willing to work, they had to work a great deal harder than they thought they should. "Both Father and I," wrote Mary Poole Wilson, "have eaten all of our white bread, and taken our ease when young and now must work more than is agreeable."[20]

Wilson was even unable to get along with the ruling element in his local community. In 1844 he was disowned for disunity from the Whitewater Quaker Meeting. Some Friends were appointed to urge him to change "his language and deportment," but they were unsuccessful.[21] Henceforth Wilson was a stranger to the Friends he had come west to join.

Mary Wilson, David's daughter, is an interesting pivotal figure in this history. She apparently did not live in Richmond for any extended period, and so she was never received by the Whitewater Meeting. She preferred to take up residence in Wilmington, Delaware, with her Aunt Elizabeth

---

[18]David Wilson to Daniel Corbit, 9 August 1842.

[19]Mary Poole Wilson to Daniel Corbit, 1 July 1847.

[20]Mary Poole Wilson to Mary Wilson Corbit, 3 March 1850.

[21]Davis, "Genealogy of David Wilson." Note copied from the minutes of the Whitewater Meeting held 26 June 1844, Wilson-Warner Papers. Wilson was disowned by the Whitewater Meeting on 28 August 1844.

Shipley, a well-to-do semi-invalid who loved her dearly. Aunt Shipley was the sister of Mary's late mother, Ann Jefferis Wilson. Mary had reached the age of thirty-six as a plain and kindly spinster, living on the fringes of her rich and powerful friends as a sympathetic, ladylike companion and visitor.

In 1846 her fortunes took a remarkable turn when she received a proposal of marriage from her cousin Daniel Corbit (1796-1877), who was fifteen years her senior and the recently widowed father of five children, not all of whom were living. The son of William Corbit, Daniel was the owner of "Castle William," the Corbit mansion next door to Mary's girlhood home. In a series of courtly, affectionate letters, which are nevertheless completely faithful to his late wife, Daniel urged Mary to marry him. He noted that his "best thoughts [had] been increasingly turned toward thee *as the one,* on whom I can place my confidence and best affection," also that "the high estimation in which [his former wife] had held thee my cousin," and the similarity of their "lovely" characters would encourage "her sainted spirit" to speak to him encouragingly for his sake and "for the sake of her dear *motherless* children." Corbit stressed their similar backgrounds in urging his suit. "Thee is no stranger to me, but belonging to a near branch of my own family—native of the same village—brought up much like myself."[22]

Mary modestly returned, "I have always looked upon thee as so much *my superior* in *all things* that *I am tempted to ask* if thee has given this affair thy most serious consideration." She accepted his proposal, however, and even grew somewhat ardent. "Do my manners appear cold to thee cousin? I have been told so very often, but it is only in manner believe me—but I guess thee will find that out for thyself—after awhile, if thee has not already."[23]

Mary Wilson and Daniel Corbit were married on 15 April 1847. Thirty-four Friends were present, including a number of Tatnalls, Bringhursts, and Shipleys. The bride's brother Jefferis was the only member of either immediate family present. David Wilson had written that he would rather have had them joined by a magistrate than "be tied . . . in meeting

---

[22]Daniel Corbit to Mary Wilson, 27 July 1846, 16 August 1846.

[23]Mary Wilson to Daniel Corbit, 13 December 1846.

by those dead ceremon[ies]." But, he told them, if they were pleased, he would be too.[24]

The new marriage set up an interesting contrast between the Odessa and Richmond families. Mary Wilson Corbit left her life as a homeless companion to become the mistress of the Corbit mansion and the wife of the respected first citizen of Cantwell's Bridge. From being the spinster and poor relation, she moved to a position from which she could dispense largesse. She became a gracious mistress and devoted wife and mother. Her husband adored her, and although she was in her mid-thirties at the time of their marriage, she was always the young wife of her older husband.

Mary became the bridge between the Wilsons and Corbits, remaining true to her past affection for her own family. Her husband, who remembered David Wilson as the cousin with whom he had grown up, was similarly loyal. Correspondence flourished after the marriage. Mary saved the letters and so documented the rich relationship and the stresses that accompanied it.

Her family, meantime, struggled on. Mary Poole Wilson remarked in 1849, two years after moving to Richmond, that "cash is at quite as low an ebb, as it ever has been." "Our brushes are decidedly better than any that the merchants bring from the east," she noted, but David was out peddling more than he ever had in the past. Mary Poole Wilson regretted that they had ever learned the brush business. "It is a miserable trade. . . . It would have been much better if they had all learned the Shoe making."[25]

In 1849 this hard-pressed family consisted of David, then sixty-two, his wife Mary Poole, fifty-four, and James, the forty-year-old invalid who lived precariously on until 1877. George had returned from the sea and settled in Indiana. He had married a Quaker from Maryland named Alethea Swiggett, and had then fathered three of the seven children eventually born to him. George was probably working as a blacksmith; he later owned his own shop.[26]

---

[24]David Wilson to Daniel Corbit, 1 July 1847.

[25]Mary Poole Wilson to Elizabeth Shipley, n.d.

[26]John T. Plummer, ed., A Directory to City of Richmond Containing Names, Business and Residence of the Inhabitants Together with a Historick Sketch (Richmond IN, 1857) 12.

Jefferis, the dashing third son, bore some of the marks of his family's changing status. Tempted into a freer life, he became known in Cincinnati for his gambling and drinking. He could not find a good way to earn a living but still spent beyond his means. He moved to Philadelphia in 1843 and was disowned by the Cherry Street Monthly Meeting five years later.[27] He went bankrupt, yet even after that event he bought a gold watch, careless of his inability to pay for it.

In 1849 Sarah Poole Wilson was twenty-five. She had been married the year before to Jeremiah Lee Meek, Jr., a quiet man who had been a saddlery apprentice and then went into the manufacture of trace chains, harnesses, and cradles. In 1857 he was a grocer and later went into business with his brother-in-law George.[28]

William Poole Wilson was twenty-one in 1849. He had studied bookkeeping in the East under his sister Mary's patronage and was again at home.

The youngest child, Daniel (called Henry), was just twelve. This boy, called "smart but willfull," and later "completely worthless" by his tolerant sister Mary, was a considerable disappointment to his family. His philosophical father explained his difficulties by saying that Henry's "*begetting* and gestation" took place when his parents were in a "very uncomfortable and reckless state of mind." Wilson would not have been surprised "had he been born idiotic." Henry served through the Civil War and was honorably discharged, but his father said, "It would have been better if he had been left with the honoured dead." When the clear-eyed old patriarch looked around his family, he noted, "We have met much disappointment in our own children."[29]

So, in 1849 the family consisted of David, Mary, James, William, and Henry. George and Sarah were married and living nearby. Mary was married and living in Delaware, and Jefferis was flitting about.

The discovery of gold in California offered glorious possibilities to these disappointed people, who had been working away for little reward. The shining promise of easy money tempted George, and he would have

---

[27]He was disowned 31 June 1848 (Davis, "Genealogy of David Wilson").

[28]Ibid.

[29]Mary Wilson Corbit to Jefferis Wilson, 14 September 1847; David Wilson to Mary Wilson Corbit, 9 July 1862.

gone west if he could have made some provision for his family. Jefferis did go. His growing reputation as a rake required him to go somewhere, and his necessary exit fortunately coincided with the gold rush. He set out for California, with ten borrowed dollars, *on foot*. He exchanged his life of urban failure for one of desperate Western adventure. His letters home, until he disappeared, a casualty of some unknown gold-field chaos, are full of his cowboy and Indian adventures. [30]

Jeremiah Lee Meek, Jr., the husband of Sarah Poole Wilson (the Wilsons' daughter Sally), also joined the gold rush. Leaving his wife and baby son, Jerry trekked across the plains in 1849. "Sarah is anxious on her husband's account," Mary Poole Wilson noted. "If she had not her Father's hopeful temperament, it would be more than she could well bear." Mary went on to say, "I believe if all the tears shed by wives for their husbands, children for their parents, were collected there would be a flood almost sufficient to wash away near all of Calif. It is a sad thing for this country that gold was discovered." [31] Jerry eventually came home again, empty-handed.

As the Wilsons toiled on, the threads that bound them to their former Eastern home were woven ever tighter. Delaware memories remained dear. Wilson wrote his cousin Daniel Corbit that he was often there in his dreams. Not a month went by without his dreaming that he was "living in my own house with plenty of money in my pocket and the old gigue [gig] at my disposal." His letters concluded with a repeated refrain that despite poverty they were happy. "Though the family is very poor indeed," he noted, "yet I do not believe there ever was a family more uniformly content than we are although some of us grumble when we find we have but one shirt or shift to our backs and not a decent pair of shoes . . . yet we endeavor to keep a light heart." [32] Twenty years later he was still singing the same song. He had long concluded that few persons could "boast of more happiness and true friends" than himself. When his wife com-

---

[30]Mary Poole Wilson to Mary Wilson Corbit, n.d. [1849?]; Jefferis Wilson to David Wilson, 4 April 1850.

[31]Mary Poole Wilson to Mary Wilson Corbit, 2 February 1850.

[32]David Wilson to Daniel Corbit, 9 August 1842.

plained that she had *"nothing to wear,"* he countered that they were "rich, very rich but she says sometimes that I am crazy."[33]

Personalities emerge clearly in this four-way correspondence between the Corbits in Cantwell's Bridge and the Wilsons in Richmond. Daniel Corbit appears courtly, polite, devoted. His letters to his wife while they were separated, although conventional and repetitive, also give evidence of his love for his family.

Mary's letters—obliging, kindly, informational—show her to be affectionate and dependable. She held the family groups together through her letters, her boxes of goods, and her visits west about every three years. Yet her voice is the quietest of all in this multidirectioned correspondence. Few people saved her letters as she saved theirs.

The Richmond pair were actually more interesting than their virtuous Delaware connections. David Wilson, articulate and a formidable stylist, optimistic and outspoken, sanguine in the face of financial disaster, never hesitated to say exactly what was on his mind. Wilson's wife, Mary Poole, wrote the best letters of the quartet. Passionate, full of specific detail, and colored by her feelings of privation and cynicism, her letters give us the most information about the life the Wilsons led in Indiana. She talked about her housekeeping activities, generally with disdain. Complaining that she had little time to write letters, Mary Poole Wilson noted,

> I am constantly cooking, washing, scrubbing, and all the other etceteras that belong to a person in my situation, I am alone and of course am "pot wallopper" and "spider hunter" all over the house, still I find some time to sit down but if I am not done over, I find so many stockings to darn, coats to mend, etc. that very little of my time is my *own*.[34]

She found little pleasure in household drudgery, but she liked to do decorative handwork, and while working a pin cushion for her daughter Sarah, she noted that the work went slowly because "I dare not take it up often, I am so fond of it I should spend too much time at it."[35] Even though

---

[33]David Wilson to Mary Wilson Corbit, 31 January 1861.

[34]Mary Poole Wilson to Mary Wilson Corbit, 11 February 1849.

[35]Mary Poole Wilson to Mary Wilson Corbit, 15 February 1849.

she was a poor frontier wife, she continued the gentle activities of the leisure class.

The Wilsons were used to considerable social interaction in the East among friends and relatives; it might be expected that they would move even more freely on the open frontier, but it was not so. Mary Poole Wilson notes repeatedly that they "never visit [others. They] only go to see the children." "I do not visit [except] among our children, if I go [into society], I must have visitors, and it is an expense, and it is to me a toilsome pleasure."[36]

Mary Corbit's world was more real to Mary Poole than her own. When Mary mentioned that the Corbits were dining at Joseph Shipley's in Wilmington, Mary Poole's reaction was dramatic. "O do dear Mary write me a full description of all and every thing that took place there . . . do not forget to tell me by letter, for it may be years ere we meet."[37]

Yearning for respect and for the graceful life she envisioned her Eastern friends living, Mary Poole had to tread a difficult line in her relations with Mary Corbit. She needed things. In fact, she needed everything, and Mary was her best source. Yet she shrank from being the constant suppliant. How to ask for what she needed, urge the things that Mary had forgotten to send, indicate further needs and still not beg, caused Mary Poole to equivocate, posture, and charm. She could only touch on her needs and then pull back. Luckily for her, Mary Corbit never challenged her stepmother's imperious stance. Mary apologized for her tardiness in writing letters and sent more boxes. She was always patient and kindly.

"When thee was here," Mary Poole reminded Mary Corbit, "thee observed I think it time, mother, thee had another black silk dress—if thee has one to spare now, I am ready for it, mine is not fit to wear. Thee also said thee intended to keep thy father in shirts, his thee brought out [on your last trip] are not fit for him to wear. I must at once get some made I cannot do it myself I ought to have told thee long ago, but I did not like to." "I guess I missed the comfortable winter bonnet thee was to send me, but if I live until another winter it will not be so out of *fashion* but that I

---

[36]Ibid.; Mary Poole Wilson to Elizabeth Shipley, n.d.

[37]Mary Poole Wilson to Mary Wilson Corbit, 20 March 1854.

can wear it," she complained faintly. "If thee could see the state of my wardrobe thee would not say 'will thee have'—thee would know I would."[38]

Back in Odessa, Mary Corbit gave birth to her first and only child, a daughter, born in 1848. Mary was thirty-seven at the time of this birth, an elderly primipara. This child, Mary Cowgill (Mollie) Corbit (1848-1923), named for Daniel's grandmother, was the only issue of the union, and the most remarkable figure of the next generation. The social differences between the two branches of the family were only too distinctly drawn in the ways the children of Mary Corbit's siblings were raised compared with the privileged young Mollie Corbit.

The Wilsons struggled valiantly to maintain appearances, though just whom they wished to impress is impossible to say. Western life was hard on individuals, and despite efforts to retain the civilized appearance of the East, differences began to appear. For one thing, the Wilsons lost their teeth. My mouth "has not had a tooth in it for more than two years and [David] has only one," announced Mary Poole Wilson. She wrote this in response to the news that Cousin Daniel had gotten a new set of teeth. Only money stood in the way of gaining this improving apparatus, which cost some $40 or $50. While Mary Poole Wilson was east on a visit, she tried on a cousin's false teeth. "I said take them away I look so handsome with them in, I shall be unhappy if I look at myself much longer."[39] Such incidents reveal only too clearly the importance of appearances rather than convenience in such matters. Similar evidence attests that David Wilson, when sent a check by Daniel and Mary, used the remainder of the funds to purchase a "tile," or a high silk hat, a rather class-definitive item for a farmer and brushmaker to choose for his peregrinations.[40] These efforts to continue with the niceties of life despite their fallen condition must have been fairly successful, though bought with greater effort than previously. On her trip west in 1859, Mary Corbit noted that her sister Sarah "lives very nicely, as indeed do all my family, it gives me great pleasure to find them all so comfortable."[41]

---

[38]Mary Poole Wilson to Mary Wilson Corbit, n.d.; 20 March 1854; 29 August [1850 or 1851].

[39]Mary Poole Wilson to Mary Wilson Corbit, 20 August 1850, 19 April [1850 or 1851].

[40]David Wilson to Mary Wilson Corbit, 31 January 1861.

[41]Mary Wilson Corbit to Daniel Corbit, 28 May 1859.

This positive evidence of success and prosperity in the face of failure was undercut by Mary Poole Wilson's constant chorus of complaints. Her litany was different. "If we could both die at once, I think we should be willing to go and be at rest. It is a continual struggle to keep in bread and meat and if thy father had been like some men, he would have given out long since."[42]

Mary Poole Wilson died in 1863. The family had been living back at the farm for some time. David Wilson acknowledged her loss with his usual equanimity. Her departure led to changes in housing arrangements. David and James, the asthmatic son who outlived his father by seven years, stayed on together in the farmhouse, sometimes with a housekeeper, sometimes with a tenant farmer who took them on as boarders. Again, in this situation class differences and their manifestations in civility rankled. In 1868 his daughter Sarah commented on her father's miseries. David boarded with "very clever farmers," that is, good enough for their station in life; but Wilson was annoyed by many little things to which he had not previously been accustomed. "The way they set the table" was singled out as a proof that the farmers had "no refinement." Sarah was hinting that more money would be welcome so that the Wilsons could move to town, which they would much prefer.[43]

Sarah Poole Wilson Meek had to take over Mary Poole Wilson's begging letters, asking Mary Corbit to send clothes for her father. She did not manage to do it with nearly the charm of her mother; indeed, she complained that she had been given a disagreeable job, thus indicating a diminution of civility in the next generation. "Nothing but dire necessity could incline the dear but proud old Father to ask for favors. Sis is it not mortifying I pity him."[44]

Just how badly off were the Wilsons? Without doubt, they had fallen from their former grand state. Without doubt, they had been used to more. Moreover, they did not prosper by local standards. They considered themselves poor. Should we consider them so? Probably not. Although in debt, they had assets. They owned the farm to the end. They had a trade that produced some profits. When the farm was rented, they had the benefit

---

[42]Mary Poole Wilson to Mary Wilson Corbit, 29 March 1853.

[43]Sarah Wilson Meek to Mary Wilson Corbit, 18 January 1868.

[44]Sarah Wilson Meek to Mary Wilson Corbit, date illegible [1860?].

of half the produce with none of the labor. Their well-off relatives were generous. Mary Poole Wilson had hired help part of the time. They maintained the badges of class in dress—David Wilson in his silk hat, Mary Poole Wilson in her hand-me-down black silks. They disdained to mix with the plain people of Indiana, preferring to keep to themselves and their children. Although they felt themselves sadly fallen, they maintained a precarious respectability that made them appear gentry to their farmer neighbors.

The Richmond children were not torn between two cultures as the parents had been: they accepted the class differences their parents could not. In becoming artisans, white-collar workers, service employees, and adventurers, the uneducated Wilson children made a living as best they could and married into similar families. David Wilson's grandchildren are listed as hotel clerks, blacksmiths, and mechanics.[45] Wilson's letters show precious little pride in them. By contrast, their cousin Mollie, the daughter of Daniel and Mary Corbit, was a lady.

The contrast was dramatic because as the Wilsons lost hopes of success, the Corbits got richer and richer. Among other interests, Daniel got in on the peach boom, and in 1862 harvested 20,000 baskets of peaches.[46] Mollie's letters make it clear that he was regarded as a "weighty Friend" by Quakers at Westtown Boarding School in Westtown, Pennsylvania.

Ironically, Mollie Corbit was the grandchild most like David Wilson. Charming and articulate, innocent and well bred, she was an earnest, if not a brilliant, student. She attended Vassar Female College before going back home to what had become Odessa. In 1876, at the age of twenty-eight, she married Edward Tatnall Warner (1835-1904). Warner was thirteen years her senior and had already been widowed twice. Three sons were born to the Warners: Daniel Corbit (1878-1895), John (1884-1911), and Edward Tatnall (1889-1890). All died fairly young and without issue. Mollie was a widow for almost twenty years.

Perhaps in an effort to perpetuate her personality and family in another way, Mollie Warner collected things. Her house in Wilmington was full of the mementos of family, travel, reading, and living. She collected

---

[45]"Wilson Family Genealogy Notes," miscellaneous notes unascribed and unpaged, filed at the Wilson-Warner House.

[46]David Wilson to Mary Wilson Corbit, 9 July 1862.

the possessions of her ancestors and marked them with their historical origin: brass tags on the furniture, paper slips on the textiles, and engravings on the silver testify to her attention to detail and filial piety.

In 1901 Mollie Corbit Warner bought back the Wilson house that her grandfather David Wilson II had lost at the forced sale so long before. She paid $2,500 for it, "boxwoods and all." She never chose to live there, but she modernized it and rented it out until her death in 1923. She left the mansion, her family relics, "and anything else of interest to the people of Odessa." The house became a museum after 1925 and for some years housed the free public library established by Dr. James Corbit in 1847. In 1969 the house was deeded to the Henry Francis du Pont Winterthur Museum of American Decorative Arts and is presently administered by that institution. The Corbit house, where Mrs. Warner actually grew up, has also come to be part of Winterthur by a different route.

Mollie Corbit Warner is singlehandedly responsible for the preservation of the Wilson house. She even managed to pull her unwilling relatives into the activity, and her mark is literally everywhere—from her portrait, to her marble plaque, to the identification labels. She took an interest in the old Corbit graveyard, walling in a section of the burial ground at the Friends' Meeting House and moving in certain selected gravestones, but not the graves, of ancestors she wanted included. Her efforts to redeem the possessions of her scattered family have also succeeded in preserving their papers at the Winterthur Library. They were a group that might easily have been lost without the saving graces of Mary Wilson Corbit and her daughter Mary Corbit Warner.[47]

What can be learned about the structure of the family from this case history? For the Wilsons, economic circumstances bore on family relations. The move west—a lateral move—was also a move down—a vertical move. For others as well, migration westward was likely to be born of economic necessity, and such relocations did not necessarily repair broken fortunes. To the strain of spatial distance, migration could also add widening social distance.

---

[47]Mrs. Earl Rosman Crowe, Mrs. Paul Jennings Nowland, Mrs. Charles Lee Reese, Jr., and Mrs. David Meredith Reese, "Mrs. Edward Tatnall Warner, 1848-1923, Reminiscences of Aunt Mollie, January 1969, by Four of Her Great-Nieces," MS on file at the Wilson-Warner House, 12.

Yet, for all this, in the Wilson case, the ties of responsibility and affection were not broken. Money and goods flowed into the Wilson household from their children back home. Though never enough and often in hand-me-down form, Eastern contributions kept the Western household afloat. The families remained close in spirit, perhaps closer than had they stayed nearby, for the Wilsons clung to their Delaware connections as to a lifeline holding them to a respectable past. Distance, changed occupations, changed interests, and the widening economic gap did not sever the ties that bound them together.

Family connections could not bear the strain forever, though. The second generation of Western Wilsons forgot the old places and the old people. The sense of obligation in Cantwell's Bridge was lost after David Wilson and Mary Poole Wilson died. The cousins had little in common and grew increasingly apart. When Mollie Warner set out to reconstruct her heritage, she sought the origins of her great-grandfather David Wilson I rather than searching for her Western cousins. Distance broke off the feeling of family membership and destroyed the strength of relationships.

The Wilson story suggests the interrelation of family and place. Ties formed in proximity in Cantwell's Bridge stretched elastically across the miles. But lacking the constant renewal of association in the next generation, family bonds weakened and broke. The David Wilsons bridged two places and two families. For all their years spent in Indiana, they were more of the old place than the new. Only the graves of the David Wilsons remain in Richmond, Indiana; however, as evidence of their deep roots in "dear old Cantwell's Bridge," their residence has been "frozen" for them on Main Street in Odessa, Delaware.

Chapter Sixteen

PROBLEMS AND POSSIBILITIES
OF INDIVIDUAL-LEVEL TRACING
IN GERMAN-AMERICAN
MIGRATION RESEARCH*

Walter D. Kamphoefner

At an international conference more than twenty years ago, Frank Thistlethwaite issued a challenge to historians of migration. Bemoaning the "salt-water curtain inhibiting [American] understanding of European origins" of immigrants and similarly obscuring for Europeans the fate of migrants once they left their native shores, Thistlethwaite urged scholars to adopt a new viewpoint "from neither the continent of origin nor from the principal country of reception . . . neither of emigrants nor immigrants, but of migrants, and to treat the process of migration as a complete sequence of experience."[1]

---

*This paper was originally presented at the Eighth International Economic History Congress, Budapest, 1982. My thanks to the session participants for their comments and suggestions.

[1]Frank Thistlethwaite, "Migration from Europe Overseas in the Nineteenth and Twentieth Centuries," *XIᵉ Congres International des Sciences Historiques, Stockholm 1960, Rapports, V; Histoire Contemporaine* (Stockholm, 1960) 32-60.

My dissertation was a response to his challenge, an attempt to break through the "salt-water curtain," to trace a group of migrants from Germany to America and study them both in their European and their American social context.[2] Moreover, in the spirit of the "New Social History," I wanted to study migration "from the bottom up," to meet on their own terms the unlettered masses who made up the bulk of the newcomers to America, rather than rely on the accounts of elite observers. One of the principal questions that interested me was whether the opportunities offered to immigrants in America matched our egalitarian rhetoric. But what I shall present here are not so much substantive findings as an overview of my tracing techniques and some suggestions for future research in this direction.

The linking of German emigrant lists with American census data can shed light on a number of important questions relating to social mobility. The most obvious of these issues is the degree to which the "American Dream" was actually fulfilled for immigrants, particularly those who came over poor or penniless. Studies of mobility that begin on the American side are forced to make assumptions about the European background on the basis of an aggregate profile that may or may not hold true for a given individual.

In fact, even at the aggregate level, German emigration statistics are usually so imprecise that they give little indication of the social origins of migrants or the selectivity of migration. Moreover, their definition of emigration was usually jurisdictional rather than socioeconomic, so that anyone who crossed the border of even a petty principality was thrown into the same category as those who braved an ocean journey.[3]

---

[2]Walter Kamphoefner, "Transplanted Westfalians: Persistence and Transformation of Socioeconomic and Cultural Patterns in the Northwest German Migration to Missouri" (dissertation, University of Missouri, 1978); revised German version under the title: *Westfalen in der Neuen Welt: Eine Sozialgeschichte der Auswanderung im 19. Jahrhundert* (Münster, 1982).

[3]In the Prussian emigration statistics from 1862 to 1871, for example, the tabulations of occupation, age, and family status lump together overseas emigrants with continental migrants and those moving to other German states. The occupational statistics enumerate Westfalians and Rhinelanders under the mostly East Elbian agricultural categories: 1. Gutsbesitzer, Pächter, Inspectoren, Verwalter; 2. Winzer, Gärtner, Jäger, Fischer; 3. Gesinde und Arbeiter bei der Land- und Forstwirtschaft. Furthermore, no distinction is made between industry and artisanship, much less between individual artisan occupations. All one learns for certain about the emigrants to North America is their absolute number. *Preussische Statistik* 26 (Berlin, 1874).

In addition to the narrow issue of socioeconomic mobility, there are a number of other questions that can be addressed by tracing individual migration paths and careers. First of all, the importance of chain migration and the degree of ethnic homogeneity at the local level can be more accurately assessed. Some answers may also be provided to the paradox that although German immigrants were predominantly rural (if not always agricultural) in origin, many of them located in American cities. German-Americans were more urban than either the American population as a whole or the countrymen they had left behind. Was this urbanization primarily the result of positive factors such as the demand for artisan skills, or does it reflect a negative factor, such as lack of enough funds to travel further or acquire land? The paths of mobility followed by Germans in America may be suggestive of the motives behind emigration. For example, it has commonly been argued that many artisans emigrated to preserve traditional skills that were being undermined by industrialization in Europe.

Germany in the nineteenth century encompassed a great deal of diversity in dialect, religion, and economic patterns, and political unification was not achieved until 1871. In selecting case-study sites for tracing, one should observe at least the tripartite division of Germany into the regions east of the Elbe and those north and south of the Main River respectively. Some account should also be taken of the degree of industrialization and urbanization in various regions of origin. On the American side a similar distinction should be maintained between rural Midwest, urban Midwest, and East Coast cities, the three main areas of German settlement. As my earlier work has demonstrated, the concentration of Germans from a given region varied widely from state to state in America. Thus it would be interesting, for example, to compare Wurttembergers in Philadelphia, where they were heavily over-represented, with those in St. Louis, where they were relatively scarce.[4] It would also be important to develop a comparative profile of the background of Germans settling in rural as opposed to urban areas. These, then, are some of the general principles that should be taken into consideration when designing tracing studies.

---

[4]Kamphoefner, "Transplanted Westfalians," ch. 4; "Transplanted Villages: Regional Distribution and Patterns of Settlement of Germans in America to 1870," paper presented at the Social Science History Association Meeting, Cambridge MA, 1979.

The first nationwide agreement to register and enumerate emigrants from Germany went into force in 1846, but many states or provinces had been collecting such information already. Moreover, even after 1846, or 1871 for that matter, there was no standard agreement as to what information should be gathered. Typically, emigrant lists recorded the name, age, occupation, and place of birth or residence of the principal emigrant, and sometimes of accompanying family members as well. Data on clandestine emigrants, if collected at all, was of necessity second hand, and thus less accurate. No emigrant list is ever 100 percent complete, though one can assume that the lower the level of jurisdiction at which information was gathered, the higher the degree of coverage and accuracy.

Such emigrant lists were gathered all over Germany, but there appear to be some regional differences as to the amount of archival material that has survived to the present day. A goodly proportion of what has survived has been transcribed and published in one form or another. Although this is a big help for researchers, it is often worthwhile to spot-check the original files as well. For example, I discovered that the lists from *Regierungsbezirk* Münster contained information on money holdings for the years 1846 to 1850, though this was in no way indicated in the publication.[5] The data situation is perhaps best in Northwest Germany and the Middle Rhine region. For the region of heaviest emigration, Baden-Wurttemberg, published material is scarce, though archival holdings appear to be plentiful. For areas east of the Elbe, very little has been published, and it is not certain how much of the archival material that once existed has been preserved. West German archives are increasingly publishing overviews of their holdings, and a genealogical guide gives an excellent summary of both archival and published sources reaching up to about 1970.[6]

---

[5]Friedrich Muller, "Westfälische Auswanderer im 19. Jahrhundert: Auswanderer aus dem Regierungsbezirk Münster, 1803-1850," *Beiträge zur Westfälischen Familienforschung* 22-24 (1964-1966): 7-484; this source also gives citation of the archival material in Staatsarchiv Münster on which it is based.

[6]For a bibliography of published emigrant lists and similar material, see Clifford Neal Smith, *Encyclopedia of German-American Genealogical Research* (New York and London, 1976) 208-32. For a similar guide to primary sources, see the companion volume, Clifford Neal Smith, *American Genealogical Resources in German Archives* (Munich, 1977). The latter volume is based on the unpublished eleven-part archival survey, "Americana in

Tracing any given German emigrant to his place of settlement in America or following any German immigrant in the U.S. back to his village of origin is quite a challenge. Tracing a large enough group to allow for social-scientific generalizations is an even more difficult task, but it is not impossible. Four possible research strategies are outlined below, three of which the author has applied in practice. Briefly categorized, they are the homogeneous American settlement, the selected small German state, the alphabetic sample, and the computer-search approach or technique.

The homogeneous-American-settlement approach is almost self-explanatory; what is not so self-evident is how one finds such a cluster in the first place. Moreover, not any settlement will do—there must be surviving emigrant lists on the German side. Thus it might seem logical to start with such lists and see which destinations were most prominent in a given area. In practice, however, destinations were recorded rather unsystematically, and were usually not very specific or accurate. The most fruitful approach is probably to start on the American side and work back. Not that the United States Census is of much help in this respect: only in rare instances does it give more than state of birth. But local-history sources, especially biographical sketches in county histories, often mention the town or county (*Kreis*) of birth.[7] A tabulation of such sources will usually bring to light such a concentration if one exists. Other local sources such as German-American parish records often provide information on town of origin, as do some early naturalization records before the process became bureaucratized and the application forms standardized.

---

deutschen Sammlungen," compiled by the Deutsche Gesellschaft für Amerikastudien in 1958-1961. As Smith cautions in his preface, "It cannot be asserted that the Handbook is complete; many small communal archives and those of most noble estates are not included; the vast archival remains in East Germany are missing entirely." Moreover, as West German archives become more thoroughly catalogued, additional material has probably come to light, and some material from local archives has been collected in regional centers. [Editor's note: for additional source material, see the Appendix to this chapter.]

[7]For more information on such county-history biographies and an evaluation of their worth as a historical source, see Archibald Hanna, "Every Man His Own Biographer," *Proceedings of the American Antiquarian Society* 80 (1970): 291-98. Although the originals are often inaccessible, a number of such volumes have been reprinted in recent years. A major microfilming project by Research Publications International has preserved more than 2,000 such titles from the states of California, Illinois, Indiana, Michigan, New York, Ohio, Pennsylvania, and Wisconsin.

One final clue that can often be helpful in determining the German area of origin is local place names. The only nationwide study of this subject dates back to the Nazi era and is grossly inadequate.[8] But a detailed late-nineteenth-century American map would probably reveal many more German namesakes than have survived to the present, especially among tiny villages or townships. Not every German name reflects a homogeneous settlement, however, especially in the case of big cities such as Hamburg or Berlin. But by using a combination of the indicators outlined above, one should be able to detect homogeneous settlements and link them up with their German roots. In the case of my first tracing study, there were two towns only six miles apart in America named after two towns only twenty miles apart in Germany; this provided the first clue of a homogeneous settlement. A tabulation of immigrant birthplaces recorded in a county history heightened my suspicion. Investigation of German emigrant lists revealed a migration chain of about 150 families from the *Kreis* or county of Tecklenberg who settled in two adjoining counties in the state of Missouri. In fact, more than 200 persons in this area could be traced back to the same village in Germany.

Although the discovery of such a homogeneous pattern of settlement was significant in itself, even more important was the opportunity this presented to study at the individual level the degree of social mobility resulting from emigration. The chances for economic advancement appear to have been excellent for this traced group. Nearly three-fourths of them had become landowning farmers according to the 1850 U.S. Census, and an even higher proportion reported real estate holdings of some kind. Former peasant proprietors did fare better than those who had been tenants in Europe, but the gap between these two classes had narrowed considerably in the New World. Although German artisans generally found their skills in demand in America, those in this group frequently gave up their trades for agricultural pursuits.[9]

One suspects, however, that ethnically homogeneous areas are subject to the same biases for social-mobility studies as they are for investi-

---

[8]Norbert Zimmer, *Der Siedlungsweg der Niedersachsen über die Erde* (Hannover, 1934); for a list of Southwest German place names, see Arnold Scheuerbrandt, "Sudwestdeutsche Einwanderung und Siedlungsgrundung in USA," in *USA und Baden-Württemberg in ihren geschichtlichen Beziehungen: Beiträge und Bilddocumente* (Stuttgart, 1976) 50-61.

[9]Walter Kamphoefner, "Transplanted Westfalians," ch. 6.

gations of voting patterns: people behave differently in homogeneous than in heterogeneous settings. Indeed, settlement in an ethnic enclave or outside it may represent a self-selection process and produce subgroups that vary systematically in important personal and sociological characteristics. It is not clear, though, whether rates of social mobility in ethnic enclaves would have been above or below average (or perhaps less extreme in both directions). Thus it would be desirable to locate and trace immigrants both within and outside of such ethnic concentrations, not only in rural areas but also in cities, where the German population tended to be more heterogeneous.

Here the fragmentation of nineteenth-century Germany into a number of sovereign states is to the historian's advantage. The U.S. Census, from 1860 on, generally recorded the German state of birth, including such tiny sovereignties as the Duchy of Brunswick or the Principality of Lippe Detmold, with areas not much bigger than American counties, and populated by only a few thousand emigrants. By selecting immigrants from such states, the process of linkage is much simpler than with immigration from some Prussian *Kreis* of the same size, which would require checking nearly half of all German-Americans as potential matches, since the census usually recorded their birthplaces simply as Prussia. Selecting a dwarf state would greatly simplify a comparison between settlers in homogeneous versus heterogeneous areas. Also, urban-history and social-mobility studies have computerized the census for several urban areas, and could provide a listing of all persons from a given birthplace.

This approach was applied in my second case study, using natives of two tiny principalities, Brunswick and Lippe Detmold, as "tracer elements," to investigate immigrant mobility.[10] Thus it was possible to deal with all the immigrants from these states, and to compare the unmatched with the matched. Using data from the 1860 Manuscript Census, immigrants in three distinctive environments were compared: four counties of rural Missouri, the Midwestern city of St. Louis, and the East Coast me-

---

[10]Walter Kamphoefner, "Predisposing Factors in German-American Urbanization," paper presented at the Organization of American Historians Meeting, Philadelphia, 1982. Sources of published emigration lists were Fritz Verdenhalven, *Die Auswanderer aus dem Fürstentum Lippe (bis 1877)* (Detmold, 1980); Fritz Gruhne, *Auswandererlisten des ehemaligen Herzogtums Braunschweig: ohne Stadt Braunschweig und Landkreis Holzminden, 1846-1871* (Braunschweig, 1971).

tropolis of Philadelphia. In the latter case the Philadelphia Social History
Project cooperated in supplying a list of all natives of Brunswick and Lippe
Detmold in the city. I ended with two data sets, each with about 1,800
individuals, including children born in America and other household
members. The success ratio in matching was about sixty percent for Lippe,
but considerably lower for Brunswick.

The mobility patterns of immigrants from Lippe in rural Missouri were
very similar to those found in my earlier study of the Tecklenburgers, as
indeed they should have been, for the two groups were very similar in regional origins and social composition. One striking feature was the homogeneity of settlement patterns: nearly all of the Lippe Detmolders were
concentrated in two of the four counties studied. Property holdings were
small, but property was widely distributed and rates of ownership high.
Social class in Germany did exert an influence on wealth, but the difference between peasant proprietors and tenants was mostly in size of holdings, and the gap narrowed with time.

Size of place of origin apparently had little influence on urban settlement in America, nor did previous occupation appear particularly important. While three-fourths of those who were artisans in America had
also been so in Germany, less than half of all emigrating artisans remained
with their trades in the New World. Perhaps more important as a factor
in urban settlement was the life-cycle stage. Germans who migrated to
American cities were much like those who moved from the countryside to
German cities: they were usually young and unmarried. Furthermore, the
urban German-American population contained a higher proportion of recent arrivals than rural immigrant settlements, suggesting that many Germans initially stopped in American cities, and moved on when they had
accumulated enough earnings to establish themselves on farms or in small-
town businesses.

Still, these approaches also have their limits. For Northwest Germany, the states of Lippe Detmold and Brunswick provide ideal case studies on the basis of published emigrant lists. For Southwest Germany, the
only state of comparable size is Nassau, but the emigrant lists from this
state, though published, are too incomplete in their information for adequate matching, and rarely include occupational data.[11]

---

[11]Struck, *Auswanderung aus Nassau*, appendix. [Editor's note: see Appendix for full
publication information.]

Two of the most interesting German states for a tracing study are the East Elbian states of Mecklenburg and the Kingdom of Saxony, for they represent the extremes of the agricultural-industrial continuum. Since each constituted about three percent of the total German emigration, they would also yield sample groups of an optimal size—small enough to be manageable but large enough for adequate generalization. A problem arises, however, when it comes to emigrant lists. Only a very few have been published for either area. In fact, there is very little published individual-level information on any East Elbian emigrants.[12] How much unpublished material has survived in archives at various levels of administration is an open question at present. If such archival sources are still extant, exploiting them for tracing purposes could be a fruitful area of East-West cooperation.

If, for any of the reasons cited above, working with emigrant lists from the area of origin does not prove feasible, then the Hamburg passenger lists might provide an attractive alternative.[13] Of course, some method of sampling would have to be devised to select from the literally millions who traveled via this port. The best approach might be a total enumeration of emigrants from Mecklenburg and Saxony combined with an alphabetic sample of the rest of the emigration. (An alphabetic sample consists of all persons whose last name begins with a given letter.) This would greatly facilitate tracing and matching on the American side, especially where alphabetized census indexes are available.[14] One could also construct an economic and occupational profile of emigrants, at least for East Elbians, by region of origin. The alphabetic approach could likewise be used to narrow down a case study of emigrants from states such as Baden, Wurt-

---

[12]For a list of emigrants from Mecklenburg-Schwerin in the years 1861-1864, see Max Wiegland, "Die Auswanderung aus Mecklenburg-Schwerin in überseeische Länder," *Jahrbuch des Vereins für Mecklenburgische Geschichte und Altertumskunde* 94 (1930): 277-94. A list of Old Lutheran emigrants, primarily from Brandenburg, Silesia, and Pommerania, in the 1830s and 1840s, is included in Wilhelm Iwan, *Die Altlutherische Auswanderung um die Mitte des 19. Jahrhunderts*, vol. 2 (Ludwigsburg, 1943) 241-96.

[13]The port of Hamburg began keeping emigration lists in 1837; those from 1850 on have been preserved. For details, see "Quellenkundliches Rundgespräch," 49-51 [Editor's note: see Appendix for full publication information]. Smith, *Encyclopedia*, 199-200.

[14]See John A. Phillips, "Achieving a Critical Mass while Avoiding an Explosion: Letter-Cluster Sampling and Nominal Record Linkage," *Journal of Interdisciplinary History* 9 (1979): 493-508; Michael D. Ornstein and A. Gordon Darroch, "National Mobility Studies in Past Time: A Sampling Strategy," *Historical Methods* 11 (1978): 152-61.

temberg, Bavaria, or Hesse, since each constituted about ten percent of the total emigration, which is too much for them to be treated in their entirety.[15]

Disappointingly, there is a considerable proportion of immigrants who only recorded their birthplace as "Germany" in the census, about fifteen percent of all German-Americans in 1870 and considerably more in other years. Moreover, it appears that information on German state of birth was gathered most systematically where Germans made up a large share of the population and had enough political influence to be appointed as census takers. American or Irish enumerators were more likely to write simply "German" rather than inquire further. There may be some social skewing in whether a person identified himself nationally or regionally. Besides, one would like to devise a system that kept at a minimum the manual searching through census microfilm rolls.

An ideal solution would be to leave most of the searching to the computer and scan a large, heterogeneous cross-section of America. Computerized indexes of the U.S. Census of 1850 have been prepared for all or most of the states, and there are scattered indexes for other years as well, especially 1860.[16] With the cooperation of the private firms that published these indexes, it would be possible to obtain a statewide list of names in machine-readable form. Because of the wide variations in spelling that result when American census takers record German names, these would have to be converted to phonetic equivalents, preferably with the Russel Soundex system. The computer program developed by the Philadelphia Social History Project to translate names into the Soundex code has produced good results.[17]

---

[15]Regional archives in Baden contain information on roughly 100,000 emigrating individuals or families; see "Quellenkundliches Rundgesprach," 10. For Wurttemberg, the holdings of Hauptstaatsarchiv Stuttgart include lists for the entire Kingdom for the years 1849-1852 and 1854. Continuous runs of emigrant lists for the period 1817-1860 have been preserved for a number of Oberämter (counties) in Staatsarchiv Ludwigsburg, and were utilized in a recent study, Wolfgang V. Hippel, Auswanderung aus Südwestdeutschland: Studien zur württembergischen Auswanderung und Auswanderungspolitik im 18. und 19. Jahrhundert (Stuttgart, 1984).

[16]Census indexes for most of the United States in 1850 can be obtained from: Ronald V. Jackson and Gary R. Teeples, Accelerated Indexing Systems, Inc., 3346 S. Orchard Dr., Bountiful UT, 84010.

[17]For an explanation of the Soundex system and a discussion of some of the problems of individual-level tracing in the United States Census, see Theodore Hershberg, "Record Linkage," Historical Methods Newsletter 9 (1976): 137-63.

Many German names are unique to certain localities or regions, so that the emigration list from a given *Kreis* or *Amt* should yield a short list of names, including many uncommon ones. If such an emigrant list were computerized and converted to Soundex, and the same done with a state-wide census index, one could then do a computerized search for names with the same phonetic code in both sources. (One would probably want to throw out such common names as Meyer, Schmidt, and Muller, and perhaps a few others; besides being very common in Germany, they also have the same Soundex code as the common English names of Moore, Smith, and Miller.) Sorting by census order, one would produce a compact list of probable matches that could be checked with one pass through the microfilmed census rolls. Once completed, this would provide a comparison of immigrants in rural and urban areas, in homogeneous German settlements and scattered among Anglo-Americans. The only remaining distortions would result from severely misspelled names or people omitted from the census. Otherwise, everyone would have the same chance of being matched. This approach would work equally well for any area of Germany where emigrant lists were available. Moreover, it might also turn up homogeneous immigrant settlements that were otherwise unsuspected.

In conclusion, the importance of individual-level tracing for an understanding of the process of migration and acculturation is becoming ever more apparent. Moreover, the strategies outlined above should make research of this type feasible for other scholars of German-America. With similar studies on Scandinavians, Dutch, Italians, and Eastern Europeans nearing completion, historians of migration may at last be in a position to fling wide open the "salt water curtain."

APPENDIX

Several published emigrant lists were either overlooked by Smith or have since appeared: Wolf Heino Struck, *Die Auswanderung aus dem Herzogtum Nassau (1806-1866)* (Wiesbaden, 1966); Norbert Scheele, "Auswanderungen aus Stadt und Amt Olpe nach Amerika in den Jahren 1834 bis 1890," *Heimatstimmen aus dem Kreise Olpe* 2 (1948): 80-114; Julius Pickert, "Auswanderungen aus der Stadt- und Landgemeinde Attendorn nach Amerika," *Heimatstimmen aus dem Kreise Olpe* 4 (1949): 201-204; name index of the two above, ibid., 224-28. Additional articles in the *Heimatstimmen* 1-17 (1948-1954) provide information on the location of settlements in America. Friedrich Blendinger, "Die Auswanderung nach Nordamerika aus dem Regierungsbezirk Oberbayern in den Jahren, 1846-1852," *Zeitschrift für bayrische Landesgeschichte* 27 (1964): 430-87; Fritz Verdenhalven, *Die Auswanderer aus dem Fürstentum Lippe (bis 1877)* (Detmold, 1980); Friedrich Muller, "Westfälische Auswanderer aus dem Regierungsbezirk Minden, 1816-1900," *Beiträge zur westfalischen Familienforschung* 38-39 (1980-1981): 1-711.

The proceeds of a 1977 conference dealing with sources and methods of German emigration research were recently published by Willi Paul Adams, ed., *Die deutschsprachige Auswanderung in die Vereinigten Staaten: Berichte über Forschungsstand und Quellenbestände* (Berlin, 1980), including reports on emigrant lists and other archival material in the German states of the Palatinate, Hesse, Hamburg, Baden, and Wurttemberg as well as Austria and Switzerland. A session of the German archivists' conference in 1978 covered much of the same ground, though not in such detail. For an abstract of the proceedings and the text of several reports, see "Quellenkundliches Rundgespräch: Die Auswanderung nach Ubersee im 19. Jahrhundert—Forschungsansätze und archivarische Quellen," *Der Archivar* 32 (1979): 9-11, 49-72.

CONTRIBUTORS

John W. Adams, Associate Professor of Anthropology, University of South Carolina, Columbia

Robert Charles Anderson, Salt Lake City, Utah, is a trained historian, author, and certified genealogist

Virginia DeJohn Anderson, Assistant Professor of History, University of Colorado, Boulder

Lee L. Bean, Professor of Sociology, University of Utah, Salt Lake City

Claudia Bushman, Newark, Delaware, historian and author, is Executive Director of the Delaware Heritage Commission

Ralph J. Crandall, Director, New England Historic Genealogical Society, Boston, Massachusetts

David Hackett Fischer, Earl Warren Professor of History, Brandeis University, Waltham, Massachusetts

Samuel P. Hays, Distinguished Service Professor of History, University of Pittsburgh, Pittsburgh, Pennsylvania

Willard Heiss, Indianapolis, Indiana, a certified genealogist, is Chairman of the Family History Section of the Indiana Historical Society

Walter D. Kamphoefner, Assistant Professor of History, University of Miami, Coral Gables, Florida

Alice Bee Kasakoff, Associate Professor of Anthropology, University of South Carolina, Columbia

Lawrence J. Kilbourne is Air Force historian at Lackland AFB, San Antonio, Texas

Dean L. May, Associate Professor of History, University of Utah, Salt Lake City

Elizabeth Shown Mills, Tuscaloosa, Alabama, is a certified genealogist, author, and teacher

Patricia Trainor O'Malley, Professor of History, Bradford College, Bradford, Massachusetts

James M. O'Toole, Archivist, Archdiocese of Boston, Brighton, Massachusetts

Andrejs Plakans, Professor of History, Iowa State University, Ames

Anita H. Rutman, Adjunct Professor of History, University of Florida, Gainesville

Darrett B. Rutman, Graduate Research Professor, History Department, University of Florida, Gainesville

John A. Schutz, Professor of History, University of Southern California, Los Angeles

Mark H. Skolnick, Associate Professor of Human Genetics, University of Utah, Salt Lake City

Robert M. Taylor, Jr., Director, Indiana Guide Project, Madison (IN) Architecture Project, Indiana Historical Society, Indianapolis

Index

Acy, Margaret, 194
Acy, William, 194
Adams, Samuel, 161
Allen, James, 161
American Antiquarian Society, 163
American Society of Genealogists, 13, 14
Anderson, Christopher, 238
Anthropology
    functionalist village studies in, 61
    genealogies in, 53, 130
    and history, 74-75, 131
Antiquarian, as term of opprobrium, 82
Apthorp, Charles, 169
Archivists, role of, in new social history, 43-51

Ball, Kezia (or Keziah), 257
Bancroft family, 178
Barker, Thomas, 197
Batchelder family, 254
Beamon, William, 274
Belcher, Andrew, 277, 278, 285
Belcher, Jonathan, 274, 278, 280
Bennett, Joanna, 195
Berlin, Ira, 102
Beverly, Robert, 91
Black genealogists, 98
Blassingame, John W., 102
Blowers, Rev. Thomas, 277
Bowdoin, James, 169
Brandon family, 96-97
Brewster family, 218
Bridge family, 281-82
Briggs, Harmon, 178
Brocklebank, Jane, 197-98

Bromfield, Edward, 280, 282
Bromfield, Mary Danforth, 278
Bureau of Refugees, Freedmen, and Abandoned Lands, records of, 98
Burpee, Thomas, 195
Byrd, William, 91, 262

Cambridge Group for the History of Population and Social Structure, 18, 35
Canon Law, New Code of (1917), 114
Cantwell's Bridge, 294, 296
Cappon, Lester J., 17
Carter, James Earl, 238
"Catholic Charities," 120
Catholic Family Movement, 112
Catholic Order of Forresters, 120
Catholic Rural Life Conference, 112
Catholic Worker Movement, 112
"Celtic Thesis" of Southern history, 91n
Census records
    computerization of, 48-50
    in family history, 21
    indexing of, 36
    migration research with, 36, 40-41, 142-43
    of Southern U.S., 96-97
Certification of genealogists, 14
Charleville family, 95
Cherokee Indians, 98
Cherry Street Monthly Meeting, Philadelphia, 297, 301
Coale, Ansley, 203
Colket, Meredith B., Jr., 13
Collective biography, 162-63
Comer, Bragg, 96

Compendium of American Genealogy, 12
Computers, in historical research, 20, 60
Cooke, Elisha, 161
Corbit family
  class differences, 308
  close ties of, 308-309
  marriage into Wilson family, 299
  Mary Corbit as bridge between the
    Wilsons and Corbits, 300
  weakening of family bonds, 309
  See also Wilson family
Cousin marriage, 58-61
Crosby, Constance, 197
Crosby, Jane Sothern, 194
Crosby, Thomas, 194
Cushing family, 169-70
Cushing, Thomas, 278

Danforth family, 272-90
  See also Migration
Daughters of the American Revolution, 38
Degler, Carl, 92, 104
Demos, John, 19
Dictionary of American Biography, 12
Dolan, Jay, 112
Dow, Josiah, 205-206, 209
Doyle, Don H., 153
Dresser, John, 198
Duck Creek Monthly Meeting, 294
Dunbar, Hannah Danforth, 283
Dupee, Captain Isaac, 279
Duty, Joseph, 189
Dwight family, 172-74, 176-77
Dyer, Gustavus W., 106

Elder, Glen, Jr., 24
Ellsworth, Hannah, 194, 199
Ellsworth, Jeremiah, 194, 199
Emerson family, 230, 235
Endogamy, defined, 62n
Essex Institute, 163
Ethnic history, 33-34
Eugenics, 9, 11. *See also* Race suicide

Fairview, Utah, 145, 147, 154
Family history, 32-33
Family-cycle model, historians' use of, in
  family history, 22
Family reconstitution, 18, 35, 64n
Family traditions, oral, questions about, 10
Farmer, John, 5

Federation of American Family Associations, 12
Fertility, in Hampton, New Hampshire
  biological factors, 208
  changes in marital fertility, 207-208
  decline in, by mid-eighteenth century,
    206-207
  land scarcity as factor, 210-11
  psychological changes of greatest
    importance, 211
  reproductive rates by class, 209
  urban-industrial explanation, 204, 209
  voluntary limitation, 208-209
"Filiopietistic antiquarianism," defined, 86
Fiske, John, 17
Fitch, Abiel Danforth, 278, 279
Fitch, John, 279
Fitch, Martha Stoddard, 279
Fitch, Thomas, 279
Folger family, 177-78
Fortes, Meyer, 128
Foxcroft, Daniel, 274
Frankfurt, Maine, 169
French, Nicholas, 280
Fulton, John, 204, 210

Gardner, Silvester, 169
Genealogical Helper, 37, 38, 39
Genealogical Journal, 21
Genealogical Society of Pennsylvania, 6,
  12, 14
Genealogical Society of Utah, 6, 7
Genealogies
  accuracy of, 24-25, 206
  adequacy of migration information in,
    68-69
  coverage of wealth differences in, com-
    pared with general population, 66-68
  in historical research, methodological
    considerations of, 24
  provincialism in, 71
  women in, 69
Genealogists
  major contributions of, 43
  and writing of family history narratives,
    25, 43, 48
Genealogy, history of
  in America, 4-15
  colonial, 4
  Revolution to Civil War, 4-6, 15, 81

Civil War to World War I, 6-11, 15,
    81-82
  1920s, 11-12
  1930s, 12-13
  World War II to present, 13-15
  lack of research in, 4
Genealogy
  analogous to mathematics, 82-83
  as auxiliary discipline of social sciences,
    84
  and blacks, 80
  and collective biography, 87
  and Jews, 79-80
  and literary critics, 1930s, 13
  overlooked by historians, reasons for, xii
  qualities of, 21
  reasons for popularity, 80-81
  relationship to field of history, 15-26,
    29-31, 39-40, and professional schol-
    ars, 81-82
  why neglected in academia, 84-87
German village genealogies (Ortssippen-
    bücher), 132
Gitksan Indians, 56, 58, 61, 76-77
Glendale, Utah, 145, 148, 154
Goody, Jack, 130
Grant, Jane, 197
Gray, William, 248
Greene, David L., 87
Greven, Philip, 18, 157
Guardianship records, 44

Haley, Alex, 3, 80, 90, 99
Hall, Van Beck, 19
Halpern, Joel M., 139
Hamilton, Ontario, Canada, 77
Hampton, New Hampshire, 205-14
Hancock, Thomas, 169
Hartwell, Elizabeth, 223
Hartwell, Ephraim, 233
Hazen, Edward, 185, 194
Hazen, Richard, 185
Hennesey, James, 112
Henretta, James, 209
Hicksite Quakers, 295
Hidden, Sarah, 199
Hobson, Ann Reyner, 196
Hobson, William, 196
Hollingsworth, T. H., 19
Holy Name Society, 119

Houtart, Francois, 122
Hutchinson-Oliver family, 175-77
Hyrum, Utah, 145, 147, 154, 155, 156
Income tax records, 46
Individual-level tracing. See Migration
Institute of Genealogical Research, 13
International Congress of Genealogy, 11
Jacobus, Donald L., 12
Jensen, Richard, 19
Johnson, Elizabeth, 181
Johnson, Frances, 199
Kamman, Michael, 19
Kanab, Utah, 145, 148, 154, 155
Katz, Michael B., 77
Kennebeck Proprietors, 168
Kin terms, 54, 58
Kinship
  analysis of, in genealogical
    reconstitution, 130
  European history of, 127
  knowledge of, 129
  need for statements of, over time, 129,
    131, 132
  rules of behavior in, 129
  studies of, genealogies in, 23
  within given communities, 41
Kinship classification, limitations of, for
  total kinship history, 139
Kinship and genealogy, relationship of, 138
Kluckhorn, Clyde, 142
Knights of Columbus, 120
Lambert, Edna, 195
Lambert, Francis, 197, 198
Lambert, Jane, 197, 198
Lambert, Thomas, 195
Land records, 45
Laslett, Peter, 22n, 140
Latter-day Saints, Church of Jesus Christ of,
  10. See also Mormons
Lehi, Utah, 144, 145, 147, 154, 155, 156
Lévi-Strauss, Claude, 58, 59
Library of Congress, 7, 163
Life-course approach, historians use of in
  family history, 22
Lockridge, Kenneth, 19
Logan, Utah, 145, 149, 153
Lowder, Elizabeth Danforth, 278
Manti, Utah, 145, 149, 150, 153

Marriage: in colonial New England, 64-65
————: in colonial Rowley, Massachusetts
age at first marriage, 188-93; divorce, 193-94; duration, 193-94; marriage order of children, 192-93; remarriage and widowhood, 194-99; source of spouses, 186-88; universality, 185-86
Marriage group, as unit of anthropological study, 62
Marriage patterns in Schwalm area, 136-37
Massachusetts Charter of 1691, 163
Massachusetts General Council, 164; duties of, 164
Massachusetts General Court
benefits of service in, 168-70
hostility of legislators from interior towns towards colleagues from port towns, 160
membership in, as standard of leadership, 159
turnover in, 167
Massachusetts House of Representatives, 163-64
average representative, 165-66
duties in, 164-65
Mayflower descendants, 57
Meek, Jeremiah, Jr., 302
Meek, Sarah Poole Wilson, 302
Metoyer family, 105
Migration
as destabilizing force, 270; as integrative mechanism, 271; in New England, patterns of, 65, 72-74; reliability of genealogical records of, 68-69; and the social history of New England, 269-70; as stabilizing force, 271; studies of, genealogies in, 23, 32, 40-43, 87
————, and Danforth family
acquisition of family land and persistence, 281-82; age at, 276-77; economic motives for, 278-80; effect of inheritance on, 280-81; and long-distance kin communication, 284-87; male, reasons for, 277-78; more common for women, 275; rates of, 273; short-distance of, 274
————, from Germany to America
concentrations of Germans in United States, 313; records of German emigra-

tion, 314-15; tracing of individuals, advantages of, 313
————, research strategies
computerized scanning of U.S. censuses, 320; dwarf-state approach, 317-18; homogeneous-American-settlement approach, 315-17; working from emigrant lists, alphabetic approach, 319. See also Corbit family; Wilson family
Military records, 44, 45
Mills, Gary B., 93, 100, 101
Minot family, 171-72
Mobility, selective process of, 42; vertical, 33
Mormons, genealogical interest of, 38, 39. See also Latter-day Saints
Murdock, G. P., 138

Nadel, S. H., 129
Names
of aid in ordering history of family, 216-17, 240-41; as clues to culture, 243-44; interest of social scientists in, 215-16
————, in Concord, New Hampshire
emerging process of giving, 1950-1980, 236-40; revolution in giving of, 1770-1820, 224-31; stable Puritan pattern of, characterized by biblical favorites, 219-24; stable Victorian pattern of, individuality expressed in, 1820-1950, 232-35
————, in colonial Middlesex County, Virginia
assigned by white owners, 264-65; and blacks, 103, 258-63; common phenomenon of sharing of, 248-51; contrast with New England patterns, 254-56; freely given, 257-58; lack of patterns of, 263; lack of sharing of, 262; pool of, established by whites, 259-60; reflect strong family orientation, 251-54; scholarly stress of African sources of, 258-59
National Archives, 12, 50
National Genealogical Society, 6, 14
Netting, Robert McC., 139
Network analysis, utility of, in researching kinship structure, 23
Newberry Library, Family and Community Center, 21, 84
New England, town studies in, 63-65

New England genealogies, wealth bias in, 66-67
New England Historic Genealogical Society, 5, 6, 12, 70, 163
New England Historical and Genealogical Register, 6, 21
"New" social history, xi, 15, 31
New York Genealogical and Biographical Society, 6
New York Genealogical and Biographical Society Register, 6
New York Public Library, 7

Obituaries, 50
Oliver, Andrew, 279
Oliver, Mary Fitch, 279
Onomastics. *See* Names
Oral genealogies, 56, 57, 77
Oral history, in family biographies, 48; as source for black genealogy, 99-102
Osterhud, Nancy, 204, 210
Otis, James, 161

Packard, Joseph, 178
Palmer, Francis, 195
Palmer, Hannah Johnson, 199
Palmer, John, 195
Parsons, Talcott, 142
Patriotic and hereditary societies, 8, 71-72, 81
Pearson, Dorcas, 199
Pearson, Hannah, 199
Pearson, John, 199
Philadelphia Social History Project, 320
Phipps, Jonathan, 278
Phipps, Samuel, 279
Phipps, Thomas, 279, 285
Pickard, John, 195
Pickard, Samuel, 195
Platts, Jonathan, 181, 198, 201
Poll records, 44
Poole, William Jr., 295
Poole, Sarah Sharpless, 295
Property records, 45, 50
Provo, Utah, 145, 147, 149, 153
Public historians, 20

Quakers, fertility of, 204.
    See also Wilson family

Race relations. *See* Southern United States
Race suicide, fears of, 8. *See also* Eugenics

Radcliffe-Brown, A. R., 130
Rayburn, Samuel Taliaferro, 237-38
Records
    access to, 48
    indexing of, by genealogists, 36
    linkage, 85, 132
    preservation of, 36, 37, 47
    See also under specific type of record
Reyner, Humphrey, 196
Ridge Runners, 40
Rivers, W. H. R., 53-55, 58
Robbins, William G., 154
Rockville, Utah, 145, 148, 154
Rogers, Rev. Ezekial, 181, 183
Roman Catholic Church
    archival resources, 112; interest in genealogy, 111-12; sacramental registers in Southern U.S., 95
    _____and records
    baptism, 113-14; cemetery, 122; communion, 116-17; confirmation, 116-17; death and burial, 122; lay organizations, 119; lay trustee, 120; marriage, 118; mission, 120; orphanage, 116; parish census, 115; private manuscripts, 121; school, 117; sick call, 122
Rowley, Massachusetts, 181-201
Russel Soundex system, 320

St. George, Utah, 145, 150, 153, 155
St. Vincent de Paul, 120
Salt Lake City, Utah, 145, 147, 148, 156, 157, 158
Sandeford, Richard, 251
Sandeford, Sarah, 251
Savage, James, 6
Saveth, Edward, 19
School records, 45, 46
Schwalm area (West Germany), data collection of, as base for historical kinship research, 132-39
Sewall family, 222
Shattuck, Lemuel, 54
Shipley, Elizabeth, 298-99
Shorter, Edward, 200
Smith, Daniel Scott, 18, 216, 254-55
Social Security records, 48
Society of Cincinnatus, 38
Society of Mayflower Descendants, 69
Sodality of the Virgin, 119

Soliday, Gerald, 126-28
Southern United States
  black slaveholders in, 105
  Celtic origins, 91-92
  errors in racial identification in 1860
    census, 96
  free blacks in, 104-105
  Indian-white miscegenation, 92
  myth of the Southern planter, 106
  nonblack slavery, 106-107
  "one-drop rule," 92
  race relations misconceived, 90,
    not addressed by genealogists, 90-91
  "racial purity" not universal concern
    in, 93
Spotswood, Alexander, 91
Stability ratios
  as index of community persistence,
    defined, 143-45, 151
  use of genealogies in, 143
Stanard, William, 263-64
Stearns, Peter, xi
Stebbins, Luke, 4
Steel, Dan, 19
Steward, George, 236, 237
Steward, Hugh, 248
Stickney family, 189-91
Swiggett, Alethea, 300
Symmes, Elizabeth Blowers, 282
Symmes, Thomas, 282

Tax records, 46, 270
Temple family, 169
Tenney, Thomas, 189, 195
Thistlethwaite, Frank, 311
Thomas, Samuel, 294
Toledot, 80
Toquerville, Utah, 145, 148, 154

United States Bureau of Indian Affairs,
  records of, 98
Utah Genealogical Society, 143
Utah towns
  persistence rates compared to other
    American towns, 153-55
  unusual stability, an effect of religious
    commitment, 157

Utah, University of, Center for Historical
  Population Studies in, 21
Vann, Richard, 18
Vinovskis, Maris, 204

Wachter, Kenneth W., 57, 140
Warner, Edward Tatnall, 307
Warner, Mollie Corbit, 308
Watts, Samuel, 174
Webb, Rev. John, 278
Wells, Robert V., 204, 211
Wendell family, 169, 175
Western Pennsylvania Historical Society,
  19
Wheeler, Joseph, 189
Wheeler, William, 234
Whitewater Quaker Meeting, 298
Whiting, John, 285
Whiting, Rev. Joseph, 274
Whitmore, William H., 6
Wilson family
  and fragmentation, 297
  in Odessa, Delaware, 292
  in Philadelphia, 296
  and Quakers, 293-98
  in Richmond, Indiana, 297-307
  in Wilmington, Delaware, 298
  See also Corbit family
Wisconsin Magazine of History, 11
Winterthur Library, 308
Women's history, 34
Wood family, 252
Wood, Peter, 259
Wood, Thomas, 189
Woodson, Carter G., 105
Works Progress Administration, "Slave
  Testimonies," 98
World Conference on Records, 1969, 14
Wright, Edmund, 286
Wright, J. Leitch, 92

Yasuba, Yasukici, 203
Young, Brigham, 148

Zelnick, Melvin, 203

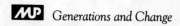 *Generations and Change*

Designed by Margaret Jordan Brown
Composition by MUP Composition Department
Production specifications:
    text paper—60-pound Warren's Olde Style
    endpapers—Multicolor Antique Bombay
    covers (on .088 boards)—Holliston Roxite B 53525 linen finish
    dust jacket—Printed two colors, PMS 116 (yellow) and PMS 307 (blue),
        on 100-pound enamel, and varnished